A-Z OLDHAM and

C000244767

CONTENT

Key to Map Pages	2-3
Map Pages	4-55

Index
Villages, Hospi...
Selected Places of Interest

REFERENCE

Motorway	**M62**	Car Park (Selected)	**P**
A Road	A62	Church or Chapel	†
B Road	B6222	Fire Station	■
Dual Carriageway		Hospital	**H**
One-way Street	→	House Numbers 'A' and 'B' Roads only	13 ... 8
Traffic flow on A Roads is also indicated by a heavy line on the driver's left.		Information Centre	**i**
Restricted Access		National Grid Reference	³95
Pedestrianized Road		Police Station	▲
Track / Footpath		Post Office	★
Railway	Level Crossing / Station / Tunnel	Toilet	▽
		with facilities for the Disabled	♿
Local Authority Boundary		Educational Establishment	
Posttown Boundary		Hospital or Health Centre	
Postcode Boundary within Posttowns		Industrial Building	
		Leisure or Recreational Facility	
		Place of Interest	
Built-up Area	MILL ST.	Public Building	
		Shopping Centre & Market	
Map Continuation	12	Other Selected Buildings	

Scale

1:15,840

0	¼	½ Mile

4 inches (10.16 cm) to 1 mile
6.31cm to 1kilometre

0	250	500	750 Metres	1 Kilometre

Copyright of Geographers' A-Z Map Company Limited

Head Office :
Fairfield Road, Borough Green, Sevenoaks, Kent TN15 8PP
Tel: 01732 781000 (General Enquiries & Trade Sales)

Showrooms :
44 Gray's Inn Road, London WC1X 8HX
Tel: 020 7440 9500 (Retail Sales)
www.a-zmaps.co.uk

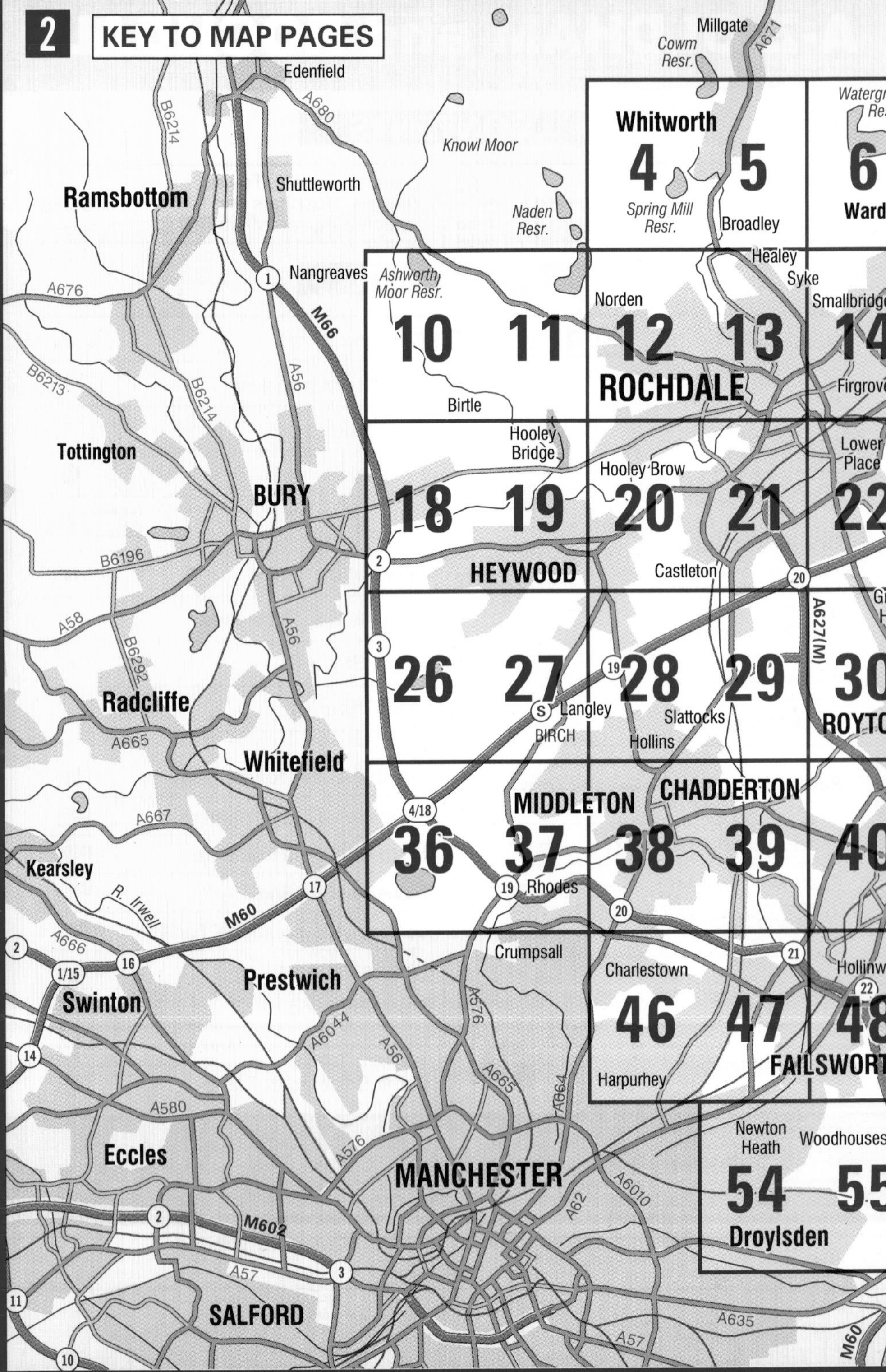

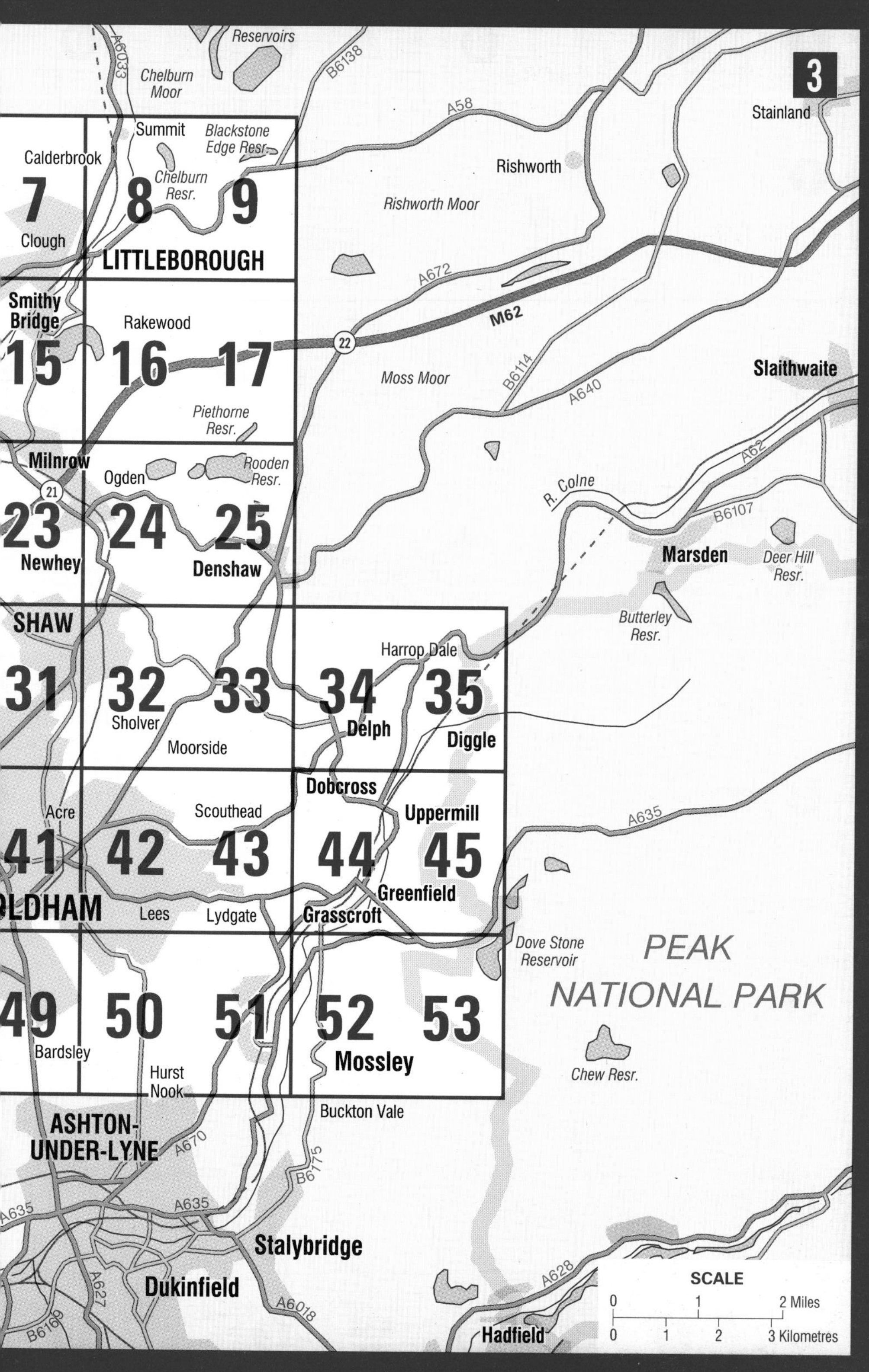

3

Stainland

Reservoirs

Chelburn
Moor

Summit   Blackstone
             Edge Resr.
Calderbrook
                           Rishworth
Chelburn
7   **8**   **9**   Resr.

Clough   Rishworth Moor

LITTLEBOROUGH

                A58

Smithy   M62
Bridge   Rakewood   **Slaithwaite**
15   **16**   **17**   ②②
                                        Moss Moor
                Piethorne
                Resr.

Milnrow   Rooden   R. Colne
         Ogden   Resr.   B6107
②①
23   **24**   **25**   **Marsden**   Deer Hill
                                                                              Resr.
Newhey   **Denshaw**
                                                      Butterley
                                                      Resr.
SHAW
                              Harrop Dale
31   **32**   **33**   **34**   **35**

         Sholver   **Delph**   **Diggle**
                Moorside

                        Dobcross
Acre   Scouthead   **Uppermill**   A635
41   **42**   **43**   **44**   **45**

OLDHAM   Lees   Lydgate   **Greenfield**
                            Grasscroft
                                          Dove Stone   **PEAK**
                                          Reservoir
                                                      NATIONAL PARK
49   **50**   **51**   **52**   **53**
Bardsley   Chew Resr.
         Hurst   **Mossley**
         Nook
                Buckton Vale
**ASHTON-
UNDER-LYNE**

                        Stalybridge

Dukinfield

                Hadfield

SCALE

0 _____ 1 _____ 2 Miles

0 ____ 1 ____ 2 ____ 3 Kilometres

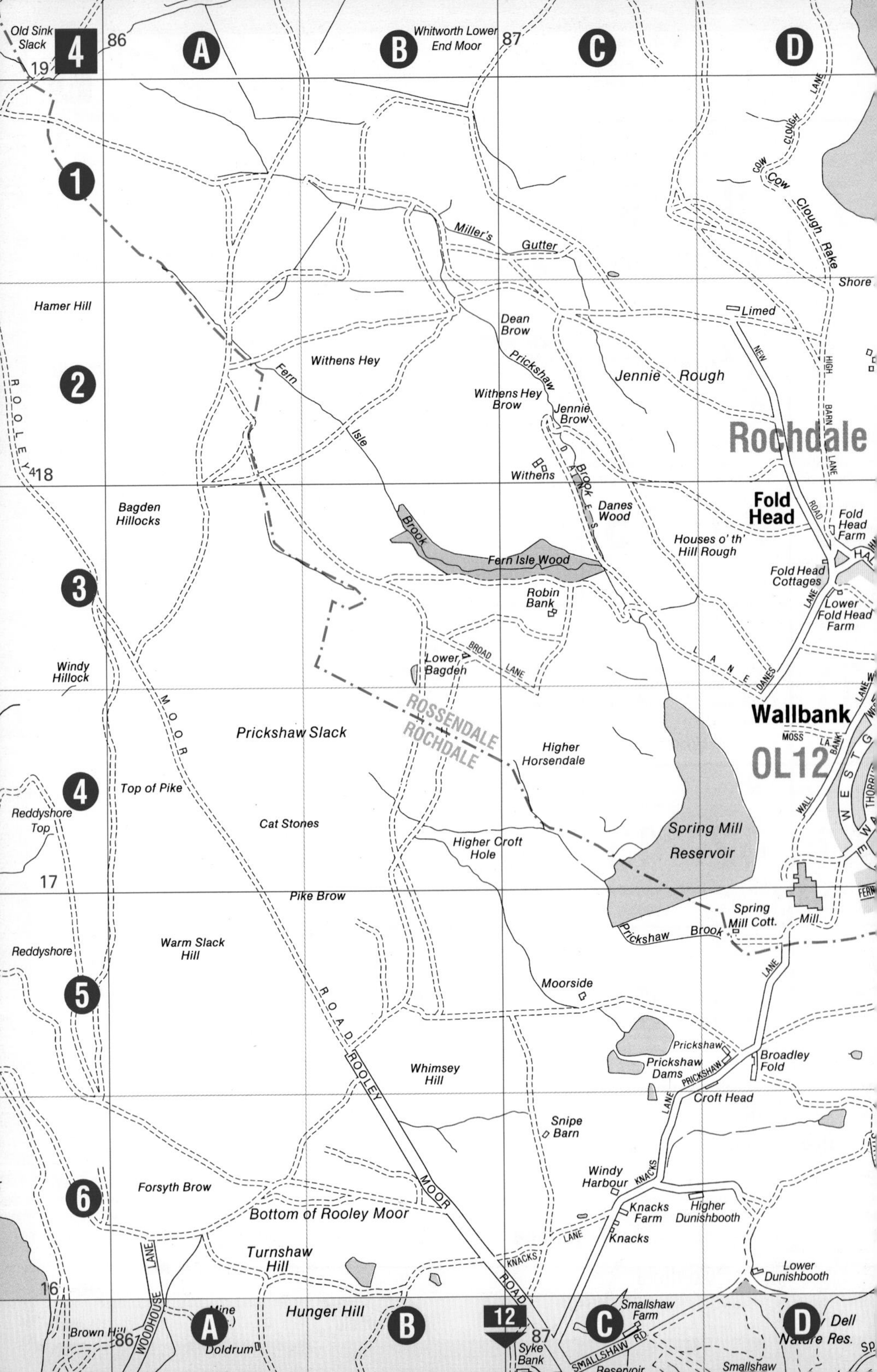
4
A
B
C
D
1
2
3
4
5
6
86
87
19
18
17
16
12
Old Sink Slack
Whitworth Lower End Moor
Hamer Hill
Withens Hey
Miller's Gutter
Dean Brow
Prickshaw
Jennie Rough
Withens Hey Brow
Jennie Brow
Withens
Rochdale
Fold Head
Fold Head Farm
Fold Head Cottages
Lower Fold Head Farm
Bagden Hillocks
Fern Isle Brook
Fern Isle Wood
Danes Brook
Danes Wood
Houses o' th' Hill Rough
Robin Bank
Lower Bagden
Broad Lane
Danes Lane
Windy Hillock
Rossendale
Rochdale
Wallbank
OL12
Prickshaw Slack
Higher Horsendale
Top of Pike
Reddyshore Top
Cat Stones
Higher Croft Hole
Spring Mill Reservoir
Pike Brow
Spring Mill Cott.
Mill
Prickshaw Brook
Reddyshore
Warm Slack Hill
Moorside
Rooley Moor Road
Prickshaw Dams
Broadley Fold
Whimsey Hill
Prickshaw Lane
Croft Head
Snipe Barn
Windy Harbour
Knacks Lane
Forsyth Brow
Knacks Farm
Higher Dunishbooth
Bottom of Rooley Moor
Knacks
Turnshaw Hill
Lower Dunishbooth
Hunger Hill
Smallshaw Farm
Brown Hill
Doldrum
Woodhouse Lane
Syke Bank
Smallshaw Rd
Reservoir
Smallshaw
Dell Nature Res.
Cow Clough Lane
Cow Clough Rake
Shore
Limed
New Road
High Barn Lane
Moss Lane
Wall Bank
West
Lane
Hall
Fern

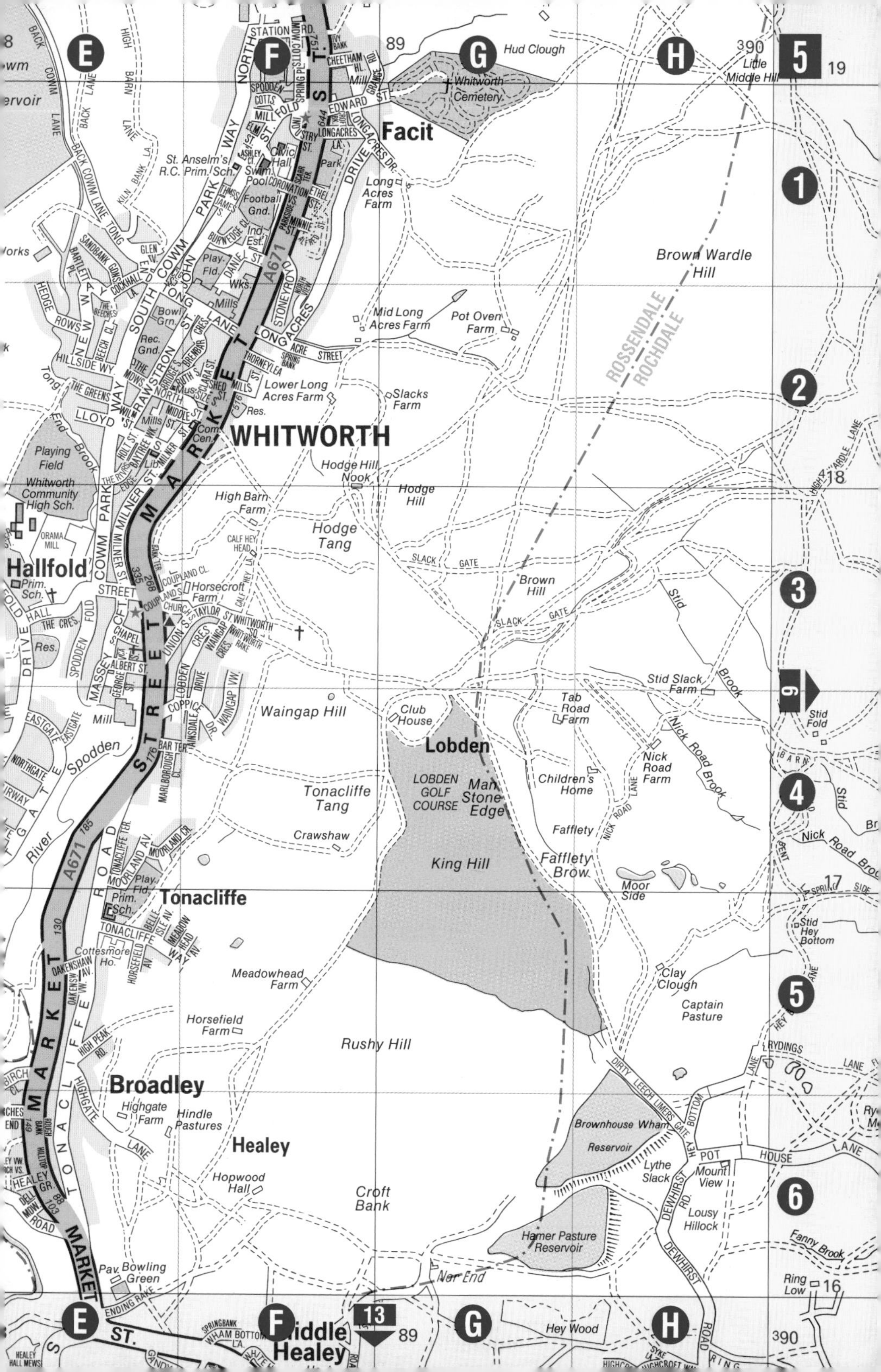
5
E
F
G
H
1
2
3
4
5
6
9
13
Facit
WHITWORTH
Hallfold
Tonacliffe
Broadley
Healey
Lobden
Middle Healey
Hud Clough
Whitworth Cemetery
Little Middle Hill
Brown Wardle Hill
ROSSENDALE
ROCHDALE
Long Acres Farm
Mid Long Acres Farm
Pot Oven Farm
Lower Long Acres Farm
Slacks Farm
Hodge Hill Nook
Hodge Hill
High Barn Farm
Hodge Tang
Brown Hill
Slack Gate
Stid Brook
Stid Slack Farm
Stid Fold
Tab Road Farm
Nick Road Farm
Nick Road Brook
Children's Home
Club House
Waingap Hill
Tonacliffe Tang
Crawshaw
LOBDEN GOLF COURSE
Man Stone Edge
King Hill
Fafflety
Fafflety Brow
Moor Side
Stid Hey Bottom
Clay Clough
Captain Pasture
Meadowhead Farm
Horsefield Farm
Rushy Hill
Highgate Farm
Hindle Pastures
Hopwood Hall
Croft Bank
Brownhouse Wham Reservoir
Hamer Pasture Reservoir
Lythe Slack
Mount View
Lousy Hillock
Fanny Brook
Ring Low
Ner End
Hey Wood
Bowling Green
Pav.
Playing Field
Whitworth Community High Sch.
Spodden
River Spodden
MARKET STREET
A671
St. Anselm's R.C. Prim. Sch.
Civic Hall
Swim. Pool
Football Gnd.
Rec. Gnd.
Bowl. Grn.
Play. Fld.
Mus.
Com. Cen.
Lib.
Res.
Horsecroft Farm
Prim. Sch.
Cottesmore Ho.
DIRTY LEECH LIMERS GATE
POT HOUSE LANE
DEWHIRST RD.
HEY BOTTOM
RYDINGS LANE
ENDING RAKE
WHAM BOTTOM LA.
390
89
19
18
17
16

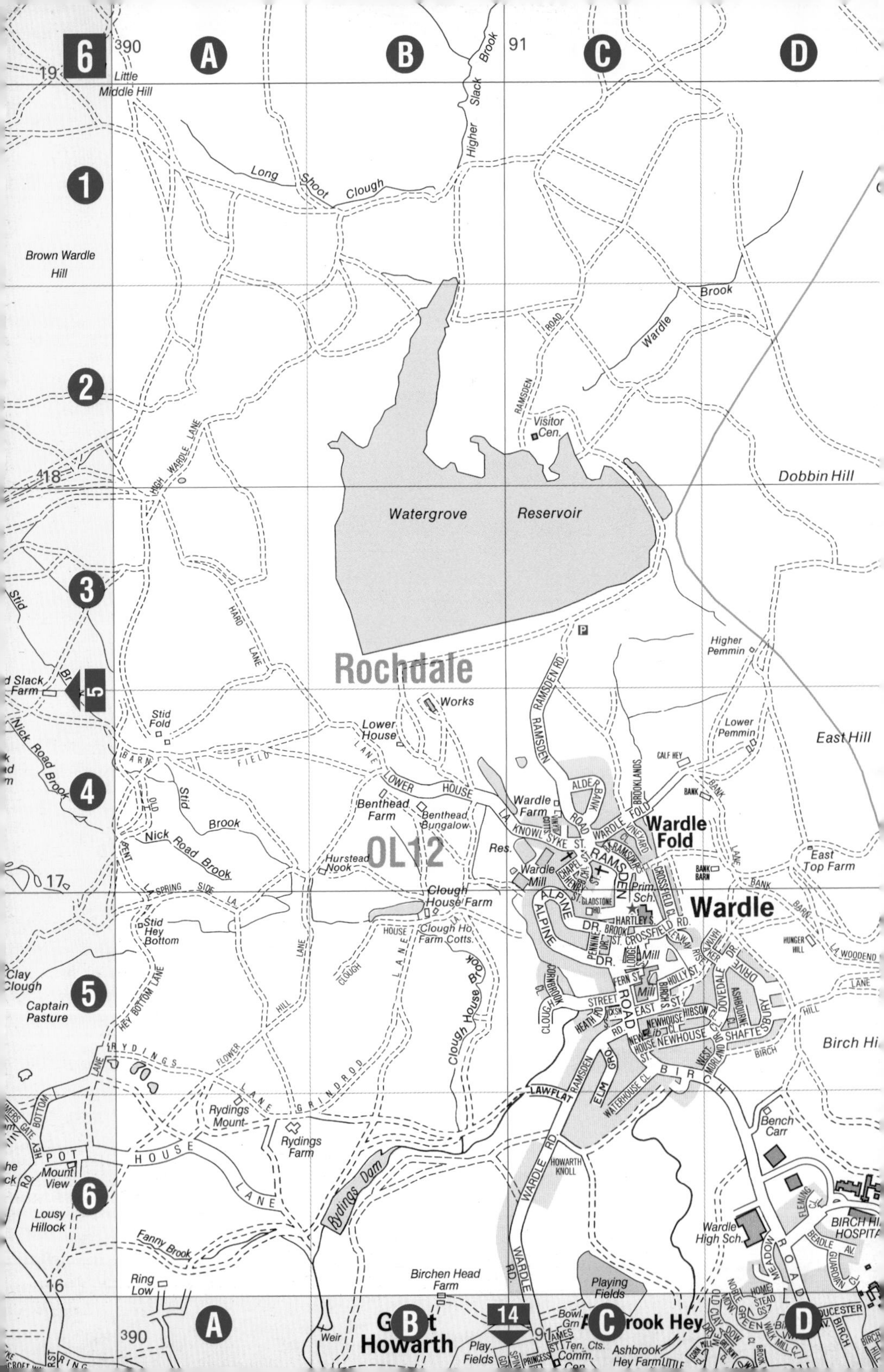

390
A
B
91
C
D
19
Little Middle Hill
Higher Slack Brook
Long Shoot Clough
1
Brown Wardle Hill
Wardle Brook
2
RAMSDEN ROAD
Visitor Cen.
HIGH WARDLE LANE
18
Dobbin Hill
Watergrove Reservoir
3
Stid
HARD LANE
Higher Pemmin
Rochdale
Slack Farm
5
Works
RAMSDEN RD.
Stid Fold
Lower House
Lower Pemmin
East Hill
BARN FIELD LANE
Nick Road Brook
4
LOWER HOUSE
CALF HEY
BROOKLANDS
BANK
Benthead Farm
Benthead Bungalow
Wardle Farm
Wardle Fold
Stid Brook
OL12
Res.
Hurstead Nook
Wardle Mill
RAMSDEN
Prim. Sch.
BANK BARN
East Top Farm
17
SPRING SIDE LA.
Clough House Farm
ALPINE
GLADSTONE
HARTLEY S.
CROSSFIELD RD.
Wardle
Stid Hey Bottom
Clough Ho. Farm Cotts.
PENNINE DR.
HUNGER HILL
WOODEND
Clay Clough
Mill
FERN ST.
HOLLY ST.
DOVEDALE
5
Captain Pasture
HEY BOTTOM LANE
Clough House Brook
CORNBROOK CL.
ASHBOURNE
STREET
EAST ST.
ROAD
HEATH RD.
NEWHOUSE
Lib.
SHAFTESBURY
Birch Hi
RYDINGS
FLOWER HILL
GRINDROD LANE
BIRCH
RAMSDEN
ELM GRO.
WATERHOUSE CL.
LAWFLAT
Rydings Mount
Rydings Farm
POT HOUSE LANE
Mount View
6
Rydings Dam
WARDLE RD.
HOWARTH KNOLL
Bench Carr
FLEMING CL.
Lousy Hillock
Wardle High Sch.
BIRCH HOSPITAL
BEADLE AV.
GUARDIAN
Fanny Brook
MEADOW
Ring Low
Birchen Head Farm
Playing Fields
16
14
A
390
B
Howarth
Weir
Play. Fields
C
Ashbrook Hey
Ten. Cts.
Comm.
Ashbrook Hey Farm
D
GLOUCESTER

7
Littleborough
OL15
Calderbrook
Clough
Gale
Shore
Caldermoor
Stubley
Littleborough
LITTLEBOROUGH
Dearnley
Turn Slack Hill
Fox Stones Hill
Pasture House Plantation
Turn Slack Dam
Old Charles Hill
Flight Hill
Cuckoo Hill
Lower Turn Slack Hill
Dearden's Pasture
Long Hill
Pike Hill
Ringing Pots Hill
Grimes
Blackbrow Hill
Higher Stone Pits
Stansfield Hill
Far Hey Head
Near Hey Head
Lower Stone Pits
Long Clough
Hey Bottom Farm
Ratcliffe Hill
High Lee Slack
Middle Newgate
Higher Newgate
Hill Top Farm
Heights Farm
Clough Ter.
Lower Newgate
Green Hill
Gorsey Hill Wood
Higher Shore Wood
High Lea
Higher Shore
Higher Shore House
Lower Town House
Town House
New Platt Farm
Playing Fields
Cricket Grd.
Football Grd.
Rec. Grd.
Hare Hill Park
Pedler Brow
Starring Wood
Higher Starring Farm
Middle Starring
Starring Hill
Pav. Sports Grd.
Cemetery
Stubley New Hall
LITTLEBOROUGH IND. ESTATE
A58
A6033
B6225
Bank Top
Works
Engineering Works

Pasture House Plantation
94
A
Scout End
B
395
C
CHELBURN MOOR
D
Solomon Cutting
Chelburn
Pasture House
Yellow Hill
1
Chelburn Bridge
TODMORDEN ROAD
Slack
Stony Field
Weir
Weir
Lock
Long Hill
Pike Hill
Lower Chelburn Reservoir
Summit
Leach Hill
Mawrode Farm
Timbercliffe
Snoddle Hill
Timbercliffe Farm
Higher Chelburn Reservoir
2
Calderbrook
Punchbowl Bridge
Leach
Pennine Trout Fishery
Handle Hall
Works
Sch.
Barrat
Handle Hall Farm
Sladen Fold
Littleborough
CALDERBROOK ROAD
A6033
Sladen Ter. Mill
3
Hill Top Farm
Whitfield Farm
Grove
Sladen Hill
Longley Hey
Green Halghs
Castle Bungalow
Castle Clough
Sports Gnd.
Whitfield
Fishery
Mill
Sladen Bridge
Weir
OL15
Newgate
Mill Race (dis.)
Rec. Gd.
7
Recn. Gnd.
Pikehouse Cotts.
Weir
Gorsey Hill Wood
Gale
Mill
Cloise
Pikehouse Bridge
LANE
Lightowlers
Subway
4
Mill
Limefield
Overdale Ho.
New Barn
Rochdale Canal (disused)
River Roch
Lightowlers Lane
Higher Swaindrod
Fence Nook
Town House
New Platt Farm
Benthouse Bridge
17
Bent House Farm
Engineering Works
Heathfield
Honresfeld (Cheshire Home)
Stormer Hill Bar
Playing Fields
Pav.
Football Grd.
Windy Bank Bridge
Stormer Hill
Lydgate Clough
5
Eng. Wks.
Windy Ridge
Rec. Grd.
A58
Gate House
BLACKSTONE EDGE OLD ROAD
Works
HALIFAX ROAD
Higher Windy Bank Farm
Humber Farm
Knowl Farm
Oil Mill Bridge
Lydgate
Durn
CHURCH STREET
Heritage Cen.
Fielden Farm
Draught Hill
Ealees
6
Littleborough
Reservoir
Mill
Ealees Wood
Ealees Brook
Owlet Hall
Shore Lane Brook
Shore Lane Farm
LITTLEBOROUGH
16
Lane Foot
A
B
16
WHITTAKER GOLF COURSE
395
C
Salmon Well
D
94
Bank Top
Clegg's Wood

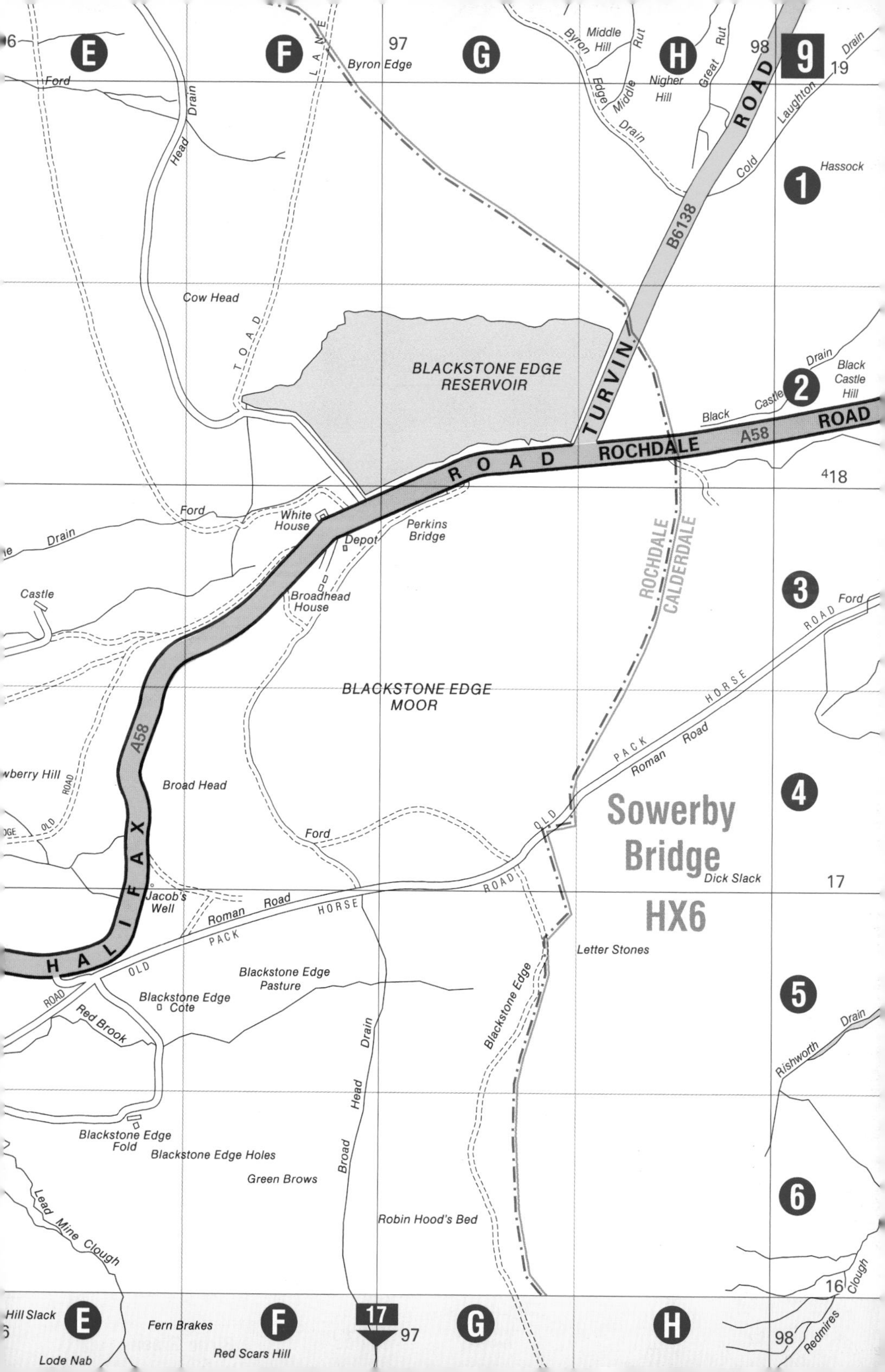

9
E
F
G
H
97
98
19
Byron Edge
Middle Hill
Rut
Nigher Hill
Great Rut
Middle Edge Drain
Byron Edge
Ford
Head Drain
LANE
ROAD
Cold Laughton Drain
Hassock
1
B6138
Cow Head
TOAD
TURVIN
BLACKSTONE EDGE RESERVOIR
Drain
Black Castle Hill
2
Black Castle
A58
ROAD
ROCHDALE
ROAD
418
Ford
Drain
White House
Depot
Perkins Bridge
ROCHDALE
CALDERDALE
Castle
Broadhead House
3
Ford
ROAD
HORSE
BLACKSTONE EDGE MOOR
PACK
Roman Road
A58
wberry Hill
ROAD
OLD
Broad Head
4
Sowerby Bridge
HX6
OLD
Ford
Dick Slack
17
HALIFAX
Jacob's Well
Roman Road
ROAD
HORSE
PACK
Letter Stones
OLD
Blackstone Edge Pasture
ROAD
Blackstone Edge Cote
5
Red Brook
Drain
Blackstone Edge
Rishworth
Broad Head Drain
Blackstone Edge Fold
Blackstone Edge Holes
Green Brows
6
Lead Mine Clough
Robin Hood's Bed
16
Clough
Hill Slack
Fern Brakes
17
97
Red Scars Hill
Lode Nab
98
Redmires

10
82
16
83
A
B
C
D
EDENFIELD
Moorlands
Ashworth Moor
Croston Close Upper Bridge
Croston Close
Croston Close Bottoms
Ashworth Moor Reservoir
Cross Gate
Kirkby's
CLOSE
ROAD
ASHWORTH ROAD
Plant Close
Buckhurst Brow
Buckhurst Farm
Rough Lee
BUCKHURST RD.
BUCKHURST RD.
LA.
Far Croft Head
Closes
ROCHDALE
ROSSENDALE
Closes Bridge
Sales's Fm.
15
SALES'S
DEEPLY
Yates Farm
Top o'th' Hill Farm
Bird Fields
Deeply Vale Higher Bridge
Deeply Hill
Lark Mount
CROSTON
Deeply Vale
Wind Hill
ASHWORTH
Wind Hill Farm
Deeply Vale Lower Bridge
VALE
Stand Lees Farm
LANE
Cob House Nab
CROSTON
Bury
Copped Farm
Copped
Cob House Farm
CLOSE
BL9
14
CARR
Shepherds Hey
Leaches
Deep Moss
Cockshouse
SCOTLAND
ROAD
LA.
Dunham Farm
LANE
Club House
(Garrett's Close)
CASTLE
Cheesden
WALMERSLEY
GOLF COURSE
Cleggs Wood
Old Birtle
Broomses Farm
HILL
Old Birtle
MILLETT TER.
BIRTLE
New Birtle Farm
Wood Barn
Moor Bank
Penn Green Farm
13
ROAD
18
Harwood Fields
83
Birtle Green
CASTLE
ROAD
1
2
3
4
5
6

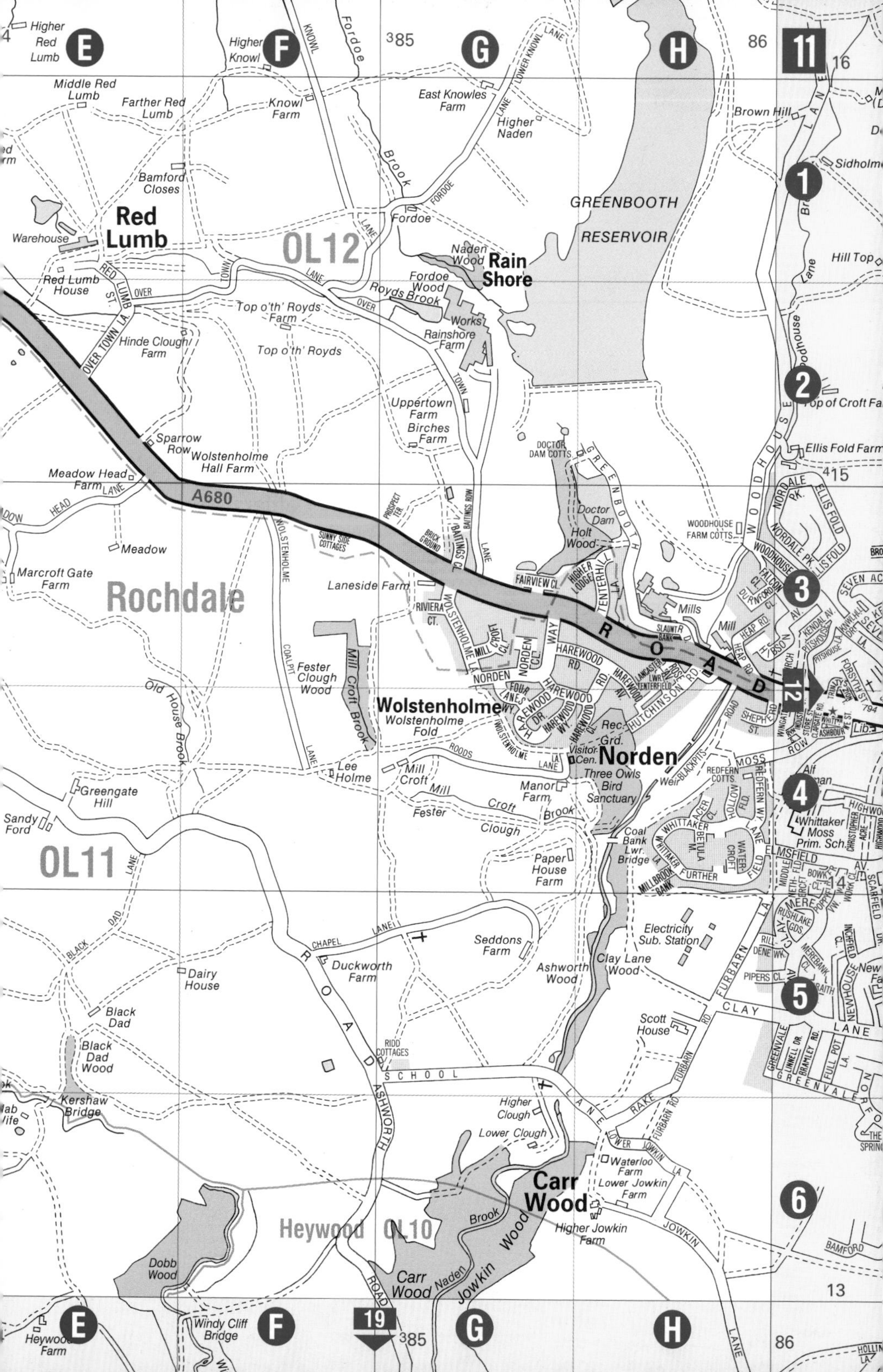

11
E
F
G
H
385
86
16
Higher Red Lumb
Higher Knowl
Middle Red Lumb
Farther Red Lumb
Knowl Farm
East Knowles Farm
Higher Naden
Brown Hill
Sidholme
Bamford Closes
Red Lumb
Warehouse
OL12
Fordoe
GREENBOOTH RESERVOIR
Naden Wood
Rain Shore
Hill Top
Red Lumb House
Fordoe Wood
Royds Brook
Top o'th' Royds Farm
Works
Rainshore Farm
Hinde Clough Farm
Top o'th' Royds
Uppertown Farm
Birches Farm
Top of Croft Farm
Ellis Fold Farm
Sparrow Row
Wolstenholme Hall Farm
Meadow Head Farm
A680
Doctor Dam
Holt Wood
Woodhouse Farm Cotts
Meadow
Marcroft Gate Farm
Rochdale
Laneside Farm
Mills
Mill
ROAD
Fester Clough Wood
Mill Croft Brook
Wolstenholme
Wolstenholme Fold
Norden
Rec. Grd.
Visitor Cen.
Three Owls Bird Sanctuary
Old House Brook
Greengate Hill
Sandy Ford
Lee Holme
Mill Croft
Manor Farm
Fester Clough
Weir
Whittaker Moss Prim. Sch.
OL11
Paper House Farm
Coal Bank Lwr. Bridge
Electricity Sub. Station
Seddons Farm
Duckworth Farm
Dairy House
Ashworth Wood
Clay Lane Wood
Black Dad
Black Dad Wood
Scott House
Kershaw Bridge
Higher Clough
Lower Clough
Waterloo Farm
Lower Jowkin Farm
Carr Wood
Higher Jowkin Farm
Heywood OL10
Dobb Wood
Jowkin Wood
Naden Brook
Heywood Farm
Windy Cliff Bridge
19
13
1
2
3
4
5
6
12
415
14

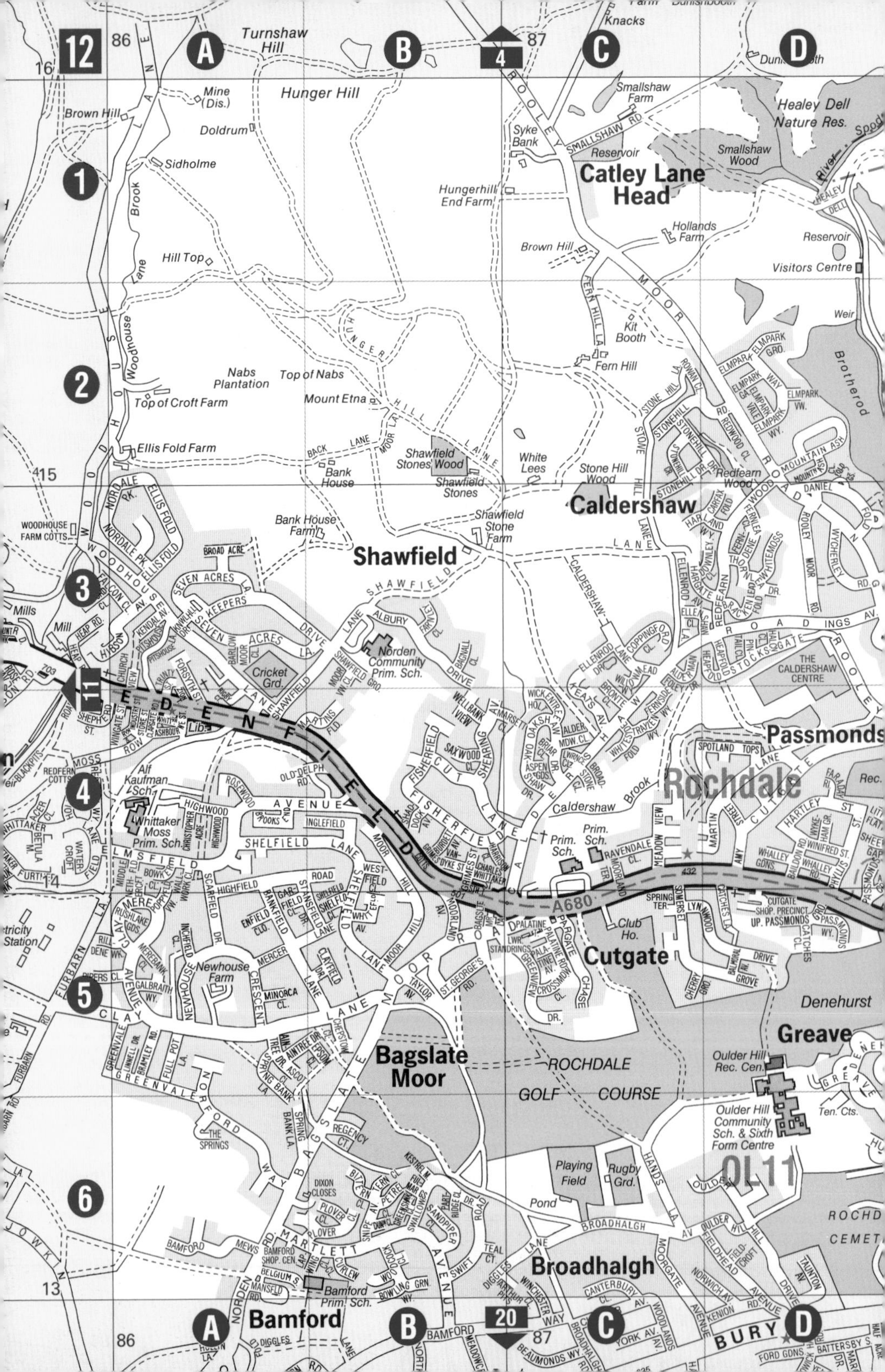

12
Turnshaw Hill
Knacks
Hunger Hill
Mine (Dis.)
Brown Hill
Doldrum
Sidholme
Smallshaw Farm
Healey Dell Nature Res.
Syke Bank
Reservoir
Smallshaw Wood
Catley Lane Head
Hungerhill End Farm
Hollands Farm
Brown Hill
Reservoir
Visitors Centre
Hill Top
Kit Booth
Weir
Fern Hill
Brotherod
Nabs Plantation
Top of Nabs
Mount Etna
Top of Croft Farm
Ellis Fold Farm
Shawfield Stones' Wood
White Lees
Stone Hill Wood
Bank House
Shawfield Stones
Redfearn Wood
Caldershaw
Woodhouse Farm Cotts
Bank House Farm
Shawfield Stone Farm
Shawfield
Mills
Mill
Cricket Grd.
Norden Community Prim. Sch.
The Caldershaw Centre
Passmonds
Lib.
Alf Kaufman Sch.
Whittaker Moss Prim. Sch.
Rochdale
Rec.
Prim. Sch.
Prim. Sch.
A680
Club Ho.
Cutgate
Cutgate Shop. Precinct
Electricity Station
Newhouse Farm
Denehurst
Greave
Bagslate Moor
Rochdale Golf Course
Older Hill Rec. Cen.
Ten. Cts.
Oulder Hill Community Sch. & Sixth Form Centre
OL11
Playing Field
Rugby Grd.
Pond
Rochdale Cemetery
Broadhalgh
Bamford Shop. Cen.
Bamford Prim. Sch.
Bamford
20
Edenfield Road
Bury Road
86
87
16
15
14
13
1
2
3
4
5
6
A
B
C
D
4
11

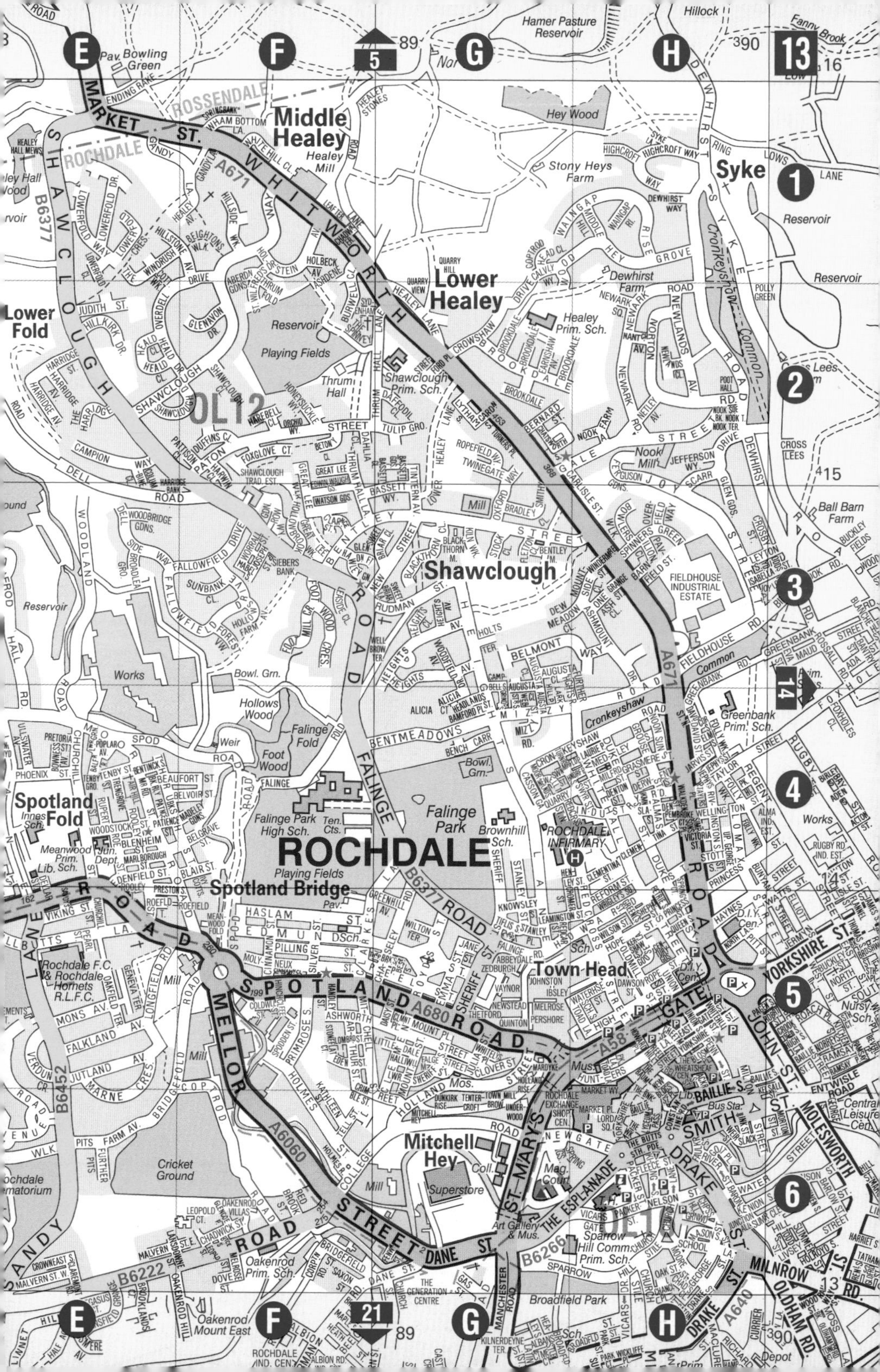

13
E
F
G
H
5
21
89
390
Hillock
Hamer Pasture Reservoir
Fanny Brook
Middle Healey
Healey Mill
Hey Wood
Stony Heys Farm
Syke
Reservoir
Lower Healey
Dewhirst Farm
Healey Prim. Sch.
Lower Fold
Playing Fields
Thrum Hall
Shawclough Prim. Sch.
OL12
Cronkeyshaw Common
Cross Lees
Ball Barn Farm
Polly Green
Nook Mill
Shawclough
FIELDHOUSE INDUSTRIAL ESTATE
Greenbank Prim. Sch.
Works
Bowl. Grn.
Hollows Wood
Falinge Fold
Foot Wood
Weir
Spotland Fold
Innes Sch.
Meanwood Prim. Sch.
Lib.
Jun. Dept.
Falinge Park High Sch.
Falinge Park
Brownhill Sch.
ROCHDALE INFIRMARY
ROCHDALE
Playing Fields
Spotland Bridge
Town Head
Rochdale F.C. & Rochdale Hornets R.L.F.C.
Mill
Cricket Ground
Mitchell Hey
Coll.
Superstore
Mag. Court
Art Gallery & Mus.
Sparrow Hill Comm. Prim. Sch.
Oakenrod Prim. Sch.
Oakenrod Mount East
THE GENERATION CENTRE
Broadfield Park
Rochdale Crematorium
RUGBY RD. IND. EST.
D.I.Y. Cen.
Central Leisure Cen.
Nursy. Sch.
Bus Sta.
ROCHDALE EXCHANGE SHOPP. CEN.
ROCHDALE IND. CEN.
A671
A680
A58
A6060
A640
B6377
B6452
B6222
B6266
ROSSENDALE
ROCHDALE
MARKET ST.
WHITWORTH ROAD
SHAWCLOUGH ROAD
SPOTLAND ROAD
FALINGE ROAD
MELLOR STREET
DANE ST.
YORKSHIRE ST.
JOHN ST.
MOLESWORTH ST.
SMITH ST.
DRAKE ST.
MILNROW RD.
OLDHAM RD.
ST. MARY'S GATE
THE ESPLANADE
MANCHESTER ROAD
SANDY LANE

14
A
B
C
D
1
2
3
4
5
6
6
13
22
Hillock
Fanny Brook
Ring Low
Syke
Great Howarth
Ashbrook Hey
Hurstead
Playing Fields
Reservoir
Cross Lees Farm
H.M.P. BUCKLEY HALL
Buckley Wood
Rydings School
OL12
Buckley
Ball Barn Farm
FIELDHOUSE INDUSTRIAL ESTATE
BUCKLEY HALL INDUSTRIAL ESTATE
Greenbank Prim. Sch.
Heybrook Prim. Sch.
Hamer Prim. Sch.
Youth Club
Alice Ingham R.C. Prim. Sch.
Howarth Cross
Rochdale
Smallbridge
Greenga
Pennine View Hostel
Greenfield
Lower Eafield
Clover Hall
Mayfield
Belfield
Belfield Prim. Sch.
FIRGROVE BUSINESS PARK
OL16
Newbold Brow
Newbold
ROCHDALE
Central Leisure Cen.
Depot
Works
Mill
Mosque
Bus Sta.
KINGSWAY RETAIL PARK
CHICHESTER BUSINESS CENTRE
HERITAGE PK.
Firgrov
A58
A664
A640
A671
B6266
YORKSHIRE STREET
HALIFAX ROAD
ALBERT ROYDS STREET
KINGSWAY
MILNROW
ENTWISTLE
MOLESWORTH
JOHN ST.
OLDHAM RD.
DRAKE ST.
SMITH
BAILLIE ST.
WHITWORTH RD.
REGENT
BELFIELD ROAD
MAYFIELD
RIVERSIDE
Beal
River Roch
Moss Brook
Hey Brook
Stanney Brook
Syke Brook
Ash Brook
390
91

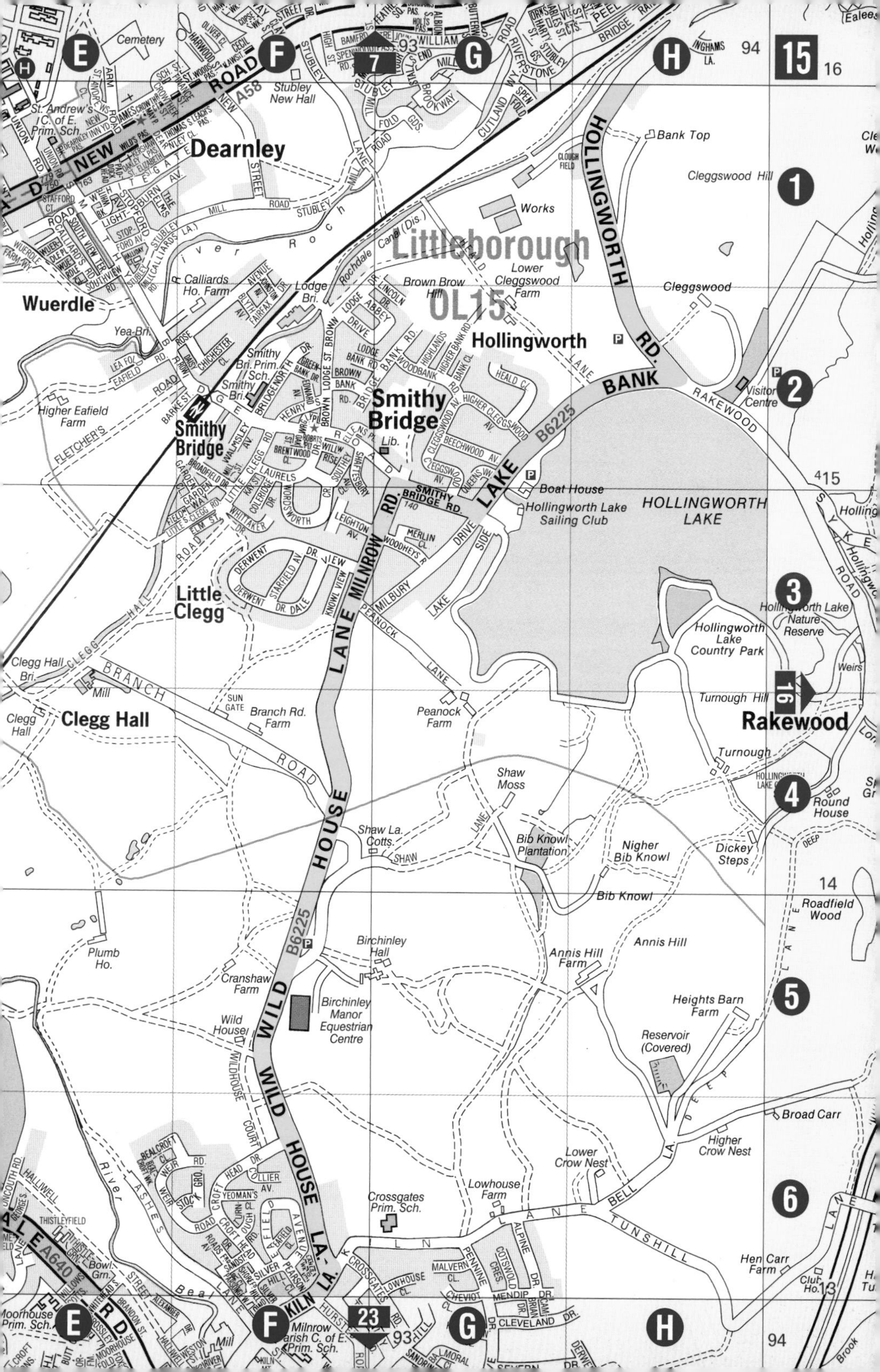

15
7
23
16
E
F
G
H
1
2
3
4
5
6
93
94
415
14
13
16
Dearnley
Littleborough
OL15
Hollingworth
Smithy Bridge
Wuerdle
Little Clegg
Clegg Hall
Rakewood
HOLLINGWORTH LAKE
HOLLINGWORTH RD.
LAKE BANK
B6225
MILNROW RD.
LANE
WILD HOUSE LANE
WILD HOUSE LA.
KILN LA.
NEW ROAD
A58
A640
Cemetery
St. Andrew's C. of E. Prim. Sch.
Stubley New Hall
Bank Top
Cleggswood Hill
Works
Lower Cleggswood Farm
Brown Brow Hill
Cleggswood
Visitor Centre
Calliards Ho. Farm
Lodge Bri.
Smithy Bri. Prim. Sch.
Smithy Bri.
Yea Bri.
Higher Eafield Farm
Boat House
Hollingworth Lake Sailing Club
Hollingworth Lake Nature Reserve
Hollingworth Lake Country Park
Turnough Hill
Turnough
Weirs
Round House
Dickey Steps
Clegg Hall Bri.
Mill
Clegg Hall
Sun Gate
Branch Rd. Farm
Peanock Farm
Shaw Moss
Shaw La. Cotts.
Bib Knowl Plantation
Nigher Bib Knowl
Bib Knowl
Roadfield Wood
Annis Hill
Annis Hill Farm
Birchinley Hall
Birchinley Manor Equestrian Centre
Plumb Ho.
Cranshaw Farm
Wild House
Heights Barn Farm
Reservoir (Covered)
Broad Carr
Higher Crow Nest
Lower Crow Nest
Lowhouse Farm
Crossgates Prim. Sch.
Hen Carr Farm
Club Ho.
Moorhouse Prim. Sch.
Milnrow Parish C. of E. Prim. Sch.
Bowl. Grn.
River Roch
Rochdale Canal (Dis.)
River Beal
Lib.
BRANCH ROAD
CLEGG HALL ROAD
FLETCHER'S
PEANOCK LANE
LAKE SIDE
DRIVE
SMITHY BRIDGE RD.
BELL LANE
TUNSHILL LANE
DEEP LANE
SYKE ROAD
RAKEWOOD
SHAW LANE
STUBLEY MILL ROAD
STUBLEY LANE
CUTLAND WY.
RIVERSTONE
WILLIAM ST.
INGHAMS LA.
WHITEGATE
STOPFORD AV.
CHICHESTER CL.
EAFIELD RD.
LEA FOLD
BARKE ST.
WALMSLEY AV.
LAURELS
COLERIDGE DR.
WORDSWORTH
LEIGHTON AV.
WHITTAKER DR.
DERWENT DR.
STARFIELD AV.
KNOWL VIEW
MILBURY DR.
MERLIN CL.
WOODHEYS R.
BRENTWOOD CL.
SHAFTESBURY
SOUTHEY
HEALD CL.
HIGHER CLEGGSWOOD AV.
CLEGGSWOOD AV.
BEECHWOOD AV.
QUEENS VW.
HIGHLANDS
WOODBANK
LODGE DRIVE
ABBEY DR.
LINCOLN DR.
LODGE ST.
BROWN ST.
BRIDGE NORTH DR.
WILDHOUSE COURT
COLLIER AV.
YEOMAN'S CL.
CROFT HEAD DR.
WEIR RD.
BEALCROFT
EAFIELD AVENUE
PEARSON
CROSSGATES RD.
LOWHOUSE CL.
MALVERN CL.
PENNINE
COTSWOLD CRES.
ALPINE DR.
MENDIP DR.
CHEVIOT CL.
CLEVELAND DR.
ASHES LANE
HALLIWELL
THISTLEYFIELD
BRANDON ST.
ALEXANDER
Brook

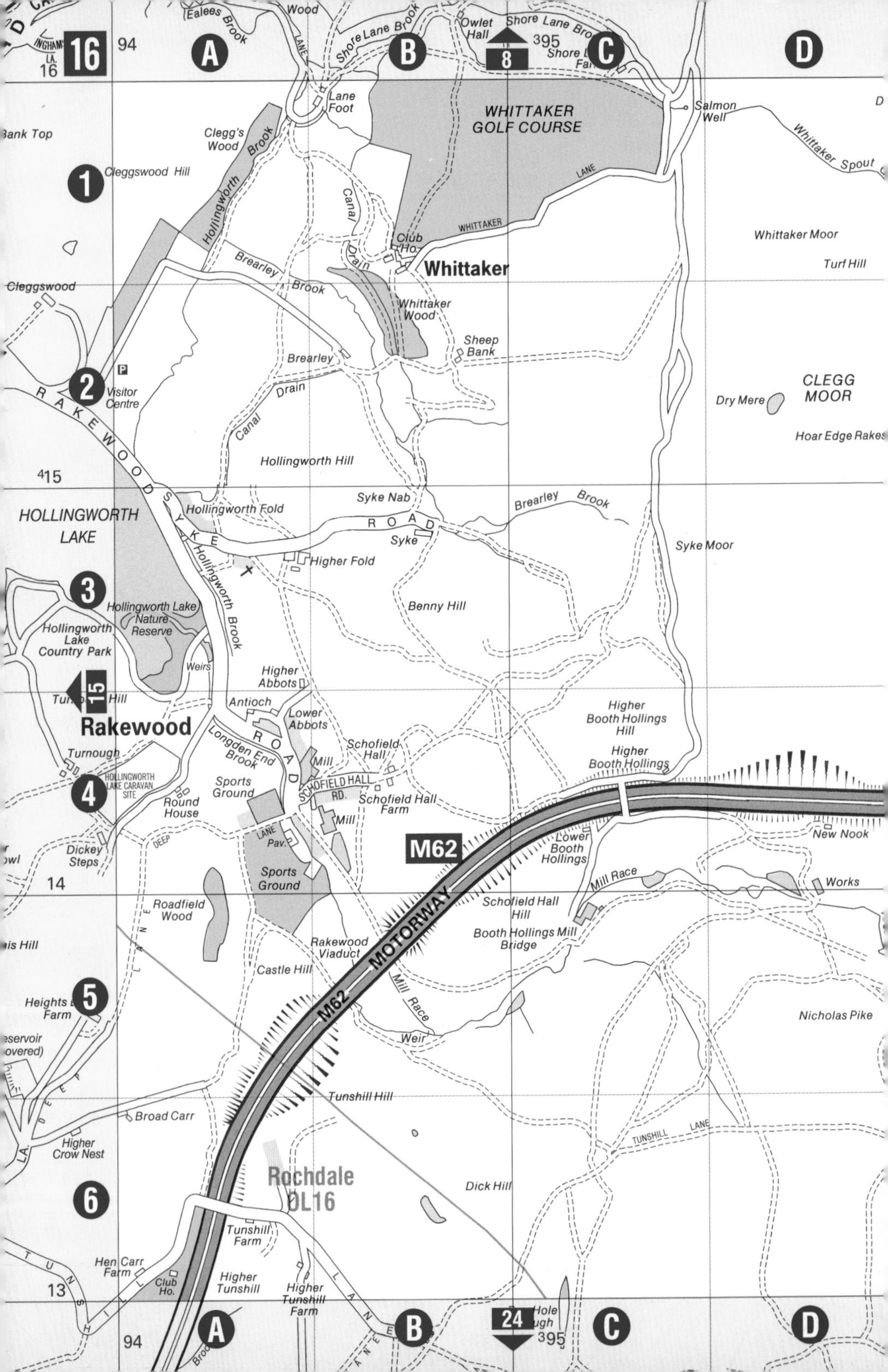
16
94
A
B
C
D
395
8
Ealees Brook
Wood
Shore Lane Brook
Owlet Hall
Shore Lane Farm
Lane Foot
WHITTAKER GOLF COURSE
Salmon Well
Whittaker Spout
Bank Top
Clegg's Wood
Hollingworth Brook
Cleggswood Hill
Canal Drain
WHITTAKER LANE
Club Ho.
Whittaker Moor
Turf Hill
Brearley Brook
Whittaker
Cleggswood
Whittaker Wood
Sheep Bank
Brearley
Visitor Centre
CLEGG MOOR
Dry Mere
Hoar Edge Rakes
RAKEWOOD
Canal Drain
Hollingworth Hill
415
Syke Nab
Brearley Brook
HOLLINGWORTH LAKE
Hollingworth Fold
SYKE ROAD
Syke
Syke Moor
Higher Fold
Hollingworth Lake Nature Reserve
Benny Hill
Hollingworth Lake Country Park
Weirs
Higher Abbots
15
Rakewood
Antioch
Lower Abbots
Higher Booth Hollings Hill
Higher Booth Hollings
Turnough
Longden End Brook
ROAD
Schofield Hall
Mill
HOLLINGWORTH LAKE CARAVAN SITE
Sports Ground
SCHOFIELD HALL RD.
Schofield Hall Farm
Round House
Mill
Lower Booth Hollings
New Nook
DEEP LANE
Pav.
M62
Dickey Steps
Sports Ground
Mill Race
Works
14
Roadfield Wood
Schofield Hall Hill
Booth Hollings Mill Bridge
Rakewood Viaduct
M62 MOTORWAY
Castle Hill
Heights Farm
Mill Race
Nicholas Pike
Weir
Tunshill Hill
TUNSHILL LANE
Broad Carr
Higher Crow Nest
Rochdale OL16
Dick Hill
Tunshill Farm
Hen Carr Farm
Club Ho.
Higher Tunshill
Higher Tunshill Farm
TUNSHILL LANE
13
24

Robin Hood's Bed
E
F
9
97
G
H
98
17
16
Mine Clough
Redmires Clough
Hill Slack
Fern Brakes
Lode Nab
Red Scars Hill
Sowerby Bridge
Redmires
HX6
1
CALDERDALE
ROCHDALE
Sun End
Ford
Ford
Slippery Moss
Longden End Clough
2
Hoar Edge
Moss Slack
Moss Slack Brook
Longden End Brook
415
Littleborough
LOW HOUSE MOOR
Low House Moor
Little Hoar Edge
Great Hoar Edge
White Isles
Black Moor
M62
3
OL15
Rook Stones Hill
Castle Shore Clough
Longden End Moor
Castle Shore Hill
M62 MOTORWAY
T.V. & Radio Station
4
Tag Heys
Windy Hill
Longden End Clough
Longden End Brook
Windy Hill
14
A672
Green Meadows
5
Axletree Edge
Windy Hills
Piethorne Clough
Brook
Weir
Ben Heys
Ashworth Clough
Griffiths Clough
Piethorne
Weir
Weir
Weir
Binns Pasture
Fool Hill
A672
6
Norman Hill Reservoir
Bleakedgate Moor
Oldham
OL3
Foxstone Edge
13
E
F
25
97
G
Rooden
H
ROAD
98

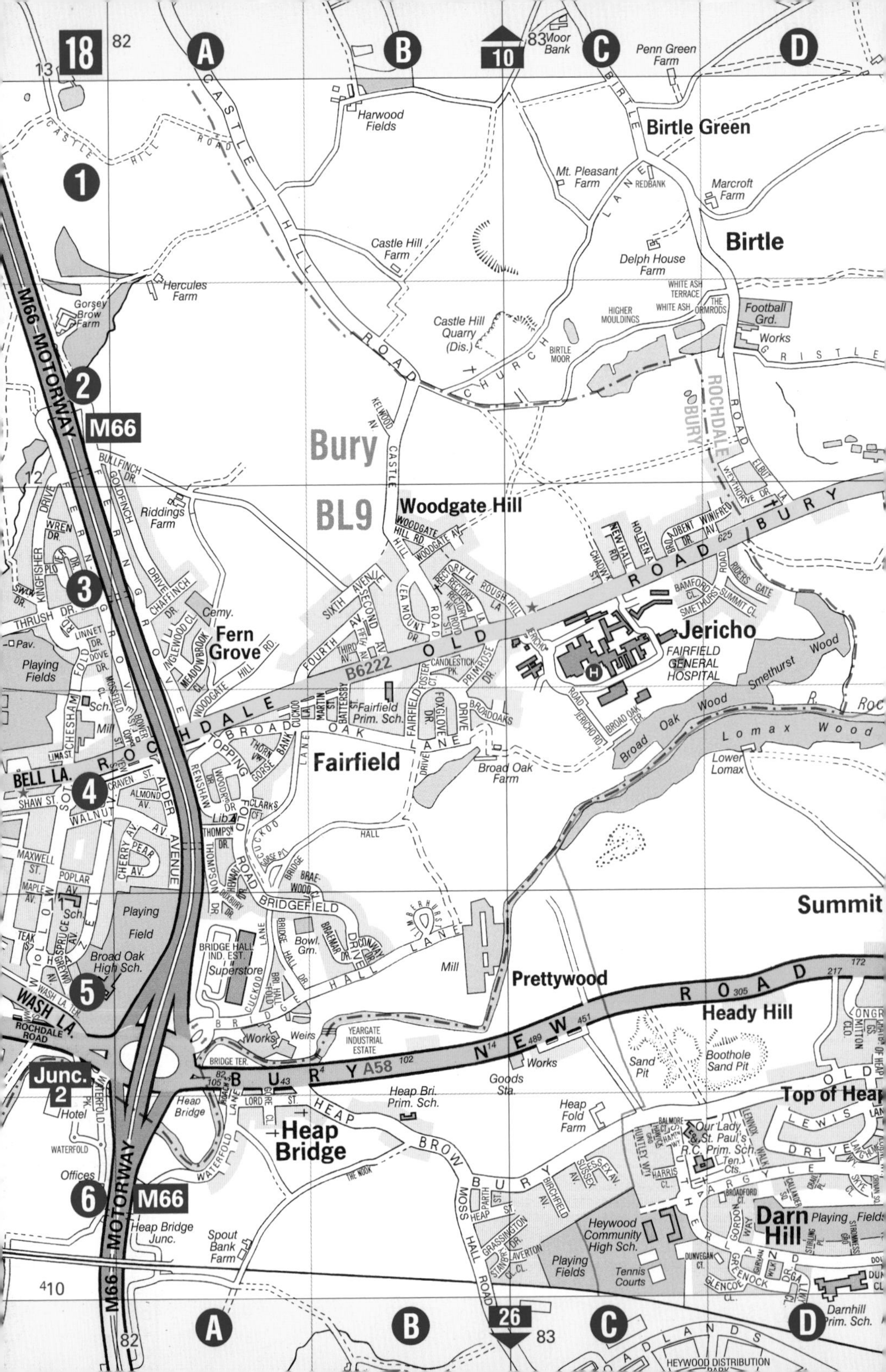

18
Birtle Green
Birtle
Harwood Fields
Moor Bank
Penn Green Farm
Mt. Pleasant Farm
Marcroft Farm
Castle Hill Farm
Delph House Farm
Hercules Farm
Gorsey Brow Farm
Castle Hill Quarry (Dis.)
Football Grd.
Works
Bury
BL9
Woodgate Hill
Riddings Farm
Cemy.
Fern Grove
Jericho
FAIRFIELD GENERAL HOSPITAL
Smethurst Wood
Broad Oak Wood
Lomax Wood
Lower Lomax
Playing Fields
Fairfield
Fairfield Prim. Sch.
Broad Oak Farm
Broad Oak High Sch.
Playing Field
BRIDGE HALL IND. EST.
Superstore
Bowl. Grn.
Mill
Prettywood
Summit
Heady Hill
Sand Pit
Boothole Sand Pit
Top of Heap
YEARGATE INDUSTRIAL ESTATE
Works
Weirs
Goods Sta.
Heap Bri. Prim. Sch.
Heap Bridge
Heap Fold Farm
Our Lady & St. Paul's R.C. Prim. Sch.
Darn Hill
Heywood Community High Sch.
Playing Fields
Tennis Courts
Darnhill Prim. Sch.
Spout Bank Farm
Heap Bridge Junc.
Junc. 2
Hotel
Offices
M66 MOTORWAY
M66
B6222
A58
ROCHDALE OLD ROAD
BURY OLD ROAD
BURY NEW ROAD
CASTLE HILL ROAD
BIRTLE LANE
CHURCH LANE
HEAP BROW
MOSS HALL ROAD
BRIDGE HALL LANE
HEYWOOD DISTRIBUTION PARK

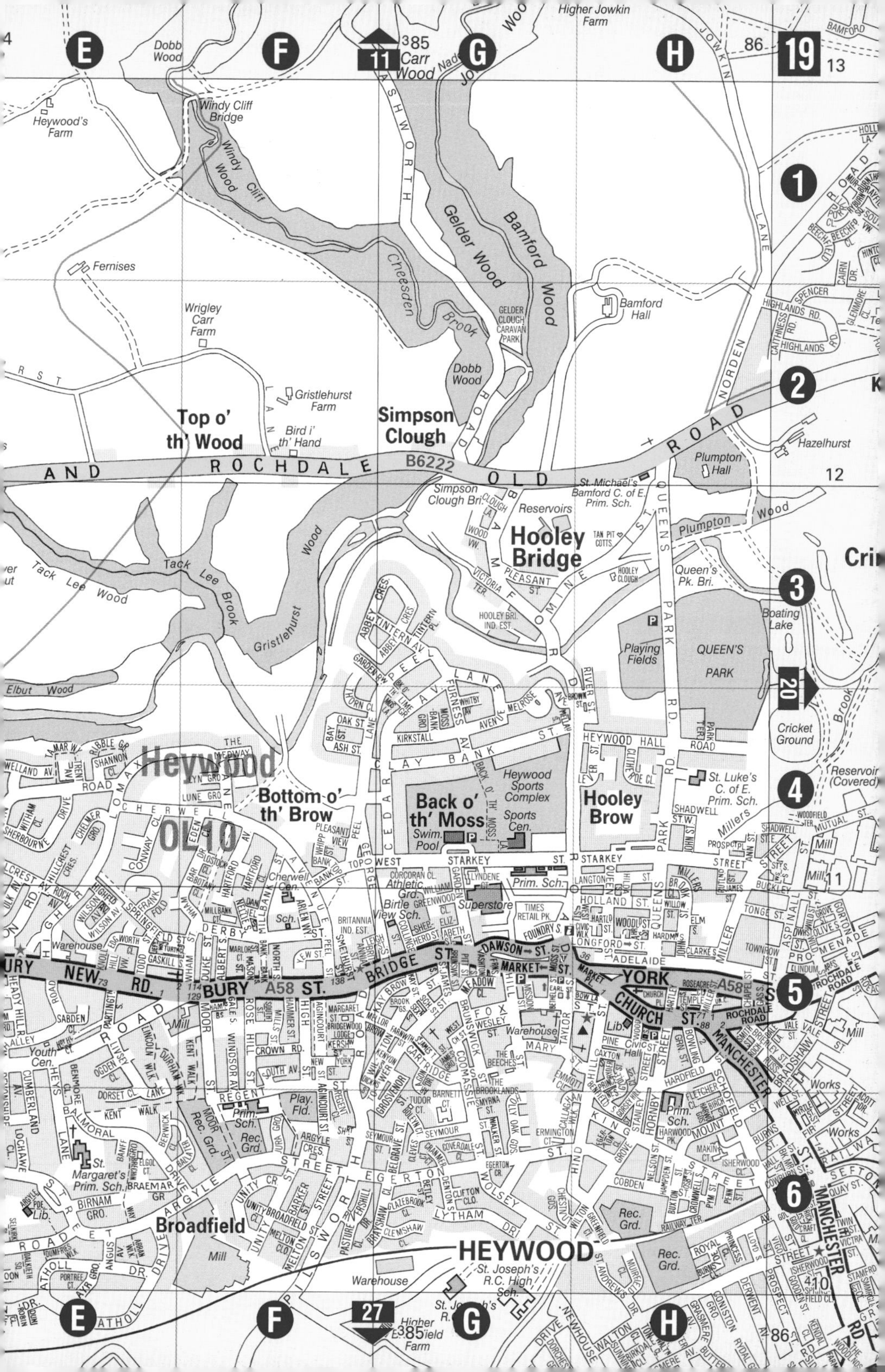
E
F
G
H
11
385
19
13
86
Higher Jowkin Farm
Dobb Wood
Carr Wood
Heywood's Farm
Windy Cliff Bridge
Windy Cliff Wood
ASHWORTH
Gelder Wood
Bamford Wood
Cheesden Brook
JOWKIN
LANE
NORDEN
Fernises
Wrigley Carr Farm
GELDER CLOUGH CARAVAN PARK
Bamford Hall
Dobb Wood
ROAD
HIGHLANDS RD.
SPENCER
CAITHNESS RD.
HIGHLANDS
GLENMORE
BEECHFIELD
CAIRN DR.
1
2
3
4
5
6
Gristlehurst Farm
Bird i' th' Hand
Top o' th' Wood
Simpson Clough
Hazelhurst
Plumpton Hall
AND ROCHDALE B6222 OLD ROAD
12
Simpson Clough Bri.
Reservoirs
St. Michael's Bamford C. of E. Prim. Sch.
Hooley Bridge
BAMFORD
ST. QUEENS
Plumpton Wood
Tack Lee Wood
Tack Lee Brook
Gristlehurst Wood
Elbut Wood
VICTORIA TER.
PLEASANT ST.
HOOLEY BRI. IND. EST.
Queen's Pk. Bri.
Boating Lake
Playing Fields
QUEEN'S PARK
20
Cricket Ground
Brook
ABBEY CRES.
TINTERN AV.
PEEL AV.
LANE
FURNESS AV.
MELROSE AVE.
KIRKSTALL AVENUE
BANK ST.
CLAY BANK
RIVER ST.
HEYWOOD HALL ROAD
PARK TER.
Heywood
Bottom o' th' Brow
Back o' th' Moss
Swim. Pool
Heywood Sports Complex
Sports Cen.
Hooley Brow
St. Luke's C. of E. Prim. Sch.
Reservoir (Covered)
OL10
CHERWELL
STARKEY ST.
STARKEY STREET
Millers
Mill
11
Cherwell Cen.
Sch.
Athletic Grd.
Birtle View Sch.
Superstore
TIMES RETAIL PK.
Prim. Sch.
HOLLAND ST.
BRITANNIA IND. EST.
Warehouse
DERBY ST.
BURY NEW RD.
BURY A58 ST.
BRIDGE ST.
DAWSON ST.
MARKET ST.
YORK ST.
CHURCH ST.
A58
ROCHDALE ROAD
MANCHESTER
Lib.
Civic Hall
FOX ST.
WESLEY ST.
MARY ST.
Warehouse
Youth Cen.
CUMBERLAND AV.
REGENT ST.
Prim. Sch.
Play. Fld.
MOOR Rec. Grd.
Rec. Grd.
Works
Prim. Sch.
KING ST.
St. Margaret's Prim. Sch.
BALMORAL
ARGYLE STREET
EGERTON STREET
Broadfield
Lib.
BIRNAM GRO.
Mill
PILLSWORTH
LYTHAM DRI.
WOLSEY ST.
HEYWOOD
Rec. Grd.
Rec. Grd.
Warehouse
St. Joseph's R.C. High Sch.
ATHOLL
27
385
86
410
MANCHESTER RD.

A
B
C
D
1
2
3
4
5
6
12
19
28
86
87
Bamford
Bamford Prim. Sch.
BAMFORD SHOP. CEN.
Broadhalgh
Kenyon Fold
Hazelhurst
Plumpton Hall
Plumpton Wood
Crimble
Crimble Hall Farm
Queen's Pk. Bri.
Boating Lake
QUEEN'S PARK
Cricket Ground
Reservoir (Covered)
Captain Fold
All Souls C. of E. Prim. Sch.
Ryecroft House
Ryecroft Farm
Heywood
HEYWOOD
OL10
Heywood Cemetery
Primrose Hill Farm
Chamberhouse Urban Farm
Matthew Moss High Sch.
Springfield Park Track
Club House
Springfield Park
Springfield Cotts.
Mereside Ho.
Marland
High Birch Sch.
MARLAND GOLF COURSE
River Roch
Mills
Ryefield
Pond
Harefield Hall
Harefield Farm
Roeacre Brook
Francil
Chamber House
Superstore
Cricket Grd.
Castleton Gabriel's F.C. Ground
Wilderness
CASTLE HAWK GOLF COURSE
Club Ho.
Rail Welding Depot
JUNCTION 19 INDUSTRIAL PARK
PHOENIX PARK INDUSTRIAL ESTATE
SOUTHGATE IND. EST.
LEMONPARK INDUSTRIAL ESTATE
Hopwood
Works
Mill
Rec. Grd.
Prim. Sch.
Ten. Cts.
BURY ROAD
B6222
BOLTON ROAD EAST
ROCHDALE ROAD
A58
MANCHESTER RD.
B6046
NORDEN ROAD
CHADWICK LANE
RAILWAY CROSS ST.

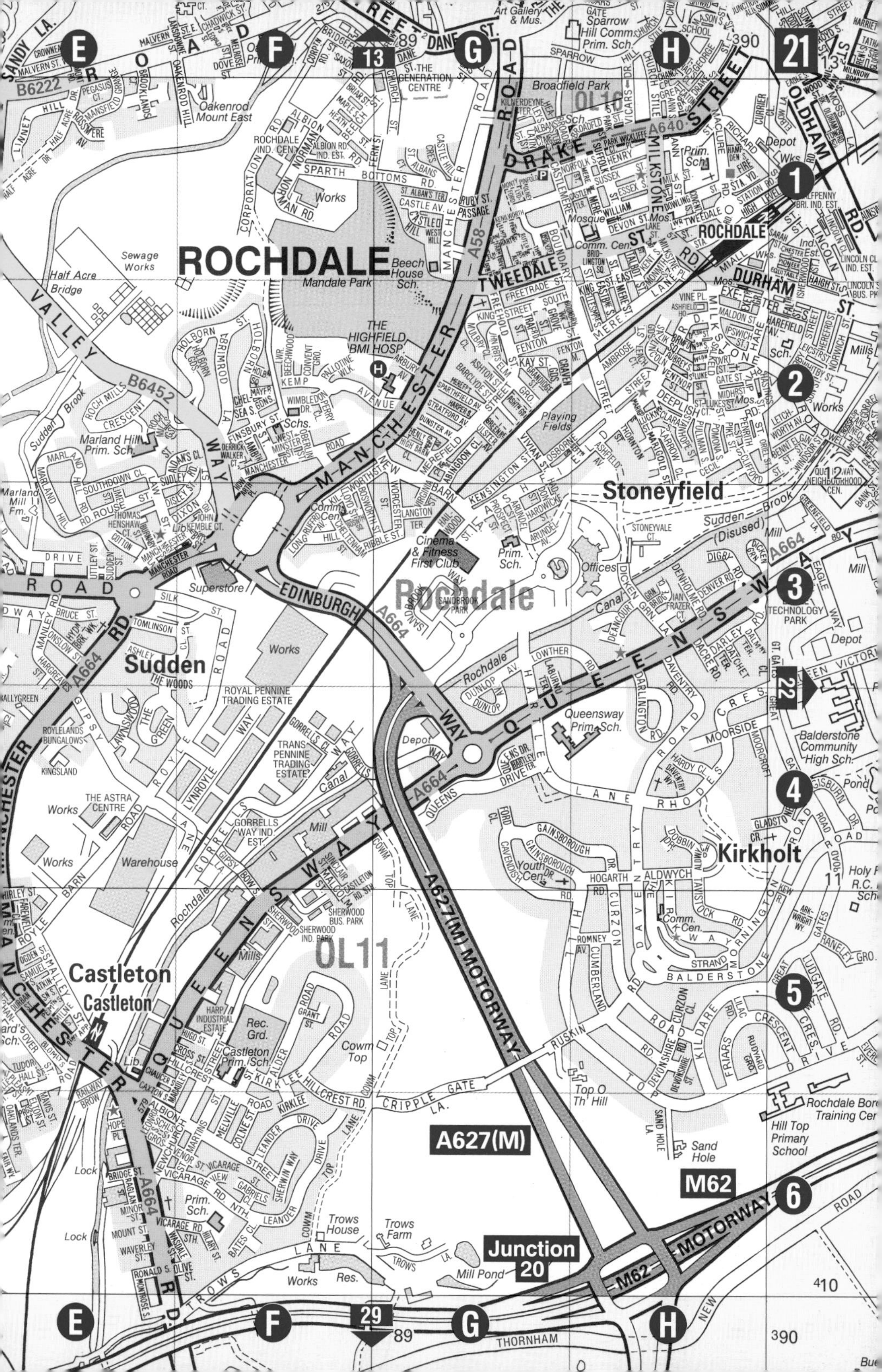

21
13
22
29
E
F
G
H
1
2
3
4
5
6
ROCHDALE
Rochdale
Stoneyfield
Sudden
Castleton
Kirkholt
OL16
OL11
MANCHESTER ROAD
EDINBURGH WAY
QUEENS WAY
DRAKE STREET
TWEEDALE ST.
ROCHDALE RD.
DURHAM ST.
OLDHAM RD.
VALLEY WAY
B6452
B6222
A58
A640
A664
A627(M)
A627(M) MOTORWAY
M62
M62 MOTORWAY
Junction 20
Broadfield Park
Mandale Park
Sewage Works
Half Acre Bridge
THE HIGHFIELD BMI HOSP.
Beech House Sch.
Oakenrod Mount East
Marland Hill Prim. Sch.
Superstore
Works
ROYAL PENNINE TRADING ESTATE
TRANS PENNINE TRADING ESTATE
GORRELLS WAY IND. EST.
THE ASTRA CENTRE
Warehouse
Cinema & Fitness First Club
Offices
Playing Fields
Queensway Prim. Sch.
Balderstone Community High Sch.
TECHNOLOGY PARK
Rochdale Canal
Rec. Grd.
Castleton Prim. Sch.
HARP INDUSTRIAL ESTATE
SHERWOOD BUS. PARK
SHERWOOD IND. PARK
Cowm Top
Top O Th Hill
Sand Hole
Trows House
Trows Farm
Mill Pond
Res.
Hill Top Primary School
Sparrow Hill Comm. Prim. Sch.
Art Gallery & Mus.
ST. THE GENERATION CENTRE
ROCHDALE IND. CEN.
THORNHAM
TROWS LANE
CRIPPLE GATE LA.
BALDERSTONE
RHODES
GAINSBOROUGH DR.
KENSINGTON ST.
SPARTH BOTTOMS RD.
390
410
89

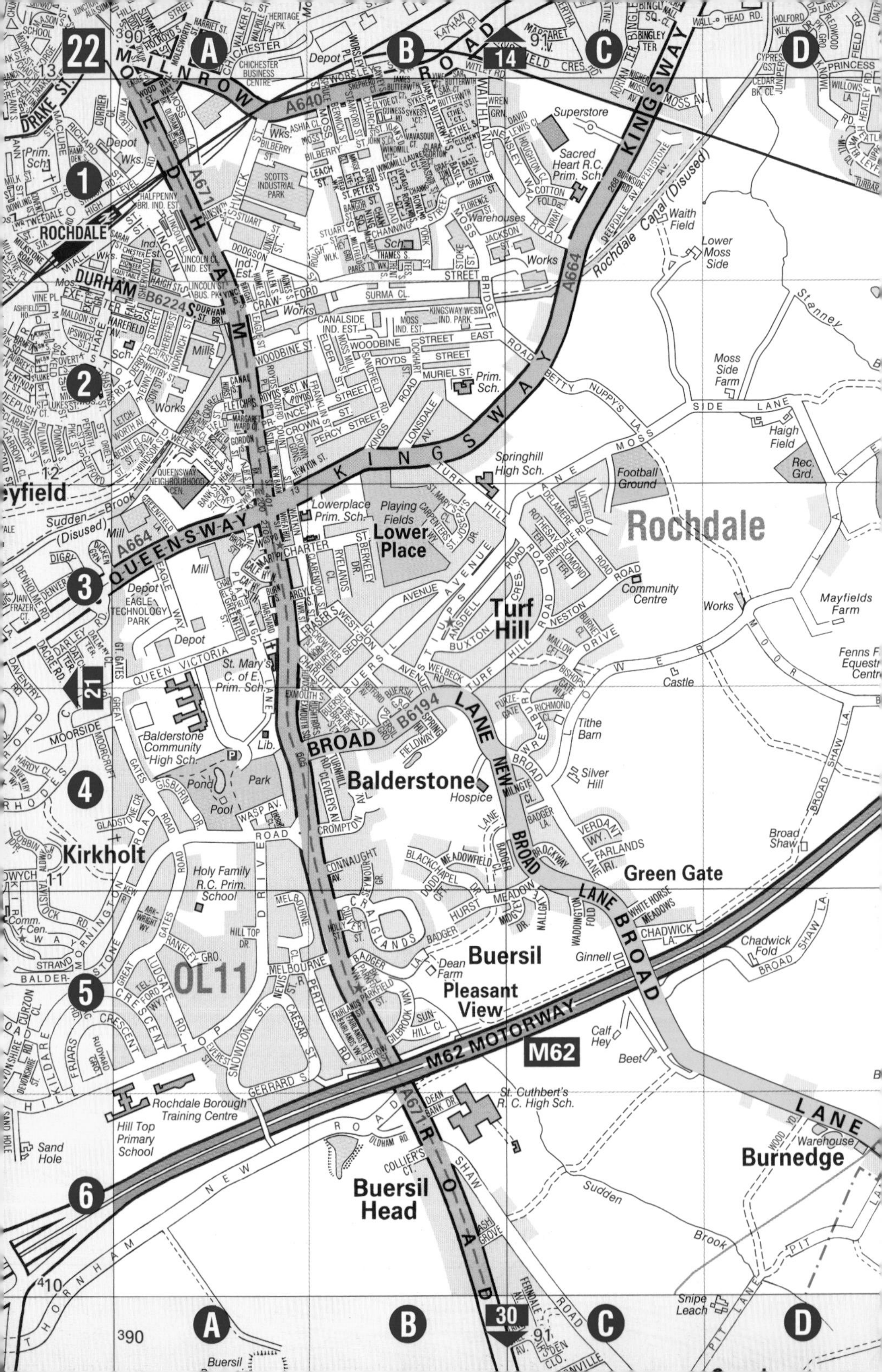

A
B
C
D
1
2
3
4
5
6
14
21
30
390
91
410
13
12
11
MILNROW ROAD
OLDHAM ROAD
A671
A640
A664
B6224
B6194
KINGSWAY
QUEENSWAY
BROAD LANE
NEW BROAD LANE
M62 MOTORWAY
M62
ROCHDALE
DURHAM ST.
DRAKE ST.
Chichester Business Centre
Scotts Industrial Park
Superstore
Sacred Heart R.C. Prim. Sch.
Rochdale Canal (Disused)
Waith Field
Lower Moss Side
Moss Side Farm
Haigh Field
Rec. Grd.
Football Ground
Rochdale
Springhill High Sch.
Lowerplace Prim. Sch.
Playing Fields
Lower Place
Queensway Neighbourhood Cen.
Eagle Technology Park
Turf Hill
Community Centre
Works
Mayfields Farm
Castle
Tithe Barn
Silver Hill
St. Mary's C. of E. Prim. Sch.
Balderstone Community High Sch.
Park
Pond
Pool
Lib.
Balderstone
Hospice
Kirkholt
Holy Family R.C. Prim. School
Green Gate
Broad Shaw
Chadwick Fold
Buersil
Dean Farm
Pleasant View
OL11
Calf Hey
Beet
St. Cuthbert's R. C. High Sch.
Rochdale Borough Training Centre
Hill Top Primary School
Sand Hole
Burnedge
Warehouse
Buersil Head
Sudden Brook
Snipe Leach
THORNHAM NEW ROAD
SHAW ROAD
PIT LANE
MOSS SIDE LANE
TURF HILL ROAD
QUEEN VICTORIA ST.
Depot
Mill
Mills

23
E
F
G
H
15
93
94
Milnrow
Moorhouse Prim. Sch.
Milnrow Parish C. of E. Prim. Sch.
Hollingworth High Sch.
Butterworth Hall
Playing Field
TUNSHILL GOLF COURSE
Tunshill Lane
Lark Hill
Moy Hill
Walk Bank
M62
MOTORWAY
Cliffe Plantation
Memorial Park
War Memorial
Newhey
Lady House
OL16
Stanney Brook Park
Cricket Grd.
Junction 21
Subway
Ellenroad
Works
Bentgate
Reservoir
Further Whitfield Bottoms Farm
Dig Gate
Garside
Knott Booth
Bryney Heys
Top o' th' Meadow
ROCHDALE
OLDHAM
Oldham
Hey Farm
Whitfield Hall
Whitefield Park Farm
Whitfield Dairy Farm
Dun Wood Park
Jep Wood
Jubilee
Green Hill
Green Hill Farm
OL2
Moss Gate
Moss Gate Fm.
Lower Rushcroft
Rushcroft Primary Sch.
Wood End
Higher
ELIZABETHAN WAY
A640
A663
B6225
B6194
HUDDERSFIELD ROAD
SHAW RD.
MILNROW RD.
ROCHDALE ROAD
NEWHEY RD.
KILN LA.
Newhey Prim. Sch.
Prim. Sch.
Rec. Grd.
Pennine Precinct
Comm. Cen.
Lib.
24
31
1
2
3
4
5
6

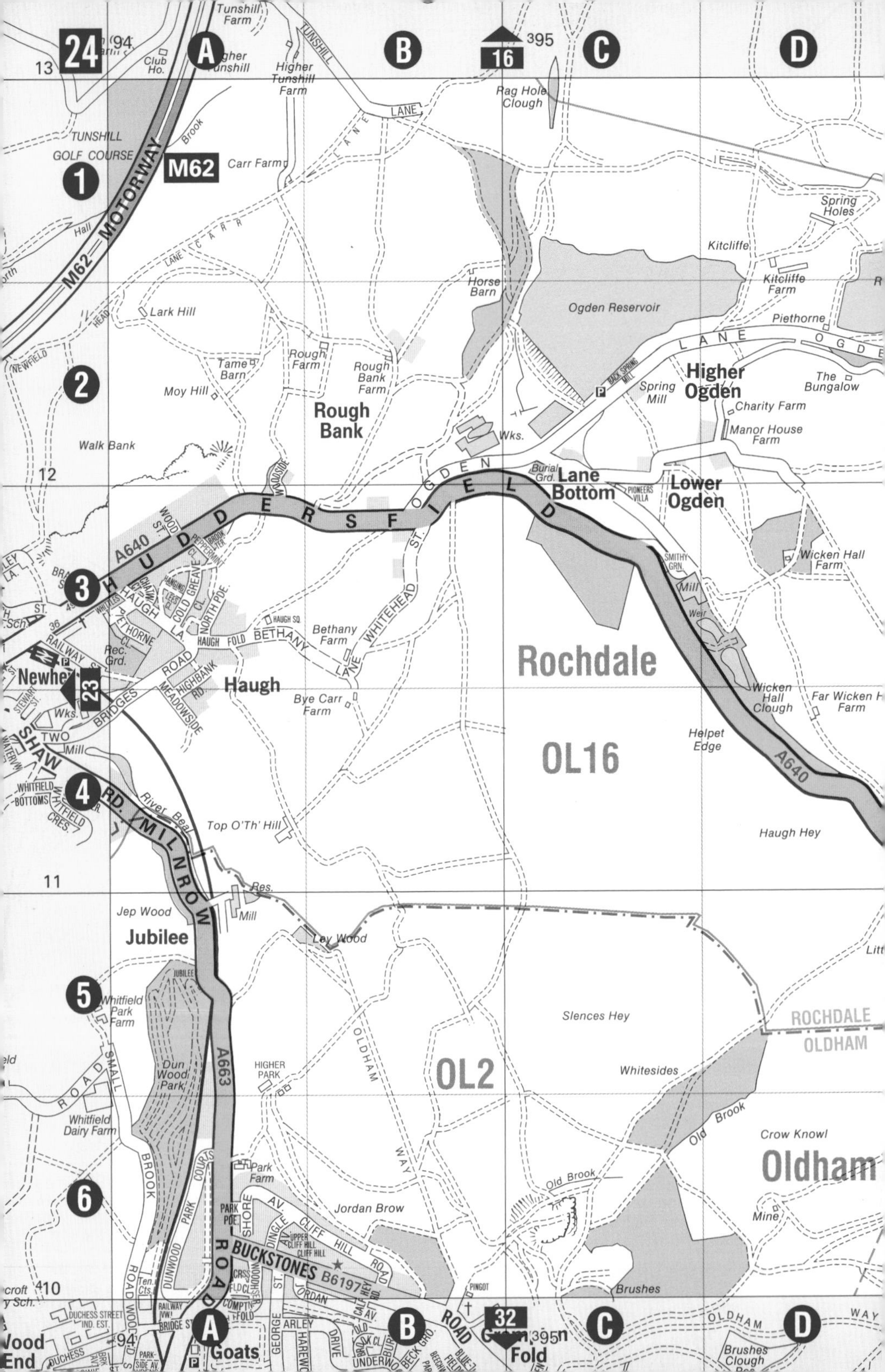

24
16
23
32
A
B
C
D
1
2
3
4
5
6
Tunshill Farm
Higher Tunshill
Higher Tunshill Farm
Club Ho.
TUNSHILL GOLF COURSE
M62
M62 MOTORWAY
Carr Farm
Rag Hole Clough
TUNSHILL LANE
CARR LANE
Lark Hill
Horse Barn
Ogden Reservoir
Spring Holes
Kitcliffe
Kitcliffe Farm
Piethorne
LANE
Rough Farm
Rough Bank Farm
Tame Barn
Moy Hill
Rough Bank
Spring Mill
Higher Ogden
The Bungalow
Charity Farm
Manor House Farm
Walk Bank
Wks.
Burial Grd.
Lane Bottom
Lower Ogden
PIONEERS VILLA
HUDDERSFIELD
A640
Wicken Hall Farm
SMITHY GRN.
Mill
Weir
HAUGH SQ.
Bethany Farm
BETHANY LANE
WHITEHEAD ST.
HAUGH FOLD
Rec. Grd.
Newhey
Haugh
Rochdale
Bye Carr Farm
Wicken Hall Clough
Far Wicken Hall Farm
Helpet Edge
OL16
TWO BRIDGES ROAD
MEADOWSIDE
HIGHBANK RD.
SHAW RD.
MILNROW
River Beal
WHITFIELD BOTTOMS
Top O'Th' Hill
Haugh Hey
Res.
Mill
Jep Wood
Jubilee
Ley Wood
Whitfield Park Farm
Dun Wood Park
A663
Slences Hey
ROCHDALE
OLDHAM
HIGHER PARK
OL2
Whitesides
OLDHAM WAY
SMALL BROOK ROAD
Whitfield Dairy Farm
Old Brook
Crow Knowl
Oldham
Park Farm
Jordan Brow
Mine
BUCKSTONES
B6197
CLIFF HILL
ROAD
PINGOT
Brushes
DUCHESS STREET IND. EST.
BRIDGE ST.
Goats
Wood End
Fold
Brushes Clough
395
94
13
12
11
410

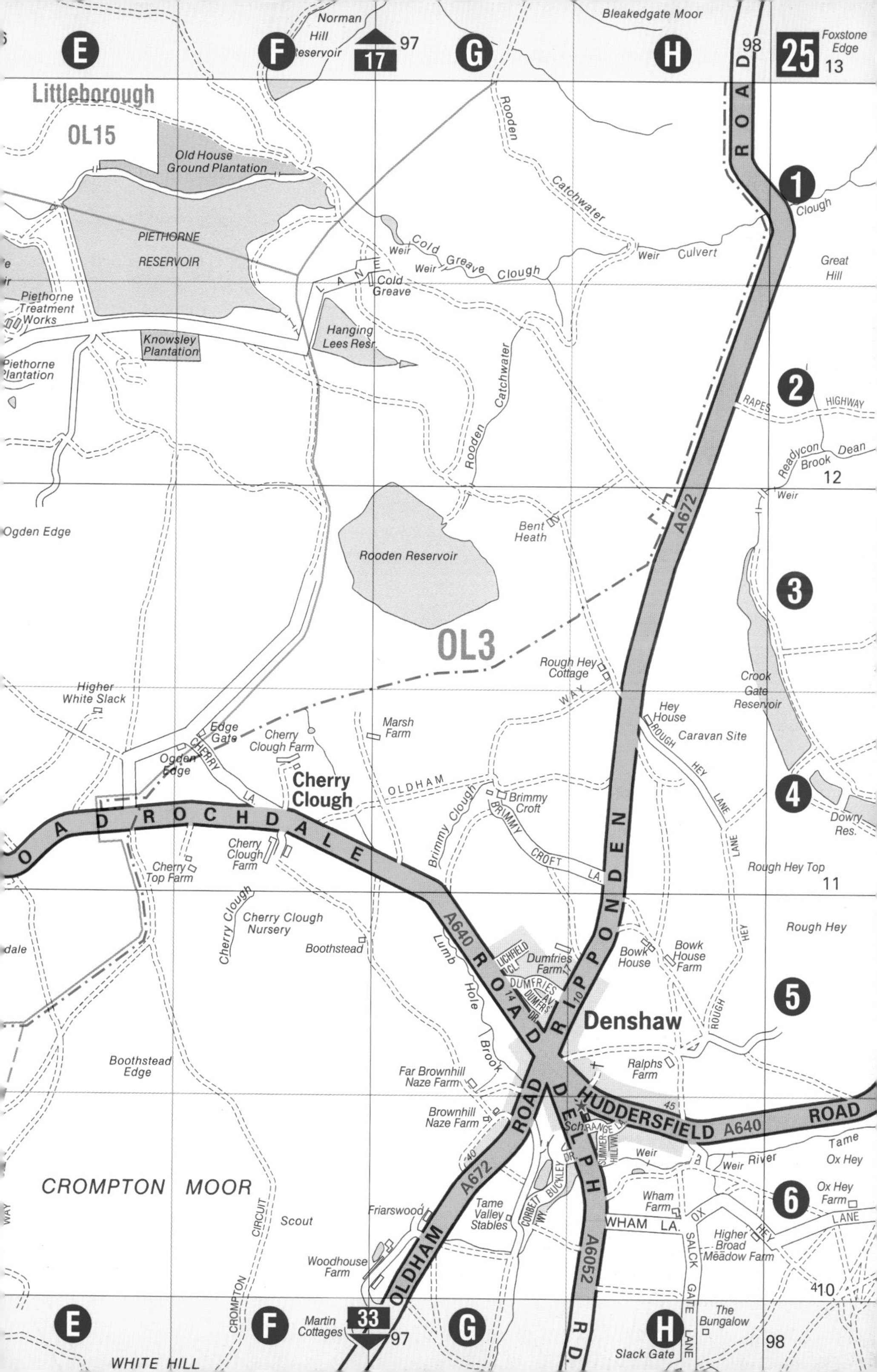

25
E
F
G
H
17
97
98
Foxstone Edge
13
Norman Hill Reservoir
Bleakedgate Moor
Littleborough
OL15
Old House Ground Plantation
PIETHORNE RESERVOIR
Piethorne Treatment Works
Knowsley Plantation
Piethorne Plantation
Hanging Lees Resr.
Cold Greave
Cold Greave Clough
Weir
LANE
Rooden
Catchwater
Clough
Culvert
Great Hill
1
2
RAPES HIGHWAY
Readycon Dean Brook
12
Rooden Reservoir
Bent Heath
A672
Ogden Edge
3
OL3
Rough Hey Cottage
Crook Gate Reservoir
Higher White Slack
Hey House
Caravan Site
ROUGH HEY LANE
Edge Gate
Cherry Clough Farm
Marsh Farm
Ogden Edge
CHERRY LA.
Cherry Clough
OLDHAM WAY
Brimmy Croft
BRIMMY CROFT LA.
Brimmy Clough
4
Dowry Res.
ROCHDALE ROAD
Cherry Top Farm
Cherry Clough Farm
Rough Hey Top
11
RIPPONDEN ROAD
Cherry Clough
Cherry Clough Nursery
Boothstead
A640
Lumb Hole Brook
LICHFIELD CL.
Dumfries Farm
DUMFRIES AV.
DUMFRS DR.
Bowk House
Bowk House Farm
Rough Hey
HEY LANE
5
Denshaw
ROUGH
Boothstead Edge
Far Brownhill Naze Farm
Ralphs Farm
Brownhill Naze Farm
DELPH ROAD
HUDDERSFIELD ROAD
A640
Sch.
RANGE LA.
SUMMER HILL VW.
Weir
Tame River
Ox Hey
6
Ox Hey Farm
CROMPTON MOOR
Tame Valley Stables
CORBETT WY.
BUCKLEY DR.
Wham Farm
OX HEY LANE
Friarswood
Scout
CIRCUIT
WHAM LA.
Higher Broad Meadow Farm
A6052
Woodhouse Farm
OLDHAM ROAD
CROMPTON
SALCK GATE LANE
410
33
Martin Cottages
The Bungalow
RD.
98
Slack Gate
WHITE HILL
WAY

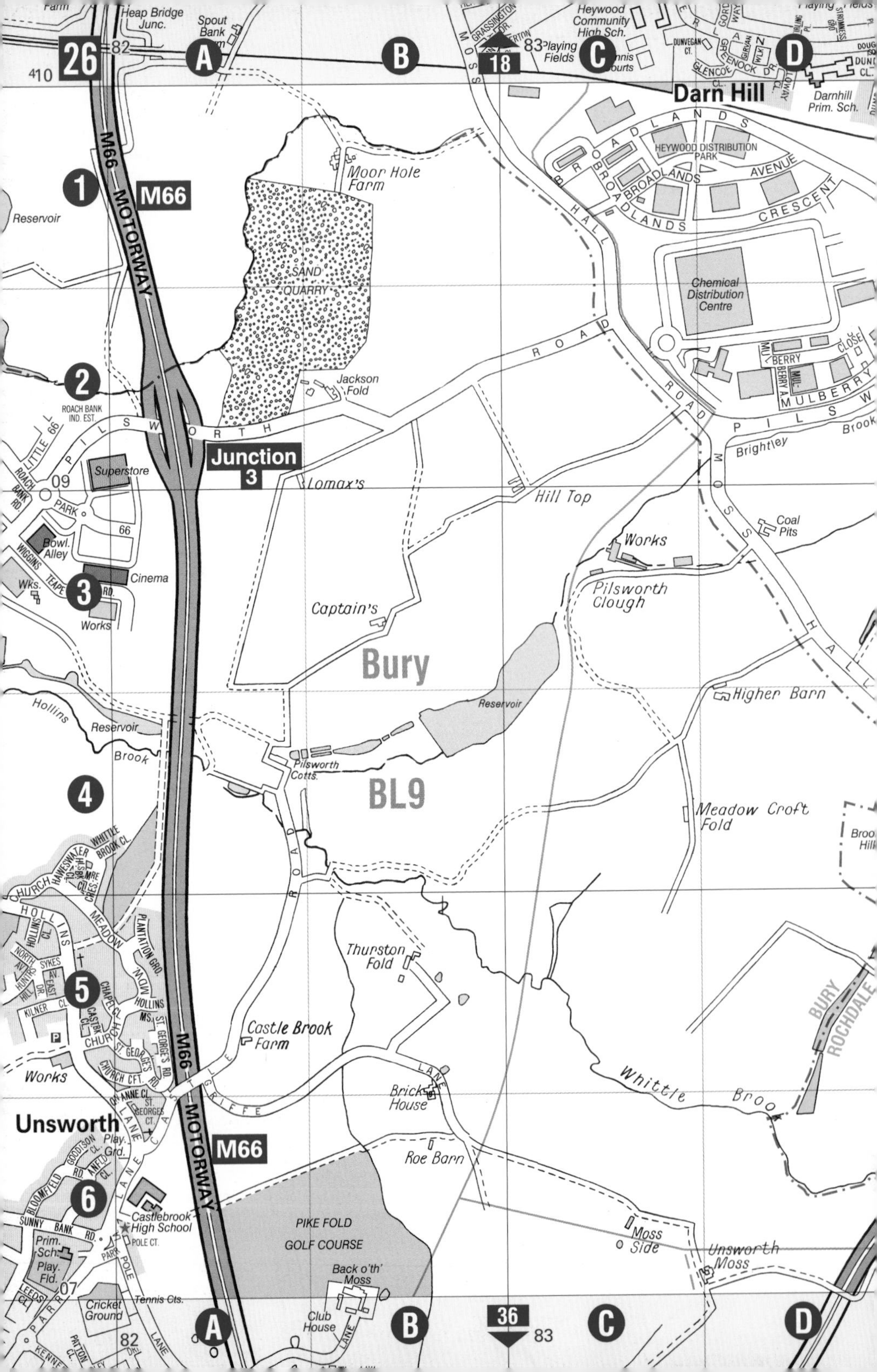

26
Heap Bridge Junc.
Spout Bank Farm
Heywood Community High Sch.
Playing Fields
Tennis Courts
Darn Hill
Darnhill Prim. Sch.
18
A
B
C
D
410
82
83
M66 MOTORWAY
M66
Reservoir
Moor Hole Farm
SAND QUARRY
HEYWOOD DISTRIBUTION PARK
BROADLANDS
BROADLANDS AVENUE
BROADLANDS CRESCENT
HALL ROAD
MOSS HALL ROAD
Chemical Distribution Centre
MULBERRY CLOSE
MULBERRY WAY
PILSWORTH ROAD
Jackson Fold
ROACH BANK IND. EST.
Junction 3
Superstore
Bowl. Alley
Cinema
Wks.
Works
Lomax's
Hill Top
Brightley Brook
Coal Pits
Pilsworth Clough
Captain's
Bury
BL9
Hollins Brook
Higher Barn
Pilsworth Cotts.
Meadow Croft Fold
Brook Hill
Thurston Fold
Castle Brook Farm
Brick House
Whittle Brook
BURY ROCHDALE
Unsworth
Castlebrook High School
Roe Barn
PIKE FOLD GOLF COURSE
Moss Side
Unsworth Moss
Back o'th' Moss
Club House
Cricket Ground
Tennis Cts.
Play. Fld.
Prim. Sch.
36
07
09
1
2
3
4
5
6

27
Broadfield
19
28
37
Junction 19
E
F
G
H
1
2
3
4
5
6
09
08
07
385
86
410
Mill
Joseph's R.C. High Sch.
St. Joseph's R.C. Prim. Sch.
Higher Broadfield Farm
HARESHILL BUSINESS PARK
Heywood
OL10
Hares Hill Farm
Siddal Moor Depot
Siddal Moor Sports College
Playing Field
Tennis Cts.
Mercer's Farm
Collop Gate Farm
Siddal Moor Farm
Brightley Brook
Higher Fields
Stock Nook
New Gap Farm
Saxons Farm
M62
Siddal Farm
Doctor Fold
Lower Whittle
BIRCH INDUSTRIAL ESTATE
Birch Service Area
M62 MOTORWAY
Mills
Siddal Fold
Top o' th' Hill
Manchester
M24
Whittle Fold
The Grange
Grange Farm
Birch
Langley Lane Farm
Greenhill Farm
Whittle Brook
Playing Fields
Green Lane End
Langley Brook
Mere Brook
Simon Lane
Furrow Community Sch.
Community Centre
Langley Prim. Sch.
Langley
MANCHESTER ROAD A6045
HEYWOOD OLD ROAD A6045
LANGLEY LANE
DOCTOR FOLD LANE
HARESHILL ROAD
WHITTLE LANE
PARKLANDS WAY

28
Hopwood
Heywood
Lane End
OL10
M62 MOTORWAY
Junction 19
M62
MANCHESTER GOLF CLUB
Glade Wood
Oaken Bank Wood
Hopwood Hall
Hopwood Hall College (Middleton Campus)
The Queen Elizabeth School
Manchester
M24
Top of Hebers
Hollins
Stanycliffe
Langley
MIDDLETON RD.
HOLLIN ROAD
HOLLIN LANE
ROCHDALE ROAD
MANCHESTER ROAD
OAKEN BANK ROAD
20
27
38

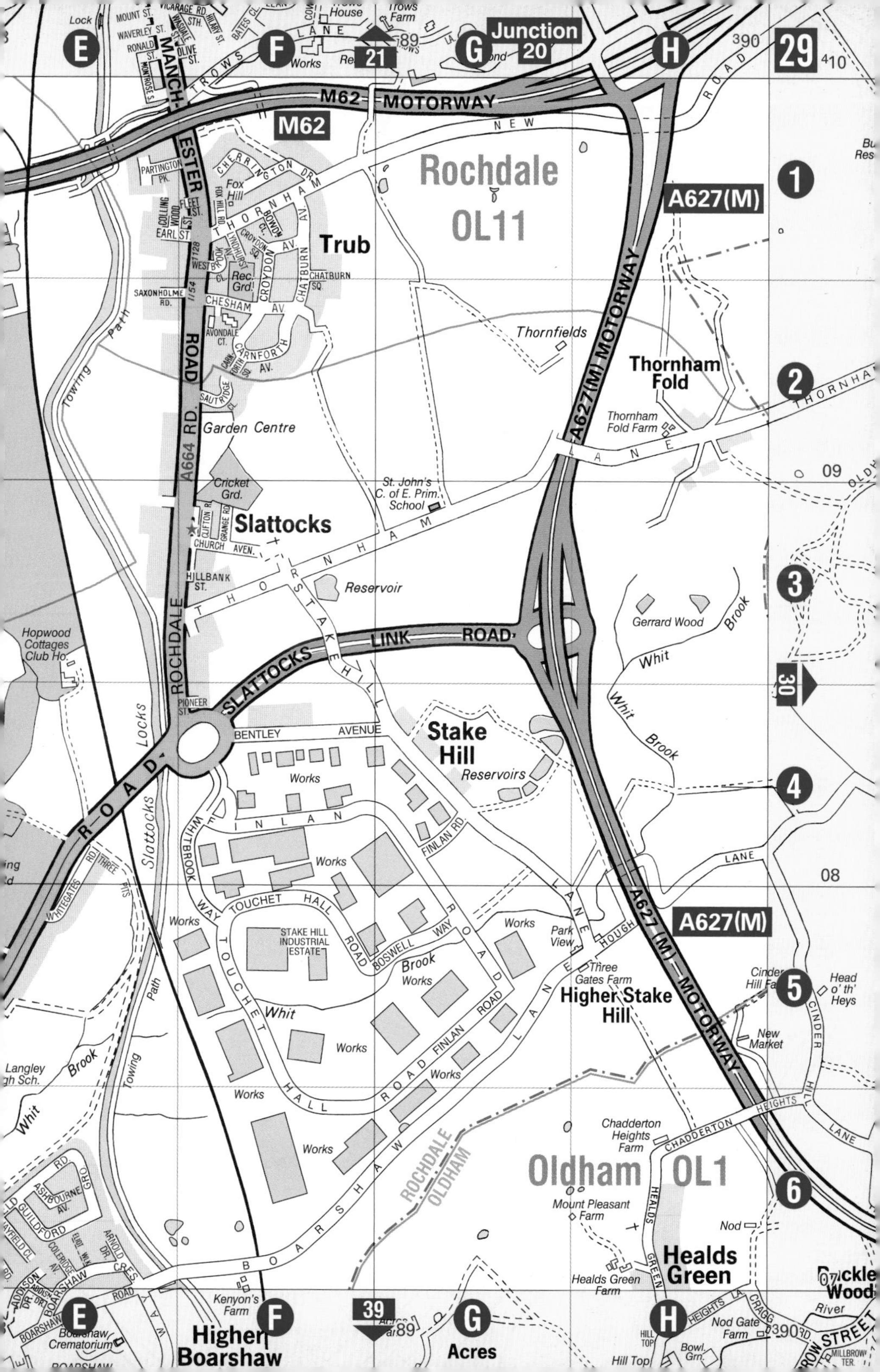

29
Junction 20
21
M62 MOTORWAY
M62
A627(M)
A627(M) MOTORWAY
Rochdale
OL11
Trub
Slattocks
Thornham Fold
Thornham Fold Farm
Thornfields
St. John's C. of E. Prim. School
Reservoir
Garden Centre
Cricket Grd.
Rec. Grd.
Fox Hill
SLATTOCKS LINK ROAD
ROCHDALE ROAD
A664 RD.
MANCHESTER ROAD
Stake Hill
Reservoirs
Gerrard Wood
Whit Brook
Hopwood Cottages Club Ho.
Slattocks Locks
Towing Path
STAKE HILL INDUSTRIAL ESTATE
Works
FINLAN RD.
TOUCHET HALL ROAD
BOSWELL WAY
WHITBROOK WAY
BENTLEY AVENUE
Park View
Three Gates Farm
Higher Stake Hill
Cinder Hill Farm
Head o' th' Heys
New Market
Chadderton Heights Farm
CHADDERTON HEIGHTS
Oldham OL1
Mount Pleasant Farm
Nod
Healds Green
Healds Green Farm
Nod Gate Farm
Hill Top
Kenyon's Farm
Boarshaw Crematorium
Higher Boarshaw
Acres
BOARSHAW LANE
ROCHDALE OLDHAM
Langley High Sch.
30
39
E F G H
1 2 3 4 5 6
09 08
390 410

A
B
C
D
1
2
3
4
5
6
22
29
40
Rochdale
OL16
OL11
OL1
ROCHDALE
OLDHAM
Buersil Reservoir
Plumpton
Gravel Hole
Snipe Leach
Thornham St. James' C. of E. Prim. Sch.
Starkey Farm
Summit
Football Grd.
High Gate
Hanging Chadder
Hanging Chadder Farm
Oldham
Firbank Prim. Sch.
Tandle Hill Countryside Centre
TANDLE HILL COUNTRY PARK
Paddling Pool
Oozewood
Lower Oozewood Farm
Dogford Park
Royton Cemetery
Thorp
Thorp Prim. Sch.
Manor Farm
Hall Play-grd.
Cricket Grd.
Bowl. Grn.
Club
Crofters
ROYTON
Brookside Farm
Millfields Farm
Haggate
Head o' th' Heys
Cinder Hill Farm
New Market
Gillotts
Lower Gillotts
Race Field
Football Grd.
Street Bridge
Sewage Works
Mills
Res.
Royley
St. Paul's C. of E. Prim. Sch.
Nether Hey Fm.
Tennis Courts
Playing Field
Holden Fold
Healds Green
Buckley Wood
Nod
Nod Gate Farm
A627(M)
A627(M) MOTORWAY
A671
A663
B6195
OLDHAM RD.
ROCHDALE
THORNHAM OLD ROAD
OLDHAM ROAD
TANDLE HILL ROAD
OOZEWOOD ROAD
CINDER HILL
CHADDERTON HEIGHTS
MIDDLETON
CASTLETON ROAD
SHAW
Thornham Fold
River Irk
Brook

23
41
32
Lower Rushcroft
Higher Rushcroft
Wood End
High Crompton
Narrow Gate Hall
Low Crompton
Cowlishaw
Luzley Brook
Heyside
Brownlow
Shaw Edge
Shaw Side
SHAW
New Town
Moss Hey
OL2
OL1
ROCHDALE ROAD
B6194
CROMPTON WAY A663
MANCHESTER RD.
SHAW ROAD
A663
OLDHAM ROAD A671
HEYSIDE
HIGGINSHAW LANE
MILNROW RD.
Crompton House School
CEMETERY
Cricket Ground Pav.
Sports Grd.
CROMPTON & ROYTON GOLF COURSE
A.T.C. Headquarters
Highbarn Jun. Sch.
Vernon Works
HOSP.
New Barn Jun. & Inf. Schs.
Source of River Irk
River Irk
Cowlishaw Farm
Rushey Fields Farm
Low Crompton Farm
Narrow Gate Farm
Royton & Crompton Sch.
Blackshaw Lane Primary School
Playing Fields
Rose View Farm
Hospice
Industrial Estate
Warehouse
Woodstock Factory
Moss Lane Ind. Est.
Bullcote Farm
Intake Farm
Birshaw Farm
Old Bank
Rushcroft Primary Sch.
Duchess Street Ind. Est.
Nursing Home
Reservoirs Rec. Grd.
Duke Mill
Bee Mill
Warehouses
River Beal
E
F
G
H
1
2
3
4
5
6
93
94
07
08
09
410

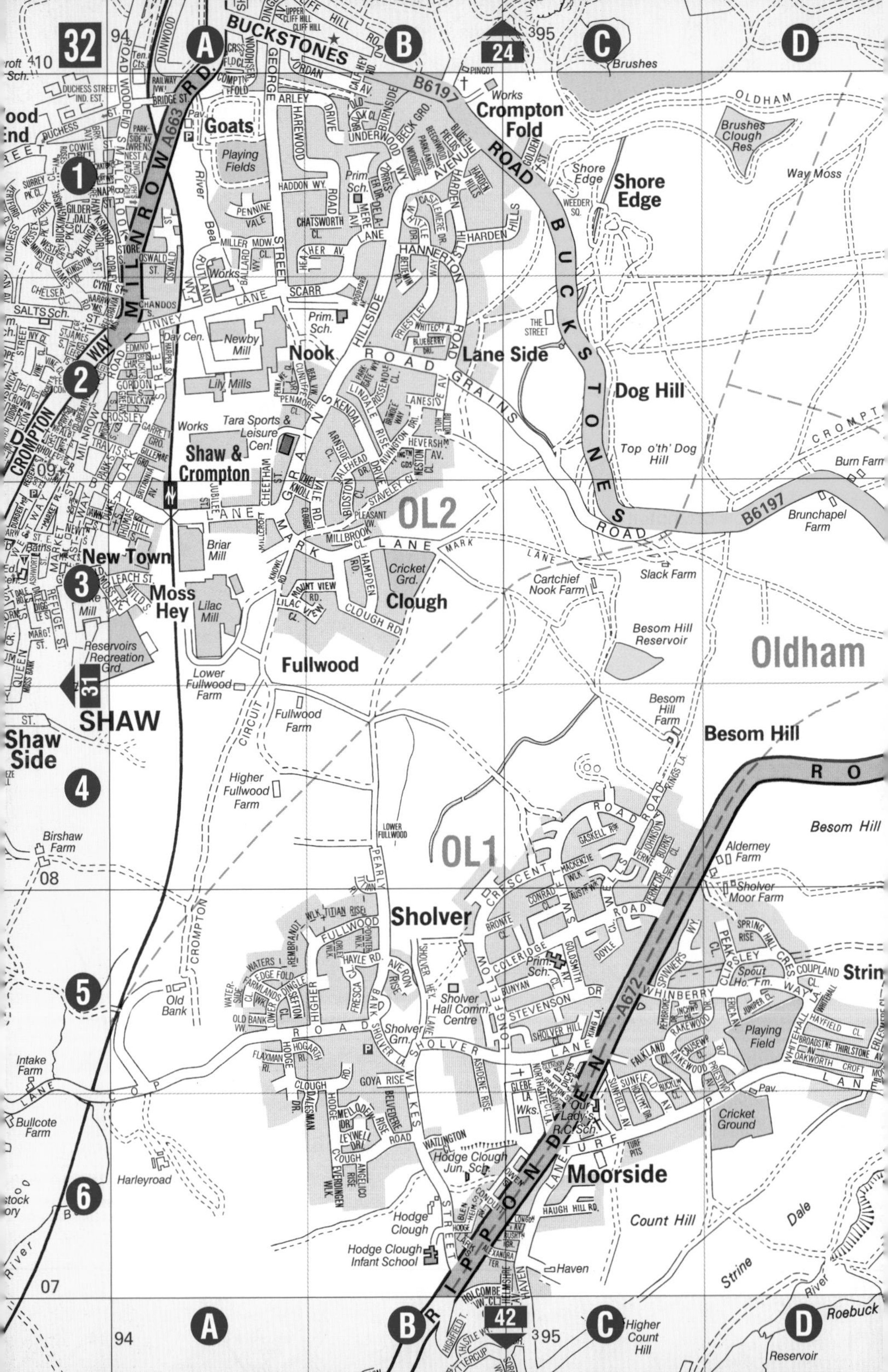

A
B
C
D
1
2
3
4
5
6
94
395
410
09
08
07
24
31
42
BUCKSTONES
BUCKSTONES ROAD
B6197
A663
MILNROW RD.
MILNROW WAY
CROMPTON WAY
A672
RIPPONDEN ROAD
Crompton Fold
Goats
Playing Fields
Brushes
Brushes Clough Res.
Way Moss
Shore Edge
OLDHAM
Works
Nook
Lane Side
Dog Hill
Top o'th' Dog Hill
Burn Farm
Brunchapel Farm
Newby Mill
Lily Mills
Tara Sports & Leisure Cen.
Shaw & Crompton
OL2
New Town
Moss Hey
Briar Mill
Lilac Mill
Cricket Grd.
Clough
Cartchief Nook Farm
Slack Farm
Besom Hill Reservoir
Oldham
Reservoirs Recreation Grd.
Lower Fullwood Farm
Fullwood
Fullwood Farm
SHAW
Shaw Side
Higher Fullwood Farm
Besom Hill Farm
Besom Hill
Birshaw Farm
OL1
Alderney Farm
Sholver Moor Farm
Sholver
Old Bank
Sholver Hall Comm. Centre
Sholver Grn.
Playing Field
Intake Farm
Bullcote Farm
Cricket Ground
Our Lady's R.C. Sch.
Hodge Clough Jun. Sch.
Moorside
Harleyroad
Hodge Clough
Hodge Clough Infant School
Count Hill
Haven
Strine Dale
River
Higher Count Hill
Roebuck
Reservoir
GRAINS ROAD
MARK LANE
CLOUGH RD.
SHOLVER LANE
CROMPTON CIRCUIT
COP LANE
TURF LANE
HAUGH HILL RD.
KINGS LA.
GASKELL RD.
MACKENZIE WLK.
CONRAD CL.
BRONTE CL.
COLERIDGE
BUNYAN
STEVENSON DR
GOLDSMITH
DOYLE
TITIAN RISE
FULLWOOD
REMBRANDT
HIGHER ROAD
HOGARTH
GOYA RISE
BELVEDERE RISE
WILKES STREET
STRINE DALE
WHINBERRY WAY
SPRING HALL CRES
CLIPSLEY CL.
COUPLAND CL.
HAYFIELD CL.
FALKLAND
RAKEWOOD

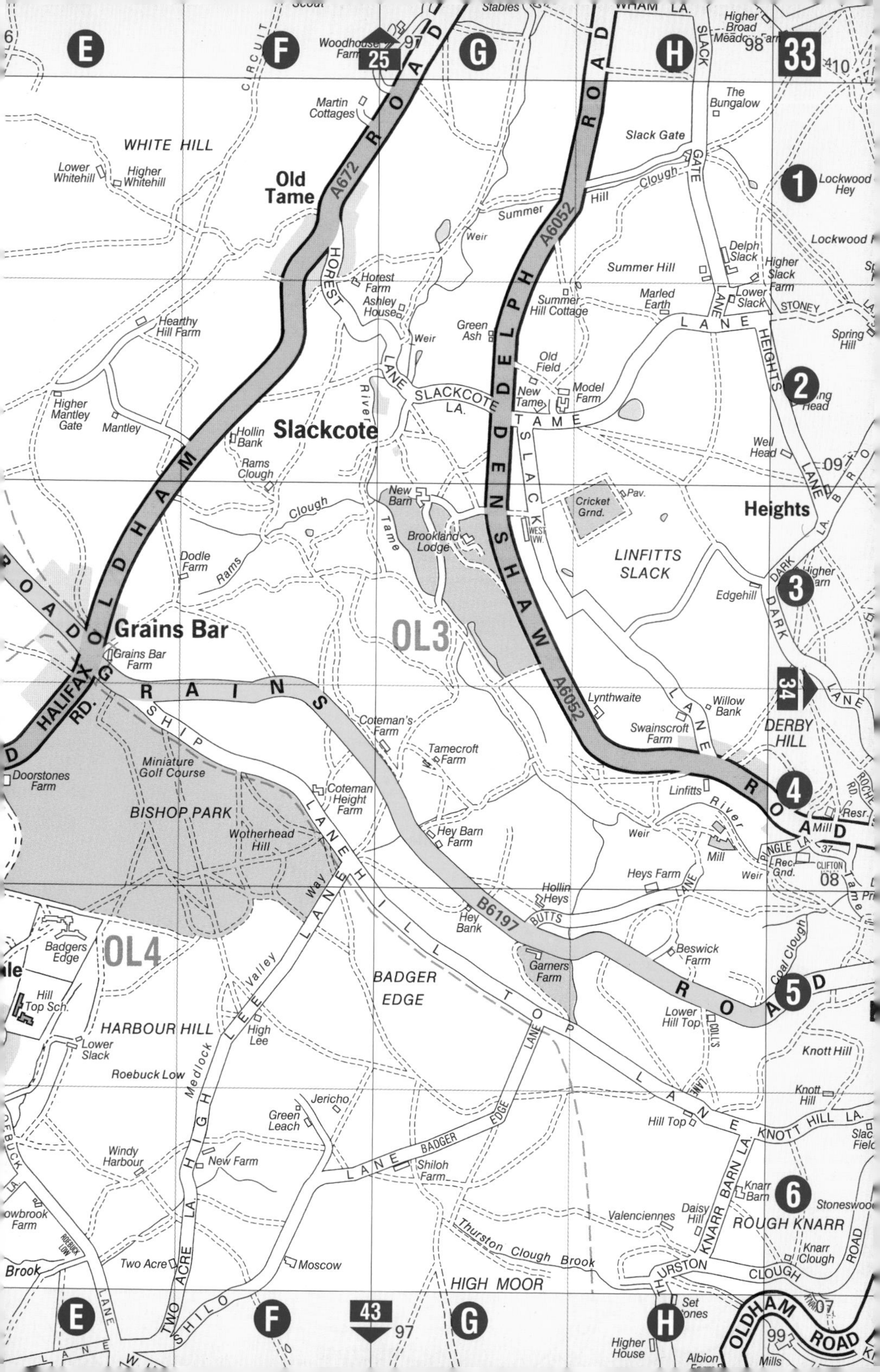

33
E
F
G
H
25
43
34
1
2
3
4
5
6
WHITE HILL
Lower Whitehill
Higher Whitehill
Old Tame
Martin Cottages
Woodhouse Farm
OLDHAM ROAD
A672
A6052
DELPH ROAD
Slack Gate
The Bungalow
Higher Broad Meadow Farm
WHAM LA.
SLACK GATE
Summer Hill
Clough
Lockwood Hey
Delph Slack
Higher Slack Farm
Lower Slack
Summer Hill Cottage
Marled Earth
STONEY LANE
Spring Hill
HEIGHTS LANE
Horest Farm
Ashley House
HOREST LANE
Weir
Green Ash
Hearthy Hill Farm
Higher Mantley Gate
Mantley
Old Field
New Tame
Model Farm
SLACKCOTE LA.
TAME
Slackcote
Hollin Bank
Rams Clough
Well Head
Heights
BROAD LA.
New Barn
River Tame
Brookland Lodge
Cricket Grnd.
Pav.
LINFITTS SLACK
WEST VW.
SLACK
DENSHAW
Dodle Farm
Rams
Edgehill
DARK LANE
Grains Bar
Grains Bar Farm
OL3
HALIFAX RD.
GRAINS ROAD
SHIP LANE
Lynthwaite
Willow Bank
Swainscroft Farm
DERBY HILL
Coteman's Farm
Tamecroft Farm
Miniature Golf Course
Doorstones Farm
Coteman Height Farm
BISHOP PARK
Wotherhead Hill
Hey Barn Farm
Linfitts
River
Resr.
Mill
PINGLE LA.
Rec. Gnd.
CLIFTON
Heys Farm
Hollin Heys
Hey Bank
B6197
BUTTS LANE
Beswick Farm
Coal Clough
Garners Farm
Badgers Edge
OL4
BADGER EDGE
Valley Way
Hill Top Sch.
HARBOUR HILL
Lower Slack
High Lee
Lower Hill Top
COLL'S.
Knott Hill
HILL TOP LANE
Roebuck Low
Medlock
HIGH LEE LA.
Jericho
Green Leach
BADGER EDGE LANE
Hill Top
KNOTT HILL LA.
Windy Harbour
New Farm
Shiloh Farm
KNARR BARN LA.
Knarr Barn
Stoneswood
Valenciennes
Daisy Hill
ROUGH KNARR
ROEBUCK LOW
Two Acre
TWO ACRE LA.
Moscow
Thurston Clough Brook
THURSTON CLOUGH ROAD
Knarr Clough
Brook
HIGH MOOR
SHILOH LANE
Set Stones
Higher House
Albion
OLDHAM ROAD
Mills
97
98
410
09
08
07
99

34
A
B
C
D
1
2
3
4
5
6
33
44
OX HEY TOP
Ox Hey Cottage
Higher Broad
The Bungalow
Lockwood Hey
Spring Hey
Friezland Hall
Delph Slack
Higher Slack Farm
Lower Slack
STONEY LANE
Spring Hill
Spring Head
Well Head
HEIGHTS LANE
Heights
BROAD LANE
DARK LANE
HEY FLAKE LANE
Higher Barn
New Barn
Delphe Greave
Grange
MILLCROFT LANE
Mill Croft
Paradise
Moor Croft
Low Bank
Wood Farm
Wood Barn
CASTLESHAW UPPER RESERVOIR
CASTLESHAW LOWER RESERVOIR
DIRTY LANE
Marld Earth Nook
Roman Fort
Castle Hill Cote
Weir
Waters
Castleshaw Centre
Waters Gate
Old Hey
Pack Horse Farm
OLD PACKHORSE RD
Pack Horse Slack
Causeway Sett
Intake Head
Oldham
OL3
HARROP EDGE
Belle Vue Farm
Harrop Farm
Green Oak Farm
Sandbed
SANDBED LA.
HULL LANE
Mill Pond
Mill
AMMON'S WY
WOOD
SEVENACRES
DELPH HILL
Upper Dale
DALE LANE
Dale
Delph Hill
Cobblers Hill
Salterhebble
DENSHAW ROAD
A6052
DERBY HILL
Linfitts
PINGLE LA.
Rec. Gnd.
CLIFTON HOLM
Delph Prim. Sch.
Spring Bridge
HILL END
Hill End
DALE FIELDS
Cricket Grnd.
Pav.
RUMBLES LA
B6197 ROAD
GRAINS ROAD
Beswick Farm
Coal Clough
Delph
Little Knott Hill
Knott Hill
WOODHOUSE KNOWL
MILLGATE
SADDLEWORTH BUSINESS PARK
Mills
HUDDERSFIELD ROAD
A62
The Barn
Larkwood
LARK HILL LANE
Lark Hill
KNOTT HILL LANE
STONESWOOD ROAD
Slack Field
Stoneswood
ROUGH KNARR
Knarr Clough
THURSTON CLOUGH ROAD
New Delph
NEW ROAD
DELPH NEW ROAD
Braeside
Gate Head
GATEHEAD
Park Field
HILL ROAD
Round Hill
Platt Hill
EDGE END
LONG LANE
Marslands
STANDEDGE
Lower Hill Top
Daisy Hill
Set Stones
OLDHAM ROAD
KNARR LA.
LOWER STONES
Ash Dene
Albion Mills
Works
Long House
Dobcross
SANDY LANE
09
08
07
98
99
10

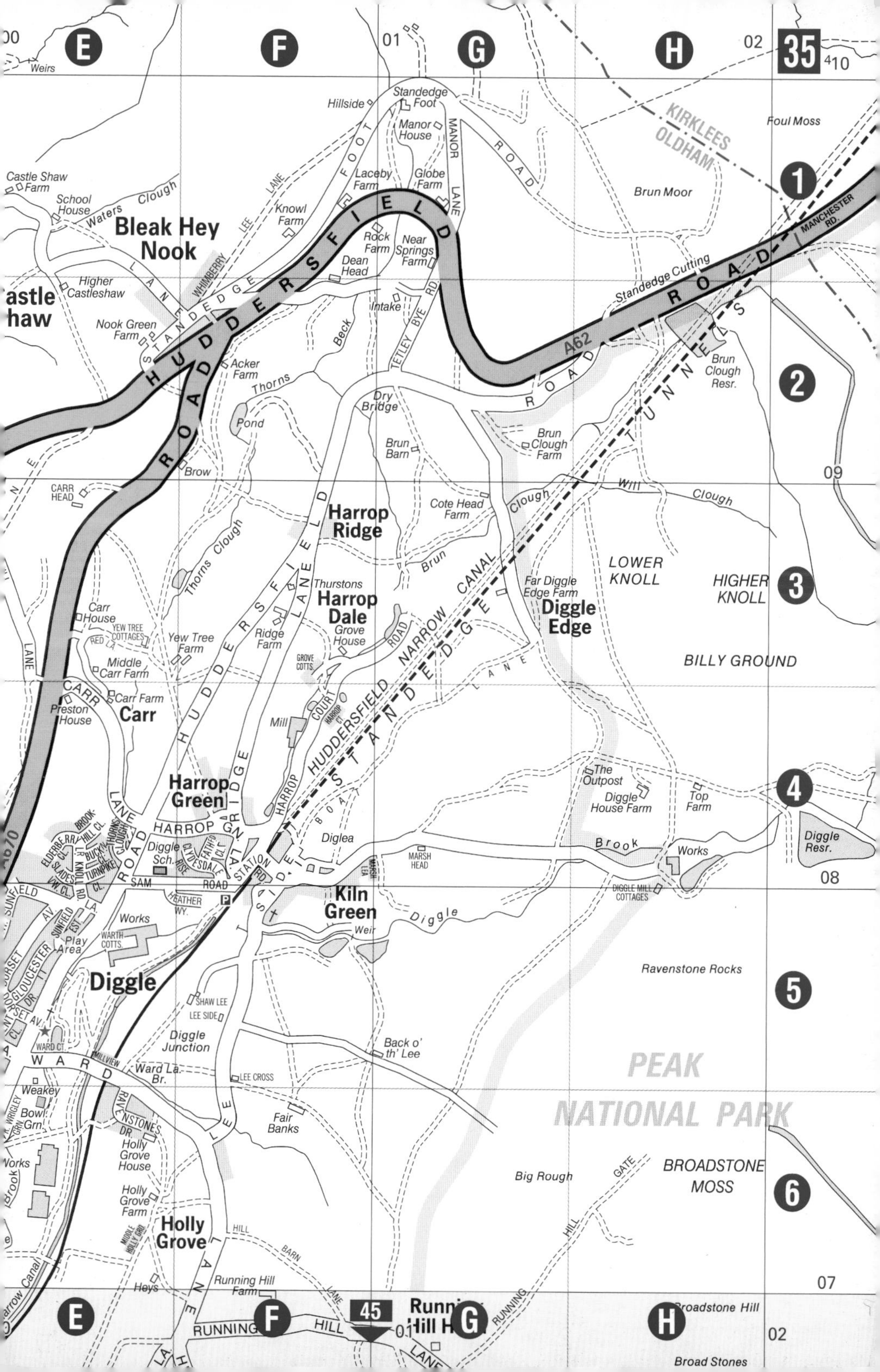

E
F
G
H
01
02
410
Weirs
Standedge Foot
Hillside
Manor House
MANOR LANE
ROAD
KIRKLEES
OLDHAM
Foul Moss
1
Brun Moor
Castle Shaw Farm
School House
Waters Clough
Bleak Hey Nook
LEE LANE
Knowl Farm
FOOT
Laceby Farm
Globe Farm
HUDDERSFIELD ROAD
Rock Farm
Near Springs Farm
Dean Head
MANCHESTER RD.
Higher Castleshaw
Castleshaw
WHIMBERRY
STANDEDGE
Intake
TETLEY BYE RD.
Standedge Cutting
ROAD
A62
Nook Green Farm
Beck
TUNNELS
Brun Clough Resr.
2
Acker Farm
Thorns
Dry Bridge
ROAD
Pond
Brun Clough Farm
Brun Barn
Brow
09
CARR HEAD
Will Clough
Clough
Cote Head Farm
Harrop Ridge
Thorns Clough
Brun
LOWER KNOLL
HIGHER KNOLL
3
Thurstons
Far Diggle Edge Farm
Harrop Dale
Diggle Edge
HUDDERSFIELD NARROW CANAL
Carr House
YEW TREE COTTAGES
RED LA.
Yew Tree Farm
Ridge Farm
Grove House
ROAD
BILLY GROUND
Middle Carr Farm
GROVE COTTS.
LANE
CARR
Carr Farm
Preston House
Carr
Mill
COURT
HARROP CT.
STANDEDGE
HUDDERSFIELD
LANE
Harrop Green
RIDGE
The Outpost
Diggle House Farm
Top Farm
4
Diggle Resr.
HARROP GN.
BOAT
Diglea
Brook
Works
Diggle Sch.
CLYDESDALE RISE
FAITHFD. CL.
STATION RD.
MARSH HEAD
MARSH LEA
08
SAM ROAD
DIGGLE MILL COTTAGES
HEATHER WY.
P
Kiln Green
Diggle
Works
WARTH COTTS.
Play Area
Weir
SUNFIELD
SUNFIELD EST.
GLOUCESTER AV.
DORSET AV.
Diggle
Ravenstone Rocks
5
SHAW LEE
LEE SIDE
Diggle Junction
WARD CT.
Back o' th' Lee
PEAK
WARD
MILLVIEW
Ward La. Br.
LEE CROSS
NATIONAL PARK
Weakey
Bowl Grn.
RAVENSTONES DR.
Holly Grove House
LEE
Fair Banks
Big Rough
GATE
BROADSTONE MOSS
6
Works
Brook
Holly Grove Farm
Holly Grove
HILL
BARN
HILL
MIDDLE HOLLY GRO.
Running Hill Farm
LANE
Heys
07
RUNNING
Narrow Canal
Broadstone Hill
RUNNING HILL
45
Running Hill Head
LANE
02
Broad Stones

36
26
A
B
C
D
Bury
BL9
Back o'th' Moss
Moss Side
Unsworth Moss
Club House
The Hills
PIKE FOLD
GOLF COURSE
M66
M66 MOTORWAY
M62
M62 MOTORWAY
M45
Junction 4
(M66)
Junction 18
(M60)
Egypt Farm
Lower Droughts Farm
Nursery
Simister
Manchester
Whitehouse Farm
Nut Lane Farm
Mount Pleasant Farm
Corday Farm
Parkwood Cottages
Heywood Farm
St. Margarets C.of E. Primary School
Clark's Cross
Parrenthorn High School
M60 MOTORWAY
M60
M25
Playing Fields
Kirkhams
BRIDLE ROAD
BURY
MANCHESTER
Dog Kennel Cottages
Fish Pond
Oak Croft Hill
HEATON PARK RESERVOIR
HEATON PARK GOLF COURSE
Radio Station
Blackfish Pond
Reservoir
Tennis Courts
Temple
Club House
Heaton Hall
Heaton House
Heaton Farm
Heaton Pk. Farm Cen.
Bowling Greens
Heaton Park Bowling Pavilion
Heaton Park Horticultural Cen.
Prestwich Prep. Sch.
HEATON PARK
Miniature Golf Course
Heaton Park Tramway
Heaton Park Tramway Museum
Pool
Heaton Park
MIDDLETON
BURY OLD ROAD
A665
Play. Fld.
Football Ground
Cricket Ground
Tennis Cts.
High School
Prim. Sch.
Pilkington Ho.
82
83
06
405
04
1
2
3
4
5
6

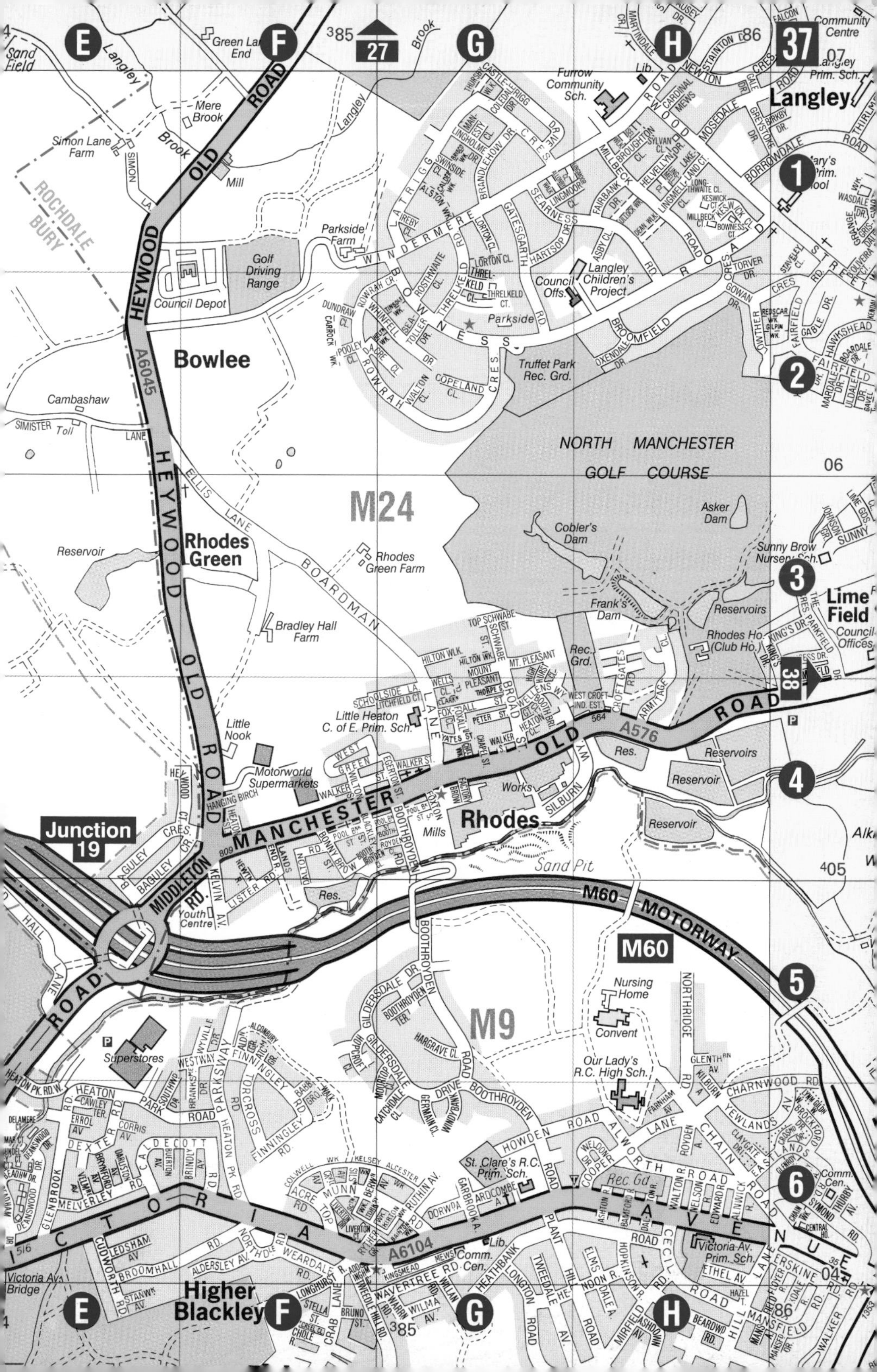

37
27
38
E
F
G
H
385
86
07
06
405
04
1
2
3
4
5
6
Langley
Bowlee
Rhodes Green
Rhodes
Higher Blackley
Lime Field
M24
M9
NORTH MANCHESTER GOLF COURSE
HEYWOOD OLD ROAD
A6045
MANCHESTER OLD ROAD
A576
M60 MOTORWAY
M60
Junction 19
MIDDLETON RD.
VICTORIA AVENUE
A6104
BOWNESS ROAD
WINDERMERE
BOARDMAN LANE
ELLIS LANE
BOOTHROYDEN ROAD
CHAIN ROAD
ALWORTH ROAD
HOWDEN ROAD
HEATON PARK ROAD
PARKSWAY
CHARNWOOD RD.
ROCHDALE
BURY
Sand Field
Green Lane End
Mere Brook
Simon Lane Farm
Mill
Golf Driving Range
Council Depot
Parkside Farm
Cambashaw
SIMISTER LANE
Toll
Reservoir
Rhodes Green Farm
Bradley Hall Farm
Little Nook
Motorworld Supermarkets
Little Heaton C. of E. Prim. Sch.
Mills
Works
Sand Pit
Youth Centre
Res.
Furrow Community Sch.
Lib.
Langley Children's Project
Council Offs.
Parkside
Truffet Park Rec. Grd.
Cobler's Dam
Asker Dam
Frank's Dam
Rec. Grd.
Reservoirs
Rhodes Ho. (Club Ho.)
Sunny Brow Nursery Sch.
Council Offices
Community Centre
Langley Prim. Sch.
Nursing Home
Convent
Our Lady's R.C. High Sch.
St. Clare's R.C. Prim. Sch.
Rec. Gd
Victoria Av. Prim. Sch.
Comm. Cen.
Superstores
Victoria Av. Bridge
Comm. Cen.
Lib.

38
A
B
C
D
28
86
87
1
2
3
4
5
6
37
46
Langley
Hollins
Community Centre
Langley Prim. Sch.
St. Mary's R.C. Prim. School
HOLLIN LANE
ROCHDALE ROAD
A6046
Cricket Grd.
Middleton Parish Prim. Sch.
Play. Fld.
Recreation Ground
Boarshaw Prim. Sch.
BOARSHAW IND. EST.
CROMER INDUSTRIAL ESTATE
Jubilee Park
Burial Ground
NORTH MANCHESTER GOLF COURSE
Asker Dam
Sunny Brow Nursery Sch.
Parkfield Prim. Sch.
John Lee Fold
Lark Hill
MIDDLETON
A669
GRIMSHAW LANE
Works
Lime Field
Recreation Ground
Council Offices
Reservoirs
Rhodes Ho. (Club Ho.)
MIDDLETON SHOP. CEN.
Bus Sta.
Little Park
MIDDLETON WAY
OLD ROAD
A576
MANCHESTER
Mc BRIDE RIVERSIDE PARK
T.A. Cen.
Mill
MILL FOLD RD.
Manchester
Ramsden Farm
St. Peter's R.C. Prim. Sch.
Kitchen Wood
Lever Bri.
River Irk
Reservoir
Alkrington Hall
Bird Sanctuary
Alkrington Wood
MOUNT RD.
M24
KINGSWAY
A664
MANCHESTER NEW ROAD
Alkrington Prim. Sch.
Alkrington Garden Village
Wood Cott.
M60
ROCHDALE MANCHESTER
M9
Nut Bank
Junc. 20
M60 MOTORWAY
MAINWAY
Library
Comm. Cen.
Youth Cen.
Playing Field
St. Thomas More R.C. Prim. Sch.
Alkrington Moss Prim. Sch.
St. Michael's C. of E. Prim. Sch.
Tennis Cts.
BLACKLEY GOLF COURSE
MOSSWAY
Comm. Cen.
Victoria Av. Prim. Sch.
VICTORIA AVENUE
A6104
ROCHDALE RD.
05
06
04
07
405

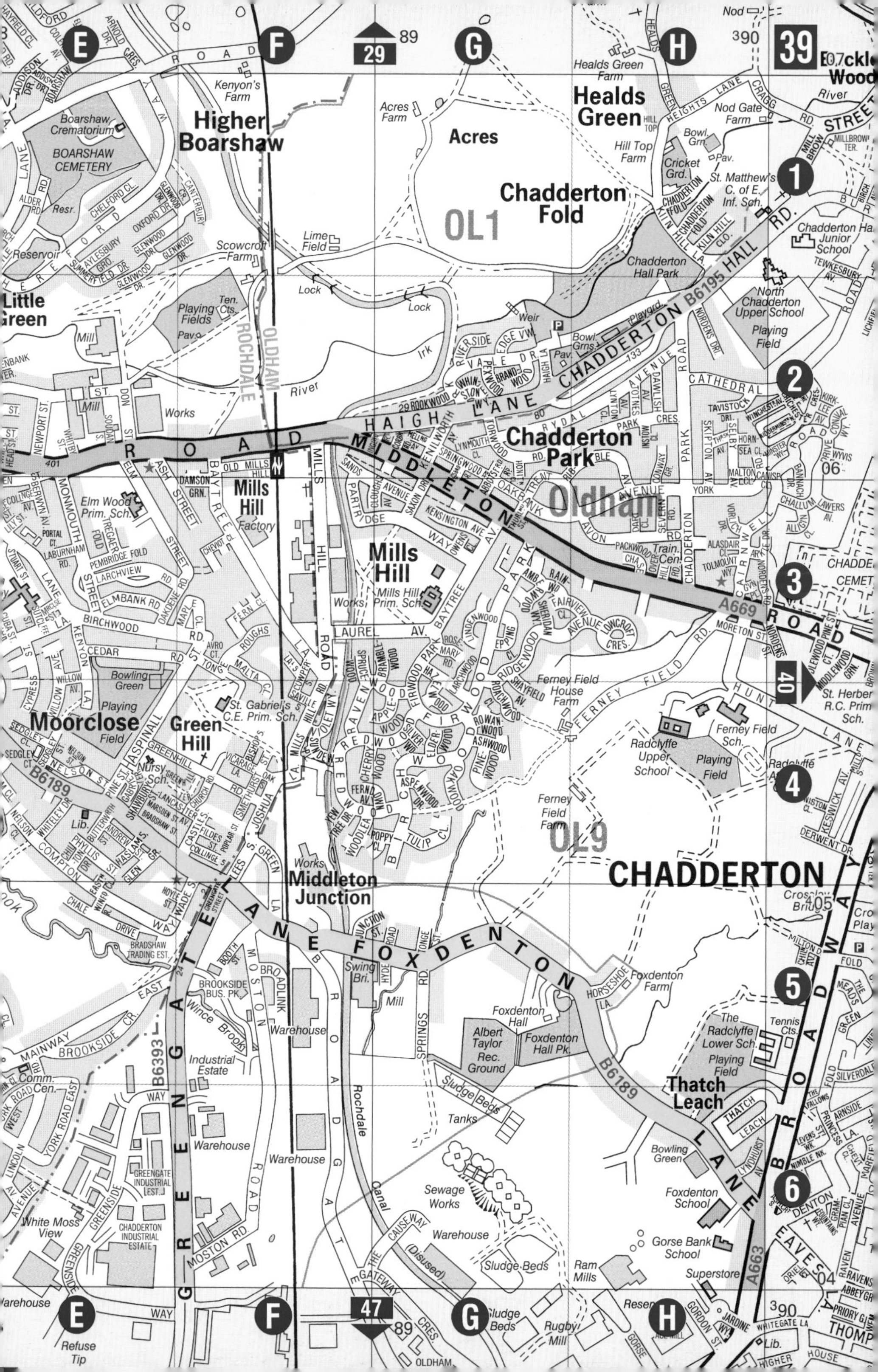
39
E
F
G
H
29
89
390
47
1
2
3
4
5
6
40
Higher Boarshaw
Boarshaw Crematorium
BOARSHAW CEMETERY
Kenyon's Farm
Healds Green
Healds Green Farm
Acres
Acres Farm
Chadderton Fold
OL1
Lime Field
Scowcroft Farm
Little Green
Playing Fields
Reservoir
Resr.
Nod Gate Farm
Hill Top Farm
Cricket Grd.
Bowl. Grn.
St. Matthew's C. of E. Inf. Sch.
Chadderton Hall Park
Chadderton Hall Junior School
North Chadderton Upper School
Playing Field
Lock
Weir
River Irk
ROCHDALE
OLDHAM
CHADDERTON HALL RD.
B6195
HAIGH LANE
ROAD
401
Mills Hill
Factory
Works
Mill
Chadderton Park
Oldham
MIDDLETON
A669
ROAD
Elm Wood Prim. Sch.
Mills Hill Prim. Sch.
Train. Cen.
Ferney Field House Farm
Ferney Field Sch.
Radclyffe Upper School
Playing Field
Ferney Field Farm
OL9
CHADDERTON
Moorclose
Green Hill
Bowling Green
Playing Field
St. Gabriel's C.E. Prim. Sch.
Lib.
B6189
Middleton Junction
FOXDENTON LANE
Swing Bri.
Mill
Foxdenton Farm
Foxdenton Hall
Albert Taylor Rec. Ground
Foxdenton Hall Pk.
The Radclyffe Lower Sch.
Playing Field
Tennis Cts.
Thatch Leach
Bowling Green
Foxdenton School
Gorse Bank School
Superstore
Ram Mills
Rugby Mill
Sludge Beds
Tanks
Sewage Works
Warehouse
Industrial Estate
BROOKSIDE BUS. PK.
Wince Brook
GREENGATE INDUSTRIAL EST.
CHADDERTON INDUSTRIAL ESTATE
BRADSHAW TRADING EST.
White Moss View
Refuse Tip
Comm. Cen.
Rochdale Canal
(Disused)
B6393
GREENGATE
A663
BROADWAY
Crossley Bri.
405
St. Herbert's R.C. Prim. Sch.
THOMP

40
A
B
C
D
30
39
48
1
2
3
4
5
6
Buckley Wood
A627(M)
A627(M) MOTORWAY
Holden Fold
ELK MILL CENTRAL RETAIL PARK
Chadderton Hall Junior School
North Chadderton Upper School
Playing Field
Clayton Playing Fields
The Clayton Arms Sports Hall
Oldham Athletic F.C. & Oldham R.L.F.C. (Boundary Park)
Football Grd.
THE ROYAL OLDHAM HOSPITAL
Superstore
West Hulme
Westwood Park
College
Burnley Brow
North Chadderton Lower School
Bare Trees Inf. & Jun. School
CHADDERTON CEMETERY
Eustace St. Prim. Sch.
FALCON ENTERPRISE CENTRE
Busk
Open Space
CHADDERTON PRECINCT
St. Herbert's R.C. Prim. Sch.
Ferney Field Sch.
Radclyffe Athletics Centre
Sports Cen.
Lib.
Town Hall
North Moor
Westwood
WESTWOOD INDUSTRIAL ESTATE
Westwood Prim. Sch.
Stock Brook
PALM BUSINESS CENTRE
CHADDERTON
OL9
St. Luke's C. of E. Prim. Sch.
Crossley Play. Fld.
Cowhill
CROSSLEY EST.
Alder Root
GLENBY ESTATE
BENTFIELD IND. UNITS
Refuse Tip
BOOTH HOUSE TRAD. EST.
Oldham Werneth
HARTFORD IND. EST.
WESTWOOD BUS. CEN.
Richmond Jun. Sch.
Richmond Inf. Sch.
The Radclyffe Lower Sch.
Christ Church C. of E. Prim. Sch.
Thatch Leach
Foxdenton School
Nimble Nook
Mona Mill
Raven Mill
Transport Depot
Freehold Prim. Sch.
Recreation Ground
Butler Green
Werneth
WERNETH PARK
Nat. Hist. Mus.
Marion Walker Ho. Cen.
Horse Bank School
MIDDLETON ROAD
A669
CHADDERTON WAY
A663
BROADWAY
A663
CHADDERTON WAY A627
FEATHERSTALL ROAD SOUTH
MANCHESTER ST.
A62
EDWARD ST. B6192
OXFORD ST. B6191
FREDERICK ST. B6192
LANSDOWNE RD.
BLOCK LANE B6190
EAVES LA. B6189
CHADDERTON HALL RD.
MILL BROW
STREET BRIDGE RD.
B6195
FOXDENTON LA.
BURNLEY LANE
PARK AVENUE
390
405
06
04
91

E
F
G
H
31
93
94
07
1
2
3
4
5
6
06
05
04
42
49
Hospice
Warehouse
Industrial Estate
Works
Woodstock Factory
Factory
Higginshaw
Broadbent
LAUREL TRADING EST.
Stoneleigh Prim. Sch.
Sacred Heart R.C. Prim. Sch.
The Pollards
OL2
Long Sight
Depot
Stoneleigh Park
Pav.
Sarah Moor
COLDHURST HOLLOW ESTATE
Playing Field
Derker
Mayfield Prim. Sch.
Greenacres Hill
Oldham Edge
Higginshaw Youth Cen.
CROMFORD BUSINESS CEN.
OLDHAM CENTRAL TRADING PARK
Oldham
Cold Hurst
Works
Inf. Sch.
Jun. Sch.
Beever Sch.
THE ACORN CEN.
ROKER IND. EST.
Bismark Ho.
Acre
Lower Moor
Ind. Est.
Blue Coat C. of E. Sch.
OL1
Mumps
Bus Depot Mumps M.
Warehouse
FORGE IND. EST.
Green-acres Prim. Sch.
The Oldham College
County Court
Civic Centre
Market Hall
Oldham Sports Cen.
Superstore
Sorting Office
SOUTHLINK IND. PK.
MOUNT PLEASANT BUSINESS CENTRE
St. Anne's C. Prim. Sch.
Castle Iron Wks.
Play. Fld.
THE SPINDLES & TOWN SQ. SHOP CEN.
Bus Sta.
Roscoe Mill
Oldham Mumps
SOUTHLINK BUS. PK.
Horton Mill Prim. Sch.
MOORHEY IND. EST.
Moorhey
Football Grd.
Bank Top
Rhodes Bank
OLDHAM
Caravan Pk.
Mills
Swim. Pool
OL4
WELLINGTON BLDGS
ALEXANDRA CEN. RETAIL PK.
OL8
Primrose Bank
Visitor Cen.
ALEXANDRA PARK
Boating Lake
Bowl. Grns.
Tennis Cts.
Pav.
Playground
Works
Glodwick Inf. Sch.
Glodwick
Roxbury
Coppice Jun. Sch.
Coppice Inf. Sch.
Alexandra Pk. Jun. Sch.
Sports Grd.
Rec. Ground
Comm. Cen.
Football Grd.
Cricket
ROCHDALE ROAD
A671
HIGGINSHAW LA.
SHAW ROAD
B6194
HUDDERSFIELD ROAD
A62
LEES ROAD
A669
MUMPS
YORKSHIRE ST.
HIGH STREET
UNION ST.
WELLINGTON ST.
ASHTON ROAD
A627
KING ST.
QUEENS ROAD
GLODWICK ROAD
ABBEY HILLS ROAD
SALMON FIELDS
MOSS LA.
MEEK ST.
MANOR ST.
STATION ROAD
BOOTH HILL LANE
EGERTON STREET
GREENACRES ROAD
CROSS ST.
BOWER ST.
STAMPSTONE ST.
SOUTHLINK STREET
ROUNDTHORN RD.
PEVERIL RD.
WHETSTONE HILL RD.
BUXTED RD.
ST. MARY'S ST.
ROCK ST.
HORSEDGE ST.
BAR GAP ROAD
CROMPTON ST.
COLDHURST ST.
MAGDALA ST.
TRAFALGAR ST.
MANCHESTER ST.
BROOK LANE
KINGS ROAD
WOODSTOCK ST.
MORRIS ST.
SCOTTFIELD RD.
PARK RD.
KINGSWAY

A
B
C
D
1
2
3
4
5
6
32
41
50
OL1
OL4
Broadbent
Watersheddings
Higher Barrowshaw
Higher Count Hill
Lower Count Hill
Counthill School
Playing Fields
Near Barrowshaw
Reservoir
Lower Strinesdale Reservoir
Gailey Hall
Waterhead Water Treatment Works
Works
Spring Hill
Waterhead Park
Waterhead
Oldham
Birks
Greenacres Hill
Littlemoor Prim. Sch.
Top Of Moor
Mills
Greenacres Lane
River Medlock
Greenacres Moor
Cross Bank
Cookcroft
Greenacres Fold
Greenacres Cemetery
Greenacres
Sun Hill
Dowry Park Estates
Hey With Zion Prim. Sch.
St. Edward's R.C. Prim. Sch.
Sacred Heart R.C. Prim. Sch.
The Pollards
Watersheddings Prim. Sch.
Mayfield Prim. Sch.
Castle Iron Wks.
Mount Pleasant Business Centre
Forge Ind. Est.
Clarksfield Jun. & Inf. Schs.
Bank Top
Glen Trading Estate
Leesbrook
Football Grd.
Moorhey
Salem
Leesfield
New Earth
Breeze Hill Sch.
Nether Lees
Roxbury
Glodwick
Roundthorn
LEES
Cemetery
Thornley
County End
Knowl Lane
Sports Grd.
Walker
A62
A672
A669
RIPPONDEN ROAD
HUDDERSFIELD ROAD
ROAD
HIGH ST.
ABBEY HILLS RD.
Low

43
33
51
44
HIGH MOOR
Thurston Clough Brook
Two Acre
Moscow
Set Stones
Higher House
Albion Farm
Greaves
Temple Bar Farm
The Bungalow
WHITEGATES
Nebo
Blunder Hall
Brighton
None Directional Radio Beacon Station
Daisy Hill Farm
DOCTOR LA. HEAD COTTS.
Res.
New Inn Farm
Heights Farm
Upper House Farm
Wall Hill
THE COTTAGES
Intake
Lower Houses
Doctor Lane Head
Doctor House
Doctor House Farm
OL3
Works
Herds Low
Daisy Hollow Farm
Higher Thorpe
Field House
Starting Chair
Old Nathan's
Vicarage
White Gate
Lower Thorpe
Wade Hill
Austerlands
The Pastures
Scouthead
New Houses
HUDDERSFIELD ROAD
OLDHAM ROAD
A62
Stone Rake
LAUREATE'S PLACE
Wood Brook
Platting Farm
Doles Pit
Ford
Knowsley Jun. Sch.
Pav.
Playing Fields
Load Hill
Hills Farm
The Nook
Burnedge Farm
Shelderslow
Stone Breaks Hill
Stone Breaks
Earnshaw Head Fm.
Lower Hills Farm
Grotton Hall
Grotton Head
Springhead
Lydgate
Prim. Sch.
Grasscroft Clough
A669
Grotton
Grasscroft Independent School
The Grange
Sharon
Prospect Farm
Lydgate Farm
Thornley Brook Farm
FERN COTTAGE
Lower Lydgate Farm
Vicarage
STOCKPORT ROAD
A6050
MOSSLEY ROAD
A670
Higher Quick Farm
Lower Quick Edge Farm
Kiln
Resr.
Aqueduct

Dobcross
Marslands
Wall Hill
Tame Water
Oldham
SADDLEWORTH
Uppermill
SADDLEWORTH GOLF COURSE
Grasscroft
OL4
Grasscroft Clough
Shaw Hall
Greenfield
Shaw Hall Bank
Frenches
Lower Arthurs
Friezland
Sharon
Wharmton
Ladcastle
Temple Bar Farm
Husteads
Wade Hill
Higher Wade Hill
Hillside Bungalow
Burnedge Bent
Springfield Farm
Burnedge House
Burnedge Farm
Albion Farm
Meg Heys
Set Stones
Knarr Clough
Ash Dene
Long House
Brown Hill
Saddleworth School
Ladbrook
Club House
Ladcastle Farm
Spring Bank
Top o' th' Croft
Churchill Playing Fields Track
Churchill Fields
Cricket Ground
Wharmton Tower
Quarry (dis.)
Rugby Football Grd.
Sewage Works
Friezland Grange
Mann's Wharf Bridge
Manns
Wellihole Bridge
Well-i-Hole Farm
Tennis Court
Aqueduct
Mill Stream
Mast
Wickens Clough
DELPH NEW ROAD
DOBCROSS NEW ROAD
OLDHAM ROAD
WOOL ROAD
HIGH STREET
CHAPEL ROAD
CHEW VALLEY ROAD
MANCHESTER ROAD
MOSSLEY ROAD
SHAW HALL BANK RD.
WELL-I-HOLE RD.
LADCASTLE ROAD
MOUNT LANE
WADE HILL LANE
BURNEDGE LANE
WALL HILL
KNARR LA.
PLATT LANE
SANDY LANE
SUGAR LANE
HIGH LANE ROAD
CHURCH ROAD
A62
A6052
A670
A669
A635
B6175
34
43
52
A B C D
1 2 3 4 5 6
98 99
07 06 405 04

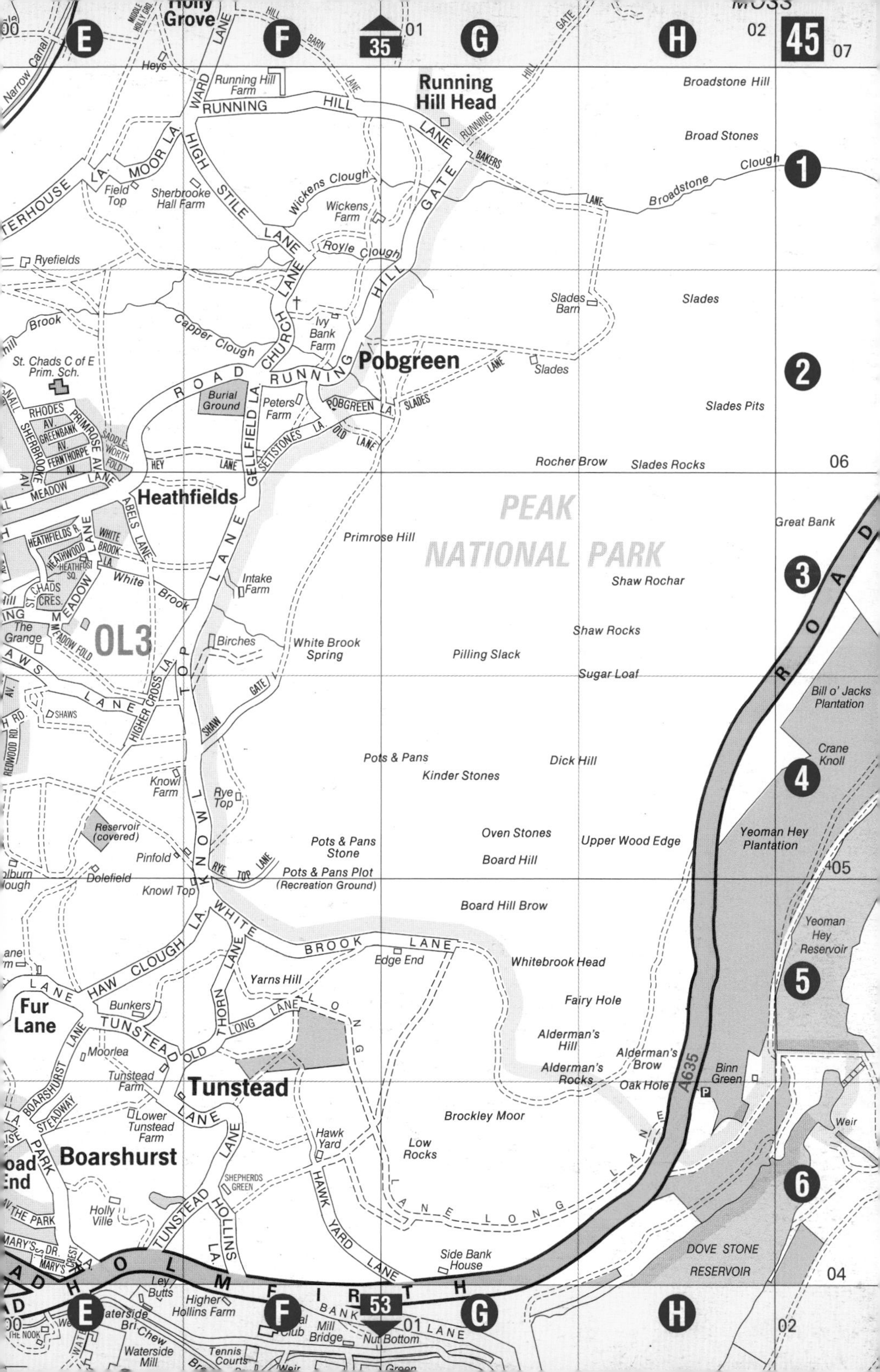

35
53
Running Hill Head
Pobgreen
Heathfields
Tunstead
Boarshurst
Fur Lane
Holly Grove
OL3
PEAK NATIONAL PARK
Broadstone Hill
Broad Stones
Broadstone Clough
Slades
Slades Barn
Slades Pits
Rocher Brow
Slades Rocks
Great Bank
Primrose Hill
Shaw Rochar
Shaw Rocks
Pilling Slack
Sugar Loaf
Bill o' Jacks Plantation
Crane Knoll
Dick Hill
Pots & Pans
Kinder Stones
Oven Stones
Board Hill
Upper Wood Edge
Yeoman Hey Plantation
Pots & Pans Stone
Pots & Pans Plot
(Recreation Ground)
Board Hill Brow
Yeoman Hey Reservoir
Whitebrook Head
Fairy Hole
Alderman's Hill
Alderman's Brow
Alderman's Rocks
Oak Hole
Binn Green
Brockley Moor
Low Rocks
Weir
DOVE STONE RESERVOIR
Side Bank House
A635
HOLMFIRTH ROAD
LONG LANE
Running Hill Farm
Heys
RUNNING HILL LANE
RUNNING HILL GATE
BAKERS LANE
MOOR LA.
HIGH STILE LANE
WARD LANE
Field Top
Sherbrooke Hall Farm
Wickens Clough
Wickens Farm
Royle Clough
Ryefields
CHURCH LANE
Ivy Bank Farm
Capper Clough
Brook
St. Chads C of E Prim. Sch.
CHURCH ROAD
RUNNING
Burial Ground
Peters Farm
GELLFIELD LA.
POBGREEN LA.
SLADES LANE
SETTSTONES LA.
OLD LANE
RHODES AV.
GREENBANK AV.
FERNTHORPE AV.
SHERBROOKE AV.
PRIMROSE AVE.
SADDLEWORTH FOLD
HEY LANE
MEADOW LANE
HEATHFIELDS R.
HEATHWOOD
HEATHFIELDS SQ.
WHITE BROOK LA.
ABELS LANE
White Brook
ST. CHADS CRES.
MEADOW LANE
MEADOW FOLD
The Grange
Intake Farm
Birches
White Brook Spring
SHAWS LANE
SHAWS
HIGHER CROSS LA.
REDWOOD RD.
SHAW GATE
KNOWL TOP LANE
Knowl Farm
Rye Top
Reservoir (covered)
Pinfold
Dolefield
Knowl Top
RYE TOP LANE
WHITE BROOK LANE
HAW CLOUGH LA.
Edge End
THORN LANE
Yarns Hill
Bunkers
TUNSTEAD LANE
LONG LANE
OLD
Moorlea
Tunstead Farm
BOARSHURST LANE
STEADWAY
Lower Tunstead Farm
Hawk Yard
HAWK YARD LANE
SHEPHERDS GREEN
PARK
THE PARK
Holly Ville
HOLLINS LA.
MARY'S DR.
MARY'S CREST
Ley Butts
Higher Hollins Farm
Waterside
Bri. Chew
Waterside Mill
THE NOOK
Club
Mill Bridge
Nut Bottom
BANK LANE
Tennis Courts
Weir
Green
Road End
Narrow Canal
00
01
02
07
06
405
04

Junc. 20
38
A
B
C
D
1
2
3
4
5
6
M60 MOTORWAY
VICTORIA AVENUE
A6104
ROCHDALE ROAD
A664
BLACKLEY GOLF COURSE
Club House
JEWS CEMY
Crosslee Prim. Sch.
Play. Fld.
Knottley Hill
St. John Bosco R.C. Prim. Sch.
Charlestown
M9
Bailey's Wood
BOOTH HALL CHILDREN'S HOSPITAL
Charlestown Prim. Sch.
Nth. Manchester High Sch. for Boys (Lwr.)
Playing Fields
Nth. Manchester High Sch. for Boys (Upper)
Manchester
CHARLESTOWN ROAD
Pav.
Sports Ground
Boggart Hole Clough Track
Playing Field
War Memorial
Oliver Clough
Fish Pond
BOGGART HOLE CLOUGH
Boating Lake
Nth. Manchester High Sch. for Girls
Tennis Courts
Bowling Green
David Lewis Rec. Grd
Playground
Boggart Hole Brook
Moston Fields Prim. Sch.
BROADHURST PARK
ST. JOSEPH'S CEMETERY
Blackley
Barnes Green
Holy Trinity Prim. Sch.
Swim. Pools
MOSTON LANE
Mkt.
HARPURHEY DISTRICT CENTRE
Manchester College
Moston
St. Dunstan's R.C. Primary Sch.
Lily La. Jun. & Inf. Schs.
Broadhurst Park
Nursing Home
LIGHTBOWNE ROAD
Dogs' Home
Moston Brook
Harpurhey
Burgess Prim. Sch.
Playing Field
Diesel Depot
Dean Lane
St. Mary's R.C. Bri
86
87
03
402
01

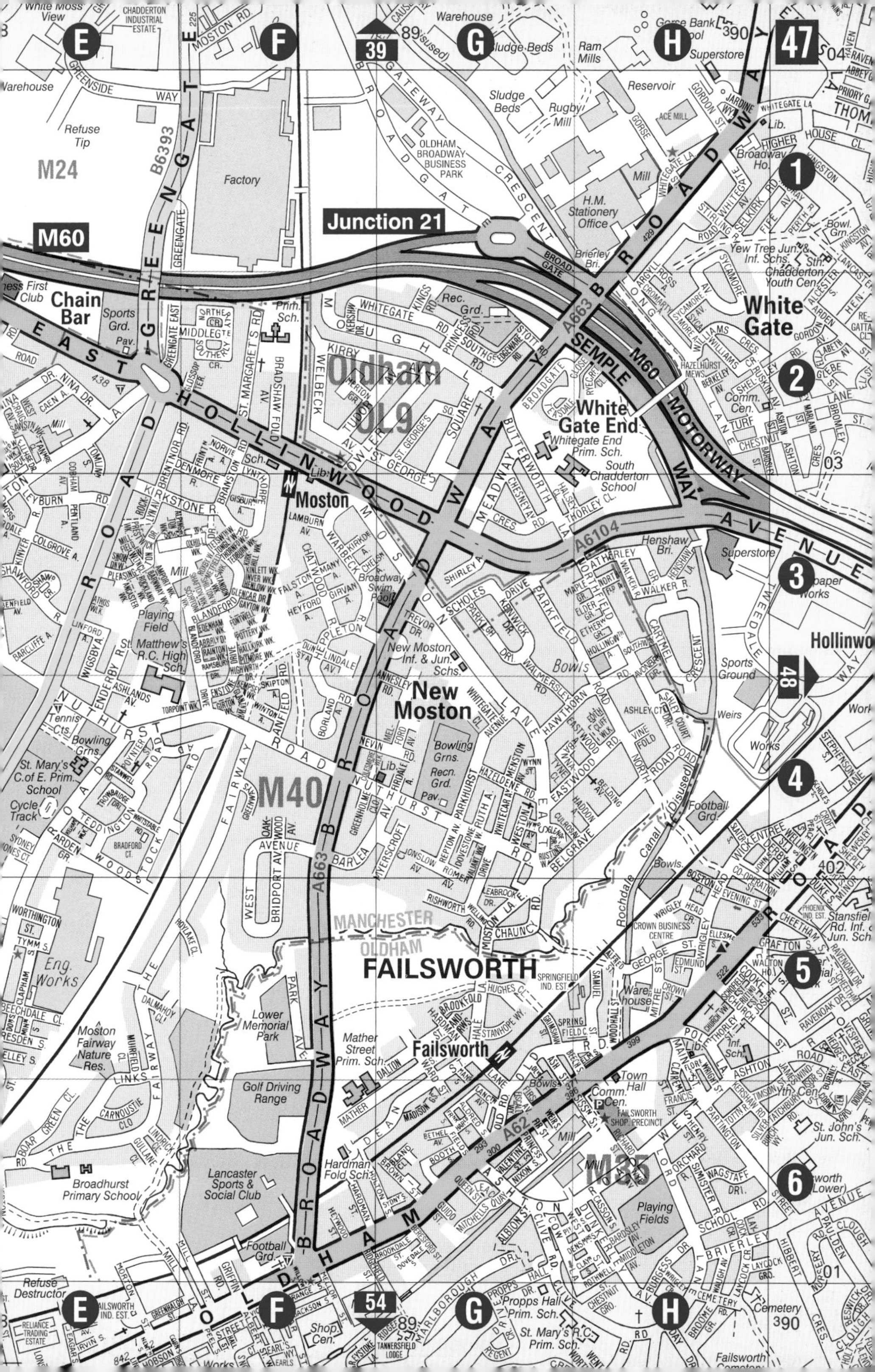

47
39
54
48
E
F
G
H
1
2
3
4
5
6
Junction 21
M60
M24
M40
M35
Oldham
OL9
Chain Bar
White Gate
White Gate End
Moston
New Moston
FAILSWORTH
Failsworth
MANCHESTER
OLDHAM
Hollinwood
Chadderton Industrial Estate
Greenside Way
Refuse Tip
Factory
Warehouse
Sludge Beds
Ram Mills
Gorse Bank School
Superstore
Reservoir
Rugby Mill
Ace Mill
Mill
H.M. Stationery Office
Oldham Broadway Business Park
Broadgate
Crescent
Brierley Bri.
Yew Tree Jun. & Inf. Schs.
Sth. Chadderton Youth Cen.
Broadway Ho.
Lib.
Comm. Cen.
Semple Way
M60 Motorway
A663
A6104
A62
B6393
Greengate
East
Hollinwood Avenue
Broadway
Whitegate End Prim. Sch.
South Chadderton School
Henshaw Bri.
Broadway Swim. Pool
Playing Field
St. Matthew's R.C. High Sch.
New Moston Inf. & Jun. Schs.
Bowls
Sports Ground
Weirs
Works
Paper Works
Rochdale Canal (Disused)
Football Grd.
Bowling Grns.
Recn. Grd.
Pav.
Nuthurst Road
Fairway
St. Mary's C.of E. Prim. School
Cycle Track
Tennis Cts.
Eng. Works
Moston Fairway Nature Res.
Lower Memorial Park
Golf Driving Range
Lancaster Sports & Social Club
Broadhurst Primary School
Mather Street Prim. Sch.
Hardman Fold Sch.
Crown Business Centre
Springfield Ind. Est.
Town Hall
Comm. Cen.
Failsworth Shop. Precinct
Playing Fields
Stansfield Rd. Inf. & Jun. Sch.
St. John's Jun. Sch.
Refuse Destructor
Failsworth Ind. Est.
Reliance Trading Estate
Shop. Cen.
Tannersfield Lodge
Propps Hall Prim. Sch.
St. Mary's R.C. Prim. Sch.
Cemetery
Failsworth Cemetery
Ashton Road
Oldham Road
390
01
03
04
89

48
A
B
C
D
40
1
2
3
4
5
6
47
55
Butler Green
Recreation Ground
Transport Depot
Werneth
Werneth Park
Tennis Cts.
Nat. Hist. Mus.
Convent
Stanley Road Prim. Sch.
Corpus Christi R.C. Prim. Sch.
St. Augustine of Canterbury R. C. Sch.
Bowling Green
Playing Fields
White Gate
Yew Tree Jun. & Inf. Schs.
Chadderton Youth Cen.
Coalshaw Grn. Park
Play. Field
Warehouses
Victoria Mill
OL9
Chapel Road Play. Fld.
St. Margaret's C. of E. Prim. Sch.
Hollins
Heron Mill
Temple
Res.
Mill
Works
Lyndhurst Prim. Sch.
The Edge
Superstore
Newspaper Works
Hollinwood
M60 MOTORWAY
HOLLINWOOD A6104 AV.
A6104
A62
B6189
B6192
MANCHESTER
HOLLINS
DRURY LA.
BOWER LA.
OLDHAM ROAD
Moss Grove
Limeside Park
Limeside Prim. Sch.
Lime Side
Lime Gate
HOLLINWOOD CEMETERY
Oldham Crematorium
Rec. Grd.
Sports Grd.
Recreation Ground
Limehurst Prim. Sch.
Holy Family R.C. Prim. Sch.
Junc. 22
Windsor Mill
Gas Works
HOLLINWOOD BUS. CEN.
MERSEY RD. IND. EST.
Kaskenmoor School
Playing Field
Playgrd.
M60
Weirs
Works
Football Grd.
Stansfield Rd. Inf. & Jun. Schs.
Higher Memorial Park
Manchester
Street End
M35
FAILSWORTH
St. John's Jun. Sch.
Failsworth Sch. (Lower)
Failsworth Sch. (Upper)
Sports Cen.
Tennis Cts.
Argyll Cricket Grd.
Holt Lane End
Cutler Hill
CUTLER HILL
M60 MOTORWAY
Woodhouse Green
Woodhouse Grn. Farm
Greenfold Farm
Crime Lake
Crime Fm.
Crime Bri.
Crime Bridge Farm
Pinch Farm
Comm. Cen.
Cemetery
Woodhouses
Woodhouses C. of E. & Free Church Prim. School
Failsworth
390
91
402
01
03
04

E
F
G
H
1
2
3
4
5
6
41
50
93
94
04
03
02
01
Glodwick
Alexandra Park
Glodwick Brook
Fenny Hill
Lees Recreation Ground
Playing Field
Snipe Clough
Fitton Hill Junior School
Fitton Hill Infant School
Fitton Hill
Hathershaw
Hathershaw School
Copster Hill
Copster Park
Oldham
Hollins Green
Playing Fields
WERNETH GOLF COURSE
Club House
COAL PIT LANE
OL8
Bardsley
Bank Top Farm
Fairbottom
Fairbottom Farm
Wester Hill
Park Dean School
Comm. Education Cen.
Marland Fold Sch.
St. Martin's C.of E. Prim. Sch.
Heritage Cen.
Dean House
Fenny Field Bridge
River Medlock
Bankfield Clough
Public Open Space
Manor Pk. (R.U. Football Grd.)
Manor House Farm
Wood Park
Wood Pk. Farm
Wood Park Clough
Slaters Farm
Riversvale Farm
Knott Lanes
Croft End Farm
Bardsley Park Golf Centre
Bardsley Fold Farm
Bardsley Sewage Works
Valley Farm
Valley Bridge
Riversvale Arboretum
DAISY NOOK COUNTRY PARK
Fairbottom Branch
OLDHAM
TAMESIDE
Canal (Disused)
Ashton-under-Lyne
Bardsley Vale Mills
Holden Clough
OL7
OL6
Limehurst Farm
Springwood Hall
Limehurst
ASHTON ROAD
OLDHAM ROAD
A627
HATHERSHAW LA.
ABBEY HILLS RD. B6194
ALEXANDRA ROAD
ROTARY ST.
PARK BRIDGE ROAD
ALT HILL LANE

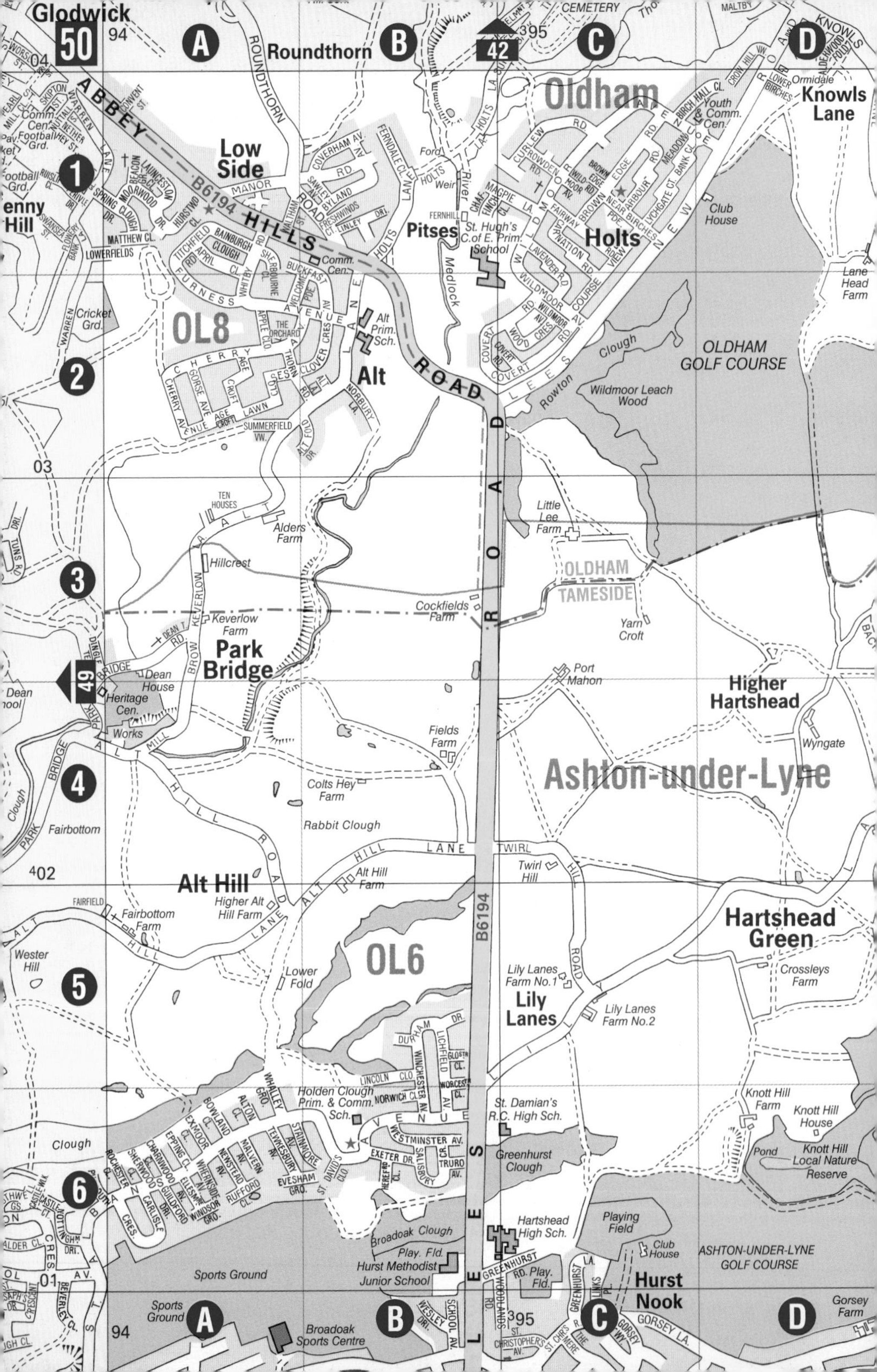

Glodwick
94
A
Roundthorn
B
42
395
C
D
Oldham
Knowls Lane
Low Side
ABBEY HILLS
B6194
ROAD
Pitses
Holts
St. Hugh's C.of E. Prim. School
Club House
Lane Head Farm
OL8
Alt Prim. Sch.
Alt
OLDHAM GOLF COURSE
Rowton Clough
Wildmoor Leach Wood
Cricket Grd.
03
Alders Farm
Hillcrest
Little Lee Farm
OLDHAM
TAMESIDE
Cockfields Farm
Keverlow Farm
Yarn Croft
Park Bridge
Dean House
Heritage Cen.
Works
49
Port Mahon
Higher Hartshead
Wyngate
Fields Farm
Colts Hey Farm
Rabbit Clough
Ashton-under-Lyne
Fairbottom
402
Alt Hill
Alt Hill Farm
Higher Alt Hill Farm
Twirl Hill
Fairbottom Farm
Hartshead Green
Wester Hill
OL6
Lower Fold
Lily Lanes Farm No.1
Lily Lanes
Lily Lanes Farm No.2
Crossleys Farm
Holden Clough Prim. & Comm. Sch.
St. Damian's R.C. High Sch.
Knott Hill Farm
Knott Hill House
Clough
Greenhurst Clough
Pond
Knott Hill Local Nature Reserve
Broadoak Clough
Hartshead High Sch.
Playing Field
Club House
ASHTON-UNDER-LYNE GOLF COURSE
Play. Fld.
Hurst Methodist Junior School
Sports Ground
Hurst Nook
01
Sports Ground
Broadoak Sports Centre
Gorsey Farm
LEES ROAD

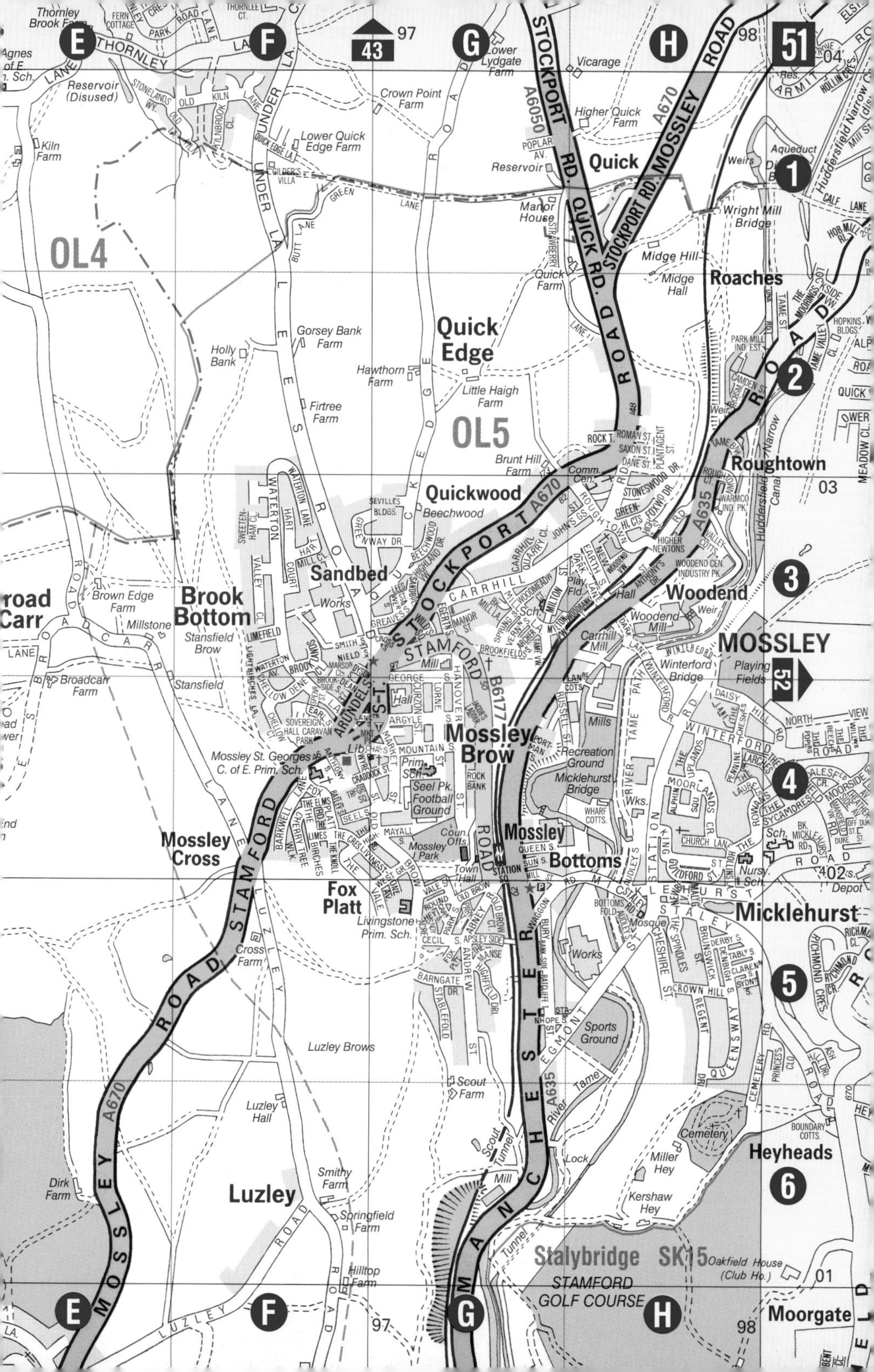
51
43
52
E
F
G
H
1
2
3
4
5
6
97
98
04
03
02
01
OL4
OL5
SK15
Quick
Quick Edge
Quickwood
Sandbed
Brook Bottom
Roaches
Roughtown
Woodend
MOSSLEY
Mossley Brow
Mossley Bottoms
Mossley Cross
Fox Platt
Micklehurst
Heyheads
Luzley
Moorgate
Stalybridge
STAMFORD GOLF COURSE
STOCKPORT RD.
MOSSLEY ROAD
QUICK RD.
STOCKPORT ROAD
STAMFORD ROAD
MANCHESTER ROAD
A670
A6050
A635
B6177
Huddersfield Narrow Canal
River Tame
Thornley Brook Farm
Reservoir (Disused)
Kiln Farm
Lower Quick Edge Farm
Crown Point Farm
Lower Lydgate Farm
Vicarage
Higher Quick Farm
Manor House
Quick Farm
Midge Hill
Gorsey Bank Farm
Holly Bank
Hawthorn Farm
Little Haigh Farm
Firtree Farm
Brunt Hill Farm
Beechwood
Brown Edge Farm
Millstone
Stansfield Brow
Broadcarr Farm
Stansfield
Mossley St. Georges C. of E. Prim. Sch.
Seel Pk. Football Ground
Mossley Park
Town Hall
Livingstone Prim. Sch.
Cross Farm
Luzley Brows
Luzley Hall
Scout Farm
Dirk Farm
Smithy Farm
Springfield Farm
Hilltop Farm
Recreation Ground
Micklehurst Bridge
Winterford Bridge
Playing Fields
Woodend Mill
Carrhill Mill
Sports Ground
Cemetery
Miller Hey
Kershaw Hey
Oakfield House (Club Ho.)
Wright Mill Bridge
Aqueduct
Scout Tunnel
Tunnel
Lock
Works
Mills
Mosque
Depot
Broadcarr

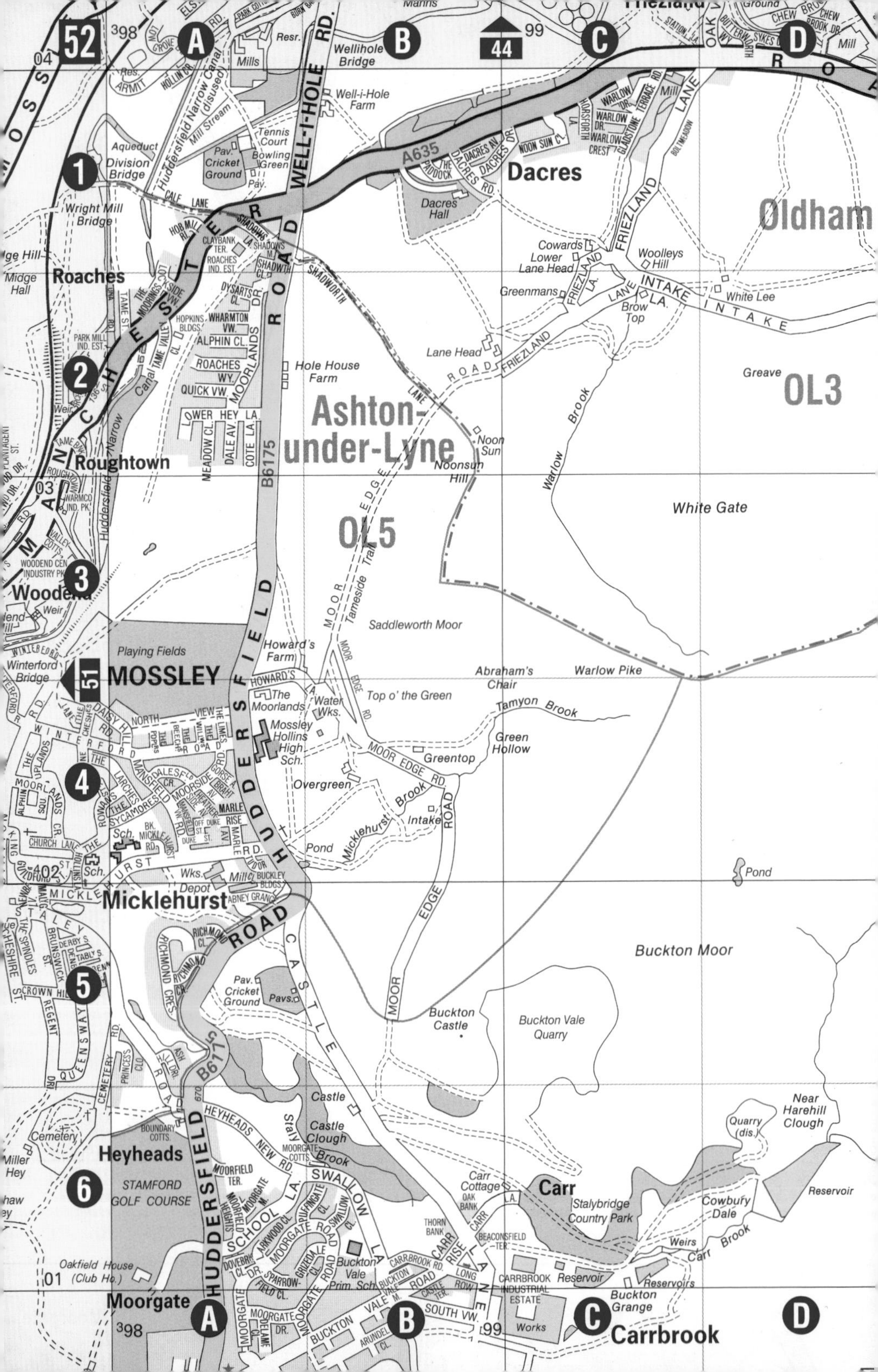

52
44
51
A
B
C
D
1
2
3
4
5
6
Dacres
Oldham
Ashton-under-Lyne
OL5
OL3
MOSSLEY
Roaches
Roughtown
Woodend
Micklehurst
Heyheads
Moorgate
Carrbrook
Carr
Saddleworth Moor
Buckton Moor
White Gate
Warlow Pike
Abraham's Chair
Top o' the Green
Green Hollow
Greentop
Overgreen
Intake
Pond
Howard's Farm
Hole House Farm
Lane Head
Greenmans
Cowards
Lower Lane Head
Woolleys Hill
White Lee
Brow Top
Greave
Noon Sun
Noonsun Hill
Dacres Hall
Well-i-Hole Farm
Wellihole Bridge
Division Bridge
Wright Mill Bridge
Aqueduct
Pav. Cricket Ground
Tennis Court
Bowling Green
Playing Fields
Winterford Bridge
Mossley Hollins High Sch.
The Moorlands
Water Wks.
Buckton Castle
Buckton Vale Quarry
Castle
Castle Clough
Stalybridge Country Park
Carr Cottage
Cowbury Dale
Near Harehill Clough
Quarry (dis.)
Reservoir
Reservoirs
Weirs
Buckton Grange
Carrbrook Industrial Estate
Works
Buckton Vale Prim. Sch.
Oakfield House (Club Ho.)
Stamford Golf Course
Cemetery
Miller Hey
Pav. Cricket Ground
Pavs.
A635
B6175
HUDDERSFIELD ROAD
WELL-I-HOLE RD.
MANCHESTER ROAD
MOOR EDGE ROAD
CASTLE LANE
FRIEZLAND LANE
INTAKE LANE
Tameside Trail
Warlow Brook
Tamyon Brook
Micklehurst Brook
Carr Brook
Stayley Brook
Huddersfield Narrow Canal (disused)
398
99
04
03
402
01

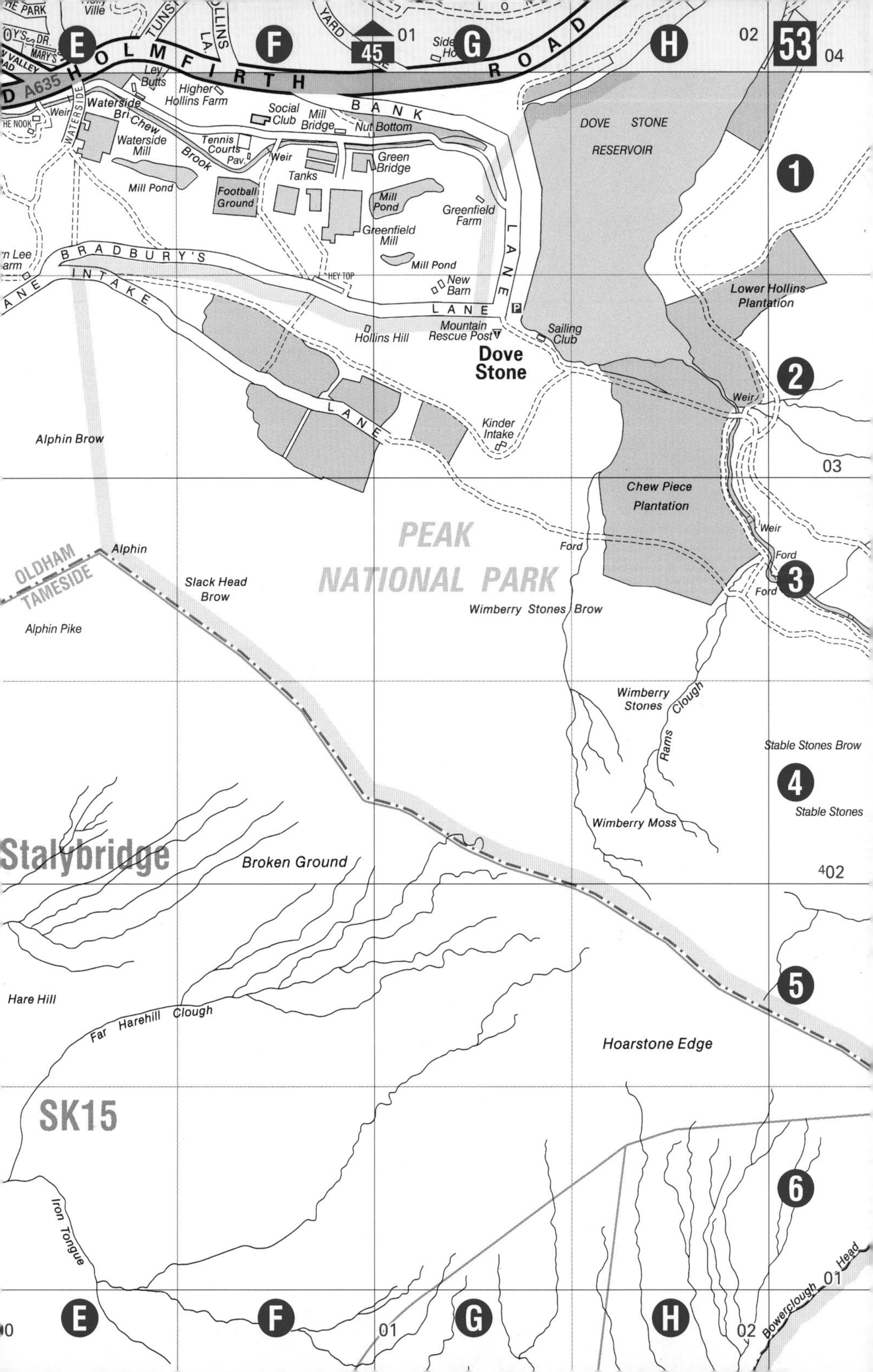
E
F
45
01
G
H
02
04
HOLMFIRTH ROAD
A635
Ley Butts
Higher Hollins Farm
Waterside
Bri
Weir
Chew Brook
Waterside Mill
Mill Pond
Tennis Courts
Pav.
Social Club
Mill Bridge
Nut Bottom
BANK
Weir
Tanks
Green Bridge
Football Ground
Mill Pond
Greenfield Farm
Greenfield Mill
Mill Pond
LANE
BRADBURY'S
INTAKE
HEY TOP
New Barn
LANE
Mountain Rescue Post
Hollins Hill
DOVE STONE RESERVOIR
Lower Hollins Plantation
Sailing Club
Dove Stone
Weir
LANE
Kinder Intake
Alphin Brow
03
Chew Piece Plantation
PEAK NATIONAL PARK
Weir
Ford
Ford
Ford
Alphin
OLDHAM
TAMESIDE
Slack Head Brow
Alphin Pike
Wimberry Stones Brow
Wimberry Stones
Rams Clough
Stable Stones Brow
Stable Stones
Wimberry Moss
Stalybridge
Broken Ground
402
Hare Hill
Far Harehill Clough
Hoarstone Edge
SK15
Iron Tongue
Bowerclough Head
01
1
2
3
4
5
6

54
88
A
B
C
D
47
89
1
2
3
4
5
6
OLDHAM ROAD
A62
Dean Lane
Refuse Destructor
Reliance Trading Estate
Failsworth Ind. Est.
Works
Lock
Mills
Shop. Cen.
Propps Hall Prim. Sch.
St. Mary's R.C. Prim. Sch.
Tannersfield Lodge
Newton Heath
Mkt.
Rec. Grd.
Sch.
Jun. & Inf. Schs.
Christ the King R.C. Prim. Sch.
Playing Field
St. Wilfred's C.of E. Primary Sch.
Cricket Grd.
Tennis Cts.
Brookdale Hall
Bowls
BROOKDALE PARK
Recreation Ground
South Failsworth Prim. Sch.
M40
Culcheth
Recreation Ground
Clayton Bridge
Sewage Works
Resrs.
Works
Weir
River
Gartside Farm
Clayton Bridge
Clayton Vale Bridge
Clayton Mill Bridge
Vauxhall Farm
Clayton Vale
St. Willibrord's R.C. Prim. Sch.
Sunny Bank Brook
Playing Field
Greenside
M11
Clayton
Liby.
Clayton Pk.
Clayton Hall
Moat
Rec. Grd.
Hewlett Playing Fields
Seymour Rd. Prim. Sch.
Rec. Grd.
Sunny Bank Park
Playground
Tennis Courts
Playing Field
Rec. Grd.
Depot
Annexe
Droylsden High Sch.
Comm. Cen.
Bowl. Grns.
ASHTON NEW ROAD
A662
MANCHESTER ROAD
Clayton Lane Bridge
Lock
Chemical Works
Comm. Cen.
Openshaw
Police Training Units
Clayton Industrial Estate
Chemical Works
Locks
Higher Openshaw Community School
Ashton Canal
Works
Res.
Failsworth Cemetery
Cemetery

55
48
E
F
G
H
Holt Lane End
Woodhouses
Crime Bridge Farm
Pinch Farm
Woodhouses C. of E. & Free Church Prim. School
Daisy Nook
DAISY NOOK COUNTRY PARK (N.T.)
Visitor Cen.
Daisy Nook Farm
M60
Bottom Field Farm
Diamond Hall Farm
Bowls Playgrd.
NEWMARKET RD.
River Medlock
M35
Bottom of Woodhouses
Cricket Grd.
Warwick Road Park
Wellstyle Farm
Canal
Hollinwood Branch
Ash Bridge
Club House
BROOKDALE GOLF COURSE
OLDHAM
TAMESIDE
Nook View Farm
Meadow View Farm
M60 MOTORWAY
Willow Bank Farm
Cinderland Bridge
Pond
Cinderland Hall Farm
Medlock Vale
Medlock Vale Farm
Bell Clough
Buckley Hill Farm
Hope Fold Farm
Jaum Farm
Littlemoss High School for Boys
The Willows
Manchester
Littlemoss
Swing Bridge
MILO INDUSTRIAL PARK
Moss Side Farm
Lumb Clough
Running Track
Cricket Ground
Ashton-under-Lyne
ASHTON MOSS
Medlock Leis. Cen.
Rec. Grd.
DROYLSDEN
M43
LEES PARK
OL7
Moorside Prim. Sch.
Droylsden F.C.
GREENSIDE TRADING CEN.
Hypermarket
Superstore
Council Offs.
M34
Playing Field
Aldwyn Primary School
Lib.
Swim Pool
ASHTON RD.
DROYLSDEN
A662
MANCHESTER ROAD
A635
SNIPE RETAIL PARK
Superstores
Works
Junc. 23
1
2
3
4
5
6
91
92
400
99
398
390

INDEX

Including Streets, Places & Areas, Hospitals & Hospices, Industrial Estates,
Selected Flats & Walkways and Selected Places of Interest.

HOW TO USE THIS INDEX

1. Each street name is followed by its Postal District (or, if outside the Manchester Postal District, by its Posttown or Postal Locality), and then by its map reference;
e.g. Abbey Dri. *L'boro* ....2F **15** is in the Littleborough Posttown and is to be found in square 2F on page **15**. The page number being shown in bold type.

2. A strict alphabetical order is followed in which Av., Rd., St., etc. (though abbreviated) are read in full and as part of the street name;
e.g. Abbey Cres. appears after Abberley Dri. but before Abbeydale.

3. Streets and a selection of flats and walkways too small to be shown on the maps, appear in the index in *Italics* with the thoroughfare to which it is connected shown in brackets; e.g. *Abbeydale. Roch....5G* **13** (off Spotland Rd.)

4. Places and areas are shown in the index in **blue type** and the map reference is to the actual map square in which the town centre or area is located and not to the place name shown on the map; e.g. **Belfield 5C 14**

5. An example of a selected place of interest is **Alexandra Pk. Vis. Cen. 6F 41**

6. An example of a hospital or hospice is **BIRCH HILL HOSPITAL....6D 6**

GENERAL ABBREVIATIONS

All : Alley	Ct : Court	Lit : Little	Rd : Road
App : Approach	Cres : Crescent	Lwr : Lower	Shop : Shopping
Arc : Arcade	Cft : Croft	Mc : Mac	S : South
Av : Avenue	Dri : Drive	Mnr : Manor	Sq : Square
Bk : Back	E : East	Mans : Mansions	Sta : Station
Boulevd : Boulevard	Embkmt : Embankment	Mkt : Market	St. : Street
Bri : Bridge	Est : Estate	Mdw : Meadow	Ter : Terrace
B'way : Broadway	Fld : Field	M : Mews	Trad : Trading
Bldgs : Buildings	Gdns : Gardens	Mt : Mount	Up : Upper
Bus : Business	Gth : Garth	Mus : Museum	Va : Vale
Cvn : Caravan	Ga : Gate	N : North	Vw : View
Cen : Centre	Gt : Great	Pal : Palace	Vs : Villas
Chu : Church	Grn : Green	Pde : Parade	Vis : Visitors
Chyd : Churchyard	Gro : Grove	Pk : Park	Wlk : Walk
Circ : Circle	Ho : House	Pas : Passage	W : West
Cir : Circus	Ind : Industrial	Pl : Place	Yd : Yard
Clo : Close	Info : Information	Quad : Quadrant	
Comn : Common	Junct : Junction	Res : Residential	
Cotts : Cottages	La : Lane	Ri : Rise	

POSTTOWN AND POSTAL LOCALITY ABBREVIATIONS

A'wrth : Ashworth	*Facit* : Facit	*Mars* : Marsden	*Shire* : Shore
Ash L : Ashton-under-Lyne	*Fail* : Failsworth	*Midd* : Middleton	*Smal* : Smallbridge
Aud : Audenshaw	*Fir* : Firgrove	*Miln* : Milnsbridge	*S'bri* : Smithybridge
Aus : Austerlands	*Grass* : Grasscroft	*Moss* : Mossley	*Sower B* : Sowerby Bridge
Bar : Bardsley	*G'fld* : Greenfield	*Most* : Moston	*S'head* : Springhead
B'edge : Burnedge	*G'ton* : Grotton	*New M* : New Moston	*Stal* : Stalybridge
Bury : Bury	*Harp* : Harpurhey	*Newt H* : Newton Heath	*S'dale* : Strinesdale
Carr : Carrbrook	*Heal* : Healey	*Oldh* : Oldham	*Summ* : Summit
Chad : Chadderton	*Heap B* : Heap Bridge	*Open* : Openshaw	*Uns* : Unsworth
Clay : Clayton	*Heyw* : Heywood	*P'wich* : Prestwich	*Upperm* : Uppermill
Del : Delph	*Hey D* : Heywood Distribution Pk.	*Rams* : Ramsbottom	*Ward* : Wardle
Dens : Denshaw	*Higg* : Higginshaw	*Roch* : Rochdale	*W'head* : Waterhead
Dent : Denton	*Hurs* : Hurstead	*Rytn* : Royton	*W'fld* : Whitefield
Dig : Diggle	*Lees* : Lees	*Sale* : Sale	*Whitw* : Whitworth
Dob : Dobcross	*L'boro* : Littleborough	*Scout* : Scouthead	
Droy : Droylsden	*Lyd* : Lydgate	*Shaw* : Shaw	

A

Abberley Dri. *M40*. 3F **47**
Abbey Cres. *Heyw* 3F **19**
Abbeydale. Roch 5G **13**
    (off Spotland Rd.)
Abbey Dri. *L'boro* 2F **15**
Abbey Gro. *Chad* 1A **48**
Abbey Hills Rd. *Oldh* 6H **41**
Abbey Rd. *Del* 4A **34**
Abbey Rd. *Droy* 4D **54**
Abbey Rd. *Fail* 5B **48**
Abbey Rd. *Midd* 5B **28**
Abbotsford. Whitw 1F **5**
    (off Millfold)
Abbotsford Dri. *Midd* 5H **27**
Abbotsford Rd. *Chad* 3G **39**
Abbotsford Rd. *Oldh* 2H **41**
Abbott St. *Roch* 4D **20**
Abels La. *Upperm*. 3E **45**
Abercorn St. *Oldh*. 5B **42**
Aberdare Wlk. *M9* 6A **38**
    (off Brockford Dri.)
Aberdeen Gdns. *Roch*. 1F **13**
Aberley Fold. *L'boro* 4F **7**
Abingdon Clo. *Chad* 1B **48**
Abingdon Rd. *Roch* 2G **21**
Abinger Wlk. *M40* 3B **54**

Abney Grange. *Moss* 5A **52**
Abney Rd. *Moss* 5G **51**
Abney Steps. *Moss* 5G **51**
    (off Apsley Side)
Aboukir St. *Roch* 5B **14**
Abson St. *Chad* 2C **40**
Acacia Rd. *Oldh* 4D **48**
Ace Mill. *Chad* 1H **47**
Acer Clo. *Roch* 4H **11**
Acker St. *Roch* 5H **13**
Acorn Cen., The. *Oldh* 3H **41**
Acorn St. *Lees* 5C **42**
Acorn Way. *Oldh* 4E **41**
Acre. **3H 41**
Acre Barn. *Shaw* 1E **31**
Acre La. *Oldh* 2G **41**
Acres. **1G 39**
Acresfield Av. *Aud* 6G **55**
Acresfield Rd. *Midd* 6D **28**
Acre St. *Chad* 3B **48**
Acre St. *Whitw* 2F **5**
Acre Top Rd. *M9* 6F **37**
Acton St. *Oldh* 3G **41**
Acton St. *Roch* 4A **14**
Adair St. *Roch* 5D **20**
Adam St. *Oldh* 3F **49**
Ada St. *M9*. 4A **46**
Ada St. *Oldh* 5G **41**
Ada St. *Roch* 3A **14**

Addingham Clo. *M9* 6F **37**
Addison Dri. *Midd* 1E **39**
Adelaide St.' *Heyw* 5H **19**
Adelaide St. *Midd*. 3C **38**
Adelaide St. E. *Heyw* 5A **20**
Aden St. *Oldh* 6B **42**
Aden St. *Roch* 4A **14**
Adlington St. *Oldh* 2B **42**
Adrian St. *M40*. 6C **46**
Adrian Ter. *Roch* 1C **22**
Adswood Clo. *Oldh*. 2B **42**
Afghan St. *Oldh* 3H **41**
Age Cft. *Oldh* 2A **50**
Agincourt St. *Heyw* 3F **19**
    (in two parts)
Agnes Clo. *Oldh* 1C **48**
Agnes St. *Chad* 6B **40**
Agnes St. *Roch* 2A **22**
Ainley Wood. *Del* 4A **34**
Ainsbrook Av. *Del*. 5B **34**
Ainsbrook Ter. *Dig* 4F **35**
    (off Harrop Ct. Rd.)
Ainsdale Clo. *Oldh* 1D **48**
Ainsdale Cres. *Rytn* 1E **41**
Ainsdale Dri. *Whitw* 4F **5**
Ainsley St. *M40* 2A **54**
Ainsworth St. *Roch* 1A **22**
Ainthorpe Wlk. *M40* 2B **54**
Aintree Dri. *Roch* 5A **12**

Aintree St. *M11* 6A **54**
Aintree Wlk. *Chad* 4C **40**
Air Hill Ter. *Roch* 4E **13**
Ajax St. *Roch*. 4D **20**
Alan Av. *Fail*. 2D **54**
Alandale Dri. *Rytn* 4C **30**
Alasdair Clo. *Chad* 3H **39**
Albany St. *Midd*. 4D **38**
Albany St. *Oldh* 2B **42**
Albany St. *Roch*. 2A **22**
Albert Av. *Shaw* 4G **31**
Albert Gdns. *M40*. 2B **54**
Albert Mt. *Oldh* 2G **41**
Albert Pl. *Lees* 5C **42**
Albert Royds St. *Roch* 3B **14**
Albert St. *Chad*. 2B **48**
Albert St. *Droy* 6F **55**
Albert St. *Heyw* 5F **19**
Albert St. *Lees* 5C **42**
Albert St. *L'boro*. 6H **7**
Albert St. *Midd*. 3C **38**
Albert St. *Miln* 2G **23**
Albert St. *Oldh*. 4B **48**
Albert St. *P'wich* 6A **36**
Albert St. *Rytn*. 5D **30**
Albert St. *Shaw* 2G **31**
Albert St. *Whitw* 3E **5**
Albert St. W. *Fail* 1B **54**
Albert St. Works. *Droy* 6F **55**

56 A-Z Oldham & Rochdale

Albine St. *M40* 5B **46**
Albion Dri. *Droy* 5E **55**
Albion Fold. *Droy* 5E **55**
Albion Gdns. Clo. *Rytn* 5F **31**
Albion Rd. *Roch* 1F **21**
Albion Rd. Ind. Est. *Roch* 1F **21**
Albion St. *Chad* 4A **40**
Albion St. *Fail* 6G **47**
Albion St. *L'boro* 6G **7**
Albion St. *Oldh* 4F **41**
(in two parts)
Albion St. *Roch* 6E **21**
Albury Dri. *Roch* 3B **12**
Alcester Clo. *Midd* 5D **38**
Alcester St. *Chad* 2A **48**
Alcester Wlk. *M9* 6G **37**
Alconbury Ct. Droy 6F ***55***
(off Williamson La.)
Alconbury Wlk. *M9* 5F **37**
Alder Av. *Bury* 4A **18**
Alderbank. *Ward* 4C **6**
Alder Clo. *Ash L* 6H **49**
Alderdale Dri. *Droy* 5C **54**
Alder La. *Oldh* 3D **48**
Alderman Foley Dri. *Roch* 3C **12**
Aldermaston Gro. *M9* 5F **37**
Alder Mdw. Clo. *Roch* 4C **12**
Alder Rd. *Fail* 2D **54**
Alder Rd. *Midd* 1E **39**
Alder Rd. *Roch* 5F **21**
Alder Root **5B 40**
Alders Ct. *Oldh* 5G **49**
Aldersley Av. *M9* 6F **37**
Alderson St. *Oldh* 4E **41**
Alderwood Fold. *Lees* 6D **42**
Aldham Av. *M40* 3A **54**
Aldred St. *Fail* 6G **47**
Aldwych. *Roch* 4H **21**
Alexander Av. *Fail* 5A **48**
Alexander Dri. *Miln* 1E **23**
Alexander St. *Roch* 5D **20**
Alexandra Cen. Retail Pk. *Oldh* 5F **41**
Alexandra Cres. *Oldh* 3H **41**
Alexandra Ho. *Oldh* 3H **41**
Alexandra M. *Oldh* 6G **41**
Alexandra Pk. Vis. Cen. 6F 41
Alexandra Rd. *Oldh* 1G **49**
Alexandra St. *Heyw* 1A **28**
Alexandra St. *Oldh* 6G **41**
Alexandra Ter. *Oldh* 6B **32**
Alford St. *Oldh* 3B **48**
Alfred St. *M9* 5A **46**
Alfred St. *Fail* 5H **47**
Alfred St. *L'boro* 5G **7**
Alfred St. *Oldh* 5C **40**
(in two parts)
Alfred St. *Shaw* 2G **31**
Alfred St. *Whitw* 1F **5**
Alfreton Wlk. M40 6C ***46***
(off Thorpebrook Rd.)
Alice Ingham Ct. *Roch* 4D **12**
Alice St. *Roch* 4B **14**
Alicia Ct. *Roch* 4G **13**
Alicia Dri. *Roch* 4G **13**
Alison Kelly Clo. *M9* 5B **46**
Alison St. *Shaw* 1G **31**
Alkrington Ct. *Midd* 6D **38**
Alkrington Garden Village **5C** 38
Alkrington Grn. *Midd* 5B **38**
Alkrington Hall Rd. N. *Midd* 4B **38**
Alkrington Hall Rd. S. *Midd* 5A **38**
Alkrington Pk. Rd. *Midd* 4A **38**
Allamaiqbal Rd. *Oldh* 6A **42**
Allenby St. *Shaw* 2G **31**
Allen Clo. *Shaw* 3G **31**
Allen St. *Oldh* 5D **40**
Allen St. *Roch* 1A **22**
Alligin Clo. *Chad* 3A **40**
Allington. *Roch* 1G **21**
Allonby Wlk. *Midd* 1G **37**
Alloway Wlk. *M9* 6C **46**
All Saint's Clo. *Rytn* 4D **30**
All Saints St. *M40* 2A **54**
All Saints Ter. *Roch* 3B **14**
Alma Ind. Est. *Roch* 4H **13**
Alma St. *Roch* 4H **13**
Alminstone Clo. *M40* 3B **54**
Almond Av. *Bury* 4A **18**
Almond Clo. *Fail* 1D **54**
Almond Clo. *L'boro* 5F **7**
Almond Rd. *Oldh* 2B **42**
Alnwick Rd. *M9* 6H **37**
Alperton Wlk. *M40* 3B **54**
Alphin Clo. *G'fld* 6D **44**
Alphin Clo. *Moss* 2A **52**
Alphin Sq. *Moss* 4H **51**
Alpine Dri. *Miln* 6G **15**
Alpine Dri. *Rytn* 6C **30**
Alpine Dri. *Ward* 5C **6**
Alpington Wlk. *M40* 3E **47**
Alresford Rd. *Midd* 6B **38**
Alston Av. *Shaw* 1H **31**
Alston Wlk. *Midd* 1G **37**
Alt **2B 50**
Alt Fold Dri. *Oldh* 2B **50**
Alt Hill **5A 50**
Alt Hill La. *Ash L* 5H **49**
Alt Hill Rd. *Ash L* 4A **50**
Althorpe Wlk. *M40* 3B **54**
Alt La. *Oldh* 3A **50**
Alton Clo. *Ash L* 6A **50**
Alton St. *Oldh* 2F **49**
Alt Wlk. *W'fld* 1A **36**
Alva Rd. *Oldh* 1B **42**
Alwin Rd. *Shaw* 1G **31**
Alworth Rd. *M9* 6H **37**
Amberley Wlk. *Chad* 4C **40**
Amberwood. *Chad* 3G **39**
Ambleside Clo. *Midd* 2A **38**
Ambleside Wlk. *M9* 3C **46**
Ambrose Cres. *Dig* 6D **34**
Ambrose St. *Roch* 2H **21**
Amesbury Rd. *M9* 1A **46**
Ammon's Way. *Del* 4B **34**
Ammon Wrigley Clo. *Oldh* 4F **41**
Amos Av. *M40* 3A **54**
Amos St. *M9* 6B **46**
Amport Wlk. *M40* 3E **47**
Amy St. *Midd* 2D **38**
Amy St. *Roch* 4D **12**
Ancaster Wlk. *M40* 3E **47**
Anchor St. *Oldh* 3F **41**
Ancoats St. *Lees* 5C **42**
Andover Av. *Midd* 6D **38**
Andre St. *M11* 5A **54**
Andrew Rd. *M9* 4A **36**
Andrew's Brow. *M40* 3B **54**
Andrews Bldgs. Moss 4A ***52***
(off Bk. Micklehurst Rd.)
Andrew St. *Chad* 3B **40**
Andrew St. *Droy* 3G **55**
Andrew St. *Fail* 5G **47**
Andrew St. *Midd* 4E **39**
Andrew St. *Moss* 5G **51**
Andy Nicholson Wlk. *M9* 5B **46**
Anfield Clo. *Bury* 6A **26**
Anfield Rd. *M40* 4F **47**
Angela Av. *Rytn* 1E **41**
Angelico Ri. *Oldh* 6B **32**
Angus Av. *Heyw* 6E **19**
Aniline St. *M11* 6A **54**
Annable Rd. *Droy* 6F **55**
Anne Line Clo. Roch 2A ***22***
(off Wellfield St.)
Annersley Av. *Shaw* 2G **31**
Annesley Rd. *M40* 4G **47**
Annie Darby Ct. *M9* 6A **46**
Annisfield Av. *G'fld* 6D **44**
Annis St. *M9* 5A **46**
Ann Sq. *Oldh* 3B **42**
Ann St. *Heyw* 4H **19**
Ann St. *Roch* 1H **21**
(in two parts)
Ansdell Dri. *Droy* 5C **54**
Ansdell Rd. *Roch* 3B **22**
Anselms Ct. *Oldh* 1C **48**
Anthony St. *Moss* 4F **51**
Anton Wlk. *M9* 6A **46**
Anvil Way. *Oldh* 4E **41**
Apfel La. *Chad* 4B **40**
Appleby Wlk. *Rytn* 5E **31**
Apple Clo. *Oldh* 2A **50**
Applecross Wlk. *Open* 6A **54**
Appledore Wlk. *Chad* 5B **40**
Apple Way. *Midd* 5D **38**
Applewood. *Chad* 4G **39**
Apprentice Ct. *M9* 5A **46**
April Clo. *Oldh* 1A **50**
Apsley Side. *Moss* 5G **51**
Aragon Dri. *Heyw* 5G **19**
Arbor Gro. *Droy* 4E **55**
Arbory Av. *M40* 5D **46**
Arbour Rd. *Oldh* 1C **50**
Arbroath St. *M11* 6B **54**
Arbury Av. *Roch* 2G **21**
Archer Pk. *Midd* 3A **38**
Archer St. *Moss* 3G **51**
Arcon Clo. *Roch* 1E **23**
Ardale Av. *M40* 3E **47**
Ardcombe Av. *M9* 6G **37**
Arden Av. *Midd* 6D **38**
Arden Gro. *M40* 4E **47**
Arden Ho. *Rytn* 5E **31**
Arden St. *Chad* 2A **48**
Argus St. *Oldh* 3C **48**
Argyle Cres. *Heyw* 6F **19**
Argyle Pde. *Heyw* 6E **19**
Argyle St. *Droy* 6E **55**
Argyle St. *Heyw* 6D **18**
Argyle St. *Moss* 4G **51**
Argyle St. *Oldh* 3H **41**
Argyle St. *Roch* 3A **22**
Argyll Clo. *Fail* 6B **48**
Argyll Pk. Rd. *Fail* 6B **48**
Argyll Rd. *Chad* 2H **47**
Arkendale Clo. *Fail* 6C **48**
Arkholme Wlk. *M40* 6D **46**
Arkle Dri. *Chad* 3H **39**
Arkwright St. *Oldh* 5C **40**
Arkwright Way. *Roch* 5A **22**
Arlen Way. *Heyw* 5F **19**
Arley Dri. *Shaw* 1A **32**
Arlington Clo. *Rytn* 1E **41**
Armadale Av. *M9* 1C **46**
Armdale Ri. *Oldh* 2C **42**
Armitage Clo. *Midd* 4H **37**
Armitage Clo. *Oldh* 2C **48**
Armitage Owen Wlk. *M40* 6C **46**
Armit Rd. *G'fld* 1A **52**
Arm Rd. *L'boro* 6E **7**
Armstrong Hurst Clo. *Roch* 2B **14**
Arncliffe Ri. *Oldh* 5D **32**
Arncott Clo. *Rytn* 5G **31**
Arne St. *Chad* 6A **40**
Arnold Av. *Heyw* 2A **28**
Arnold Dri. *Droy* 6E **55**
Arnold Dri. *Midd* 6E **29**
Arnold St. *Oldh* 3G **41**
Arnside Av. *Chad* 5A **40**
Arnside Clo. *Shaw* 2B **32**
Arnside Dri. *Roch* 2A **20**
Arran Av. *Oldh* 2F **49**
Arran St. *M40* 5B **46**
Arran Wlk. *Heyw* 6E **19**
Arthington St. *Roch* 5B **14**
Arthur Pits. *Roch* 6B **12**
Arthur St. *Heyw* 5H **19**
Arthur St. *Roch* 5F **13**
Arthur St. *Shaw* 2G **31**
Arundel Av. *Roch* 3G **21**
Arundel Av. *W'fld* 4A **36**
Arundel Clo. *Carr* 6B **52**
Arundel Ct. *M9* 6E **37**
Arundel St. *Moss* 4F **51**
Arundel St. *Oldh* 4A **42**
Arundel St. *Roch* 3G **21**
Arundel Wlk. *Chad* 5A **40**
Asby Clo. *Midd* 1H **37**
Ascot Clo. *Chad* 4C **40**
Ascot Clo. *Roch* 5A **12**
Ascot Rd. *M40* 3A **54**
Ascroft Ct. *Oldh* 5F **41**
Ascroft St. *Oldh* 5F **41**
Ashbourne Av. *Midd* 6E **29**
Ashbourne Clo. *Ward* 5D **6**
Ashbourne Sq. *Oldh* 6E **41**
Ashbourne St. *Roch* 4A **12**
Ashbridge Rd. *Fail* 1F **55**
Ashbrook Clo. *W'fld* 3A **36**
Ashbrook Cres. *Roch* 2C **14**
Ashbrook Hey **1C 14**
Ashbrook Hey La. *Roch* 1C **14**
Ashbrook Rd. *S'head* 6D **42**
Ashburn Flats. Heyw 5G ***19***
(off School St.)
Ash Clo. *Roch* 1C **14**
Ashcroft. *Roch* 1D **14**
Ashcroft St. *Chad* 6A **40**
Ashdale Cres. *Droy* 6D **54**
Ashdene. *Roch* 2F **13**
Ashdene Clo. *Chad* 2C **40**
Ashdene Clo. *S'head* 4D **42**
Ashdene Ri. *Oldh* 5B **32**
Ashdown Av. *M9* 6H **37**&1A **43**
Ashdown Ter. *M9* 1A **46**
Ashdown Way. *Shaw* 1E **31**
Ashes La. *Miln* 6E **15**
Ashes La. *S'head* 5D **42**
Ashfield Av. *Roch* 2H **21**
Ashfield Cres. *S'head* 5D **42**
Ashfield Dri. *M40* 3B **54**
Ashfield Ho. *Roch* 2H **21**
Ashfield La. *Miln* 3F **23**
Ashfield Rd. *Roch* 3G **21**
Ashfield Sq. *Droy* 6D **54**
Ashfield St. *Oldh* 2C **48**
Ashford Ct. *Oldh* 2B **42**
Ashford St. *Heyw* 5D **18**
Ashford Wlk. *Chad* 5B **40**
Ashgill Wlk. M9 6A ***46***
(off Fernclough Rd.)
Ash Gro. *L'boro* 6F **7**
Ash Gro. *Miln* 4G **23**
Ash Gro. *Roch* 6B **22**
Ash Gro. *Rytn* 3D **30**
Ash Gro. *S'head* 4E **43**
(in two parts)
Ash Hill Dri. *Moss* 5A **52**
Ashia Clo. *Roch* 1A **22**
Ashlands Av. *M40* 4E **47**
Ashlea Gro. *G'ton* 5F **43**
Ashleigh Clo. *Rytn* 1E **41**
Ashley Clo. *Roch* 3E **21**
Ashley Ct. *M40* 4H **47**
Ashley Ct. *Whitw* 1F **5**
Ashley Ct. Dri. *M40* 4H **47**
Ashley La. *M9* 5B **46**
Ashley Rd. *Droy* 5C **54**
Ashley St. *Oldh* 3C **40**
Ashmond. *S'head* 5D **42**
Ashmond Rd. *S'head* 5D **42**
Ashmount Dri. *Roch* 3H **13**
Ashness Dri. *Midd* 6H **27**
Ash Rd. *Droy* 5D **54**
Ash Sq. *Oldh* 3B **42**
Ash St. *Fail* 5G **47**
Ash St. *Heyw* 4F **19**
Ash St. *Midd* 2E **39**
Ash St. *Oldh* 5H **41**
Ash St. *Roch* 5E **21**
Ashton Cres. *Chad* 2A **48**
Ashton Gdns. *Roch* 2G **21**
Ashton Hill La. *Droy* 6E **55**
Ashton La. *Midd* 3C **38**
Ashton New Rd. *M11* 5A **54**
Ashton Rd. *M9* 6H **37**
Ashton Rd. *Droy* 6F **55**
Ashton Rd. *Fail* 1G **55**
Ashton Rd. *Oldh* 6E **41**
Ashton Rd. E. *Fail* 5H **47**
Ashton Rd. W. *Fail* 6G **47**
Ashton St. *M9* 5B **46**
Ashton St. *Chad* 2A **48**
Ashton St. *Heyw* 5G **19**
Ashton St. *Roch* 2G **21**
Ash Tree Av. *Droy* 5D **54**
Ash Tree Gro. *Droy* 4D **54**
Ashurst Av. *M11* 5A **54**
Ashville Ter. *M40* 4B **46**
Ash Wlk. *Chad* 3B **40**
Ash Wlk. *Midd* 5B **38**
Ashwater Wlk. M9 6A 38
(off Brockford Dri.)
Ashwood. *Chad* 4G **39**
Ashwood Dri. *L'boro* 6F **7**
Ashwood Dri. *Rytn* 4C **30**
Ashworth Clo. *Chad* 1B **48**
Ashworth Clo. *L'boro* 4G **7**
Ashworth Clo. *Rytn* 5F **31**
Ashworth Ct. Shaw 3H ***31***
(off Ashworth St.)
Ashworth Gdns. *G'fld* 6D **44**
Ashworth Rd. *Roch & Heyw* 2C **10**
Ashworth St. *Fail* 1B **54**
Ashworth St. *Heyw* 1H **27**
Ashworth St. *Oldh* 5F **41**
Ashworth St. *Roch* 5F **13**
Ashworth St. *Shaw* 3H **31**
Askett Clo. *M40* 1B **54**
Aspell Clo. *Midd* 2B **38**
Aspen Gdns. *Roch* 4C **12**
Aspenwood Dri. *Chad* 4G **39**
Aspinall St. *Heyw* 5A **20**
Aspinall St. *Midd* 4E **39**
Aspull St. *Oldh* 6A **42**
Assheton Av. *Aud* 6G **55**
Assheton Cres. *M40* 3B **54**
Assheton Rd. *M40* 3B **54**
Assheton Rd. *Shaw* 2F **31**
Assheton St. *Midd* 2C **38**
(Clarke Brow)
Assheton St. *Midd* 1C **38**
(King St.)
Assheton Way. *Midd* 3C **38**
Assumption Rd. *Midd* 6H **27**
Astan Av. *Droy* 4B **54**
Astbury Av. *Aud* 6H **55**
Astbury Clo. *S'head* 5D **42**
Aster Ho. *Oldh* 2E **41**
Aster St. *Oldh* 2E **41**

Astley Clo. Shaw . . . 2F 31
Astley St. M11 . . . 6A 54 (in two parts)
Aston Ct. Oldh . . . 3E 41
Astra Cen., The. Roch . . . 4E 21
Atcham Gro. M9 . . . 5F 37
Athens Way. Lees . . . 5C 42
Atherley Gro. M40 & Chad . . . 3H 47
Atherstone. Roch . . . 5H 13 (off Redcross St.)
Atherton Clo. Fail . . . 2F 55
Atherton St. Lees . . . 6C 42
Atherton St. S'head . . . 5D 42 (in two parts)
Athlone Av. M40 . . . 5C 46
Atholl Dri. Heyw . . . 6E 19
Athol St. Roch . . . 4B 14
Athos Wlk. M40 . . . 3E 47
Atkinson St. Oldh . . . 3D 40
Atkinson St. Roch . . . 5E 21
Attleboro Rd. M40 . . . 6C 46
Aubrey St. Roch . . . 2H 21
Audax Wlk. M40 . . . 3A 54
Auden Clo. M11 . . . 6B 54
Auden Ct. M11 . . . 6B 54 (off Auden Clo.)
Audley St. Moss . . . 4H 51 (in two parts)
Audrey St. M9 . . . 6B 46
Augusta Clo. Roch . . . 3G 13 (in two parts)
Augusta St. Roch . . . 4G 13
Augustine Webster Clo. M9 . . . 5A 46
Austen Wlk. Oldh . . . 5C 32
Austerlands . . . 3E 43
Avenue, The. Shaw . . . 3G 31
Averill St. M40 . . . 2B 54
Averon Ri. Oldh . . . 5B 32
Avis St. Shaw . . . 2H 31
Avonbrook Dri. M40 . . . 3H 47
Avon Clo. Miln . . . 1G 23
Avondale Ct. Roch . . . 2F 29
Avon Flats. Heyw . . . 5G 19 (off Kay St.)
Avonlea Rd. Droy . . . 5C 54
Avonleigh Gdns. Oldh . . . 2A 42 (off Clyde St.)
Avon Rd. Chad . . . 3H 39
Avon Rd. Heyw . . . 5E 19
Avon Rd. Shaw . . . 1H 31
Avon St. Oldh . . . 1F 49
Avro Ct. Midd . . . 3F 39
Aylesbury Gro. Midd . . . 1E 39
Aylestone Wlk. M40 . . . 6C 46
Ayr Av. Oldh . . . 2F 49
Ayr Gro. Heyw . . . 6E 19
Aysgarth. Roch . . . 4B 14

B

Babbacombe Gro. M9 . . . 6F 37
Bk. Albany St. Roch . . . 2A 22
Bk. Bradshaw St. Roch . . . 5A 14
Bk. Chapel St. Ward . . . 4C 6
Bk. Cowm La. Whitw . . . 1E 5 (in two parts)
Bk. Dale St. Miln . . . 2F 23
Bk. Drake St. Roch . . . 1H 21
Bk. Gladstone St. Oldh . . . 5H 41
Bk. High St. Heyw . . . 5F 19 (off High St.)
Bk. Hope St. Oldh . . . 4H 41
Bk. King St. Oldh . . . 5E 41
Back La. Ash L . . . 2H 55 (in two parts)
Back La. Oldh & Moss . . . 2E 51
Back La. Roch . . . 2B 12
Back La. Scout . . . 2G 43
Bk. Lee St. Upperm . . . 3D 44
Bk. Louise St. Roch . . . 2B 14
Bk. Manchester St. Heyw . . . 6A 20 (off Hall St.)
Bk. Micklehurst Rd. Moss . . . 4A 52
Bk. Mill La. Moss . . . 3G 51
Bk. Nook Ter. Roch . . . 2H 13
Bk. Oldham Rd. Roch . . . 1A 22
Back o' th' Low Rd. Oldh . . . 3D 42
Back o' th' Moss . . . 4G 19
Bk. o' th' Moss La. Heyw . . . 4G 19 (Clay Bank St.)
Bk. o' th' Moss La. Heyw . . . 4G 19 (Lime Gro.)
Bk. Parkfield Vw. Roch . . . 5B 22
Bk. Patience St. Roch . . . 4E 13
Bk. Pine St. Miln . . . 3H 23 (off Newhey Rd.)
Bk. Ramsden Rd. Roch . . . 4C 6
Bk. Rochdale Old Rd. N. Bury . . . 3B 18 (off Rectory La.)
Bk. Rochdale Old Rd. N. Bury . . . 4A 18 (off Coppice St.)
Bk. Rochdale Old Rd. S. Bury . . . 4A 18 (off Rochdale Old Rd.)
Bk. Rochdale Old Rd. S. Bury . . . 4A 18 (off Topping Fold Rd.)
Bk. Rochdale Old Rd. S. Bury . . . 4A 18 (Cuckoo La.)
Bk. Rooley Moor Rd. Roch . . . 4E 13
Bk. Royds St. Roch . . . 2A 22
Bk. St James St. Oldh . . . 4H 41
Bk. Scott St. Oldh . . . 6F 41 (off Scott St.)
Bk. Spring Mill. Miln . . . 2C 24
Bk. Union Rd. Roch . . . 1E 15
Back Whitegate. L'boro . . . 1E 15
Bacup St. M40 . . . 5C 46
Bader Dri. Heyw . . . 2H 27
Badger Clo. Roch . . . 4B 22
Badger Edge La. Oldh . . . 6G 33
Badger La. Roch . . . 5B 22 (in three parts)
Bagnall Clo. Roch . . . 3B 12
Bagnall Clo. Upperm . . . 2E 45
Bagot St. M11 . . . 5A 54
Bagslate Moor . . . 5B 12
Bagslate Moor La. Roch . . . 5B 12
Bagslate Moor Rd. Roch . . . 6A 12
Baguley Cres. Midd . . . 4E 37
Baguley St. Droy . . . 6F 55
Baildon Rd. Roch . . . 4D 12
Baildon St. M40 . . . 4C 46
Bailey St. M11 . . . 6B 54
Bailey St. Oldh . . . 4G 41
Bailey St. P'wich . . . 6A 36
Baillie St. Roch . . . 6H 13 (in three parts)
Baillie St. E. Roch . . . 5A 14
Bainbridge Rd. Oldh . . . 2B 42
Bainburgh Clough. Oldh . . . 1A 50
Bainton Wlk. M9 . . . 6G 37
Baitings Clo. Roch . . . 3G 11
Baitings Row. Roch . . . 3G 11
Baker Ho. Rytn . . . 5E 31 (off Royton Hall Wlk.)
Bakers La. Dig . . . 1G 45
Baker St. Heyw . . . 1A 28
Baker St. Midd . . . 3D 38
Bakewell Rd. Droy . . . 5C 54
Balderstone . . . 4B 22
Balderstone Rd. Roch . . . 5H 21
Balfour Rd. Roch . . . 4E 13
Balfour St. Oldh . . . 4A 42
Balfour St. Shaw . . . 2H 31
Ballantine St. M40 . . . 3A 54
Ballard Clo. L'boro . . . 4H 7
Ballard Way. Shaw . . . 1A 32
Ballater Clo. Heyw . . . 6F 19
Ball St. Roch . . . 5A 14
Ballygreen. Roch . . . 4E 21
Balmoral Av. Roch . . . 5D 12
Balmoral Av. Rytn . . . 5F 31
Balmoral Clo. Miln . . . 1G 23
Balmoral Ct. M8 . . . 6D 36
Balmoral Dri. Heyw . . . 6E 19
Balmore Ct. Heyw . . . 6C 18
Bamford . . . 1A 20
Bamford Av. Midd . . . 1C 38
Bamford Clo. Bury . . . 3C 18
Bamford Ct. Roch . . . 1D 20 (off Half Acre M.)
Bamford M. Roch . . . 6A 12
Bamford Pl. Roch . . . 4G 13
Bamford Rd. M9 . . . 6H 37
Bamford Rd. Heyw . . . 3G 19
Bamford Shop. Cen. Roch . . . 6A 12
Bamfords Pas. L'boro . . . 5H 7
Bamford St. M11 . . . 5A 54
Bamford St. Chad . . . 3C 40
Bamford St. L'boro . . . 6F 7 (Featherstall Rd.)
Bamford St. L'boro . . . 5E 7 (Shore Rd.)
Bamford St. Rytn . . . 6E 31
Bamford Way. Roch . . . 1A 20
Bampton Wlk. Midd . . . 1A 38
Banbury Rd. Fail . . . 3C 54
Banbury Rd. Midd . . . 6B 38
Banff Gro. Heyw . . . 6E 19
Bangor St. Roch . . . 1B 22
Bank. Roch . . . 4C 6
Bank Barn. Ward . . . 4D 6
Bank Barn La. Ward . . . 4D 6
Bank Clo. L'boro . . . 2G 15
Bankfield Av. Droy . . . 5E 55
Bankfield Cotts. Dob . . . 1B 44
Bankfield Dri. Oldh . . . 3H 49
Bankfield La. Roch . . . 5A 12
Bankhall Wlk. M9 . . . 6A 46 (off Broadwell Dri.)
Bank Hill St. Oldh . . . 4A 42
Bank La. G'fld . . . 1F 53
Bank La. Ward . . . 4D 6
Banks Cft. Heyw . . . 2H 27
Bank Side. Moss . . . 5G 51
Bankside Av. Upperm . . . 4E 45
Bankside Clo. Oldh . . . 5D 40
Bank St. Heyw . . . 5F 19 (in two parts)
Bank St. Oldh . . . 5B 42
Bank St. Roch . . . 3A 22
Bank St. Shaw . . . 2G 31
Bank Ter. Whitw . . . 3E 5
Bank, The. Roch . . . 6H 13
Bank Top . . . 5B 42 **(Greenacres)**
Bank Top . . . 5E 41 **(Oldham)**
Bank Top Pk. Oldh . . . 5B 42
Bank Top St. Heyw . . . 4F 19
Bannach Dri. Chad . . . 2A 40
Bannatyne Clo. M40 . . . 4G 47
Bannerman Rd. Droy . . . 6F 55
Bantry St. Roch . . . 3A 14
Barathea Clo. Roch . . . 4C 20
Barcliffe Av. M40 . . . 3E 47
Barclyde St. Roch . . . 2G 21
Barcombe Clo. Oldh . . . 1B 42
Barcombe Wlk. M9 . . . 6A 46 (in two parts)
Bardsley . . . 5G 49
Bardsley Av. Fail . . . 6H 47
Bardsley St. M40 . . . 2B 54
Bardsley St. Chad . . . 2H 47
Bardsley St. Lees . . . 6C 42
Bardsley St. Midd . . . 2C 38
Bardsley St. Oldh . . . 3C 42
Bardsley Va. Av. Oldh . . . 5G 49
Barehill St. L'boro . . . 5H 7
Bar Gap Rd. Oldh . . . 3F 41
Barker St. Heyw . . . 6F 19
Barker St. Oldh . . . 4E 41
Barke St. L'boro . . . 2E 15
Barkwell La. Moss . . . 4F 51
Barkworth Wlk. M40 . . . 1A 54
Barlea Av. M40 . . . 4F 47
Barleyfield Wlk. Midd . . . 2B 38
Barley Hall St. Heyw . . . 4A 20
Barlow Ho. Oldh . . . 6F 41
Barlow Moor Clo. Roch . . . 3A 12
Barlow St. Heyw . . . 1A 28
Barlow St. Oldh . . . 5G 41
Barlow St. Roch . . . 6A 14
Barmeadow. Dob . . . 1B 44
Barmouth Wlk. Oldh . . . 3B 48
Barnes Green . . . 4A 46
Barnes Meadows. L'boro . . . 2A 8
Barnett Ct. Heyw . . . 6G 19
Barnfield. L'boro . . . 5B 8
Barn Fld. La. Ward . . . 4A 6
Barnfield Ri. Shaw . . . 6G 23
Barnfield St. Heyw . . . 5A 20
Barnfield St. Roch . . . 3H 13
Barn Fold. Lees . . . 6C 42
Barngate Dri. Moss . . . 5G 51
Barnside. Whitw . . . 3E 5
Barnside Way. Fail . . . 1G 55
Barn St. Oldh . . . 5E 41
Barnswell St. M40 . . . 2A 54
Barnway Wlk. M40 . . . 3E 47
Barons Ct. Fail . . . 1B 54
Baron St. Oldh . . . 6H 41
Baron St. Roch . . . 6H 13
Barratt Gdns. Midd . . . 5H 27
Barrett St. Oldh . . . 6H 41
Barrington Av. Droy . . . 6D 54
Barrington St. M11 . . . 5A 54
Barrowfields. Midd . . . 1C 38
Barrowfield Wlk. Midd . . . 2C 38
Barry St. Oldh . . . 3H 41
Bar Ter. Whitw . . . 4E 5
Bartlam Pl. Oldh . . . 4F 41
Bartlemore St. Oldh . . . 2G 41
Bartlett Rd. Shaw . . . 3G 31
Barton Rd. Midd . . . 3B 38
Barton St. Oldh . . . 3D 40
Basil Ct. Roch . . . 1B 22
Basil St. Roch . . . 1B 22
Baslow Rd. Droy . . . 4C 54
Bassett Clo. Roch . . . 2G 13
Bassett Gdns. Roch . . . 2G 13
Bassett Way. Roch . . . 3G 13
Bates Clo. Roch . . . 6F 21
Bateson Dri. S'head . . . 5D 42
Bateson Way. Oldh . . . 6F 41
Bath St. Chad . . . 4B 40
Bath St. Oldh . . . 6C 40
Bath St. Roch . . . 4A 14
Batley St. M9 . . . 5A 46
Batley St. Moss . . . 4F 51
Battersby St. Bury . . . 4B 18
Battersby St. Roch . . . 1D 20
Baum, The. Roch . . . 5H 13
Baxter St. Oldh . . . 3B 48
Bayfield Gro. M40 . . . 4C 46
Baysdale Dri. Rytn . . . 4C 30
Bay St. Heyw . . . 4F 19
Bay St. Oldh . . . 4D 40
Bay St. Roch . . . 4A 14
Bayswater Av. M40 . . . 3A 54
Baytree Av. Chad . . . 3G 39
Baytree La. Midd . . . 3F 39
Baytree Wlk. Whitw . . . 2E 5
Beacon Gro. Oldh . . . 1A 50
Beaconsfield Ter. Stal . . . 6B 52
Beadham Dri. M9 . . . 6E 37
Beadle Av. Roch . . . 6D 6
Bealbank Clo. Miln . . . 4G 23
Beal Cres. Roch . . . 4C 14 (in two parts)
Bealcroft Clo. Miln . . . 6E 15
Bealcroft Wlk. Miln . . . 6E 15
Beal La. Shaw . . . 3H 31
Beal Ter. Miln . . . 1F 23
Beal Vw. Shaw . . . 2B 32
Beal Wlk. W'fld . . . 3A 36
Beard St. Droy . . . 6D 54
Beard St. Rytn . . . 6E 31
Beardwood Rd. M9 . . . 6H 37 & 1A 46
Beatrice St. Roch . . . 6F 13
Beaufont Dri. Oldh . . . 6A 42
Beaufort St. Roch . . . 4E 13
Beaumonds Way. Roch . . . 1C 20
Beaumont Clo. L'boro . . . 6F 7
Bebbington St. M11 . . . 6A 54
Becket Meadows. Oldh . . . 5H 41
Becket Mdw. St. Oldh . . . 5H 41
Beckett St. Lees . . . 4C 42
Beck Gro. Shaw . . . 1B 32
Beckley Clo. Rytn . . . 5G 31
Bedfont Wlk. M9 . . . 4A 46 (off Polworth Rd.)
Bedford Av. Shaw . . . 2F 31
Bedford St. Heyw . . . 5A 20
Bedford St. P'wich . . . 6A 36
Beech Av. Chad . . . 1A 40
Beech Av. Droy . . . 6D 54
Beech Av. G'fld . . . 5D 44
Beech Av. Oldh . . . 3B 42
Beech Clo. Whitw . . . 2E 5
Beechdale Clo. M40 . . . 5E 47
Beeches, The. Heyw . . . 5G 19
Beeches, The. Moss . . . 4A 52
Beeches, The. Whitw . . . 2E 5
Beechey Sq. Oldh . . . 4G 41
Beechfield. Grass . . . 5H 43
Beechfield. Roch . . . 1A 20
Beechfield Clo. Roch . . . 1A 20
Beechfield Clo. S'head . . . 5D 42
Beechfield Rd. Miln . . . 2E 23
Beech Hill Rd. Grass . . . 5H 43
Beech Ho. Shaw . . . 4H 31
Beech La. Grass . . . 6H 43
Beech St. Chad . . . 2B 48
Beech St. Fail . . . 5G 47
Beech St. Midd . . . 3B 38
Beech St. Miln . . . 3G 23
Beech St. Oldh . . . 4G 41
Beech St. Roch . . . 1F 21 (in two parts)
Beech Wlk. Midd . . . 5B 38
Beechwood. Shaw . . . 1B 32
Beechwood Av. L'boro . . . 2G 15
Beechwood Dri. Moss . . . 3G 51
Beechwood Dri. Rytn . . . 3C 30
Beechwood Gro. M9 . . . 6A 46
Beechwood Rd. Oldh . . . 3F 49
Beehive St. Oldh . . . 2F 49
Beeston Gro. W'fld . . . 5A 36
Beeston St. M9 . . . 5A 46

Beever St. *Oldh* 4G **41**
Beightons Wlk. *Roch* 1F **13**
Belding Av. *M40* 4H **47**
Belfairs Clo. *Ash L* 6H **49**
Belfield **5C 14**
Belfield Clo. *Roch* 5C **14**
Belfield La. *Roch* 6C **14**
(Milnrow Rd.)
Belfield La. *Roch* 6D **14**
(Rochdale Rd.)
Belfield Lawn. *Roch* 5D **14**
Belfield Mill La. *Roch* 5C **14**
Belfield Old Rd. *Roch* 5C **14**
Belfield Rd. *Roch* 5B **14**
Belgian Ter. *Rytn* 5F **31**
Belgium St. *Roch* 6A **12**
Belgrave Av. *Fail* 5B **48**
Belgrave Av. *Oldh* 1G **49**
Belgrave Ct. *Oldh* 6F **41**
Belgrave Rd. *M40* 4G **47**
Belgrave Rd. *Oldh* 1F **49**
Belgrave St. *Heyw* 6G **19**
(in two parts)
Belgrave St. *Roch* 4F **13**
Belgravia M. *Shaw* 2A **32**
Bell Clough Rd. *Droy* 4F **55**
Belle Isle Av. *Roch* 5E **5**
Bellfield Av. *Oldh* 3F **49**
Bellingham Clo. *Shaw* 1H **31**
Bell La. *Bury* 4A **18**
Bell La. *Miln* 6H **15**
Bell Mdw. Dri. *Roch* 2B **20**
Bellott Wlk. *Oldh* 3E **41**
Bellscroft Av. *M40* 6D **46**
Bellshill Cres. *Roch* 4C **14**
(in two parts)
Bell St. *Droy* 5F **55**
Bell St. *Oldh* 4G **41**
Bell St. *Roch* 5H **13**
Belmont Av. *S'head* 4D **42**
Belmont St. *Lees* 6C **42**
Belmont St. *Oldh* 3E **41**
Belmont Way. *Chad* 3C **40**
Belmont Way. *Roch* 3G **13**
*Belsyde Wlk. M9 6A **46***
(off Craigend Dri.)
Belthorne Av. *M9* 3C **46**
Belton Av. *Roch* 4C **14**
Belton Wlk. *Oldh* 5D **40**
Belvedere Ri. *Oldh* 6B **32**
Belvoir Meadows. *Roch* 1E **15**
Belvoir St. *Roch* 4F **13**
Ben Brierley Way. *Oldh* 4F **41**
Bench Carr. *Roch* 4G **13**
Benfield Av. *M40* 3E **47**
Benfield St. *Heyw* 5H **19**
Benfield Wlk. *Midd* 6H **27**
Benin Wlk. *M40* 2A **54**
Benmore Clo. *Heyw* 5E **19**
Benmore Rd. *M9* 1B **46**
Bennett St. *Roch* 2A **22**
Benny La. *Droy* 4G **55**
Bentfield Cres. *Miln* 3G **23**
Bentfield Ind. Units. *Chad* 5B **40**
Bentgate **4G 23**
Bentgate Clo. *Miln* 3G **23**
Bentgate St. *Miln* 4G **23**
Bentinck St. *Oldh* 1F **49**
Bentinck St. *Roch* 4E **13**
Bentley Av. *Midd* 4F **29**
Bentley M. *Roch* 3G **13**
Bentley St. *Chad* 4B **40**
Bentley St. *Oldh* 3H **41**
Bentley St. *Roch* 3F **13**
Bentmeadows. *Roch* 4G **13**
Benton St. *M9* 6B **46**
Bents Farm Clo. *L'boro* 6F **7**
Bentworth Wlk. *M9* 6A **46**
Benyon St. *Lees* 5C **42**
Beresford Cres. *Oldh* 3B **42**
Beresford St. *Fail* 6G **47**
Beresford St. *Miln* 3H **23**
Beresford St. *Oldh* 3B **42**
Berger St. *M40* 2B **54**
Berkeley Av. *Chad* 2H **47**
Berkeley Dri. *Roch* 3B **22**
Berkeley Dri. *Rytn* 1D **40**
Berkeley St. *Rytn* 4D **30**
Berkley Wlk. *L'boro* 6F **7**
Berkshire Clo. *Chad* 6B **40**
Berkshire Pl. *Oldh* 6C **40**
Bernard St. *M9* 5A **46**
Bernard St. *Roch* 2G **13**
Berne Clo. *Chad* 5C **40**
Bernice Av. *Chad* 5B **40**
Berry Brow. *M40* 3B **54**
(in two parts)
Berry St. *G'fld* 6D **44**
Bertha Rd. *Roch* 6C **14**
Bertha St. *Shaw* 4H **31**
Bertie St. *Roch* 3F **21**
Berwick Clo. *Heyw* 6E **19**
Berwick St. *Roch* 1B **22**
Berwyn Av. *M9* 6F **37**
Berwyn Av. *Midd* 3E **39**
Berwyn Clo. *Oldh* 2E **49**
Besom Hill **4D 32**
Bessemer Way. *Oldh* 4E **41**
Beswick Dri. *Fail* 1E **55**
Beswicke Royds St. *Roch* 4B **14**
Beswicke St. *L'boro* 6A **8**
Beswicke St. *Roch* 5G **13**
Beswick St. *Droy* 6F **55**
Beswick St. *Rytn* 1E **41**
Bethany La. *Miln* 3A **24**
Bethel Av. *Fail* 6G **47**
*Bethel Grn. L'boro 2A **8***
(off Calderbrook Rd.)
Bethel St. *Heyw* 5G **19**
Bethesda St. *Oldh* 1F **49**
Betjeman Pl. *Shaw* 1B **32**
Betley St. *Heyw* 6G **19**
Betony Clo. *Roch* 2F **13**
Betty Nuppy's La. *Roch* 2C **22**
Betula M. *Roch* 4H **11**
Beverley Clo. *Ash L* 6H **49**
*Beverley Flats. Heyw 5G **19***
(off Wilton St.)
Beverley Pl. *Roch* 5A **14**
Beverley St. *M9* 4A **46**
Beverley Wlk. *Oldh* 6E **41**
Beverston. *Roch* 1G **21**
Bewley St. *Oldh* 3D **48**
Bewley Wlk. *M40* 6C **46**
Bexhill Wlk. *Chad* 5B **40**
Bexley St. *Oldh* 6C **40**
Bickerstaffe Clo. *Shaw* 3G **31**
Bickerton Ct. *Chad* 2C **48**
Bideford Rd. *Roch* 4D **20**
Bidston Clo. *Shaw* 3B **32**
Biggin Gdns. *Heyw* 2A **28**
*Bigginwood Wlk. M40 6C **46***
(off Halliford Rd.)
Bilberry St. *Roch* 1A **22**
(in two parts)
Bill Williams Clo. *M11* 6A **54**
Billy Whelan Wlk. *M40* 2A **54**
Bilsland Wlk. *M40* 2A **54**
Bilson Sq. *Miln* 2G **23**
*Bindon Wlk. M9 6A **46***
(off Carisbrook St.)
Bingley Rd. *Roch* 6C **14**
Bingley Sq. *Roch* 6C **14**
Bingley Ter. *Roch* 6C **14**
Binns Nook Rd. *Roch* 3A **14**
*Binn's Ter. L'boro 5H **7***
(off Lodge St.)
Birch **5G 27**
Birch Av. *Chad* 1A **40**
Birch Av. *Fail* 1D **54**
Birch Av. *Midd* 4C **38**
Birch Av. *Oldh* 3D **48**
Birch Av. *Roch* 1D **14**
Birch Clo. *Whitw* 5E **5**
*Birch Ct. Heyw 6A **20***
(off Twin St.)
Birch Cres. *Miln* 4G **23**
Birch Dri. *Lees* 6D **42**
Birchenall St. *M40* 5B **46**
Birchenlea St. *Chad* 2A **48**
Birches End. *Whitw* 6E **5**
Birches, The. *Moss* 4F **51**
Birchfield Av. *Bury* 6C **18**
Birchfield Dri. *Roch* 2E **21**
Birch Hall Clo. *Oldh* 1C **50**
Birch Hey Clo. *Roch* 1C **14**
Birch Hill Cres. *Roch* 1D **14**
BIRCH HILL HOSPITAL **6D 6**
Birch Hill La. *Ward* 5D **6**
Birch Hill Wlk. *L'boro* 6F **7**
Birch Ind. Est. *Heyw* 4E **27**
Birchinlee Av. *Rytn* 6B **30**
Birchinley Manor Equestrian Cen. 5F **15**
Birch Mt. *Roch* 1D **14**
Birch Rd. *Midd* 1E **39**
Birch Rd. *Upperm* 4E **45**
Birch Rd. *Ward & Roch* 5C **6**
Birch St. *Droy* 6F **55**
Birch St. *Heyw* 6H **19**
Birch St. *Ward* 5C **6**
Birch Vs. *Whitw* 6E **5**
Birchwood. *Chad* 4G **39**
Birchwood. *Droy* 4F **55**
Birchwood Rd. *Midd* 3E **39**
Birkby Dri. *Midd* 1A **38**
Birkdale Av. *Rytn* 1E **41**
Birkdale Clo. *Heyw* 1H **27**
Birkdale Rd. *Roch* 3C **22**
Birks **3D 42**
Birks Av. *Lees* 3D **42**
Birley St. *Roch* 4A **14**
Birnam Gro. *Heyw* 6E **19**
Birshaw Clo. *Shaw* 4H **31**
Birtle **1D 18**
Birtle Green **1C 18**
Birtle Moor. *Bury* 2C **18**
Birtle Rd. *Bury* 6C **10**
Bishopdale Clo. *Rytn* 4D **30**
Bishop Marshall Way. *Midd* 5H **27**
Bishops Ga. St. *Chad* 5A **40**
Bishopsgate Wlk. *Roch* 3C **22**
Bishops Mdw. *Midd* 6H **27**
Bishop St. *Midd* 4F **39**
Bishop St. *Roch* 4B **14**
Bisley St. *Oldh* 5D **40**
Bismark St. *Oldh* 6G **41**
Bittern Clo. *Roch* 6B **12**
Bittern Dri. *Droy* 4G **55**
Blackchapel Dri. *Roch* 4B **22**
Black Dad La. *Roch* 5E **11**
Blackdown Gro. *Oldh* 2E **49**
Black Leach. *S'head* 4E **43**
Blackley **4A 46**
Blackley Pk. Rd. *M9* 4A **46**
Blackley St. *Midd* 4F **37**
Blackpits Rd. *Roch* 4H **11**
Blackpool St. *M11* 5B **54**
(Powell St.)
Blackpool St. *M11* 5A **54**
(Walsden St.)
Black Sail Wlk. *Oldh* 2G **41**
Blackshaw La. *Rytn* 5F **31**
Blacksmith La. *Roch* 3D **20**
Blackstone Av. *Roch* 5C **14**
Blackstone Edge Ct. *L'boro* 5A **8**
Blackstone Edge Old Rd. *L'boro* 5A **8**
Blackstone Wlk. *M9* 6A **46**
Blackthorn Clo. *Roch* 3G **13**
Blackthorn M. *Roch* 3G **13**
Blackthorn Rd. *Oldh* 5D **48**
Blair Clo. *Shaw* 2H **31**
Blairhall Av. *M40* 6C **46**
Blair St. *Roch* 4F **13**
Blakelock St. *Shaw* 2H **31**
Blake St. *Roch* 5A **14**
Blanche St. *Roch* 3A **14**
Blanche Wlk. *Oldh* 3G **41**
Bland Clo. *Fail* 6G **47**
Blandford Dri. *M40* 3F **47**
Bleak Hey Nook **1E 35**
Bleasby St. *Oldh* 4A **42**
Bleasdale St. *Rytn* 4D **30**
Blencarn Wlk. *M9* 6A **46**
Blenheim Av. *Oldh* 6B **32**
Blenheim Clo. *Heyw* 5A **20**
*Blenheim Ct. M9 6E **37***
(off Deanswood Dri.)
Blenheim St. *Roch* 4E **13**
Block La. *Chad* 6B **40**
Blomley St. *Roch* 5E **21**
Bloomfield Dri. *Bury* 6A **26**
Bloom St. *Oldh* 5E **41**
Blossom Pl. *Roch* 5H **13**
Bloxham Wlk. *M9* 2B **46**
Blue Bell Av. *M40* 4C **46**
Bluebell Dri. *Roch* 4D **20**
Blueberry Dri. *Shaw* 2B **32**
Bluefields. *Shaw* 1B **32**
Bluestone Rd. *M40* 5C **46**
Blunn St. *Oldh* 1F **49**
Blyth Av. *L'boro* 2F **15**
Boardale Dri. *Midd* 2A **38**
Boardman Fold Clo. *Midd* 6C **38**
Boardman Fold Rd. *Midd* 6B **38**
Boardman La. *Midd* 3F **37**
Boar Grn. Clo. *M40* 6E **47**
Boarshaw Clough. *Midd* 1D **38**
Boarshaw Clough Way. *Midd* 1D **38**
Boarshaw Crematorium. *Midd* 1E **39**
Boarshaw Cres. *Midd* 1E **39**
Boarshaw Ind. Est. *Midd* 1D **38**
Boarshaw La. *Midd* 6F **29**
Boarshaw Rd. *Midd* 2C **38**
Boarshurst **6E 45**
Boarshurst Bus. Pk. *G'fld* 6D **44**
Boarshurst La. *G'fld* 6D **44**
Boat La. *Dig* 4F **35**
Bobbin Wlk. *Oldh* 5G **41**
Bob Massey Clo. *Open* 6A **54**
Bodley St. *M11* 5A **54**
Bodmin Clo. *Rytn* 6G **31**
Bolderrod Pl. *Oldh* 3G **41**
Boleyn Ct. *Heyw* 6G **19**
Bollin Wlk. *W'fld* 1A **36**
Bollin Way. *W'fld* 1A **36**
Boltmeadow. *G'fld* 1C **52**
Bolton Rd. *Roch* 3C **20**
Bolton St. *Oldh* 5H **41**
(in two parts)
Boltons Yd. *Upperm* 3D **44**
Bond St. *Roch* 3A **14**
Bonny Brow St. *Midd* 4F **37**
Bonscale Cres. *Midd* 6A **28**
Bookham Wlk. *M9* 5A **46**
Booth Bri. Clo. *Midd* 4G **37**
BOOTH HALL CHILDREN'S HOSPITAL 2B **46**
Booth Hall Rd. *M9* 2C **46**
Booth Hill La. *Oldh & Rytn* 2E **41**
Booth Ho. Trad. Est. *Oldh* 5C **40**
Boothroyden Clo. *Midd* 4F **37**
(in two parts)
Boothroyden Rd. *M9* 5G **37**
Boothroyden Rd. *Midd* 4G **37**
(in two parts)
Boothroyden Ter. *M9* 5G **37**
Booth St. *Fail* 6G **47**
Booth St. *Lees* 5C **42**
Booth St. *Midd* 5F **39**
Booth St. *Oldh* 5E **41**
Bordale Av. *M9* 6B **46**
Borland Av. *M40* 4F **47**
Borrowdale Clo. *Rytn* 3D **30**
Borrowdale Dri. *Roch* 3D **20**
Borrowdale Rd. *Midd* 1H **37**
Bossall Av. *M9* 1A **46**
Boston Clo. *Fail* 4H **47**
Boston St. *Oldh* 1F **49**
Boswell Av. *Aud* 6H **55**
Boswell Way. *Midd* 5G **29**
Bosworth Clo. *W'fld* 3A **36**
Bosworth Sq. *Roch* 3F **21**
Bosworth St. *Roch* 3F **21**
Botany Clo. *Heyw* 4F **19**
Botesworth Grn. *Miln* 2G **23**
Bottomfield Clo. *Oldh* 2G **41**
Bottom of Woodhouses **2E 55**
Bottom o' th' Brow **4F 19**
Bottom o' th' Moor. *Oldh* 4H **41**
Bottoms **5H 51**
Bottoms Fold. *Moss* 5H **51**
Boundary Cotts. *Carr* 6A **52**
Boundary Gdns. *Oldh* 2E **41**
Boundary Pk. Rd. *Oldh* 2C **40**
Boundary St. *Roch* 1G **21**
Boundary Wlk. *Roch* 2G **21**
Bourne Dri. *M40* 4D **46**
Bourne Rd. *Shaw* 1G **31**
Bourne St. *Chad* 3B **48**
Bowden Clo. *Roch* 1F **29**
Bower Av. *Roch* 1D **14**
Bower La. *Chad* 3A **48**
Bower St. *Bury* 4A **18**
Bower St. *Oldh* 4H **41**
Bower Ter. *Droy* 4G **55**
Bowfield Wlk. *M40* 2A **54**
Bowker Clo. *Roch* 4A **12**
Bowland Clo. *Ash L* 6A **50**
Bowland Clo. *Shaw* 2E **31**
Bowland Gro. *Miln* 3F **23**
Bow La. *Heyw* 5H **19**
Bowlee **2F 37**
Bowler St. *Shaw* 2H **31**
Bowlers Wlk. *Roch* 3H **13**
Bowling Grn. St. *Heyw* 5H **19**
Bowling Grn. Way. *Roch* 6B **12**
Bowling St. *Chad* 3B **48**
Bowness Av. *Roch* 4E **13**
Bowness Ct. *Midd* 1H **37**
Bowness Rd. *Midd* 2G **37**
*Bowness Wlk. Rytn 5E **31***
(off Shaw St.)
Bow St. *Oldh* 4F **41**
Bow St. *Roch* 4F **21**
Box St. *L'boro* 6G **7**
Bracken Clo. *Droy* 5G **55**
Bracken Clo. *Heyw* 1H **27**
Bracken Clo. *S'head* 5D **42**

Brackenhall Ct. Heyw 5E 19
(off Todd St.)
Brackenhurst Av. Moss 4A 52
Brackenlea Fold. Roch 3D 12
Bracken Lodge. Rytn 2E 41
Brackenwood Clo. Rytn 1C 40
Brackley Dri. Midd 6C 38
Brackley Sq. Oldh 3G 41
Brackley St. Oldh 3G 41
Bradbury's La. G'fld 1E 53
Bradbury Wlk. Rytn 5E 31
(off Shaw St.)
Braddocks Clo. Roch 1D 14
Braddon St. M11 6A 54
Bradford Ct. M40 4E 47
Bradford St. Oldh 3E 41
Bradley Dri. Bury 1A 36
Bradley Ho. Oldh 6F 41
Bradley La. Miln 3H 23
Bradley Smithy Clo. Roch 3G 13
Bradley St. Miln 3H 23
Bradshaw Av. Fail 2C 54
Bradshaw Fold Av. M40 2F 47
Bradshaw St. Heyw 5A 20
(in two parts)
Bradshaw St. Midd 4E 39
Bradshaw St. Oldh 4F 41
Bradshaw St. Roch 5A 14
Bradshaw Trad. Est. Midd 5E 39
Braemar Ct. M9 6E 37
Braemar Dri. Bury 5B 18
Braemar Gro. Heyw 6E 19
Braemore Clo. Shaw 1E 31
Brae Side. Oldh 3E 49
Braewood Clo. Bury 4A 18
Braithwaite Rd. Midd 5H 27
Brakehouse Clo. Miln 1E 23
Bramber Way. Chad 5B 40
Bramble Av. Oldh 2B 42
Bramble Clo. L'boro 6F 7
Bramblewood. Chad 3G 39
Brambling Clo. Aud 5G 55
Bramhall Clo. Miln 1E 23
Bramley Rd. Roch 5A 12
Branch Rd. L'boro 3E 15
Brandlehow Dri. Midd 1G 37
Brandon Brow. Oldh 3E 41
Brandon Cres. Shaw 1G 31
Brandon St. Miln 1E 23
(off Nall St.)
Brandram Rd. P'wich 6A 36
Brandwood. Chad 2G 39
Branksome Dri. M9 6F 37
Bransby Av. M9 1A 46
Bransdale Av. Rytn 5C 30
Branston Rd. M40 3F 47
Brantwood Clo. Rytn 4C 30
Brantwood Ter. M9 6B 46
Brassey St. Midd 2C 38
Brattray Dri. Midd 6A 28
Braxton Wlk. M9 5A 46
Brayshaw Clo. Heyw 6G 19
Brechin Wlk. Open 6A 54
Brechin Way. Heyw 6E 19
Brecon Clo. Rytn 3C 30
Brecon Cres. Ash L 6H 49
Brecon Wlk. Oldh 3B 48
Bredbury St. Chad 5B 40
Bredon Way. Oldh 2E 49
Breeze Hill. Shaw 4H 31
Breeze Hill Rd. Oldh 6B 42
Brellafield Dri. Shaw 6F 23
Brenbar Cres. Whitw 2F 5
Brendon Av. M40 6C 46
Brendon Dri. Aud 6H 55
Brendon Hills. Rytn 6D 30
Brenley Wlk. M9 5A 46
(off Maybrook Wlk.)
Brennan Ct. Oldh 3C 48
Brentford St. M9 6A 46
Brentnor Rd. M40 3E 47
Brentwood Clo. L'boro 2F 15
Brewerton Rd. Oldh 6A 42
Brewster St. M9 5A 46
Brewster St. Midd 1C 38
Brian Av. Droy 4G 55
Brian St. Roch 5D 20
Briar Av. Oldh 2B 42
Briar Clo. Roch 4C 12
Briarfield Rd. Dob 1C 44
Briar Gro. Chad 2B 40
Briarmere Wlk. Chad 4C 40
Briar St. Roch 1F 21
Briarwood Av. Droy 4C 54
Brickfield St. Roch 3B 14
Brick Ground. Roch 3G 11
Brideoak St. Oldh 3C 42
Bri. Bank Rd. L'boro 2F 15
Bridge End. Del 5B 34
Bridgefield Cres. S'head 5D 42
Bridgefield Dri. Bury 5A 18
Bridgefield St. Roch 6F 13
Bridgefold Rd. Roch 6E 13
Bri. Hall Dri. Bury 4A 18
(in two parts)
Bri. Hall Fold. Bury 5A 18
Bri. Hall Ind. Est. Heap B 5A 18
Bri. Hall La. Bury 5A 18
Bridgenorth Dri. L'boro 2F 15
Bridge St. Heyw 5G 19
Bridge St. Midd 3C 38
Bridge St. Miln 1F 23
Bridge St. Oldh 5G 41
Bridge St. Roch (OL11) 6E 21
Bridge St. Roch (OL12) 2C 14
Bridge St. Shaw 1A 32
Bridge St. S'head 5D 42
Bridge St. Upperm 4D 44
Bridge St. Whitw 2E 5
Bridge Ter. Bury 5A 18
Bridgewater St. Oldh 3G 41
Bridgewood Lodge. Heyw 5F 19
Bridle Clo. Droy 4G 55
Bridle Rd. P'wich 4B 36
Bridlington Clo. M40 1A 54
Bridlington Sq. Roch 1H 21
Bridport Av. M40 5F 47
Bridson St. Oldh 4A 42
Brierfields. Fail 6A 48
(off Brierley Av.)
Brierley Av. Fail 6H 47
Brierley Dri. Midd 4C 38
Brierleys Pl. L'boro 5G 7
Brierley St. Chad 3C 40
Brierley St. Heyw 5H 19
Brierley St. Oldh 2F 49
Brierley Wlk. Chad 3C 40
Brierwood Clo. Oldh 2E 41
Brigham St. M11 6A 54
Brighton Rd. Scout 3E 43
Bright St. Chad 1A 48
Bright St. Droy 6F 55
Bright St. Oldh 6D 40
Bright St. Roch 2A 22
Brimfield Wlk. M40 1A 54
Brimmy Cft. La. Dens 4G 25
Brimrod La. Roch 2F 21
Brindle Way. Shaw 2B 32
Brindley Av. M9 6F 37
Brinston Wlk. M40 6C 46
Briony Clo. Rytn 1E 41
Briscoe La. M40 2A 54
Briscoe St. Oldh 3F 41
Briscoe Wlk. Midd 1G 37
Bristol Av. Ash L 6H 49
Bristowe St. M11 4B 54
Britannia Av. Shaw 3A 32
Britannia Ind. Est. Heyw 5F 19
Britannia St. Heyw 5F 19
Britannia St. Oldh 4G 41
Briton St. Roch 5A 14
Briton St. Rytn 1E 41
Britton St. Oldh 4C 40
Brixworth Wlk. M9 2A 46
(off Greendale Dri.)
Broad Acre. Roch 3A 12
Broadbent. 1H 41
Broadbent Clo. Rytn 4G 31
Broadbent Dri. Bury 3C 18
Broadbent Rd. Oldh 1A 42
Broad Carr. 3E 51
Broadcarr La. Moss 3E 51
Broadfield. 6E 19
Broadfield Dri. L'boro 2F 15
Broadfield Stile. Roch 1G 21
Broadfield St. Heyw 6F 19
Broadfield St. Roch 1H 21
Broadford Ct. Heyw 6D 18
Broadgate. Chad 2G 47
Broadgate. Dob 2A 44
Broadgate. Midd & Chad 5F 39
Broadgate Wlk. M9 5A 46
(off Roundham Wlk.)
Broadhalgh. 6C 12
Broadhalgh Av. Roch 6C 12
Broadhalgh Rd. Roch 1C 20
Broadhead Wlk. W'fld 2A 36
Broadhurst Av. Oldh 2B 40
Broad Ing. Roch 4E 13
Broadlands Av. Hey D 1C 26
Broadlands Cres. Hey D 1C 26
Broadlands Wlk. M40 6C 46
Broadlands Way. Hey D 1C 26
Broad La. Del 2A 34
Broad La. Roch 4B 22
Broad La. Whitw 3B 4
Broadlea Gro. Roch 3E 13
Broadley. 5E 5
Broadley Vw. Whitw 6E 5
Broad Link. Midd 5F 39
Broadmoss Dri. M9 2C 46
Broadmount Ter. Oldh 1B 48
(off Devon St.)
Broadoak Cres. Oldh 3G 49
Broad Oak La. Bury 4A 18
Broadoak Rd. Roch 1A 20
Broadoaks. Bury 4B 18
Broadoak Sports Cen. 6B 50
Broad Oak Ter. Bury 4C 18
Broad Shaw La. Miln 5D 22
(in two parts)
Broadstone Av. Oldh 5D 32
Broadstone Clo. Roch 4C 12
Broad St. Midd 4G 37
Broadway. M40 & Chad 4F 47
Broadway. Chad 6A 40
Broadway. Fail 6F 47
Broadway. Rytn 1C 40
Broadway St. Oldh 1F 49
Broadway Swimming Pool. 3G 47
Broadwell Dri. M9 6A 46
Broche Clo. Roch 4D 20
Brockford Dri. M9 6A 38
Brockledale Rd. Roch 6D 14
Brocklehurst St. M9 5C 46
Brockway. Roch 4C 22
Brodick St. M40 5B 46
Bromfield. Roch 5H 13
(off Redcross St.)
Bromley Av. Rytn 3C 30
Bromley St. Chad 2A 48
Bromlow St. M11 6A 54
Brompton Av. Fail 5B 48
Brompton St. Oldh 6G 41
Bromwich Dri. M9 6A 46
Bronte Clo. Oldh 5B 32
Bronte Clo. Roch 4C 12
Bronville Clo. Chad 2C 40
Brook Av. Droy 6D 54
Brook Av. Shaw 1H 31
Brook Av. Upperm 3E 45
Brookbank Clo. Midd 4D 38
Brook Bottom. 3F 51
Brook Clo. W'fld 3A 36
Brookdale. Roch 2G 13
Brookdale Av. M40 2B 54
Brookdale St. Fail 6G 47
Brook Dri. W'fld 3A 36
Brookes St. Midd 1D 38
Brookfield. Shaw 6G 23
Brook Fld. Av. Rytn 6D 30
Brookfield Dri. L'boro 5E 7
Brookfields. Moss 3G 51
Brookfield St. Oldh 6F 41
Brookfold. Fail 5G 47
Brook Gdns. Heyw 5G 19
Brook Hey Clo. Roch 1D 14
Brookhill Clo. Dig 4E 35
Brooklands. Roch 4C 6
Brooklands Av. Chad 6B 40
Brooklands Clo. Moss 3F 51
Brooklands Ct. Roch 1E 21
Brooklands Dri. Droy 4G 55
Brooklands Dri. G'ton 5F 43
Brooklands Pde. G'ton 5F 43
Brooklands St. Midd 2C 38
Brooklands St. Rytn 4D 30
Brooklands, The. Heyw 5G 19
Brookland St. Roch 4B 22
Brook La. Dob 1B 44
Brook La. Lees 5C 42
Brook La. Oldh 1G 49
(in five parts)
Brook La. Roch 4B 22
Brooklawn Dri. P'wich 5A 36
Brooklet Clo. S'head 6D 42
Brooklyn Av. L'boro 4G 7
Brooklyn Av. Roch 1D 14
Brooklyn St. Oldh 2A 42
Brooks Dri. Fail 1C 54
Brooks End. Roch 4A 12
Brook Side. Lees 5B 42
Brookside. Moss 4F 51
Brookside Av. Droy 4G 55
Brookside Av. G'ton 5F 43
Brookside Bus. Pk. Midd 5F 39
Brookside Cres. Midd 5E 39
Brookside Rd. M40 4C 46
Brookside Ter. Del 5A 34
(off High St.)
Brook's Pl. Oldh 1E 49
Brook's Pl. Roch 5G 13
Brook St. Chad 3B 40
Brook St. Fail 1A 54
Brook St. L'boro 6A 8
Brook St. Oldh 4G 41
Brook St. Rytn 6D 30
Brook St. Ward 5C 6
Brook Ter. Miln 3A 24
Brook, The. L'boro 2A 8
Brook Vs. M9 6A 46
Brookville Flats. Whitw 2E 5
(off Rawstron St.)
Brookway. Grass 5A 44
Brookway. Lees 6C 42
Brookway. L'boro 1G 15
Broome Gro. Fail 1D 54
Broome St. Oldh 5D 40
Broomfield Cres. Midd 2H 37
Broomfield Sq. Roch 2H 21
Broomfield Ter. Miln 3H 23
Broomhall Rd. M9 6E 37
Broomhill Ho. Moss 3G 51
(off Manor St.)
Broomhurst Av. Oldh 1D 48
Broom St. Miln 3H 23
Brotherdale Clo. Rytn 4D 30
Brotherod Hall Rd. Roch 3E 13
Broughton Clo. Midd 1H 37
Brow Av. Midd 5D 38
Browbeck. Oldh 4E 41
Browfield Way. Oldh 2E 41
Brown Bank Rd. L'boro 2F 15
Brown Edge Rd. Oldh 1C 50
Brownhill Countryside Cen. 2C 44
Brownhill Dri. Aus 4E 43
Brownhill La. Upperm 2D 44
Browning Av. Droy 6E 55
Browning Rd. Midd 1D 38
Browning Rd. Oldh 2H 41
Brown Lodge Dri. L'boro 2F 15
Brown Lodge St. L'boro 2F 15
Brownlow. 6H 31
Brownlow Av. Rytn 6G 31
Brownson Wlk. M9 5A 46
Brown St. Chad 3A 40
Brown St. Fail 6G 47
Brown St. Heyw 4H 19
Brown St. L'boro 6H 7
Brown St. Midd 1C 38
Brown St. Oldh 4G 41
Browside Clo. Roch 2C 14
Brow St. Roch 3A 22
Bruce St. Roch 3E 21
Bruno St. M9 6F 37
Brunswick St. Heyw 5G 19
(in two parts)
Brunswick St. Moss 5H 51
Brunswick St. Oldh 5E 41
Brunswick St. Roch 5A 14
Brunswick St. Shaw 2H 31
Bryan St. Oldh 2A 42
Brynford Av. M9 6E 37
Buckfast Rd. Midd 6B 28
Buckhurst Rd. M19 2A 10
(in two parts)
Buckingham Rd. Droy 6C 54
Buckinghamshire Pk. Clo. Shaw 1H 31
Buckingham St. Roch 5A 14
Buckley. 2B 14
Buckley Barn Ct. Roch 6E 21
(off Heape St.)
Buckley Brook St. Roch 3B 14
Buckley Bldgs. Moss 4A 52
Buckley Chase. Miln 2E 23
Buckley Dri. Dens 6G 25
Buckley Farm La. Roch 2B 14
Buckley Fields. Roch 3A 14
Buckley Hall Ind. Est. Roch 2B 14
Buckley Hill La. Miln 2E 23
Buckley La. Roch 2B 14
Buckley Rd. Oldh 3B 42
Buckley Rd. Roch 3B 14
Buckley St. Chad 4A 40
Buckley St. Droy 6E 55
Buckley St. Heyw 4H 19
Buckley St. Lees 6C 42
Buckley St. Roch 5A 14
Buckley St. Shaw 2A 32

Buckley St.—Centre Va. Clo.

Buckley St. Upperm 3D 44
Buckley Ter. Roch 2B 14
Buckley Vw. Roch 2B 14
Buckley Wood 6A 30
Bucklow Clo. Oldh 5C 32
Buckstones Rd. Shaw & Oldh 6A 24
Buckton Clo. Dig 4E 35
Buckton Va. M. Carr 6B 52
Buckton Va. Rd. Carr 6B 52
Budworth Gdns. Droy 6F 55
Buersil 5B 22
Buersil Av. Roch 3B 22
Buersil Gro. Roch 4B 22
(in two parts)
Buersil Head 6B 22
Buersil St. Roch 4B 22
Buerton Av. M9 6E 37
Buile Dri. M9 1B 46
Bullcote Grn. Rytn 5G 31
Bullcote La. Oldh 5G 31
Buller St. Droy 6F 55
Buller St. Oldh 3B 42
Bullfinch Dri. Bury 2A 18
Bulwer St. Roch 5A 14
Bunyan Clo. Oldh 5C 32
Bunyan St. Roch 4H 13
Burchall Fld. Roch 6B 14
Burder St. Oldh 3C 48
Burdett Av. Roch 4B 12
Burgess Dri. Fail 6H 47
Burghley Av. Oldh 5B 42
Burlington Av. Oldh 1E 49
Burlington St. Roch 3A 22
Burnaby St. Oldh 6C 40
Burnaby St. Roch 3E 21
Burn Bank. G'fld 6A 44
Burnedge 6D 22
Burnedge Clo. Whitw 1F 5
Burnedge Fold Rd. Grass 5H 43
Burnedge La. Grass & Dob 5G 43
Burnedge M. Oldh 5H 43
Burnell Ct. Heyw 2H 27
Burnet Clo. Roch 3C 22
Burnley Brow 3D 40
Burnley La. Chad 1A 40
(in two parts)
Burnley St. Chad 4B 40
Burnley St. Fail 5A 48
Burnsall Gro. Rytn 5D 30
Burns Clo. Oldh 4C 32
Burns Gro. Droy 5E 55
Burnside. Shaw 1B 32
Burnside Clo. Heyw 6H 19
Burnside Cres. Midd 6A 28
Burnside Rd. Roch 1C 22
Burns St. Heyw 6H 19
Burnthorpe Clo. Roch 1A 20
Burntwood Wlk. M9 5A 46
(off Naunton Wlk.)
Burton St. Lees 6C 42
Burton St. Midd 3B 38
(in two parts)
Burtonwood Ct. Midd 2B 38
Burwell Clo. Roch 2F 13
Bury & Rochdale Old Rd.
Bury & Heyw 3D 18
Bury New Rd. Bury & Heyw 5A 18
Bury Old Rd. Bury & Heyw 6B 18
Bury Old Rd. W'fld & P'wich 5A 36
Bury Pl. M11 5A 54
Bury Rd. Roch 2A 20
Bury St. Heyw 5F 19
Bury St. Moss 5G 51
Bushgrove Wlk. M9 6H 37
(off Claygate Dri.)
Bushnell Wlk. M9 6H 37
(off Eastlands Rd.)
Busk 3C 40
Busk Rd. Chad 3C 40
(in two parts)
Busk Wlk. Chad 3C 40
Butcher La. Rytn 4C 30
Bute Av. Oldh 2F 49
Bute St. M40 5B 46
Butler Green 1A 48
Butler Grn. Chad 1A 48
Buttercup Dri. Oldh 1B 42
Buttercup Dri. Roch 4D 20
Butterhouse La. Dob 1E 45
Buttermere Av. Heyw 1H 27
Buttermere Dri. Midd 1A 38
Buttermere Gro. Rytn 2D 30
Buttermere Rd. Oldh 3B 42
Butterworth Hall 2G 23
Butterworth Hall. Miln 2G 23
Butterworth La. Chad 2G 47
Butterworth Pl. Shire 5G 7
Butterworth St. Chad 4B 40
Butterworth St. L'boro 6G 7
Butterworth St. Midd 4E 39
Butterworth St. Oldh 4A 42
Butterworth Way. G'fld 6D 44
Butt La. Moss 1F 51
Button Hole. Shaw 2B 32
Butts Av, The. Roch 6H 13
(off Butts, The)
Butts La. Del 5G 33
Butts, The. Roch 6H 13
Buxted Rd. Oldh 2H 41
Buxton Cres. Roch 3B 22
Buxton La. Droy 6C 54
Buxton Pl. Oldh 6E 41
Buxton St. Heyw 6H 19
Bycroft Wlk. M40 3B 54
Byland Av. Oldh 1B 50
Byng St. Heyw 1A 28
Byrom Ct. Droy 6D 54
Byron Av. Droy 5E 55
Byron Rd. Midd 1D 38
Byron St. Oldh 3B 48
Byron St. Rytn 5E 31
Byron Wlk. Rytn 5E 31
(off Shaw St.)
Byrth Rd. Oldh 5F 49

C

Cabin La. Oldh 6D 32
Cadleigh Wlk. M40 6C 46
Caen Av. M40 2E 47
Caesar St. Roch 5A 22
Cairn Dri. Roch 1A 20
Cairnwell Rd. Chad 3H 39
Caistor Wlk. Oldh 4F 41
Caithness Rd. Roch 2A 20
Cajetan Ho. Midd 6B 38
Caldbeck Dri. Midd 2A 38
Caldecott Rd. M9 6E 37
Calder Av. L'boro 4G 7
Calderbrook 2A 8
Calderbrook Rd. L'boro 5G 7
Calderbrook Ter. L'boro 3A 8
Calderbrook Wlk. M9 6A 46
Calderbrook Way. Oldh 6H 41
Calder Cres. W'fld 1A 36
Calder Flats. Heyw 5G 19
(off Wilton St.)
Calder Gro. Shaw 1G 31
Caldermoor 5G 7
Caldershaw 3D 12
Caldershaw Cen., The. Roch 3D 12
Calder Shaw La. Roch 3C 12
Caldershaw Rd. Roch 4C 12
Calder St. Roch 3B 14
Calder Wlk. Midd 1G 37
Calder Wlk. W'fld 1A 36
Calder Way. W'fld 1A 36
Caledon Av. M40 5C 46
Calf Hey. L'boro 5F 7
Calf Hey. Roch 4C 6
Calf Hey Head. Whitw 3F 5
Calf Hey La. Whitw 3F 5
Calf Hey N. Roch 3A 22
Calf Hey Rd. Shaw 1B 32
Calf Hey S. Roch 3A 22
Calgarth Dri. Midd 6H 27
Callaghan Wlk. Heyw 6G 19
Callander Sq. Heyw 6D 18
Calliards La. L'boro 1E 15
Calliard's Rd. Roch 1E 15
Calverley Way. Roch 1G 13
Calverton Dri. M40 6E 47
Camberley Dri. Roch 1B 20
Camberwell Dri. Ash L 6G 49
Camberwell St. Oldh 1E 49
Camberwell Way. Rytn 5C 30
Cambrian Dri. Miln 1G 23
Cambrian Dri. Rytn 6C 30
Cambria St. Oldh 4B 42
Cambridge Av. Roch 1C 20
Cambridge Rd. M9 4A 46
Cambridge Rd. Droy 4D 54
Cambridge Rd. Fail 2D 54
Cambridge St. Oldh 6B 40
Camden Av. M40 3A 54
Camden St. Moss 2H 51
Cameron Ct. Rytn 3D 30
Campania St. Rytn 1E 41
Campbell St. Roch 3G 13
Campion Way. Roch 2E 13
Canalside Ind. Est. Roch 2B 22
Canal St. Chad 2B 48
Canal St. Droy 6E 55
Canal St. Heyw 1A 28
Canal St. L'boro 6H 7
Canal St. Roch 2A 22
Canberra St. M11 5A 54
Candlestick Pk. Bury 3B 18
Canisp Clo. Chad 2H 39
Cannon St. Oldh 4E 41
Canon Flynn Ct. Roch 6C 14
Canon St. Roch 3B 14
Canon Tighe Ct. Chad 4A 40
Canterbury Clo. Roch 6C 12
Canterbury Cres. Midd 1F 39
Canterfield Clo. Droy 5H 55
Cantrell St. M11 6A 54
Capesthorne Dri. Shaw 2F 31
Capstan St. M9 5A 46
Captain Fold 4A 20
Captain Fold. Heyw 5A 20
Cardale Wlk. M9 6A 46
(off Conran St.)
Carders Ct. Roch 4D 20
Cardiff Clo. Oldh 3B 48
Cardigan Rd. Oldh 3B 48
Cardigan St. Roch 2G 13
Cardigan St. Rytn 5E 31
Cardinal M. Midd 1H 37
Cardinal St. Oldh 4G 41
Cardwell St. Oldh 2F 49
Carfax Fold. Roch 3D 12
Carforth Av. Chad 5A 40
Carill Av. M40 4C 46
Carisbrook St. M9 6A 46
Carlburn St. M11 5B 54
Carlisle Clo. W'fld 4A 36
Carlisle Cres. Ash L 6A 50
Carlisle St. Oldh 1C 48
(in two parts)
Carlisle St. Roch 3H 13
Carlton Av. Oldh 2B 42
Carlton Flats. Heyw 5G 19
(off Brunswick St.)
Carlton Way. Rytn 1D 40
Carmel Ct. M9 4A 46
Carmine Fold. Midd 1B 38
Carnaby St. M9 4B 46
Carnarvon St. Oldh 3B 48
Carnation Rd. Oldh 1C 50
Carnforth Av. Roch 2F 29
Carnforth Sq. Roch 2F 29
Carnoustie Clo. M40 6E 47
Carnwood Clo. M40 3B 54
Carpenters Wlk. Droy 6D 54
Carpenters Way. Roch 3B 22
Carr 4E 35
(Oldham)
Carr 6B 52
(Stalybridge)
Carradale Wlk. M40 6C 46
Carrbrook 6B 52
Carrbrook Dri. Rytn 2E 41
Carrbrook Ind. Est. Carr 6C 52
Carrbrook Rd. Carr 6B 52
(in two parts)
Carr Gro. Miln 1G 23
Carr Head. Dig 3E 35
Carrhill Quarry Clo. Moss 3G 51
Carrhill Rd. Moss 3G 51
Carr Ho. Rd. S'head 4D 42
Carriage Dri. L'boro 4A 8
Carrick Gdns. Midd 5B 28
Carrington Clo. Roch 2D 14
Carrington St. Chad 2B 48
Carr La. Carr 6B 52
Carr La. Dig 4E 35
Carr La. G'fld 5D 44
Carr La. Miln 1A 24
Carrmel Ct. Del 6B 34
Carrock Wlk. Midd 2F 37
Carron Av. M9 4B 46
Carr Ri. Carr 6B 52
Carruthers Clo. Heyw 4B 20
Carr Wood 6G 11
Car St. Oldh 4G 41
Carter St. Moss 5G 51
Carthage St. Oldh 1F 49
Cartmel. Roch 5H 13
(off Redcross St.)
Cartmel Av. Miln 3F 23
Cartmel Clo. Oldh 2D 48
Cartmel Cres. Chad 3H 47
Cartmell Ct. M9 1C 46
Cartmel Wlk. M9 6A 46
(in two parts)
Cartmel Wlk. Midd 1A 38
Cartridge St. Heyw 5G 19
Carver Av. P'wich 6A 36
Carville Rd. M9 2D 46
Cash Ga. Ct. Oldh 2D 48
Cassidy Gdns. Midd 5H 27
Casson Ga. Roch 4G 13
Casson St. Fail 6H 47
Castle Av. Roch 1G 21
Castlebrook Clo. Bury 5A 26
Castle Clo. Droy 5F 55
Castle Ct. Ash L 6H 49
Castleford St. Chad 2C 40
Castle Hill. Roch 1G 21
Castle Hill Cres. Roch 1G 21
Castle Hill Rd. Bury 5A 10
(in two parts)
Castle La. Carr 5A 52
Castlemere Dri. Shaw 1B 32
Castlemere St. Roch 1G 21
Castlemere Ter. Roch 1H 21
Castle Mill St. Oldh 4H 41
Castle Pk. Ind. Est. Oldh 3H 41
Castlerigg Dri. Midd 1G 37
Castlerigg Dri. Rytn 3C 30
Castle Rd. Bury 6A 26
Castle Shaw 1E 35
Castle Shaw Roman Fort 1D 34
(Roman Remains)
Castle St. Midd 4F 39
Castle Ter. Carr 6B 52
Castleton 5E 21
Castleton Rd. Rytn 1C 30
Castleton Rd. S. Roch 4F 21
Castleton St. Oldh 5C 40
Castleton Swimming Pool 5D 20
Castle Wlk. Ash L 6H 49
Castleway. Roch 6D 20
Catchdale Clo. M9 6G 37
Catches Clo. Roch 5D 12
Catches La. Roch 5D 12
Cathedral Rd. Chad 2H 39
Catherine St. Lees 5C 42
Catley Lane Head 1C 12
Caton St. Roch 1H 21
Cattlin Way. Oldh 3C 48
Causeway, The. Chad 6G 39
Causewood Clo. Oldh 5C 32
Causey Dri. Midd 6H 27
Cavannah Ct. Oldh 6C 32
Cavendish Ct. M9 6E 37
(off Deanswood Dri.)
Cavendish Rd. Roch 4G 21
Cavendish St. Oldh 5E 41
Cavendish Way. Rytn 1C 40
Caversham Dri. M9 5A 46
Cawley Ter. M9 6E 37
Caxton St. Heyw 5H 19
Caxton St. Roch 5E 21
Cayley St. Roch 6B 14
Cecil Rd. M9 6H 37 & 1A 46
Cecil St. L'boro 6F 7
Cecil St. Moss 5G 51
Cecil St. Oldh 6E 41
Cecil St. Roch 2H 21
Cecil St. Rytn 6C 30
Cedar Av. Heyw 4G 19
Cedar Bank Clo. Fir 1D 22
Cedar Cres. Chad 3B 40
Cedar Dri. Droy 5G 55
Cedar Gro. Rytn 3D 30
Cedar Gro. Shaw 3H 31
Cedar La. Grass 5H 43
Cedar La. Miln 4G 23
Cedar Rd. Fail 1D 54
Cedar Rd. Midd 3E 39
Cedar St. Oldh 4A 42
(in two parts)
Cedar St. Roch 4H 13
Cedric Rd. Oldh 4A 42
Celandine Clo. L'boro 5F 7
Cemetery Rd. Droy 6D 54
Cemetery Rd. Fail 1D 54
Cemetery Rd. Moss 6H 51
Cemetery Rd. Rytn 4C 30
Cemetery St. Midd 2C 38
Cennick Clo. Oldh 5B 42
Ceno St. Oldh 2G 41
Central Av. G'fld 6D 44
Central Av. L'boro 5H 7
Central Ho. M9 6A 38
Centre Va. L'boro 4A 8
Centre Va. Clo. L'boro 4A 8

A-Z Oldham & Rochdale 61

Century Gdns. Roch. 5H 13
Ceylon St. Oldh 6B 42
Chadderton. 4H 39
Chadderton Fold. 1H 39
Chadderton Fold. Chad. 1H 39
(in two parts)
Chadderton Hall Rd. Chad 2H 39
Chadderton Heights. Chad 6H 29
Chadderton Ind. Est. Midd 6E 39
Chadderton Park. 2G 39
Chadderton Pk. Rd. Chad 3H 39
Chadderton Precinct. Chad 3B 40
Chadderton Sports Cen. 4B 40
Chadderton Way.
Oldh & Chad 1B 40
Chadwick Clo. Miln 2G 23
Chadwick Fold. Heyw 5B 20
(off Chadwick La.)
Chadwick Hall Rd. Roch 1D 20
Chadwick La. Heyw & Roch 5B 20
(in three parts)
Chadwick La. Roch. 5C 22
Chadwick St. Bury 3C 18
Chadwick St. Roch (OL11) 6F 13
Chadwick St. Roch (OL16) 6D 14
Chadwick Ter. Roch 1F 13
Chaffinch Clo. Droy 4G 55
Chaffinch Clo. Oldh 1B 50
Chaffinch Dri. Bury 3A 18
Chain Bar. 2E 47
Chain Rd. M9 6H 37
Chain Wlk. M9 6A 38
Chale Dri. Midd 5E 39
Chalfont Clo. Oldh 1H 49
Challum Dri. Chad 3A 40
Chamber Hall Clo. Oldh 1D 48
Chamber Ho. Dri. Roch 3D 20
Chamberhouse Urban Farm.
3C 20
Chamber Rd. Oldh 2C 48
Chamber Rd. Shaw 2G 31
Champness Hall. Roch 6H 13
Champneys Wlk. M9 6A 46
Chancel Pl. Roch 6H 13
Chancery La. Dob. 1C 44
Chancery La. Shaw 2A 32
Chancery St. Chad 3C 40
Chancery St. Oldh 5A 42
Chancery Wlk. Chad. 3C 40
Chandos St. Shaw 2A 32
Channing Ct. Roch 1B 22
Channing Sq. Roch 1B 22
Channing St. Roch 1B 22
Chapel Clo. Uns 5A 26
Chapel Ct. M9 4A 46
Chapel Cft. Rytn 5D 30
Chapel Ga. Miln 1F 23
Chapel Hill. L'boro 6H 7
Chapel La. Roch 5F 11
Chapel La. Rytn 5D 30
Chapel Rd. G'fld 5C 44
Chapel Rd. Oldh 2C 48
Chapel St. Droy 6F 55
Chapel St. Heyw 5H 19
(in two parts)
Chapel St. Lees 5C 42
Chapel St. L'boro 1B 8
Chapel St. Midd 4G 37
(Manchester Old Rd.)
Chapel St. Midd 3B 38
(Sadler St., in two parts)
Chapel St. Moss 4G 51
Chapel St. Roch 3A 22
Chapel St. Rytn 5D 30
Chapel St. Shaw 2H 31
Chapel St. Upperm 3D 44
(in two parts)
Chapel St. Ward 4C 6
Chapel St. Whitw 3E 5
Chapel Wlk. Midd. 4G 37
Chapel Wlk. W'fld. 2A 36
Chapelway Gdns. Rytn 3D 30
Chappell Rd. Droy 5E 55
Charcon Wlk. Rytn 5E 31
Charfield St. M40 2B 54
Charlbury Way. Rytn 4G 31
Charles La. Miln 2G 23
Charles M. Miln 2G 23
Charles Morris Clo. Fail 5B 48
Charles Morris Ho. Fail. 6A 48
(off Gildenhall)
Charles Shaw Clo. Oldh 2B 42
(off Adswood Clo.)
Charles St. Droy 6C 54
Charles St. Heyw 1A 28
Charles St. L'boro 6G 7
Charles St. Oldh 5C 40
Charles St. Rytn 5D 30
Charleston St. Oldh. 1F 49
Charlestown. 2C 46
Charlestown Rd. M9 3A 46
Charles Whittaker St. Roch 4B 12
Charlotte La. Grass 6A 44
Charlotte St. Roch 3B 22
Charnwood Clo. Ash L 6A 50
Charnwood Clo. Shaw 1E 31
Charnwood Rd. M9 6H 37
Charter St. Oldh 3G 41
Charter St. Roch 3A 22
Chaseley Rd. Roch 5G 13
Chatburn Av. Roch 2F 29
Chatburn Ct. Shaw 1H 31
Chatburn Gdns. Heyw 5D 18
Chatburn Sq. Roch 1F 29
Chatsworth Av. P'wich 6A 36
Chatsworth Clo. Droy 4B 54
Chatsworth Clo. Shaw 1B 32
Chatsworth Ct. M9 6E 37
(off Deanswood Dri.)
Chatsworth Rd. Droy 5C 54
Chatsworth St. Oldh 6A 42
Chatsworth St. Roch 2G 13
Chatwell Ct. Miln 3A 24
Chatwood Rd. M40 3F 47
Chaucer Av. Droy 6E 55
Chaucer Rd. Midd 1D 38
Chaucer St. Oldh 5E 41
Chaucer St. Roch 5E 21
Chaucer St. Rytn 4E 31
Chauncy Rd. M40 5G 47
Chaytor Av. M40 6C 46
Cheap Side. Midd 1C 38
Cheapside. Oldh 4E 41
Cheesden Edge. Roch 1C 10
Cheesden Wlk. W'fld 2A 36
Cheetham Av. Midd 2D 38
Cheetham Hill. Shaw 3H 31
Cheetham Hill. Whitw 1F 5
Cheethams Cres. Rytn 5G 31
Cheetham St. Fail 5A 48
(in two parts)
Cheetham St. Midd. 3B 38
Cheetham St. Oldh 4H 41
Cheetham St. Roch 5H 13
Cheetham St. Shaw 3A 32
Chelbourne Dri. Oldh 3B 48
Chelburn Vw. L'boro 2A 8
Cheldon Wlk. M40 1A 54
Chelford Clo. Midd 1E 39
Chellow Ct. Moss 4F 51
Chellow Dene. Moss 4F 51
Chelmer Gro. Heyw 4E 19
Chelmsford Av. M40 3A 54
Chelmsford St. Oldh 6E 41
Chelsea Clo. Shaw 2H 31
Chelsea Rd. M40 2A 54
Chelsea St. Roch 2F 21
Chelston Av. M40 3F 47
Cheltenham Grn. Midd 5C 38
Cheltenham Rd. Midd. 5C 38
Cheltenham St. Oldh 2H 41
Cheltenham St. Roch 3F 21
Chelwood Dri. Droy 5D 54
Chendre Rd. M9 2D 46
Chepstow Clo. Roch 5B 12
Chepstow Dri. Oldh 2H 41
Cherrington Dri. Roch 1F 29
Cherry Av. Bury 4A 18
Cherry Av. Oldh 2A 50
Cherry Clough. 4F 25
Cherry Gro. Roch 5C 12
Cherry Gro. Rytn 3C 30
Cherry Hall Dri. Shaw 2E 31
Cherry Hinton. Oldh 3D 40
Cherry La. Dens 4F 25
Cherry St. P'wich 6A 36
Cherry Tree Wlk. Moss 4F 51
Cherrywood. Chad 4F 39
Chertsey Clo. Shaw 1H 31
Cherwell Av. Heyw 4E 19
Cherwell Clo. Oldh 4C 48
Cherwell Ct. Heyw 4F 19
(off Peel La.)
Chesham Av. Roch 2F 29
Chesham Fold Rd. Bury 4A 18
(in two parts)
Chesham Rd. Oldh 5A 42
Cheshires, The. Moss. 4H 51
Cheshire St. Moss 5H 51
Chesney Av. Chad 3G 47
Chester Av. Roch 1C 20
Chesterfield St. Oldh 5H 41
Chester Pl. Rytn 5D 30
Chester St. Oldh 6C 40
Chester St. Roch 1A 22
Chesterton Gro. Droy 5E 55
Chesterton Rd. Oldh 1H 41
Chestnut Av. Droy 4C 54
Chestnut Clo. Oldh 3B 42
Chestnut Cres. Oldh 3G 49
Chestnut Gdns. Heyw 6G 19
Chestnut Gro. Fail 1D 54
Chestnut Pl. Roch 5B 14
Chestnut St. Chad 2H 47
Chestnut Way. L'boro 5F 7
Chesworth Ct. Droy 6D 54
Chetwyn Av. Rytn 5C 30
Cheviot Av. Oldh 2E 49
Cheviot Av. Rytn 6C 30
Cheviot Clo. Chad 6A 40
Cheviot Clo. Midd 3F 39
Cheviot Clo. Miln 1G 23
Cheviot Ct. Oldh 2E 49
Cheviots Rd. Shaw 1G 31
Chevron Clo. Roch 4D 20
Chew Brook Dri. G'fld 6D 44
Chew Va. G'fld 6D 44
Chew Valley Rd. G'fld 5C 44
Chichester Bus. Cen. Roch 6A 14
Chichester Clo. L'boro 2F 15
Chichester Cres. Chad 2A 40
Chichester St. Roch 6A 14
Chief St. Oldh 5G 41
Chilcombe Wlk. M9 6A 38
(off Brockford Dri.)
Chiltern Clo. Shaw 1F 31
Chiltern Dri. Rytn 5C 30
Chilton Av. Chad 5A 40
Chilton Dri. Midd 4E 39
Chinley Av. M40 5C 46
Chipping Fold. Miln 2F 23
Chirton Wlk. M40 6C 46
Chisholm Ct. Midd 2B 38
Christine St. Shaw 2H 31
(in two parts)
Christopher Acre. Roch 4A 12
Christopher St. M40 3B 54
Church Av. M40 2A 54
Church Av. Midd 3F 29
Church Brow. Midd 2C 38
Church Ct. Chad 6C 40
Church Cft. Bury 5A 26
Churchdale Rd. M9 6F 37
Churchfields. Dob 1C 44
Churchill Clo. Heyw 1A 28
Churchill St. Oldh 5G 41
Churchill St. Roch 4E 13
(in two parts)
Churchill St. E. Oldh 5G 41
Church La. M9 6A 46
(Kingscliffe St.)
Church La. M9 5A 46
(Water St.)
Church La. Bury 2B 18
Church La. Moss 4H 51
Church La. Oldh 4F 41
Church La. Roch 6H 13
Church La. Upperm 2F 45
Church Mdw. G'fld 6A 44
Church Mdw. Uns 4A 26
Church Pl. Heyw 5H 19
Church Pl. Oldh 4F 41
Church Rd. G'fld 6A 44
Church Rd. Midd 4F 39
Church Rd. Roch 1B 22
Church Rd. Shaw 3H 31
Church Rd. Upperm 3D 44
Church Stile. Roch 6H 13
Church St. Del 5A 34
Church St. Droy 6F 55
Church St. Fail 5H 47
Church St. Heyw 5H 19
Church St. Lees 6C 42
Church St. L'boro 6G 7
Church St. Midd 1C 38
Church St. Miln 3H 23
Church St. Oldh 4F 41
Church St. Roch (OL11) 1G 21
Church St. Roch (OL16) 2D 14
Church St. Rytn 5D 30
Church St. Whitw 3E 5
Church St. E. Oldh 3C 42
Church St. Ind. Est. Midd 1C 38
Church Ter. Miln 2G 23
Church Ter. Oldh 4F 41
Church Ter. Ward 4C 6
Church Vw. Droy 6F 55
Church Vw. Fail 5H 47
Church Vw. Roch 3A 12
Church Wlk. Rytn 5D 30
Churston Av. M9 1A 46
Cicero St. M9 5B 46
Cicero St. Oldh 2G 41
Cilder's Villa. Oldh 1F 51
Cinder Hill La. Chad 5A 30
Cinnabar Dri. Midd 2B 38
Cinnamon Clo. Roch 5F 13
Cinnamon St. Roch 5F 13
Civic Wlk. Heyw 5H 19
Claife Av. M40 3D 46
Clapgate Rd. Roch 4A 12
Clapham St. M40 5E 47
Clara Gorton Ct. Roch 1B 22
Clara St. Oldh 1C 48
Clara St. Roch 2H 21
Claremont Rd. Miln 2E 23
Claremont Rd. Roch 6E 13
Claremont St. Chad 2C 40
Claremont St. Fail 5H 47
Claremont St. Oldh 3F 49
Clarence Av. Oldh 1D 48
Clarence St. Roch 3F 13
Clarence St. Rytn 6G 31
Clarendon St. Moss 5H 51
Clarendon St. Roch 3B 22
Clarke Brow. Midd 2C 38
Clarkes Cft. Bury 4A 18
Clarke's La. Roch 5F 13
Clarke St. Heyw 5H 19
Clarke St. Roch 3B 14
Clarksfield Rd. Oldh 5A 42
Clarksfield St. Oldh 5A 42
Clarkson Clo. Midd 4G 37
Clarkwell Clo. Oldh 3E 41
Clatford Wlk. M9 6A 46
(off Fernclough Rd.)
Claxton Av. M9 2A 46
Clay Bank. Droy 6D 54
Clay Bank St. Heyw 4G 19
Claybank Ter. Moss 1A 52
Clay Cft. Ter. L'boro 4G 7
Clayfield Dri. Roch 5B 12
Claygate Dri. M9 6H 37
Clayhill Wlk. M9 4A 46
Clay La. Roch 5H 11
Claymere Av. Roch 5A 12
Clay St. L'boro 6F 7
Clay St. Oldh 1E 49
Clayton. 5A 54
Clayton Bridge. 3C 54
Claytonbrook Rd. M11 6A 54
Clayton Community Farm. 6A 54
(off Turner St.)
Clayton Hall Rd. M11 5A 54
Clayton Ind. Est. M11 6B 54
Clayton La. M11 6A 54
Clayton's Clo. S'head 4D 42
Clayton St. M11 4A 54
(in two parts)
Clayton St. Chad 2A 48
Clayton St. Fail. 6H 47
Clayton St. Roch 3B 14
Cleeve Rd. Oldh 5A 42
Clegg Hall. 4E 15
Clegg Hall Rd. Roch & L'boro 3D 14
(in two parts)
Clegg's Av. Whitw 1E 5
(off Clegg St.)
Clegg St. Droy 6D 54
Clegg St. L'boro 4F 7
Clegg St. Miln 2G 23
Clegg St. Oldh 5F 41
(in two parts)
Clegg St. S'head 5E 43
Clegg St. Whitw 1E 5
Cleggswood Av. L'boro 2G 15
Clement Ct. Roch 1B 22
Clementina St. Roch 4H 13
(in two parts)
Clement Pl. L'boro 6A 8
Clement Pl. Roch 5G 13
Clement Royds St. Roch 5G 13
Clement Stott Clo. M9 1B 46
Clement St. Chad 2B 48
Clemshaw Clo. Heyw 6G 19
Clevedon Rd. Chad 2A 40
Clevedon St. M9 6A 46
Cleveland Dri. Miln 1G 23
Cleveland Gro. Rytn 6C 30
Clevelands Clo. Shaw 1G 31

Cleveleys Av. *Roch* 4B **22**
Cleves Ct. *Heyw* 6G **19**
Cleworth Rd. *Midd* 1B **38**
Cliffe St. *L'boro* 1B **8**
Cliff Hill. *Shaw* 6A **24**
Cliff Hill Rd. *Shaw* 6B **24**
Clifford St. *Roch* 2H **21**
Cliff St. *Roch* 4B **14**
Clifton Av. *Oldh* 6H **41**
Clifton Clo. *Heyw* 6G **19**
Clifton Clo. *Oldh* 6H **41**
Clifton Holm. *Del* 4A **34**
Clifton Rd. *Midd* 3F **29**
Clifton St. *Fail* 4A **48**
Clifton St. *G'fld* 6D **44**
Clifton St. *Miln* 1F **23**
Clifton Vs. *Fail* 4A **48**
Cliftonville Rd. *Roch* 1C **30**
Clifton Wlk. *Midd* 6H **27**
Clinton Wlk. *Oldh* 5G **41**
Clipsley Cres. *Oldh* 5D **32**
Clitheroe Clo. *Heyw* 4H **19**
Clito St. *M9* 5B **46**
Clive Rd. *Fail* 6G **47**
Clive St. *Oldh* 3D **48**
(in two parts)
Clock Ho. Av. *Droy* 4C **54**
Clockhouse M. *Droy* 4C **54**
Clock St. *Chad* 3B **48**
Cloisters, The. *Roch* 4B **14**
Cloister St. *M9* 5B **46**
Close, The. *Midd* 6D **28**
Clough. 3G 7
(Littleborough)
Clough. 3B 32
(Oldham)
Clough. *Shaw* 3B **32**
Clough Bank. *M9* 3A **46**
Clough Bank. *L'boro* 3G **7**
Clough Clo. *Oldh* 5A **44**
Clough Fld. *L'boro* 1G **15**
Clough Ct. *Midd* 1D **38**
Clough Flats. Heyw 5G 19
(off Brunswick St.)
Clough Ga. *Oldh* 3D **48**
Clough Head. L'boro 1A 8
(off Higher Calderbrook Rd.)
Clough Ho. La. *Ward* 5B **6**
Clough La. *Grass* 5H **43**
Clough La. *Heyw* 3G **19**
Clough Pk. Av. *Grass* 5A **44**
Clough Rd. *M9* 5B **46**
Clough Rd. *Droy* 5E **55**
Clough Rd. *Fail* 6A **48**
Clough Rd. *L'boro* 3G **7**
Clough Rd. *Midd* 1C **38**
Clough Rd. *Shaw* 3B **32**
Cloughs Av. *Chad* 3F **39**
Clough Side. *M9* 4B **46**
Clough St. *M40* 3A **54**
Clough St. *Midd* 1D **38**
Clough St. *Ward* 5C **6**
Cloughton Wlk. *M40* 2B **54**
Clough Top Rd. *M9* 3C **46**
Clovelly Av. *Oldh* 3C **48**
Clovelly St. *M40* 2B **54**
Clovelly St. *Roch* 4D **20**
Clover Cres. *Oldh* 2B **50**
Clover Hall. 4C 14
Clover Hall Cres. *Roch* 4C **14**
Clover St. *Roch* 5G **13**
Clover Vw. *Roch* 5C **14**
Clowes St. *Chad* 3B **48**
Clyde Ct. *Roch* 1B **22**
Clydesdale Ri. *Dig* 4F **35**
Clydesdale St. *Oldh* 1E **49**
Clyde St. *Oldh* 2A **42**
Coach La. *Roch* 2A **20**
Coal Pit La. *Oldh* 6C **48**
Coalshaw Grn. Rd. *Chad* 2A **48**
Coatbridge St. *M11* 5A **54**
Cobblestones. *Del* 6B **34**
Cobden Lodge. Roch 5E 21
(off Tudor Hall St.)
Cobden St. *M9* 5A **46**
Cobden St. *Chad* 4B **40**
Cobden St. *Heyw* 6H **19**
Cobden St. *Oldh* 2B **42**
Cobham Av. *M40* 3E **47**
Coblers Hill. *Del* 4B **34**
Cockcroft St. *M9* 4A **46**
Cocker Mill La. *Shaw* 4F **31**
Cockhall La. *Whitw* 2E **5**
Coghlan Clo. *M11* 5A **54**
Colby Wlk. *M40* 6C **46**

Colchester Wlk. *Oldh* 4F **41**
Colclough Clo. *M40* 6D **46**
Cold Greave Clo. *Miln* 3A **24**
Cold Hurst. 3E 41
Coldhurst Hollow Est. *Oldh* . . . 2E **41**
Coldhurst St. *Oldh* 3E **41**
Coldstream Av. *M9* 1A **46**
Coldwall St. *Roch* 5F **13**
Colebrook Rd. *M40* 6C **46**
Coledale Dri. *Midd* 1G **37**
Colenso St. *Oldh* 2D **48**
Coleridge Av. *Midd* 6E **29**
Coleridge Dri. *L'boro* 3F **15**
Coleridge Rd. *Oldh* 5B **32**
Coleridge St. *M40* 3A **54**
Colesmere Wlk. *M40* 4F **47**
Cole St. *M40* 5B **46**
Colgrove Av. *M40* 3E **47**
Colindale Av. *M9* 1A **46**
College Av. *Oldh* 2D **48**
College Rd. *Oldh* 1D **48**
College Rd. *Roch* 6F **13**
Collett St. *Oldh* 3A **42**
Colley St. *Roch* 4A **14**
Collier Av. *Miln* 6F **15**
Collier Hill. *Oldh* 2D **48**
Collier Hill Av. *Oldh* 2C **48**
Collier's Ct. *Roch* 6B **22**
Collinge Av. *Midd* 3E **39**
Collinge St. *Heyw* 5G **19**
Collinge St. *Midd* 4F **39**
Collinge St. *Shaw* 2H **31**
Collingwood Av. *Droy* 4C **54**
Collingwood St. *Roch* 1E **29**
Collingwood Way. *Oldh* 3F **41**
Collop Dri. *Heyw* 2A **28**
Coll's La. *Del* 5H **33**
Colmore Dri. *M9* 1C **46**
Colne St. *Roch* 6F **21**
Colson Dri. *Midd* 4B **38**
Colsterdale Clo. *Rytn* 4E **31**
Colt Hill La. *Upperm* 3A **44**
Coltness Wlk. *M40* 2A **54**
Columbia St. *Oldh* 1F **49**
Columbine Clo. *Roch* 2E **13**
Colville Rd. *Oldh* 2D **40**
Colwell Wlk. *M9* 6F **47**
Colwyn Av. *Midd* 5C **38**
Colwyn St. *Oldh* 6A **40**
Colwyn St. *Roch* 5D **20**
Commercial Rd. *Oldh* 5F **41**
Commercial St. *Oldh* 5C **40**
Compton Fold. *Shaw* 1A **32**
Compton Way. *Midd* 4E **39**
Condor Clo. *Droy* 4G **55**
Conduit St. *Oldh* 6B **32**
Congreave St. *Oldh* 3E **41**
Coningsby Dri. *M9* 5A **46**
Conisborough. *Roch* 1G **21**
Coniston Av. *M9* 5A **46**
Coniston Av. *Oldh* 2D **48**
Coniston Dri. *Midd* 1A **38**
Coniston Gro. *Heyw* 1H **27**
Coniston Gro. *Rytn* 3D **30**
Coniston St. *M40* 2A **54**
Conival Way. *Chad* 2A **40**
Connaught Av. *Roch* 4B **22**
Connaught St. *Oldh* 5C **14**
Connell Way. *Heyw* 4B **20**
Connington Clo. *Rytn* 5C **30**
Conrad Clo. *Oldh* 5C **32**
Conran St. *M9* 6A **46**
Consort Av. *Rytn* 3C **30**
Constable Wlk. *Oldh* *6B 32*
(off Hodge Clough Rd.)
Constantine Rd. *Roch* 6H **13**
Constantine St. *Oldh* 5B **42**
Convent Gro. *Roch* 2F **21**
Convent St. *Oldh* 1A **50**
Conway Clo. *Heyw* 4E **19**
Conway Clo. *Midd* 4C **38**
Conway Dri. *Bury* 5B **18**
Conway Gro. *Chad* 2H **39**
Cookcroft. 4D 42
Cooke St. *Fail* 5H **47**
Cook St. *Oldh* 5A **42**
Cook St. *Roch* 4B **14**
Cook Ter. *Roch* 4B **14**
Coomassie St. *Heyw* 5G **19**
Cooperas La. *Droy* 6C **54**
(in three parts)
Co-operation St. *Fail* 4H **47**
Co-operative St. *Shaw* 2H **31**
Co-operative St. *S'head* 5D **42**

Co-operative St. *Upperm* 3D **44**
Cooper Fold. *Midd* 5C **28**
Cooper La. *M9* 6H **37**
Cooper La. *Midd* 6B **28**
Cooper St. *Roch* 1D **14**
Cooper St. *S'head* 4E **43**
Coopers Wlk. *Roch* 3C **14**
Cooper Ter. *Roch* 5B **14**
Coop Ter. *Roch* 6D **14**
Copeland Clo. *Midd* 2G **37**
Copenhagen Sq. *Roch* 5A **14**
Copenhagen St. *Roch* 5A **14**
(in two parts)
Copley St. *Shaw* 1A **32**
Coppice. 1E 49
Coppice Dri. *Whitw* 4E **5**
Coppice Ind. Est. *Oldh* 6D **40**
Coppice St. *Bury* 4A **18**
Coppice St. *Oldh* 6D **40**
(in two parts)
Coppice, The. *M9* 3C **46**
Coppice, The. *Midd* 5D **38**
Coppingford Clo. *Roch* 3C **12**
Cop Rd. *Oldh* 5A **32**
Copse Wlk. *L'boro* 6F **7**
Copster Hill. 2E 49
Copster Av. *Oldh* 2E **49**
Copster Hill Rd. *Oldh* 2E **49**
Copster Pl. *Oldh* 2E **49**
Copthorne Clo. *Heyw* 1H **27**
Coptrod Head Clo. *Roch* 1G **13**
Coptrod Rd. *Roch* 5F **13**
Coral M. *Rytn* 6E **31**
Corbett St. *Roch* 5B **14**
Corbett Way. *Dens* 6G **25**
Corbrook Rd. *Chad* 2G **39**
Corcoran Clo. *Heyw* 4G **19**
Corday La. *P'wich* 3B **36**
Cordingley Av. *Droy* 6D **54**
Corgi Heritage Centre, The. . . . 5H 19
(off York St.)
Cormallen Gro. *Fail* 6A **48**
Cornbrook Clo. *Ward* 5C **6**
Cornfield St. *Miln* 2F **23**
Cornhill St. *Oldh* 1B **42**
Cornish Way. *Rytn* 6F **31**
Corn Mill Clo. *Roch* 1C **14**
Corn St. *Fail* 1A **54**
Corn St. *Oldh* 4G **41**
Cornwall Cres. *Dig* 5D **34**
Cornwall Rd. *Droy* 4E **55**
Cornwall St. *Oldh* 6B **40**
Corona Av. *Oldh* 2D **48**
Coronation Av. *Heyw* 1A **28**
Coronation Rd. *Droy* 4D **54**
Coronation Rd. *Fail* 1C **54**
Coronation Vs. *Whitw* 1F **5**
Corporation Rd. *Roch* 1F **21**
(in two parts)
Corporation St. *Midd* 3C **38**
Corris Av. *M9* 6E **37**
Corry St. *Heyw* 5A **20**
Corston Wlk. *M40* 1A **54**
Corwen Clo. *Oldh* 3B **48**
Corwen St. *M9* 5A **46**
Cosgrove Cres. *Fail* 2C **54**
Cosgrove Rd. *Fail* 2C **54**
Costabeck Wlk. *M40* 3B **54**
Cotaline Clo. *Roch* 4D **20**
Cote La. *Dig* 1D **34**
Cote La. *L'boro* 5F **7**
Cote La. *Moss* 2A **52**
Cotswold Av. *Chad* 6A **40**
Cotswold Av. *Shaw* 1F **31**
Cotswold Clo. *P'wich* 6A **36**
Cotswold Cres. *Miln* 6G **15**
Cotswold Dri. *Rytn* 6B **30**
Cottages, The. *S'head* 2F **43**
Cottage, The. *Heyw* 5G **27**
Cottage Wlk. *Droy* 4D **54**
Cottage Wlk. *Roch* 1E **13**
Cottam St. *Oldh* 3D **40**
Cotton Fold. *Roch* 1C **22**
Cotton La. *Roch* 3E **21**
(in two parts)
Cotton Mill Cres. *Oldh* 1B **48**
Cotton Tree Clo. *Oldh* 3B **42**
Coulsden Dri. *M9* 2A **46**
Coulton Clo. *Oldh* 3G **41**
Counthill Rd. *Oldh* 2B **42**
(in two parts)
Count St. *Roch* 2A **22**
County End. 6D 42
County End Bus. Cen. *S'head* . . 5D **42**
County St. *Oldh* 3C **48**

Coupland Clo. *Oldh* 5D **32**
Coupland Clo. *Whitw* 3E **5**
Coupland St. *Whitw* 3E **5**
Course Vw. *Oldh* 2C **50**
Court Dri. *M40* 3C **54**
Courtfield Av. *M9* 1A **46**
Court Ho. Way. Heyw 5H 19
(off Longford St.)
Court St. *Upperm* 3D **44**
Coventry Gro. *Chad* 2A **40**
Coventry St. *Roch* 1H **21**
Coverdale Av. *Rytn* 4C **30**
Coverdale Clo. *Heyw* 6G **19**
Coverham Av. *Oldh* 1B **50**
Coverhill Rd. *G'ton* 6F **43**
Covert Rd. *Oldh* 2B **50**
Cowburn St. *Heyw* 6A **20**
Cow Clough La. *Whitw* 1D **4**
Cowhill. 5B 40
Cow Side. *Shaw* 1H **31**
Cow La. *Fail* 6G **47**
Cow La. *Oldh* 4A **42**
Cowley St. *M40* 1A **54**
Cowling St. *Oldh* 1F **49**
Cowlishaw. 3G 31
Cowlishaw. *Shaw* 4G **31**
Cowlishaw La. *Shaw* 4G **31**
Cowm Pk. Way N. *Whitw* 1E **5**
Cowm Pk. Way S. *Whitw* 3E **5**
Cowm Top La. *Roch* 4G **21**
(in two parts)
Cowper St. *Midd* 4F **39**
Crab La. *M9* 6F **37**
Crabtree La. *M11* 6B **54**
(in two parts)
Crabtree Rd. *Oldh* 3H **41**
Craddock St. *Moss* 4F **51**
Cragg Pl. *L'boro* 6H **7**
Cragg Rd. *Chad* 1H **39**
(in two parts)
Craigend Dri. *M9* 6A **46**
Craiglands. *Roch* 5B **22**
Craig Wlk. *Oldh* 6E **41**
Crail Pl. *Heyw* 6D **18**
Crammond Clo. *M40* 1B **54**
Cranberry St. *Oldh* 5H **41**
Cranbourne Rd. *Roch* 1A **20**
Cranbrook Pl. *Oldh* 5A **42**
Cranbrook St. *Oldh* 5H **41**
Cranbrook Wlk. *Chad* 5A **40**
Cranleigh Clo. *Oldh* 2C **42**
Cranmer Ct. *Heyw* 6G **19**
Cranwell Ct. Droy 6F 55
(off Williamson La.)
Craven Gdns. *Roch* 2G **21**
Cravenhurst Av. *M40* 3A **54**
Craven Pl. *M11* 5A **54**
Craven St. *Bury* 4A **18**
Craven St. *Droy* 6E **55**
Craven St. *Oldh* 2E **41**
Crawford Sq. *Heyw* 6E **19**
Crawford St. *M40* 2A **54**
Crawford St. *Roch* 2A **22**
Crawley Way. *Chad* 5A **40**
Cray, The. *Miln* 1E **23**
(in two parts)
Creaton Way. *Midd* 5G **27**
Creel Clo. *M9* 6F **37**
Crescent Rd. *Chad* 3G **47**
Crescent Rd. *Roch* 3D **20**
Crescent, The. *Droy* 6D **54**
Crescent, The. *Midd* 3A **38**
Crescent, The. *Moss* 4F **51**
Crescent, The. *Shaw* 3G **31**
Crescent, The. *Whitw* 3E **5**
Crete St. *Oldh* 1F **49**
Crib Fold. *Dob* 1C **44**
Crib La. *Dob* 1C **44**
Cricket Vw. *Miln* 2F **23**
Crimble. 3A 20
Crimble La. *Roch* 2A **20**
(in two parts)
Crimbles St. *Oldh* 3C **42**
(in two parts)
Crimble St. *Roch* 5F **13**
Crime La. *Fail & Oldh* 6D **48**
Crime Vw. Cotts. *Fail* 6D **48**
Crinan Sq. *Heyw* 6D **18**
Cripple Ga. La. *Roch* 6G **21**
Croal Wlk. *W'fld* 2A **36**
Croasdale Dri. *Rytn* 4E **31**
Crocker Wlk. *M9* 6A **46**
Crocus Dri. *Rytn* 4G **31**
Croft Av. *P'wich* 3D **36**
Croft Bank. *Whitw* 1F **5**

Croft Brow. Oldh 3E 49
Croft Edge. G'fld. 6C 44
Crofters Hall Wlk. M40. 6D 46
(off Kenyon La.)
Cft. Gates Rd. Midd 4H 37
Crofthead. L'boro 4H 7
Cft. Head Dri. Miln 6F 15
Crofthill Ct. Roch 1D 14
Cft. Hill Rd. M40 4C 46
Crofton St. Oldh 2E 49
(in two parts)
Croft Sq. Roch 2C 14
Croft St. M11 6A 54
Croft St. Fail 4A 48
Croft St. Roch 2C 14
Croft, The. Oldh 3E 49
Cromarty Av. Chad 2H 47
Cromarty Sq. Heyw 6E 19
Cromer Ind. Est. Midd 2D 38
Cromer St. M11 6B 54
Cromer St. Midd 2D 38
Cromer St. Roch 5G 13
Cromer St. Shaw 2H 31
Cromford Bus. Cen. Oldh 3H 41
Cromford St. Oldh 3G 41
Crompton Av. Roch 4B 22
Crompton Circuit. Oldh & Dens 2D 32
(Grains Bar)
Crompton Circuit. Oldh & Shaw 5A 32
(Sholver)
Crompton Circuit. Rytn 2E 31
Crompton Fold. 1B 32
Crompton Pool 3H 31
Crompton St. Chad 4C 40
(in two parts)
Crompton St. Oldh 3E 41
Crompton St. Rytn 6E 31
Crompton St. Shaw 2H 31
Crompton Way. Shaw 3H 31
Cromwell Ct. Oldh 5F 41
(off Cromwell St.)
Cromwell Rd. P'wich 6A 36
Cromwell Rd. Rytn 3C 30
Cromwell St. Heyw 6H 19
Cromwell St. Oldh 5F 41
Cronkeyshaw Rd. Roch 4G 13
Cronshaw Ind. Est. Roch 1A 22
(off Durham St.)
Crook St. Roch 5A 14
Crosby Rd. M40 2A 54
Crosby St. Roch 3H 13
Cross Bank. 4D 42
Crossbank Av. Lees 4D 42
Crossbank St. Oldh 5E 41
(in two parts)
Crossbank Way. Midd 2B 38
Crossby Clo. Midd 6B 38
Crossdale Rd. M9 1B 46
Crossfell Av. M9 6F 37
Cross Fld. Clo. Shaw 6A 24
Crossfield Clo. Ward 4C 6
Crossfield Pl. Roch 2A 22
Crossfield Rd. Ward 5C 6
Crossgates Rd. Miln 6F 15
Crossland Rd. Droy 5F 55
Cross La. Droy 3H 55
Cross Lees. Roch 2A 14
Crossley Est. Chad 5B 40
Crossley St. Miln 1E 23
Crossley St. Rytn 1E 41
Crossley St. Shaw 2A 32
Crossmead Dri. M9 6A 38
Crossmeadow Clo. Roch 5C 12
Cross St. Fir 6D 14
Cross St. Heyw 6A 20
Cross St. Lees 5C 42
Cross St. Midd 3B 38
(Kemp St.)
Cross St. Midd 2B 38
(Whittaker St.)
Cross St. Moss 3G 51
Cross St. Oldh 4H 41
Cross St. Roch 5F 21
Cross St. S'head 5E 43
Cross Ways. Oldh 4G 49
Croston Clo. Rd. Bury & Rams 3A 10
(in two parts)
Crowden Rd. M40 3D 46
Crow Hill N. Midd 5B 38
Crow Hill S. Midd 5B 38
Crow Hill Vw. Oldh 1D 50
Crowley La. Oldh 2B 42
Crowley Rd. M9 5B 46
Crown Bus. Cen. Fail 5H 47
Crowneast St. Roch 6E 13
Crown Gdns. Roch 2A 22
Crown Hill. Moss 5H 51
Crownhill Ct. Droy 5E 55
(off Chappell Rd.)
Crownhill Dri. Droy 5E 55
Crown Point Av. M40 2A 54
Crown Rd. Heyw 5F 19
Crown St. M40 2A 54
Crown St. Fail 5H 47
Crown St. Roch 2A 22
Crown St. Shaw 2H 31
Crowshaw Dri. Roch 2G 13
Crowther Ct. L'boro 1E 15
Crowther St. L'boro 1E 15
Crowther St. Roch 3B 22
Croxdale Wlk. M9 6H 37
(off Claygate Dri.)
Croxton Av. Roch 5B 14
Croydon Av. Roch 2F 29
Croydon Av. Rytn 3C 30
Croydon Dri. M40 3A 54
Croydon Sq. Roch 1F 29
Crummock Dri. Midd 6A 28
Cryer St. Droy 3G 55
Cuba St. Midd 3E 39
Cuckoo Gro. P'wich 5A 36
Cuckoo La. Bury 5A 18
(Bri. Hall La., in two parts)
Cuckoo La. Bury 4A 18
(Rochdale Old Rd.)
Cuckoo La. W'fld & P'wich 5A 36
Cuckoo Nest. P'wich 4A 36
Cudworth Rd. M9 6E 37
Culcheth. 2A 54
Culcheth La. M40 2A 54
Culgaith Wlk. M9 6A 46
Cullen Gro. M9 1B 46
(in two parts)
Culross Av. M40 4G 47
Culvert St. Oldh 3C 42
Culvert St. Roch 5B 22
Cumberland Av. Heyw 5E 19
Cumberland Dri. Oldh & Rytn 2D 40
Cumberland Rd. M9 4A 46
Cumberland Rd. Roch 5H 21
Cumbrian Clo. Shaw 1F 31
Cummings St. Oldh 3C 48
Cunliffe Dri. Shaw 2A 32
Cunningham Way. Oldh 3F 41
Curlew Clo. Roch 6B 12
Curlew Rd. Oldh 1C 50
Curzon Clo. Roch 5H 21
Curzon Rd. Roch 5H 21
Curzon St. Moss 4G 51
Curzon St. Oldh 4F 41
Cutgate. 5C 12
Cutgate Rd. Roch 4D 12
Cutgate Shop. Precinct. Roch 5D 12
Cuthbert Mayne Ct. Roch 1G 21
Cuthill Wlk. M40 3B 54
Cutland Way. L'boro 1G 15
Cut La. Roch 4B 12
Cutler Hill. 6C 48
Cutler Hill Rd. Fail 6B 48
Cutler St. Chad 4C 40
Cypress Av. Chad 3B 40
Cypress Gdns. Fir 6D 14
Cypress Rd. Droy 4E 55
Cypress Rd. Oldh 3B 42
Cypress St. Midd 4E 39
Cyprus Clo. Oldh 6B 42
Cyril St. Shaw 2H 31

D

Dacre Clo. Midd 2F 37
Dacre Rd. Roch 3H 21
Dacres. 1B 52
Dacres Av. G'fld 1B 52
Dacres Dri. G'fld 1B 52
Dacres Rd. G'fld 1B 52
Daffodil Clo. Roch 2G 13
Dahlia Clo. Roch 2F 13
Daintry Rd. Oldh 4C 40
Dairy St. Chad 4B 40
Daisey Hill Ct. Oldh 3C 42
Daisy Bank. M40 2A 54
Daisy Hill Rd. Moss 4H 51
Daisy Nook. 1H 55
Daisy Nook Country Pk. 6E 49 & 1H 5
Daisy Row. L'boro 2F 15
Daisy St. Chad 3A 40
Daisy St. Oldh 4D 40
Daisy St. Roch 5G 13
Dakerwood Clo. M40 2A 54
Dalbeattie St. M9 4A 46
Dale. 4B 34
Dale Av. Moss 2A 52
Dalebeck Clo. W'fld 3A 36
Dalebeck Wlk. W'fld 3A 36
Dale End. Oldh 3G 49
Dalefields. Del 5B 34
Dalehead Dri. Shaw 2B 32
Dale Ho. Midd 2D 38
Dale Ho. Shaw 3H 31
Dale La. Del 4B 34
Dale Rd. Midd 1D 38
Dalesfield Cres. Moss 4A 52
Dalesman Clo. M9 5B 46
Dalesman Dri. Oldh 6B 32
Dale Sq. Rytn 5F 31
Dale St. Midd 4D 38
Dale St. Miln 1F 23
Dale St. Roch 6C 14
Dale St. Shaw 3H 31
Dale Vw. L'boro 3F 15
Dalham Av. M9 3C 46
Dalkeith Sq. Heyw 6E 19
Dalmahoy Clo. M40 5E 47
Dalmeny Ter. Roch 3H 21
Dalston Av. Fail 5B 48
Dalton Av. Roch 6D 14
Dalton Clo. Roch 6D 14
Dalton Rd. M9 6H 37
Dalton Rd. Midd 4F 37
Dalton St. Chad 4B 40
Dalton St. Fail 5G 47
Dalton St. Oldh 4H 41
Daltrey St. Oldh 3G 41
Dam Head Dri. M9 2A 46
Damson Grn. Midd 3F 39
Danby Ct. Oldh 3E 41
Danby Wlk. M9 4A 46
(off Polworth Rd.)
Dane Bank. Midd 3D 38
Daneshill. P'wich 5A 36
Danes La. Whitw 2C 4
Dane St. Moss 2H 51
Dane St. Oldh 4A 42
Dane St. Roch 6G 13
Daneswood Av. M9 1B 46
Daneswood Av. Whitw 3E 5
Daneswood Clo. Whitw 3D 4
Daniel Fold. Roch 3D 12
Daniel St. Heyw 5F 19
Daniel St. Oldh 3H 41
Daniel St. Rytn 6G 31
Daniel St. Whitw 1F 5
Danisher La. Oldh 5F 49
Dantall Av. M9 2C 46
Dargai St. M11 6B 54
Dark La. Del 3A 34
Dark La. Moss 3H 51
(in two parts)
Darley Rd. Roch 3H 21
Darlington Rd. Roch 4H 21
Darliston Av. M9 6E 37
Darlton Wlk. M9 5A 46
Darn Hill. 6D 18
Dart Clo. Chad 3H 39
Dartmouth Clo. Oldh 1F 49
Darwin St. Oldh 6A 42
Datchet Ter. Roch 3H 21
Davenport St. Droy 6C 54
Davenport Ter. M9 5A 46
Daventry Rd. Roch 3H 21
Daventry Way. Roch 4H 21
David Lewis Clo. Roch 1C 22
David Pegg Wlk. M40 1A 54
David's Farm Clo. Midd 4E 39
David's La. S'head 4D 42
Davidson Dri. Midd 5D 38
David's Rd. Droy 5C 54
David St. Oldh 5E 41
David St. Roch 4H 13
David St. N. Roch 4H 13
Davies St. Oldh 3D 40
Davyhulme St. Roch 4B 14
Dawley Flats. Heyw 5G 19
(off Brunswick St.)
Dawlish Av. Chad 2H 39
Dawlish Av. Droy 5C 54
Dawn St. Shaw 3H 31
Dawson St. Heyw 5G 19
Dawson St. Lees 6C 42
Dawson St. Oldh 5B 42
Dawson St. Roch 5H 13
Day Dri. Fail 1D 54
Deacon St. Roch 3B 14
Deal Clo. M40 2B 54
Deal Wlk. Chad 5A 40
Dean Av. Newt H 6D 46 & 1A 54
Dean Bank Dri. Roch 6B 22
Dean Brook Clo. M40 6D 46
Deancourt. Roch 3H 21
Dean Head. L'boro 1B 8
Dean La. M40 6D 46 & 1A 54
Deanshut Rd. Oldh 3G 49
Dean St. Fail 6G 47
Dean St. Moss 4F 51
Dean St. Roch 4B 14
Deanswood Dri. M9 6E 37
Dean Ter. Ash L 3A 50
Dean Wlk. Midd 1H 37
Deanway. M40 5C 46
Dearden St. L'boro 5H 7
Dearnley. 1E 15
Dearnley Clo. L'boro 1E 15
Dearnley Pas. L'boro 1E 15
Debenham Av. M40 3A 54
Deepdale. Oldh 5B 42
Deepdale Av. Roch 1C 22
Deepdale Av. Rytn 1C 30
Deepdale Ct. M9 2D 46
Deep La. L'boro 6H 15
(in two parts)
Deeplish Cotts. Roch 2H 21
(off Clifford St.)
Deeplish Rd. Roch 2H 21
Deeplish St. Roch 2H 21
Deeply Va. La. Bury 3A 10
Delaford Wlk. M40 3B 54
Delamere Av. Shaw 1B 32
Delamere Clo. Carr 6A 52
Delamere Ct. M9 6E 37
Delamere Rd. Roch 3C 22
Delamere St. Oldh 6H 41
Dellar St. Roch 4E 13
Dell Clo. S'head 6D 42
Dell Gdns. Roch 3D 12
Dellhide Clo. S'head 5E 43
Dell Mdw. Whitw 6E 5
Dell Rd. Roch 2D 12
(in two parts)
Dell Side Way. Roch 3E 13
Delph. 5A 34
Delph La. Del 4B 34
Delph New Rd. Del & Dob 6A 34
Delph Rd. Dens 2G 33
Delph St. Miln 1F 23
Delside Av. M40 5C 46
Delta Clo. Rytn 1C 40
Delta Wlk. M40 6C 46
Denbigh Dri. Shaw 3F 31
Denbigh St. Moss 5H 51
Denbigh St. Oldh 2F 49
Denbydale Way. Rytn 5C 30
(in two parts)
Dene Dri. Midd 4B 38
Denehurst Rd. Roch 5D 12
Deneside Wlk. M9 5A 46
(off Dalbeattie St.)
Den Hill Dri. S'head 5D 42
Denholme Rd. Roch 3H 21
Denhurst Rd. L'boro 5H 7
Den La. S'head 4D 42
Den La. Upperm 2C 44
Denmark St. Chad 3C 40
Denmark St. Oldh 4A 42
Denmark St. Roch 5A 14
Denmark Way. Chad 3C 40
Denmore Rd. M40 2F 47
Denshaw. 5G 25
Denshaw Rd. Del 2G 33
Densmore St. Fail 6H 47
Denstone Wlk. M9 2A 46
(off Woodmere Dri.)
Denton La. Chad 6A 40
Denton St. Heyw 6G 19
Denton St. Roch 4H 13
Denver Rd. Roch 3H 21
Derby Ct. Oldh 6C 40
Derbyshire Rd. M40 3B 54
Derby St. Chad 2B 48
Derby St. Fail 4A 48
Derby St. Heyw 5F 19
Derby St. Moss 5H 51
Derby St. Oldh 6C 40
Derby St. Roch 2A 22
Derker St. Oldh 3G 41
Derrick Walker Ct. Roch 2F 21

Derry St. *Oldh* 5F **41**
Derwent Av. *Droy* 6C **54**
Derwent Av. *Heyw* 6H **19**
Derwent Av. *Miln* 1H **23**
Derwent Av. *W'fld* 3A **36**
Derwent Clo. *W'fld* 3A **36**
Derwent Dri. *Chad* 4A **40**
Derwent Dri. *L'boro* 3F **15**
Derwent Dri. *Shaw* 1G **31**
Derwent Rd. *Midd* 6A **28**
Derwent St. *Droy* 6B **54**
Derwent St. *Roch* 4H **13**
Derwent Wlk. *Oldh* 4B **42**
Deva Sq. *Oldh* 6C **40**
Devine Clo. *Rytn* 3D **30**
Devon Clo. *Shaw* 2F **31**
Devon Dri. *Dig* 5D **34**
Devonport Cres. *Rytn* 5F **31**
Devon Rd. *Droy* 4E **55**
Devon Rd. *Fail* 1C **54**
Devonshire Clo. *Heyw* 5E **19**
Devonshire Rd. *Roch* 5H **21**
Devonshire St. *Roch* 5H **21**
Devonshire St. E. *Fail* 1B **54**
Devon St. *Oldh* 1B **48**
(in two parts)
Devon St. *Roch* 1H **21**
Dewhirst Rd. *Roch* 1H **13**
(in three parts)
Dewhirst Way. *Roch* 1H **13**
Dewhurst St. *Heyw* 5A **20**
Dew Mdw. Clo. *Roch* 3G **13**
Dew Way. *Oldh* 4D **40**
Dexter Rd. *M9* 6E **37**
Dicken Grn. *Roch* 3H **21**
Dicken Grn. La. *Roch* 3H **21**
Dickens St. *Oldh* 5C **32**
Dickinson St. *Oldh* 4H **41**
Dickins St. *Heyw* 5F **19**
Digby Rd. *Roch* 3H **21**
Dig Ga. La. *Miln* 4D **22**
Diggle 5E 35
Diggle Edge 3G 35
Diggle Mill Cotts. *Dig* 5H **35**
Diggles La. *Roch* 6B **12**
(Arthur Pits)
Diggles La. *Roch* 1A **20**
(Dixon Fold)
Diggle St. *Shaw* 3H **31**
Dillicar Wlk. *M9* 6A **46**
Dilworth Clo. *Heyw* 5D **18**
Dingle Av. *Shaw* 6A **24**
Dingle Dri. *Droy* 4F **55**
Dingle Rd. *Midd* 5A **38**
Dingle Ter. *Ash L* 3H **49**
Dirty La. *Del* 1D **34**
Dirty La. *S'dale* 2F **43**
Dirty Leech. *Whitw* 5H **5**
Disley St. *Roch* 3E **21**
Ditton Mead Clo. *Roch* 3B **14**
Division St. *Roch* 3B **14**
Dixon Closes. *Roch* 6B **12**
Dixon Fold. *Roch* 1A **20**
Dixon St. *M40* 1A **54**
(in two parts)
Dixon St. *Lees* 3C **42**
Dixon St. *Midd* 1C **38**
(in two parts)
Dixon St. *Oldh* 3E **41**
Dixon St. *Roch* 3F **21**
Dobbin Dri. *Roch* 4H **21**
Dob Brook Clo. *M40* 1A **54**
Dobcross 1C 44
Dobcross New Rd. *Dob* 2C **44**
Dobson Ct. *M40* 3A **54**
Doctor Dam Cotts. *Roch* 2G **11**
Doctor Fold La. *Heyw* 3F **27**
Doctor La. *Scout* 2G **43**
Doctor Lane Head 2G 43
Doctor La. Head Cotts. *Oldh* 2G **43**
Dodd Cft. *Roch* 4B **22**
Dodgson St. *Roch* 1A **22**
Dogford Rd. *Rytn* 4D **30**
Dog Hill 2C 32
D'Oliveira Ct. *Midd* 1A **38**
Dollond St. *M9* 4A **46**
Doncaster Wlk. *Oldh* 4F **41**
Donleigh St. *M40* 1B **54**
Donnington. *Roch* 1G **21**
Don St. *Midd* 2E **39**
Dorchester Dri. *Rytn* 1D **40**
Dorchester Gro. *Heyw* 1G **27**
Doris St. *Midd* 1C **38**
Dorset Av. *Dig* 5E **35**
Dorset Av. *Shaw* 2F **31**
Dorset Clo. *Heyw* 6E **19**
Dorset Rd. *Droy* 4D **54**
Dorset Rd. *Fail* 1D **54**
Dorset St. *Oldh* 6C **40**
Dorset St. *Roch* 1H **21**
Dorstone Clo. *M40* 3A **54**
Dorwood Av. *M9* 6G **37**
Douglas Clo. *W'fld* 2A **36**
Douglas Sq. *Heyw* 6D **18**
Douglas St. *M40* 6C **46**
Douglas St. *Fail* 6A **48**
Douglas St. *Oldh* 3G **41**
Douglas Wlk. *W'fld* 2A **36**
Douglas Way. *W'fld* 2A **36**
Doulton St. *M40* 5E **47**
Dovebrook Clo. *Carr* 6A **52**
Dovecote. *Droy* 4H **55**
Dovecote La. *Lees* 4D **42**
Dovedale Av. *Droy* 5C **54**
Dovedale Ct. Midd 1A 38
(off Grisdale Dri.)
Dovedale Dri. *Ward* 5D **6**
Dovedale St. *Fail* 6G **47**
Dove Dri. *Bury* 3A **18**
Dover St. *Oldh* 6C **40**
Dover St. *Roch* 3B **14**
Dove Stone 2G 53
Dovestone Wlk. *M40* 4G **47**
Dove St. *Oldh* 5A **42**
Dove St. *Roch* 6F **13**
Dowling St. *Roch* 1H **21**
Downham Clo. *Rytn* 1C **40**
Downham Rd. *Heyw* 5E **19**
Downhill Clo. *Oldh* 2E **41**
Downley Clo. *Roch* 3D **12**
Downs, The. *Midd* 5D **38**
(in two parts)
Dowry Pk. Estates. *Oldh* 4C **42**
Dowry Rd. *Lees* 4C **42**
Dowry St. *Oldh* 2F **49**
Doyle Clo. *Oldh* 5C **32**
Drake Clo. *Oldh* 3F **41**
Drake Rd. *L'boro* 2A **8**
Drake St. *Roch* 6H **13**
Drayfields. *Droy* 5H **55**
Drefus Av. *M11* 5A **54**
Dresden St. *M40* 5E **47**
DR. KERSHAW'S HOSPICE 6F **31**
Droughts La. *P'wich* 3B **36**
Droylsden 6E 55
Droylsden Rd. *M40* 1A **54**
Droylsden Rd. *Aud* 6F **55**
Droylsden Swimming Pool 6E 55
Drury La. *Chad* 2A **48**
Dry Clough La. *Upperm* 4C **44**
Dryclough Wlk. *Rytn* 6E **31**
Dry Cft. La. *Dig* 2D **34**
Drygate Wlk. M9 6A 46
(off Bentworth Wlk.)
Drymoss. *Oldh* 4G **49**
Duchess Pk. Clo. *Shaw* 1H **31**
Duchess St. *Shaw* 1G **31**
Duchess St. Ind. Est. *Shaw* 1H **31**
Ducie St. *Oldh* 3F **49**
Duckworth St. *Shaw* 2A **32**
Duddon Clo. *W'fld* 3A **36**
(in two parts)
Duddon Wlk. *Midd* 1A **38**
Dudley St. *Oldh* 5B **42**
Duffield Ct. *Midd* 6B **38**
Duffield Gdns. *Midd* 6B **38**
Duffield Rd. *Midd* 6B **38**
Duffins Clo. *Roch* 2F **13**
Dufton Wlk. *Midd* 1A **38**
Dugdale Av. *M9* 1A **46**
Duke St. *Fail* 5A **48**
Duke St. *Heyw* 5F **19**
Duke St. *L'boro* 6G **7**
Duke St. *Moss* 4A **52**
Duke St. *Roch* 4H **13**
(in two parts)
Duke St. *Shaw* 3A **32**
Dulverton St. *M40* 1A **54**
Dumbarton Dri. *Heyw* 6E **19**
Dumfries Av. *Dens* 5G **25**
Dumfries Dri. *Dens* 5G **25**
Dumfries Hollow. *Heyw* 4B **20**
Dumfries Wlk. *Heyw* 6E **19**
Dunbar Gro. *Heyw* 1D **26**
Dunbar St. *Oldh* 3E **41**
Dunblane Gro. *Heyw* 1E **27**
Duncan Edwards Ct. M40 2A 54
(off Mitchell St.)
Duncombe Dri. *M40* 6D **46**
Duncote Gro. *Rytn* 4F **31**
Dundee Clo. *Heyw* 6D **18**
Dundraw Clo. *Midd* 2F **37**
Dunham St. *Lees* 3C **42**
Dunkerley Av. *Fail* 6H **47**
Dunkerley St. *Oldh* 3A **42**
Dunkerley St. *Rytn* 5D **30**
Dunkirk Ri. *Roch* 6G **13**
Dunkirk St. *Droy* 6F **55**
Dunlin Clo. *Roch* 6B **12**
Dunlop Av. *Roch* 4G **21**
Dunmail Dri. *Midd* 6A **28**
Dunoon Clo. *Heyw* 6E **19**
Dunrobin Clo. *Heyw* 1E **27**
Dunsford Ct. *S'head* 6D **42**
Dunsley Av. *M40* 3F **47**
Dunstable. Roch 5H 13
(off Redcross St.)
Dunstan Ct. *M40* 5C **46**
Dunster Av. *M9* 1A **46**
Dunster Av. *Roch* 2G **21**
Dunsterville Ter. Roch 2G 21
(off New Barn La.)
Dunvegan Ct. *Heyw* 6C **18**
Dunwood Av. *Shaw* 1A **32**
Dunwood Pk. Courts. *Shaw* 6A **24**
Durban Clo. *Shaw* 3G **31**
Durban St. *Oldh* 2C **48**
Durban St. *Roch* 5E **21**
Durden M. *Shaw* 3H **31**
Durham Cres. *Fail* 1E **55**
Durham Dri. *Ash L* 5B **50**
Durhams Pas. *L'boro* 6G **7**
Durham St. *M9* 6A **46**
Durham St. *Droy* 6E **55**
Durham St. *Oldh* 1C **48**
(in two parts)
Durham St. *Roch* 1H **21**
Durham St. Bri. *Roch* 2A **22**
Durham Wlk. *Heyw* 5E **19**
Durn 5A 8
Durnford Clo. *Roch* 3H **11**
Durnford St. *Midd* 2B **38**
Durnlaw Clo. *L'boro* 6A **8**
Durn St. *L'boro* 5A **8**
Durrington Wlk. M40 2E 47
(off Moston La.)
Duxbury Dri. *Bury* 5A **18**
Duxford Wlk. *M40* 2E **47**
Dye Ho. La. *Roch* 2C **14**
Dyers Ct. *L'boro* 5G **7**
Dymchurch St. *M40* 3A **54**
Dysarts Clo. *Moss* 2A **52**
Dyson Gro. *Lees* 3D **42**
Dyson St. *Moss* 3F **51**
Dyson St. *Oldh* 5F **41**

E

Eafield Av. *Miln* 6F **15**
Eafield Clo. *Miln* 6F **15**
Eafield Rd. *L'boro* 2E **15**
Eafield Rd. *Roch* 4C **14**
Eagar St. *M40* 1A **54**
Eagle Ct. *Del* 4A **34**
Eagle St. *Oldh* 4E **41**
Eagle St. *Roch* 1A **22**
Eagle Technology Pk. *Roch* 3A **22**
Eagle Way. *Roch* 3A **22**
Ealees 6A 8
Ealees. *L'boro* 6A **8**
Ealees Rd. *L'boro* 6A **8**
Eamont Wlk. *M9* 6A **46**
Earby Gro. *M9* 2B **46**
Earls Lodge. *Fail* 1B **54**
Earl St. *Heyw* 5G **19**
Earl St. *Moss* 4F **51**
Earl St. *Roch* 1E **29**
Earl's Way. *Fail* 1B **54**
Earnshaw Av. *Roch* 2G **13**
Easby Rd. *Midd* 6B **28**
Easington Wlk. *M40* 6C **46**
Eastbourne St. *Oldh* 1H **49**
Eastbourne St. *Roch* 2H **21**
E. Church Way. *Heyw* 2B **28**
East Cres. *Midd* 4B **38**
East Dri. *Bury* 5A **26**
Easterdale. *Oldh* 5A **42**
Eastern By-Pass. *M11* 6B **54**
(Crabtree La.)
Eastern By-Pass. *M11* 5A **54**
(Stanton St.)
Eastfield Av. *Midd* 4C **38**
E. Garth Wlk. *M9* 2A **46**
Eastgate. *Whitw* 4E **5**
E. Gate St. *Roch* 5H **13**
E. Grange Av. *M11* 4A **54**
Easthaven Av. *M11* 4A **54**
E. Hill St. *Oldh* 5G **41**
Eastlands Rd. *M9* 6H **37**
Eastmoor Dri. *M40* 3B **54**
Easton Clo. *Midd* 5E **39**
Easton Rd. *Droy* 5C **54**
East St. *Fir* 6D **14**
(in two parts)
East St. *L'boro* 6A **8**
East St. *Roch* 5A **14**
(in two parts)
East St. *Ward* 5C **6**
East Vw. *Midd* 3B **38**
Eastway. *Midd* 2B **38**
Eastway. *Shaw* 3H **31**
Eastwood Av. *M40* 4H **47**
Eastwood Av. *Droy* 6C **54**
Eastwood Rd. *M40* 4G **47**
Eastwood St. *L'boro* 6H **7**
Eaves La. *Chad* 6A **40**
Ebor Clo. *Shaw* 1G **31**
Ebor St. *L'boro* 6H **7**
Ebsworth St. *M40* 5B **46**
Eccleshall St. *M11* 6A **54**
(in three parts)
Eccleston St. *Fail* 5A **48**
Eclipse Clo. *Roch* 6C **14**
Edale Av. *M40* 5C **46**
Eddie Colman Clo. *M40* 2A **54**
Eden Clo. *Heyw* 4F **19**
Edenfield Rd. *Roch* 1B **10**
Edenfield St. *Roch* 4E **13**
Edenham Wlk. *M40* 3F **47**
Eden St. *Oldh* 4E **41**
Eden St. *Roch* 5F **13**
Eden Way. *Shaw* 1G **31**
Edgar St. *Roch* 3C **14**
Edge End. *Dob* 6C **34**
Edgefield Av. *M9* 1A **46**
Edge Hill Av. *Rytn* 1E **41**
Edge Hill Rd. *Rytn* 6E **31**
Edge La. *Droy & M11* 5B **54**
Edge La. Rd. *Oldh* 3F **41**
Edge La. St. *Rytn* 5E **31**
Edgemoor Clo. *Oldh* 2B **42**
Edgemoor Dri. *Roch* 2B **20**
Edge, The 3C 48
Edge Vw. *Chad* 2G **39**
Edgeware Rd. *Chad* 2G **47**
Edgworth Clo. *Heyw* 5E **19**
Edinburgh Way. *Roch* 3F **21**
Edington. Roch 5H 13
(off Redcross St.)
Edith Cavell Clo. *Open* 6A **54**
Edith Cliff Wlk. *M40* 4H **47**
Edith St. *Oldh* 2F **49**
Edlingham. *Roch* 1G **21**
Edlington Wlk. *M40* 1A **54**
Edmonds St. *Midd* 2D **38**
Edmunds Fold. *L'boro* 5F **7**
Edmunds Pas. *L'boro* 4G **7**
Edmund St. *Droy* 6E **55**
Edmund St. *Fail* 5H **47**
Edmund St. *Miln* 1F **23**
Edmund St. *Roch* 5F **13**
Edmund St. *Shaw* 2A **32**
Edward Av. *L'boro* 2F **15**
Edward Grant Ct. M9 4A 46
(off Hemsley St. S.)
Edward M. *Oldh* 6C **40**
Edward Rd. *M9* 6H **37**
Edward Rd. *Shaw* 3G **31**
Edward St. *M9* 5A **46**
Edward St. *Chad* 4A **40**
Edward St. *Droy* 6E **55**
Edward St. *Midd* 1C **38**
Edward St. *Oldh* 5C **40**
Edward St. *Roch* 5A **14**
Edward St. *Ward* 1D **14**
Edward St. *Whitw* 1F **5**
Edwin Waugh Gdns. *Roch* 3F **13**
Edzell Wlk. *Open* 6A **54**
Egbert St. *M40* 6C **46**
Egerton Clo. *Heyw* 6H **19**
Egerton Cres. *Heyw* 6G **19**
Egerton Pl. *Shaw* 3G **31**
Egerton St. *Droy* 6F **55**
Egerton St. *Heyw* 6G **19**
Egerton St. *L'boro* 6A **8**
Egerton St. *Midd* 4G **37**
Egerton St. *Moss* 3G **51**
Egerton St. *Oldh* 4F **41**
Egmont St. *Moss* 5G **51**

Egremont Rd. Miln 3E 23
Egypt La. P'wich 2B 36
Eighth Av. Oldh 4D 48
Elaine Av. M9 3D 46
Elbain Wlk. M40 2A 54
Elbow La. Roch 1A 22
Elbut La. Bury 2D 18
Elderberry Clo. Dig 4E 35
Elder Gro. M40 3H 47
Elder Rd. Lees 5C 42
Elder St. Roch 2B 22
Elderwood. Chad 4G 39
Eldon Precinct. Oldh 6E 41
Eldon St. Oldh 6F 41
Eleanor Rd. Rytn 1E 41
Eleanor St. Oldh 3D 40
Elgin Rd. Oldh 6A 42
Elgin St. Roch 2A 22
Elgol Ct. Heyw 6E 19
Elim St. L'boro 4A 8
Elim Ter. L'boro 4A 8
Eliot Wlk. Midd 6E 29
Eli St. Chad 2A 48
Elizabethan Way. Miln 1F 23
Elizabeth Av. Chad 2A 48
Elizabeth Av. Rytn 6C 30
Elizabeth Gro. Shaw 2H 31
Elizabeth St. Heyw 5G 19
Elizabeth St. L'boro 1E 15
Elizabeth St. Roch 4E 21
Elk Mill Central Retail Pk.
Rytn 1B 40
Ellenroad App. Miln 3G 23
Ellenroad St. Miln 3G 23
Ellenrod Dri. Roch 3C 12
Ellenrod La. Roch 3C 12
Ellenshaw Clo. Roch 3C 12
Ellens Pl. L'boro 2F 15
Ellen St. Droy 6F 55
Ellen St. Oldh 3D 40
Elleray Rd. Midd 6B 38
Ellesmere Av. Ash L 6A 50
Ellesmere St. Fail 5H 47
Ellesmere St. Roch 2H 21
Elliot Sq. Oldh 3G 41
Elliott St. Lees 5C 42
Elliott St. Roch 5A 14
Ellis Fold. Roch 3A 12
Ellisland Wlk. M40 6C 46
Ellis La. Midd 3F 37
Ellon Wlk. Open 6A 54
Elly Clough. Rytn 6C 30
Elmbank Rd. Midd 3E 39
Elmbridge Wlk. M40 6C 46
Elm Gro. Droy 5B 54
Elm Gro. G'ton 5F 43
Elm Gro. Miln 4G 23
Elm Gro. Roch 2G 21
Elm Gro. Ward 6C 6
Elmore Wood. L'boro 5E 7
Elm Pk. Ga. Roch 2D 12
Elm Pk. Gro. Roch 2D 12
Elm Pk. Va. Roch 2D 12
Elm Pk. Vw. Roch 2D 12
Elm Pk. Way. Roch 2D 12
Elm Rd. Oldh 4D 48
Elmsdale Av. M9 6H 37
Elmsfield Av. Roch 4A 12
Elms, The. L'boro 1E 15
Elms, The. Moss 4F 51
Elm St. Fail 5H 47
Elm St. Heyw 5H 19
Elm St. L'boro 3F 15
Elm St. Midd 2E 39
Elm St. Roch 4H 13
Elm St. Whitw 1F 5
Elmton Rd. M9 2A 46
Elm Tree Clo. Fail 6B 48
Elmwood Dri. Rytn 4C 30
Elmwood Gro. M9 6B 46
Elrick Wlk. Open 6A 54
Elsie St. M9 5A 46
Elsinore Clo. Fail 6B 48
Elsma Rd. M40 3C 54
Elsted Rd. G'fld 6A 44
Elstree Av. M40 3A 54
Elton St. Roch 6E 21
Elverston Way. Chad 3C 40
Elvira Clo. Fail 6B 48
Ely Cres. Fail 2D 54
Ely St. Chad 6B 40
Ember St. M11 5B 54
Emerson Dri. Midd 2B 38
Emily Beavan Clo. M11 6A 54
Emily Pl. Droy 6D 54
Emma St. Oldh 2F 49
Emma St. Roch 5G 13
Emmott Clo. Heyw 5G 19
Emmott St. Oldh 5F 41
Ena St. Oldh 2A 42
Enderby Rd. M40 4E 47
Ending Rake. Whitw 1E 13
Enfield Av. Oldh 2E 49
Enfield Clo. Roch 5A 12
Enfield Dri. M11 5A 54
Engine St. Chad 1B 48
Ennerdale Av. Rytn 2C 30
Ennerdale Rd. Midd 1B 38
Ennerdale Rd. Roch 3D 20
Enstone Dri. M40 4F 47
Entron Ho. Shaw 2F 31
Entwisle Rd. Roch 5A 14
Entwisle St. Miln 1E 23
Enville Rd. M40 4D 46
Epping Clo. Ash L 6A 50
Epping Clo. Chad 3G 39
Epsom Clo. Roch 5B 12
Epsom Wlk. Chad 4C 40
Equitable St. Miln 2F 23
Equitable St. Oldh 3B 42
Equitable St. Roch 1A 22
Erica Av. Oldh 5D 32
Eric St. L'boro 5G 7
Eric St. Oldh 4A 42
Erith Rd. Oldh 5A 42
Erlesmere Clo. Oldh 5D 32
Ermington Ct. Heyw 6G 19
Ernest Ter. Roch 4B 14
Errol Av. M9 6E 37
Erskine Rd. M9 6A 38
Eskdale Av. G'fld 6D 44
Eskdale Av. Oldh 1D 48
Eskdale Av. Roch 4D 20
Eskdale Av. Rytn 2D 30
Eskdale Dri. Midd 6B 28
Eskdale M. G'fld 6D 44
Esmont Dri. Midd 6A 28
Esplanade, The. Roch 6G 13
Essex Av. Bury 6C 18
Essex Av. Droy 4E 55
Essex Clo. Fail 2D 54
Essex Clo. Shaw 2F 31
Essex St. Roch 1H 21
Estate St. Oldh 1F 49
Estate St. S. Oldh 1F 49
Esther St. L'boro 6F 7
(off Featherstall Rd.)
Esther St. Oldh 4B 42
Eswick St. M11 6A 54
Ethel Av. M9 6H 37
Ethel Ct. Roch 1B 22
Ethel St. Oldh 2F 49
Ethel St. Roch 1B 22
Ethel St. Whitw 1F 5
Etherow Gro. M40 3H 47
Eton Av. Oldh 2E 49
Eton Clo. Roch 1D 20
Eustace St. Chad 2B 40
Euston Av. M9 2C 46
Evans St. Midd 3D 38
Evans St. Oldh 3F 41
Evanton Wlk. M9 6A 46
(off Nethervale Dri.)
Eva St. Roch 3A 14
Evelyn St. Oldh 2H 41
Evening St. Fail 5H 47
Everdingen Wlk. Oldh 6B 32
Everest St. Roch 5A 22
Everglade. Oldh 4G 49
Everton Rd. Oldh 1D 48
Evesham Clo. Midd 6D 38
Evesham Gdns. Midd 6C 38
Evesham Gro. Ash L 6A 50
Evesham Rd. M9 3C 46
Evesham Rd. Midd 6C 38
Evesham Wlk. Midd 6D 38
Evesham Wlk. Oldh 6E 41
Eve St. Oldh 3F 49
Ewood. Oldh 5G 49
Exbridge Wlk. M40 3B 54
Exbury. Roch 5G 13
(off Falinge Rd.)
Excelsior Ter. L'boro 2F 15
(off Barke St.)
Exchange St. Oldh 4H 41
Exeter Ct. Midd 2B 38
Exeter Dri. Ash L 6B 50
Exeter Gro. Roch 2H 21
Exeter St. Roch 2H 21
Exmoor Clo. Ash L 6A 50
Exmouth Pl. Roch 3A 22
Exmouth Sq. Roch 4A 22
Exmouth St. Roch 4A 22

F

Facit 1F 5
Factory Brow. Midd 4G 37
Factory La. M9 5A 46
Factory St. Midd 3B 38
Failsworth 6H 47
Failsworth Ind. Est. Fail 1A 54
Failsworth Rd. Fail 6B 48
Failsworth Shop. Precinct.
Fail 6H 47
Failsworth Sports Cen. 6A 48
Fairbank Dri. Midd 1H 37
Fairbottom St. Oldh 4F 41
Fairbottom Wlk. Droy 6E 55
Fairfax Dri. L'boro 2F 15
Fairfield 4B 18
Fairfield. Ash L 5H 49
Fairfield Dri. Bury 4B 18
FAIRFIELD GENERAL HOSPITAL.
3C 18
Fairfield Ho. Droy 6E 55
(off Manchester Rd.)
Fairfield Rd. Midd 2A 38
Fairfields. Oldh 3E 49
Fairlands Pl. Roch 5B 22
Fairlands St. Roch 5B 22
Fairlands Vw. Roch 5B 22
Fairlee Av. Aud 6G 55
Fair Vw. L'boro 4A 8
Fairview Clo. Chad 3G 39
Fairview Clo. Roch 3G 11
Fairway. Miln 1G 23
Fair Way. Roch 6D 20
Fairway. Whitw 4E 5
Fairway Cres. Rytn 3D 30
Fairway Rd. Oldh 1C 50
Fairway, The. M40 6E 47
Falcon Clo. Roch 3H 11
Falcon Dri. Chad 3C 40
Falcon Dri. Midd 6A 28
Falcon Enterprise Cen. Chad 3C 40
Falcon St. Oldh 6E 41
Falcon's Vw. Oldh 2E 49
Falinge Fold. Roch 4F 13
Falinge M. Roch 5G 13
Falinge Rd. Roch 4F 13
Falkirk St. Oldh 4A 42
Falkland Av. Roch 5E 13
Falkland Clo. Oldh 5C 32
Fallowfield Dri. Roch 3F 13
Fallows, The. Chad 6A 40
Falmouth St. Oldh 1F 49
Falmouth St. Roch 2A 22
Falside Wlk. M40 2A 54
Falston Av. M40 3F 47
Faraday Ri. Roch 4D 12
Fardale. Shaw 3H 31
Farewell Clo. Roch 5E 21
Fargner St. M11 6B 54
Farholme. Rytn 1C 40
Faringdon. Roch 1G 21
Farlands Ri. Roch 4C 22
Farm La. P'wich 3C 36
Farm Rd. Oldh 5C 48
Farmstead Clo. Fail 1G 55
Farm St. Chad 2B 40
Farm St. Fail 1B 54
Farm St. Heyw 1A 28
Farm Wlk. L'boro 6F 7
Farm Wlk. Roch 4C 14
Farmway. Midd 4C 38
Farnborough Av. Oldh 5B 42
Farndale Wlk. M9 5A 46
(off Up. Conran St.)
Farnham Av. M9 6H 37
Farnley Clo. Roch 3B 12
Farnworth St. Heyw 5G 19
Farrand Rd. Oldh 3B 48
Farrar Rd. Droy 6D 54
Farriers La. Roch 3D 20
Farrowdale Av. Shaw 3H 31
Farrow St. Shaw 3H 31
(in two parts)
Farrow St. E. Shaw 3H 31
(off Market St.)
Fatherford Clo. Dig 4F 35
Faulkenhurst M. Chad 2C 40
Faulkenhurst St. Chad 2C 40
Faulkner St. Roch 6H 13
Faversham Brow. Oldh 3E 41
Faversham St. M40 6D 46
Faversham St. Oldh 3E 41
Fay Av. M9 3D 46
Fearn St. Heyw 5G 19
Featherstall Ho. Oldh 6C 40
(off Featherstall Rd. S.)
Featherstall Rd. L'boro 6F 7
Featherstall Rd. N. Oldh 4D 40
Featherstall Rd. S. Oldh 6C 40
Featherstall Sq. L'boro 6G 7
Fellside. Oldh 4E 41
Fellside Gdns. L'boro 4F 7
Felltop Ct. Lyd 6G 43
Fenchurch Av. M40 3A 54
Fenny Hill 1H 49
Fenstock Wlk. M40 3B 54
Fenton M. Roch 2G 21
Fenton St. Oldh 5H 41
Fenton St. Roch 2G 21
Fenton St. Shaw 4H 31
Fenwick St. Roch 6G 13
Ferguson Gdns. Roch 2H 13
Ferguson Way. Oldh 2B 42
Fern Clo. Midd 3F 39
Fern Clo. S'head 5D 42
Fernclough Rd. M9 6A 46
Fern Comn. Shaw 2H 31
Fern Cottage. G'ton 6E 43
Ferndale Av. Roch 1C 30
Ferndale Clo. Oldh 1B 50
Ferndene. Roch 3D 12
Ferndene Rd. W'fld & P'wich 4A 36
Ferndown Av. Chad 4F 39
Ferney Fld. Rd. Chad 4H 39
Fern Grove 3A 18
Ferngrove. Bury 2A 18
(Bullfinch Dri.)
Ferngrove. Bury 3A 18
(Kingfisher Dri.)
Fernhill. Oldh 1B 50
Fern Hill La. Roch 2C 12
Fernholme Ct. Oldh 1C 48
Fernhurst St. Chad 2C 40
Fern Isle Clo. Whitw 5D 4
Fernlea Av. Chad 2C 40
Fernlea Clo. Roch 3D 12
Fernside Way. Roch 4C 12
Fern St. Chad 3A 40
Fern St. Oldh 6D 40
Fern St. Roch 1F 21
Fern St. Ward 5C 6
Fernthorpe Av. Upperm 2E 45
Ferrand Lodge. L'boro 4A 8
Ferrand Rd. L'boro 5H 7
Ferring Wlk. Chad 5B 40
Fieldcroft. Roch 6D 12
Fielden St. L'boro 3E 15
Fieldfare Av. M40 3A 54
Fieldfare Way. Ash L 6G 49
Fieldhead Av. Roch 6D 12
Fieldhouse Ind. Est. Roch 3H 13
Fieldhouse Rd. Roch 3H 13
Fielding St. Midd 1C 38
(in two parts)
Field Rd. Roch 6D 14
Fields New Rd. Chad 1A 48
Field St. Fail 6G 47
Field St. Roch 3A 22
Fieldsway. Oldh 3E 49
Fieldway. Roch 4B 22
Fife Av. Chad 1H 47
Fifield Clo. Oldh 2G 49
Fifth Av. M11 5A 54
Fifth Av. Bury 3B 18
Fifth Av. Oldh 3C 48
Filbert St. Oldh 2A 42
Fildes St. Midd 4F 39
Filey St. Roch 2C 14
Finance St. L'boro 1F 15
Finchcroft. Oldh 4E 41
Finchley Av. M40 3A 54
Finchley Gro. M40 4C 46
Finlan Rd. Midd 4F 29
Finningley Rd. M9 5F 37
Finsbury Av. M40 3A 54
Finsbury Clo. Oldh 1H 49
Finsbury St. Roch 2F 21
Fir Bank Rd. Rytn 3D 30
Firbarn Clo. Fir 6D 14
Fircroft Rd. Oldh 3G 49
Firdale Av. M40 4G 47
Firdale Wlk. Chad 4C 40
Firdon Wlk. M9 6A 46
(off Nethervale Dri.)

Fire Sta. Yd. Roch 1H 21
Firgrove. 6D 14
Fir Gro. Chad 3B 40
Firgrove Av. Roch 5D 14
Firgrove Bus. Pk. Miln 4D 14
Firgrove Gdns. Roch 5D 14
Fir La. Rytn 3D 30
Firs Av. Fail 6G 47
First Av. M11 5B 54
First Av. Oldh 3D 48
Fir St. Fail 6G 47
Fir St. Heyw 6A 20
Fir St. Rytn 3D 30
Firswood Dri. Rytn 3C 30
Firth St. Oldh 5F 41
Fir Tree Av. Oldh 3F 49
Firwood Pk. Chad 4G 39
Fiscall Way. Fail 6G 47
Fisherfield. Roch 4B 12
Fisher St. Oldh 3F 41
Fishwick St. Roch 1A 22
Fitness First Club 2E 47 (Manchester)
Fitness First Club 3G 21 (Rochdale)
Fitton Hill 3H 49
Fitton Hill Rd. Oldh 1G 49
Fitton Hill Shop. Precinct. Oldh 3G 49
Fitton St. Roch 5A 14
Fitton St. Rytn 5F 31
Fitton St. Shaw 2F 31
Five Fold Ind. Pk. Oldh 5D 40
Fiveways. Droy 5E 55
Flake La. Rytn 4D 30
Flannel St. Roch 5A 14
Flash St. M40 1A 54
Flaxman Ri. Oldh 5A 32
Fleece St. Oldh 4H 41
Fleece St. Roch 6H 13
Fleet St. Oldh 4A 42
Fleet St. Roch 1F 29
Fleming Clo. Roch 6D 6
Fleming Pl. Oldh 5D 40
Fletcher Clo. Heyw 6H 19
Fletcher Clo. Oldh 5D 40
Fletchers Pas. L'boro 5G 7
Fletcher's Rd. L'boro 2E 15
Fletchers Sq. L'boro 5H 7 (off Sutcliffe St.)
Fletcher St. L'boro 5G 7
Fletcher St. Roch 2A 22
Fletton Clo. Roch 3G 13
Flexbury Wlk. M40 3B 54
Flint Clo. M11 5A 54
Flint St. Droy 5F 55
Flint St. Oldh 3A 42
Flora St. Oldh 4E 41
Florence St. Droy 6F 55
Florence St. Fail 5H 47
Florence St. Roch 1B 22
Florida St. Oldh 6E 41
Flower Hill La. Ward 5A 6
Flowery Bank. Oldh 1H 49
Floyer Rd. M9 6A 38
Fold Av. Droy 5F 55
Fold Gdns. Roch 2D 12
Fold Grn. Chad 5A 40
Fold Head 3D 4
Fold St. M40 5C 46
Fold St. Heyw 4A 20
Fold, The. Rytn 5G 31
Fold Vw. Oldh 3G 49
Foleshill Av. M9 6A 46
Foley Gdns. Heyw 2A 28
Folkestone Rd. M11 5B 54
Folkestone Rd. E. M11 5B 54
Folkestone Rd. W. M11 4A 54
Folly Wlk. Roch 4H 13 (in three parts)
Fontwell La. Oldh 2G 41
Fontwell Wlk. M40 3F 47
Foot Mill Cres. Roch 3F 13
Foot Wood Cres. Roch 3F 13
Ford Gdns. Roch 1D 20
Fordoe La. Roch 1G 11
Forest St. Oldh 3F 49
Forest Vw. Roch 3F 13
Forge Ind. Est. Oldh 4H 41
Forge St. Oldh 4H 41
Forrester Dri. Shaw 1B 32
Forsyth St. Roch 3A 12
Foster Ct. Bury 3B 18
Foster St. Oldh 4A 42
Foundry St. Heyw 5G 19
Foundry St. Oldh 5E 41
Fountain St. Midd 3B 38
Fountain St. Oldh 4E 41
Fountains Wlk. Chad 6A 40
Four Lanes Way. Roch 4G 11
Four Stalls End. L'boro 6G 7
Fourth Av. M11 4A 54
Fourth Av. Bury 3B 18
Fourth Av. Chad 6A 40
Fourth Av. Oldh 4C 48
Fourways Wlk. M40 3D 46
Fowler St. Oldh 2C 48
Foxall Clo. Midd 4G 37
Foxall St. Midd 4G 37
Foxcroft St. L'boro 6F 7
Foxdale St. M11 6A 54
Foxdenton La. Midd & Chad 5G 39
Foxfield Dri. Oldh 4C 48
Foxglove Ct. Roch 2F 13
Foxglove Dri. Bury 4B 18
Foxhill. Shaw 1E 31
Fox Hill Rd. Roch 1F 29
Foxholes Clo. Roch 4A 14
Foxholes Rd. Roch 4A 14
Foxley Clo. Droy 6C 54
Fox Pk. Rd. Oldh 3C 48
Fox Platt 5G 51
Fox Platt Rd. Moss 4F 51
Fox Platt Ter. Moss 5G 51
Fox St. Heyw 5G 19
Fox St. Miln 1E 23
Fox St. Oldh 3C 48
Fox St. Roch 5B 14
Foxton St. Midd 4G 37
Foxwood Dri. Moss 3H 51
Frampton Clo. Midd 4D 38
Fram St. M9 5B 46
Frances St. Oldh 2G 41 (in two parts)
Frances St. Roch 2D 14
Francis St. Fail 6H 47
Frank Fold. Heyw 5E 19
Franklin Av. Droy 6E 55
Franklin Clo. Oldh 3E 41
Franklin St. Oldh 3E 41
Franklin St. Roch 2B 22
Franklin Ter. L'boro 6G 7 (off William St.)
Frank St. Fail 6G 47
Franton Rd. M11 5A 54
Fraser St. Roch 3B 22
Fraser St. Shaw 1G 31
Fraternitas Ter. Droy 4C 54
Frederick Av. Shaw 4H 31
Frederick St. Chad 3B 40
Frederick St. L'boro 5G 7
Frederick St. Oldh 6C 40
Freehold St. Roch 2G 21
Freetrade St. Roch 2G 21
French Av. Oldh 2A 42
Frenches 5D 44
Fresca Rd. Oldh 5B 32
Freshfield Av. P'wich 5A 36
Freshfield Clo. Fail 1E 55
Freshfield Wlk. M11 5A 54
Freshwinds Ct. Oldh 1B 50
Frew Clo. M40 3D 46
Friarmere Rd. Del 4A 34
Friars Cres. Roch 5H 21
Frieston. Roch 5H 13 (off Redcross St.)
Friezland 6C 44
Friezland La. G'fld 2C 52
Frinton Av. M40 2F 47
Frobisher Rd. L'boro 2A 8
Frome St. Oldh 5A 42
Frost St. Oldh 1E 49
Fulham St. Oldh 5A 42
Full Pot La. Roch 5A 12
Fullwood 3A 32
Fulmar Gdns. Roch 6B 12
Fulton's Ct. Lees 6C 42
Fulwood Av. M9 1B 46
Furbarn La. Roch 5H 11
Furbarn Rd. Roch 6H 11 (in two parts)
Fur Lane 5E 45
Furness Av. Heyw 4G 19
Furness Av. L'boro 5G 7
Furness Av. Oldh 2A 50
Furness Clo. Miln 1E 23
Furness Rd. Midd 6B 28
Further Fld. Roch 4H 11
Further Heights Rd. Roch 3H 13
Further Hey Clo. Lees 4C 42
Further Pits. Roch 6E 13
Furtherwood Rd. Oldh 2C 40
Furzegate. Roch 4C 22
Furze La. Oldh 2B 42 (in two parts)

G

Gable Dri. Midd 2A 38
Gabriels Ter. Midd 4E 39
Gabriels, The. Shaw 2F 31
Gail Clo. Fail 2C 54
Gainford Gdns. M40 4D 46
Gainsboro Rd. Aud 6H 55
Gainsborough Av. Oldh 1E 49
Gainsborough Dri. Roch 4G 21
Gainsborough Rd. Chad 2G 39
Galbraith Way. Roch 5A 12
Gale 4A 8
Gale Dri. Midd 1H 37
Gales Ter. Roch 2G 21 (off New Barn La.)
Gale St. Heyw 5F 19
Gale St. Roch 2H 13
Galland St. Oldh 4B 42
Galloway Clo. Heyw 6D 18
Galway St. Oldh 5F 41
Game St. Oldh 6A 42
Gamma Wlk. M11 5A 54
Gandy La. Roch 1E 13
Garbrook Av. M9 6G 37
Garden Av. Droy 5F 55
Garden Clo. L'boro 2F 15
Garden Ct. Roch 5C 14
Gardenfold Ho. Droy 5F 55 (off Fold Av.)
Garden La. Roch 5A 14
Garden M. L'boro 6H 7 (off Industry St.)
Garden Row. Heyw 3F 19
Garden Row. Roch 3F 13
Garden St. Heyw 4G 19
Garden St. Miln 3H 23
Garden St. Oldh 4G 41
Garden St. S'head 6D 42
Garden Ter. Rytn 2C 30
Garden Way. L'boro 3F 15
Garfield Clo. Roch 5A 12
Garforth Cres. Droy 4F 55
Garforth St. Chad 4C 40
Gargrave St. Oldh 5H 41
Garlick St. Oldh 5E 41 (in two parts)
Garnant Clo. M9 5B 46
Garnet St. Oldh 3H 41
Garrett Gro. Shaw 2A 32
Garrowmore Wlk. M9 2A 46
Garthwaite Av. Oldh 2E 49
Gartside St. Del 5A 34
Gartside St. Oldh 6H 41
Gaskell Clo. L'boro 5G 7
Gaskell Ri. Oldh 4C 32
Gaskell St. M40 2A 54
Gaskell Swimming Pool 4G 19
Gaskill St. Heyw 5E 19
Gas St. Heyw 5H 19
Gas St. Roch 6G 13
Gaston Wlk. M9 6H 37 (off Eastlands Rd.)
Gatehead Cft. Del 6B 34
Gatehead M. Del 6B 34
Gatehead Rd. Del 1B 44
Gate Keeper Fold. Ash L 6G 49
Gatesgarth Rd. Midd 1G 37
Gateside Wlk. M9 6A 38 (off Brockford Dri.)
Gate St. Roch 2H 21
Gateway Cres. Chad 6F 39
Gatley Brow. Oldh 3E 41
Gavel Wlk. Midd 2A 38
Gawsworth Clo. Shaw 2F 31
Gawsworth Ct. M9 6E 37 (off Deanswood Dri.)
Gayford Wlk. M9 6A 38 (off Brockford Dri.)
Gayton Wlk. M40 3F 47
Gee La. Oldh 3B 48
Gelder Clough Cvn. Pk. Heyw 2G 19
Gellfield La. Upperm 2F 45
Generation Cen., The. Roch 6G 13
Geneva Ter. Roch 5E 13
Geneva Wlk. Chad 5C 40
Geoff Bent Wlk. M40 2A 54
George Sq. Oldh 5E 41
George St. Chad 4A 40
George St. Fail 5H 47
George St. Fir 6E 15
George St. Heyw 4F 19
George St. L'boro 5H 7
George St. Moss 3G 51
George St. Oldh 5E 41
George St. Roch 5A 14
George St. Shaw 6A 24
George St. Smal 2D 14
George St. Whitw 4E 5
Germain Clo. M9 6G 37
Gerrard St. Roch 5A 22
Gibraltar St. Oldh 6B 42
Gibson St. Oldh 5A 42
Gibson St. Roch 5C 14
Gifford Av. M9 1B 46
Gilbrook Way. Roch 5B 22
Gildenhall. Fail 6A 48
Gilden Wlk. M9 6A 38
Gilderdale Clo. Shaw 1H 31
Gildersdale Dri. M9 5F 37
Gillemere Gro. Shaw 2A 32
Gillford Av. M9 4B 46
Gill St. M9 5B 46
Gilmerton Dri. M40 2A 54
Gilmore Dri. P'wich 6A 36
Gilmour St. Midd 3C 38
Gilmour Ter. M9 4B 46 (in two parts)
Gilpin Wlk. Midd 2A 38
Gilwood Gro. Midd 5B 28
Gipsy La. Roch 4E 21 (in two parts)
Girton Wlk. M40 4F 47
Girvan Av. M40 3F 47
Girvan Wlk. Heyw 6D 18
Gisburn Dri. Roch 4A 22
Gisburne Av. M40 3F 47
Givvons Fold. Oldh 2B 42
Glade Brow. G'ton 5E 43
Glade Wood Dri. Fail 5B 48
Gladstone Cres. Roch 4H 21
Gladstone Ho. Roch 5C 6
Gladstone St. Oldh 5H 41
Gladstone Ter. Rd. G'fld 1C 52
Glaisdale. Oldh 5B 42
Glamis Av. M11 4A 54
Glamis Av. Heyw 1A 28
Glamorgan Pl. Oldh 6C 40
Glanton Wlk. M40 4F 47
Glasson Wlk. Chad 5A 40
Glastonbury. Roch 5G 13 (off Redcross St.)
Glazebrook Clo. Heyw 6G 19
Glazedale Av. Rytn 5C 30
Glaze Wlk. W'fld 1A 36
Glebe Ho. Midd 1C 38 (off Rochdale Rd.)
Glebelands Rd. E. P'wich 6A 36
Glebe La. Oldh 5C 32
Glebe St. Chad 2A 48
Glebe St. Shaw 2H 31
Gledhill Clo. Shaw 6G 23
Glen Av. M9 4A 46
Glenavon Dri. Roch 2F 13
Glenavon Dri. Shaw 1F 31
Glenbrook Rd. M9 6E 37
Glenby Est. Chad 5C 40
Glencar Dri. M40 3F 47
Glencoe Clo. Heyw 6D 18
Glencoe Pl. Roch 6F 13
Glencoe St. Oldh 3C 48
Glendale Clo. Heyw 5H 19
Glendale Ct. Oldh 1F 49
Glendene Av. Droy 4G 55
Glenden Foot. Roch 3F 13
Glendon Ct. Oldh 5C 32
Glendon Cres. Ash L 6H 49
Gleneagles Av. M11 5A 54
Gleneagles Av. Heyw 1H 27
Glenfield Clo. Oldh 5B 42
Glen Gdns. Roch 3H 13
Glengarth. Upperm 4D 44
Glen Gro. Midd 4E 39
Glen Gro. Rytn 4D 30
Glenmore Clo. Roch 2A 20
Glenmore Dri. Fail 5B 48
Glenolden St. M11 5B 54
Glenpark Wlk. M9 6A 46 (off Craigend Dri.)
Glenridding Clo. Oldh 2G 41
Glen Rd. Oldh 5A 42
Glen Royd. Roch 4E 13
Glenroy Wlk. M9 6A 38
Glensdale Dri. M40 4G 47

Glenside Gdns. *Fail.* 6A 48
Glen, The. *Midd* 5D 38
Glenthorn Av. *M9* 5H 37
Glen Trad. Est. *Oldh* 5B 42
Glen Vw. *L'boro* 4A 8
Glen Vw. *Rytn* 4D 30
Glen Vw. *Whitw* 1E 5
Glenville Ter. Droy 4C 54
(off Greenside La.)
Glenwood Dri. *M9* 6A 46
Glenwood Dri. *Midd* 1E 39
Glenwyn Av. *M9* 1A 46
Glodwick. 6H 41
Glodwick. *Oldh* 6H 41
Glodwick Brook. 2G 49
Glodwick Rd. *Oldh* 6H 41
Glodwick Swimming Pool. 5H 41
Glossop Ter. *M40* 2F 47
Gloucester Av. *Heyw* 1G 27
Gloucester Av. *Roch* 1D 14
Gloucester Clo. *Ash L* 5B 50
Gloucester Dri. *Dig* 5E 35
Gloucester Rd. *Droy* 4E 55
Gloucester Rd. *Midd* 5C 38
Gloucester St. N. *Oldh* 6C 40
Gloucester St. S. *Oldh* 6C 40
Gnat Bank Fold. *Roch* 2B 20
Goats. 1A 32
Goddard St. *Oldh* 1F 49
Godfrey Av. *Droy* 4B 54
Godson St. *Oldh* 2E 41
Goit Pl. *Roch* 6H 13
Golborne Dri. *Shaw* 1H 31
Golborne Ho. Shaw 1H 31
(off Cowie St.)
Goldbrook Clo. *Heyw* 6A 20
Goldcraft Clo. *Heyw* 6A 20
Goldenhill Av. *M11* 4A 54
Golden St. *Shaw* 1C 32
Goldfinch Dri. *Bury* 2A 18
Goldfinch Way. *Droy* 4G 55
Goldsmith Av. *Oldh* 5C 32
Gooden St. *Heyw* 6A 20
Good Intent. *Miln* 2G 23
Goodison Clo. *Bury* 6A 26
Goodman St. *M9* 5A 46
Goodrich. *Roch* 1G 21
Good Shepherd Clo. *Roch* 5B 14
Goodwin Ct. *Chad* 1C 48
Goodwood Dri. *Oldh* 2H 41
Goodworth Wlk. M40 6C 46
(off Hanson Rd.)
Goose La. *Roch* 5H 13
Gordon Av. *Chad* 2A 48
Gordon Av. *Oldh* 5H 41
Gordon St. *Chad* 1H 47
Gordon St. *Lees* 6C 42
Gordon St. *Miln* 4H 23
Gordon St. *Roch* 2A 22
Gordon St. *Shaw* 2A 32
(in two parts)
Gordon St. *S'head* 5E 43
Gordon Ter. *M9* 5A 46
Gordon Way. *Heyw* 6D 18
Gore Av. *Fail* 5B 48
Gore Clo. *Heap B* 5A 18
Gorrells Clo. *Roch* 4F 21
Gorrell St. *Roch* 2A 22
Gorrells Way. *Roch* 4F 21
(in two parts)
Gorrells Way Ind. Est. *Roch* 4F 21
Gorse Av. *Droy* 5G 55
Gorse Av. *Moss* 4A 52
Gorse Av. *Oldh* 2A 50
Gorse Bank. *Bury* 4A 18
Gorse Pit. *Bury* 4A 18
Gorse Rd. *Miln* 1G 23
Gorse St. *Chad* 1H 47
Gorsey Bank. *L'boro* 4A 8
Gorsey Hill St. *Heyw* 6H 19
Gorsey La. *Ash L* 6C 50
Gorsey Way. *Ash L* 6C 50
Gorton St. *Chad* 5B 40
Gorton St. *Heyw* 5A 20
Gosforth Clo. *Oldh* 2G 41
Goss Hill St. *Oldh* 5A 42
Gough St. *Heyw* 5A 20
Gould St. *Oldh* 3H 41
Gowan Dri. *Midd* 2H 37
Gowers St. *Roch* 5B 14
Gower St. *Oldh* 4G 41
Gowran Pk. *Oldh* 5B 42
Goya Ri. *Oldh* 5B 32
Goyt Wlk. *W'fld* 1A 36
Grace St. *Roch* 3A 14
Gracie Av. *Oldh* 2H 41
Grafton Ct. *Roch* 1B 22
Grafton St. *Fail* 5A 48
Grafton St. *Oldh* 5C 32
Grafton St. *Roch* 1B 22
Grains Bar. 3E 33
Grains Rd. *Del* 3E 33
Grains Rd. *Shaw* 3A 32
Grammar School Rd. *Oldh* 3B 48
Grampian Clo. *Chad* 6A 40
Grampian Way. *Shaw* 1F 31
Granby St. *Chad* 2A 48
Grandidge St. *Roch* 2G 21
Grange. 3B 34
Grange Av. *Miln* 3F 23
Grange Av. *Oldh* 1C 48
Grange Ct. *Oldh* 1D 48
Grange Dri. *M9* 2B 46
Grange La. *Del* 3B 34
Grange Mill Wlk. *M40* 6D 46
Grange Pk. Rd. *M9* 2B 46
Grange Rd. *Midd* 3F 29
Grange Rd. *Whitw* 1F 5
Grange St. *Fail* 1B 54
Grange St. *Oldh* 4E 41
Grange St. *Roch* 3H 13
Grange, The. *Oldh* 3H 41
Grange Wlk. *Midd* 1A 38
Granite St. *Oldh* 3H 41
Grantham St. *Oldh* 6G 41
Grant St. *Roch* 5F 21
Granville Clo. *Chad* 4C 40
Granville Ct. *Miln* 4H 23
Granville Rd. *Aud* 6F 55
Granville St. *Chad* 3C 40
Granville St. *Oldh* 2E 41
Granville Wlk. *Chad* 3C 40
Grasdene Av. *M9* 2A 46
Grasmere Av. *Heyw* 1H 27
Grasmere Rd. *Oldh* 5A 42
Grasmere Rd. *Rytn* 3C 30
Grasmere St. *Roch* 4H 13
Grasmere Wlk. *Midd* 1B 38
Grasscroft. 5A 44
Grasscroft Clough. 5A 44
Grassington Av. *M40* 4C 46
Grassington Dri. *Bury* 6B 18
Gravel Hole. 1C 30
Gravel Walks. *Oldh* 4H 41
Graver La. *M40* 2B 54
(in three parts)
Grayrigg Wlk. *M9* 6A 46
Grayson Way. *G'fld* 5D 44
Gt. Arbor Way. *Midd* 2B 38
(in two parts)
Gt. Bent Clo. *Roch* 1D 14
Great Flatt. *Roch* 4D 12
Gt. Gable Clo. *Oldh* 3G 41
Gt. Gates Clo. *Roch* 3A 22
Gt. Gates Rd. *Roch* 4A 22
Gt. George St. *Roch* 1H 21
(in two parts)
Gt. Heaton Clo. *Midd* 4G 37
Great Howarth. 1B 14
Great Howarth. *Roch* 1B 14
Great Lee. *Roch* 2F 13
Gt. Lee Wlk. *Roch* 2F 13
(in two parts)
Great Meadow. *Shaw* 1F 31
Gt. Newton St. *M40* 2A 54
Greave. 5D 12
Greave Av. *Roch* 5D 12
Greave Pk. *Upperm* 4D 44
Greaves Av. *Fail* 1B 54
Greaves St. *Lees* 5D 42
Greaves St. *Moss* 3G 51
Greaves St. *Oldh* 4F 41
Greaves St. *Shaw* 2A 32
Greenacres. 4B 42
Greenacres Ct. *Roch* 1D 14
Greenacres Hill. 3A 42
Greenacres Moor. 3A 42
Greenacres Rd. *Oldh* 4H 41
Greenbank. Whitw 6E 5
(off Tonacliffe Rd.)
Greenbank Av. *Upperm* 2E 45
Greenbank Dri. *L'boro* 2F 15
Greenbank Rd. *Roch* 4H 13
(in two parts)
Greenbank Ter. *Midd* 2E 39
Greenbooth Rd. *Roch* 2H 11
Grn. Bridge Clo. *Roch* 3H 21
Grn. Bridge La. *G'fld* 6C 44
Green Clough. *L'boro* 3B 8
Greencroft Mdw. *Rytn* 4F 31
Greencroft Way. *Smal* 2D 14
Greendale Dri. *M9* 2A 46
Greenfield. 6D 44
Greenfield Ct. *Heyw* 6H 19
Greenfield La. *Roch* 3A 22
Greenfield La. *Shaw* 3H 31
Greenfield La. *Smal* 2D 14
Greenfield St. *Roch* 3A 22
Green Gate. 4C 22
(Balderstone)
Greengate. 2D 14
(Smallbridge)
Greengate. *M24 & Midd* 2E 47
Greengate Clo. *Roch* 1D 14
Greengate E. *M40* 2E 47
Greengate Ind. Est. *Midd* 6E 39
Greengate St. *Midd* 5F 39
Greengate St. *Oldh* 5G 41
(in three parts)
Greengrove Bank. *Roch* 2C 14
Greenhalgh St. *Fail* 1A 54
Greenheys. *Droy* 5E 55
Green Hill. 4F 39
(Manchester)
Green Hill. 6E 23
(Oldham)
Greenhill Av. *Roch* 5G 13
Grn. Hill Av. *Shaw* 6E 23
Greenhill Cotts. *Moss* 3H 51
Greenhill Pas. *Oldh* 5G 41
Greenhill Rd. *Midd* 4E 39
Greenhill Ter. *Midd* 4E 39
Greenhill Terraces. *Oldh* 5G 41
Greenholme Clo. *M40* 4F 47
Greenhurst Cres. *Oldh* 3G 49
Greenhurst La. *Ash L* 6C 50
Greenhurst Rd. *Ash L* 6B 50
Green La. *Del* 5A 34
Green La. *Fail* 3C 54
Green La. *Heyw* 5A 20
Green La. *Midd* 1D 38
(Hilton Fold La.)
Green La. *Midd* 4F 39
(Joshua La.)
Green La. *Moss* 1F 51
Green La. *Oldh* 3D 48
(Middle Ga.)
Green La. *Oldh* 1D 42
(Waterworks Rd.)
Green La. *Roch* 5G 13
Greenlees St. *Roch* 5H 13
Green Mdw. *Roch* 1D 14
Greenmount Dri. *Heyw* 2B 28
Greenock Dri. *Heyw* 6D 18
Grn. Park Vw. *Oldh* 1B 42
Greenroyde. *Roch* 2G 21
Greenshank Clo. *Roch* 6B 12
Greenside. 5D 54
Greenside Av. *Oldh* 1B 42
Greenside Cres. *Droy* 5D 54
Greenside La. *Droy* 4C 54
Greenside St. *M11* 6A 54
Greenside Trad. Cen.
Droy 6E 55
Greenside Way. *Midd* 6E 39
Greenson Dri. *Midd* 4A 38
Greens, The. *Whitw* 2E 5
Green St. *Midd* 2D 38
(in two parts)
Green St. *Oldh* 5D 40
Green, The. *Oldh* 2G 49
Green, The. *Roch* 4E 21
Greenvale. *Roch* 5A 12
Greenvale Cotts. *L'boro* 3B 8
Greenview Dri. *Roch* 5C 12
Greenway. *Midd* 6B 38
Green Way. *Roch* 6D 20
Greenway. *Shaw* 6F 23
Greenway Dri. *Moss* 3F 51
Greenways. *M40* 4F 47
Greenwich Clo. *M40* 3B 54
Greenwich Clo. *Roch* 1B 20
Greenwood Pl. L'boro 6H 7
(off Hare Hill Rd.)
Greenwood St. *Bar* 4F 49
Greenwood St. *L'boro* 6H 7
Greenwood St. *Oldh* 3A 42
(in two parts)
Greenwood St. *Roch* 6H 13
Greenwood St. *S'head* 6D 42
Greetland Dri. *M9* 1B 46
Gregge St. *Heyw* 6A 20
(in two parts)
Gregory St. *Oldh* 2C 48
Gregson St. *Oldh* 5F 41
Grendon Av. *Oldh* 1E 49
Grenville Wlk. L'boro 2A 8
(off Drake Rd.)
Gresham Dri. *Oldh* 4C 40
Gretton Clo. *Rytn* 5F 31
Greystoke Dri. *Midd* 1H 37
Greystoke La. *Fail* 1B 54
Grey St. *Midd* 2B 38
Grey St. *P'wich* 6A 36
Greywood Av. *Bury* 5A 18
Griffe La. *Bury* 6A 26
Griffin Rd. *Fail* 6F 47
Griffiths St. *M40* 2A 54
Grimes Cotts. *Roch* 4B 12
Grimes St. *Roch* 4B 12
Grimscott Clo. *M9* 4B 46
Grimshaw Av. *Fail* 5A 48
Grimshaw La. *Midd* 3D 38
Grimshaw St. *Fail* 5G 47
Grindall Av. *M40* 3D 46
Grindrod La. *Roch* 6B 6
Grindrod St. *Roch* 4G 13
Grisdale Dri. *Midd* 1A 38
Grisebeck Way. *Oldh* 4E 41
Grisedale Av. *Rytn* 1C 30
Grisedale Ct. *M9* 1C 46
Grisedale Rd. *Roch* 3D 20
Gristlehurst La. *Bury* 2D 18
Grizedale Clo. *Carr* 6A 52
Groby St. *Oldh* 2G 49
Grosvenor St. *Heyw* 6G 19
Grosvenor St. *Roch* 6E 21
Grosvenor Way. *Rytn* 1D 40
Grotton. 6F 43
Grotton Hollow. *G'ton* 5E 43
Grotton Meadows. *G'ton* 6F 43
Grouse St. *Roch* 4H 13
Grove Av. *Fail* 2C 54
Grove Cotts. *Dig* 3F 35
Grove Rd. *Midd* 1D 38
Grove Rd. *Upperm* 4D 44
Grove St. *G'fld* 6D 44
Grove St. *Heyw* 5A 20
Grove St. *Roch* 2G 21
Grove Ter. *Oldh* 3C 42
Grove, The. *Dob* 2B 44
Grove, The. *Shaw* 3G 31
Grundy St. *Heyw* 1A 28
Grundy St. *Oldh* 4G 41
Guardian Clo. *Roch* 6D 6
Guido St. *Fail* 6G 47
Guildford Dri. *Ash L* 6A 50
Guildford Gro. *Midd* 6E 29
Guildford St. *Moss* 4H 51
Guildford St. *Roch* 6A 14
(in two parts)
Guiness Ho. *Roch* 1B 22
Gullane Clo. *M40* 6E 47
Gulvain Pl. *Chad* 3H 39

H

Hackle St. *M11* 5A 54
Hackney Av. *M40* 3A 54
Haddington Dri. *M9* 2A 46
Haddon Av. *M40* 4H 47
Haddon Hall Rd. *Droy* 5C 54
Haddon St. *Roch* 3G 21
Haddon Way. *Shaw* 1A 32
Hadfield Av. *Chad* 6B 40
Hadfield St. *Oldh* 2E 49
Haggate. 6C 30
Haggate. *Rytn* 6C 30
Haggate Cres. *Rytn* 6C 30
Hague Ho. *Oldh* 6F 41
Hague St. *Oldh* 3C 42
Haigh La. *Chad* 2G 39
Haigh St. *Roch* 1A 22
Hailwood St. *Roch* 3G 21
Halcyon Clo. *Roch* 3D 12
Hale La. *Fail* 5G 47
Hales Clo. *Droy* 4D 54
Half Acre Dri. *Roch* 1E 21
(in two parts)
Half Acre La. *Roch* 1D 20
Half Acre M. *Roch* 1D 20
Half Acre Rd. *Roch* 1D 20
Halford Dri. *M40* 5D 46
Halfpenny Bri. Ind. Est. *Roch* 1A 22
Half St. *Midd* 2B 38
Halifax Rd. *L'boro* 6A 8
Halifax Rd. *Oldh* 4E 33
Halifax Rd. *Roch* 4B 14
Hallcroft Gdns. *Miln* 1E 23

Hall Dri. Midd. 4B 38
Hallfold. 3E 5
Hall Fold. Whitw 3D 4
Hall Gdns. Roch 3E 13
Halliday Ct. L'boro 1E 15
Halliford Rd. M40 6C 46
Halliwell Av. Oldh 2E 49
Halliwell St. Chad 4A 48
Halliwell St. Fir & Miln 6E 15
(in two parts)
Halliwell St. L'boro 6A 8
Halliwell St. Roch 5G 13
(in two parts)
Hallkirk Wlk. M40 3F 47
Hall Moss Rd. M9 2C 46
Hallroyd Brow. Oldh 3E 41
Halls Cotts. G'fld 5D 44
Hall's Pl. S'head 5D 42
Hall St. Fail 1B 54
Hall St. Heyw 6A 20
Hall St. Midd 3C 38
Hall St. Oldh 4H 41
Hall St. Rytn 5D 30
Hall St. Whitw 3E 5
Halls Way. G'fld 5D 44
Hallworth Av. Aud 6F 55
Halsey Clo. Chad 3G 47
Halsmere Dri. M9 2A 46
Halton Flats. Heyw 5G 19
(off Pitt St.)
Halton Rd. M11 5A 54
Hamer Ct. Roch 4B 14
Hamer Hall Cres. Roch 3B 14
Hamer La. Roch 4B 14
Hamer's Bldgs. Heyw 5F 19
Hamilton Av. Rytn 6B 30
Hamilton St. Chad 4A 40
Hamilton St. Oldh 5G 41
Hamilton Way. Heyw 6C 18
Hammer St. Heyw 5F 19
Hammond Flats. Heyw 5G 19
(off Ashton St.)
Hamnett St. M11 6B 54
Hampden Rd. P'wich 6A 36
Hampden Rd. Shaw 3B 32
Hampden St. Heyw 6H 19
Hampden St. Roch 1H 21
Hampshire Rd. Chad 6B 40
Hampshire Rd. Droy 4E 55
Hampson Av. Heyw 5G 19
Hampson St. Droy 5E 55
Hampton Rd. Fail 5A 48
Hampton St. Oldh 1D 48
Handel St. Whitw 3D 4
Handley St. Roch 5F 13
Hands La. Roch 6C 12
Hanging Birch. Midd 4F 37
Hanging Chadder. 2C 30
Hanging Chadder La. Rytn 2C 30
Hanging Lees Clo. Miln 3A 24
Hanley Clo. Midd 6C 38
Hannerton Rd. Shaw 1B 32
Hanover St. L'boro 6G 7
Hanover St. Moss 4G 51
Hanover St. Roch 5E 21
Hansby Clo. Oldh 2E 41
Hanslope Wlk. M9 5A 46
(off Swainsthorpe Dri.)
Hanson Clo. Midd 2C 38
Hanson Clo. Ind. Est. Midd 2C 38
Hanson Rd. M40 6C 46
Hanson St. Midd 2C 38
(in two parts)
Hanson St. Oldh 4A 42
Harbord St. Midd 3C 38
Harbour La. Miln 2F 23
Harbour La. N. Miln 1F 23
Harcourt St. Oldh 3H 41
Hardcastle St. Oldh 4F 41
Harden Hills. Shaw 1B 32
Hardfield Rd. Midd 6C 38
Hardfield St. Heyw 5H 19
Hard La. Ward 3A 6
Hardman La. Fail 5G 47
Hardman St. Chad 2B 48
Hardman St. Fail 6F 47
Hardman St. Heyw 5H 19
Hardman St. Miln 2G 23
Hardrush Fold. Fail 1E 55
Hardwicke St. Roch 3G 21
Hardy Clo. Roch 4H 21
Hardy St. Oldh 6G 41
Harebell Clo. Roch 2F 13
Harefield Av. Roch 2A 22
Harefield Dri. Heyw 5B 20
Hare Hill Ct. L'boro 5H 7
Hare Hill Rd. L'boro 5G 7
Hareshill Bus. Pk. Heyw 1F 27
Hareshill Rd. Heyw 1F 27
Hare St. Roch 2H 21
(in two parts)
Harewood Av. Roch 3H 11
Harewood Clo. Roch 4H 11
Harewood Ct. M9 6E 37
(off Deanswood Dri.)
Harewood Dri. Roch 4G 11
Harewood Dri. Rytn 4C 30
Harewood Rd. Roch 3G 11
Harewood Rd. Shaw 1A 32
Harewood Way. Roch 4G 11
Hargate Av. Roch 3C 12
Hargrave Clo. M9 5G 37
Hargreaves St. Oldh 5C 40
(Arkwright St.)
Hargreaves St. Oldh 4F 41
(Henshaw St.)
Hargreaves St. Roch 3E 21
Harland Way. Roch 3C 12
Harlech Av. W'fld 5A 36
Harley Ct. Midd 2B 38
Harley Rd. Midd 2B 38
Harmony St. Oldh 5G 41
Harold Lees Rd. Heyw 4B 20
Harold St. Fail 6G 47
Harold St. Midd 2A 38
Harold St. Oldh 4D 40
Harold St. Roch 3C 14
Harper Sq. Shaw 2A 32
Harper St. Oldh 1E 49
Harper St. Roch 2G 21
Harp Ind. Est. Roch 5F 21
Harpurhey. 6A 46
Harpurhey District Cen. M9 5A 46
Harpurhey Swimming Pools. 5A 46
Harridge Av. Roch 2E 13
(in two parts)
Harridge Bank. Roch 3E 13
Harridge St. Roch 2E 13
Harridge, The. Roch 2E 13
Harriet St. Roch 6A 14
Harringay Rd. M40 2A 54
Harris Clo. Heyw 6C 18
Harris Dri. Bury 1A 36
Harrison Clo. Roch 4B 12
Harrison St. Oldh 5F 41
Harrop Ct. Dig 4F 35
Harrop Ct. Rd. Dig 4F 35
Harrop Dale. 3F 35
Harrop Edge La. Del 5C 34
Harrop Fold. Oldh 4G 49
Harrop Green. 4F 35
Harrop Grn. La. Dig 4E 35
Harrop Ridge. 3F 35
Harrow Av. Oldh 2D 48
Harrow Av. Roch 1C 20
Harrow M. Shaw 2H 31
Harrow St. Roch 5B 22
Harry St. Oldh 5C 40
Harry St. Roch 4D 20
Harry St. Rytn 1E 41
Hart Av. Droy 6F 55
Hart Ct. Moss 3F 51
Hartford Av. Heyw 4F 19
Hartford Clo. Heyw 4F 19
Hartford Grange. Oldh 1D 48
Hartford Ind. Est. Oldh 5C 40
Hartford Sq. Oldh 5C 40
Hartington Ct. Rytn 5E 31
Hartington Dri. M11 4A 54
Hartland St. Heyw 5H 19
Hartlebury. Roch 1G 21
Hartley La. Roch 4G 21
Hartley Pl. Fir 6D 14
Hartley St. M40 5B 46
Hartley St. Fir 6D 14
Hartley St. Heyw 5H 19
Hartley St. L'boro 6G 7
Hartley St. Roch 4D 12
Hartley St. Ward 5C 6
Hartley Ter. L'boro 6G 7
(off William St.)
Hartley Ter. Roch 4G 21
Hart Mill Clo. Moss 3F 51
Harton Clo. Shaw 2G 31
Hartshead Cres. Fail 1G 55
Hartshead Green. 5D 50
Hartshead Pike Tower. 4E 51
Hartshead St. Lees 6D 42
Hartsop Dri. Midd 1G 37
Hart St. Droy 5E 55
Harvard St. Roch 3A 22
(in two parts)
Harvey Ct. L'boro 5A 8
Harvey St. Roch 3B 14
Harwin Clo. Roch 2F 13
Harwood Gdns. Heyw 6H 19
Harwood Pk. Heyw 6H 19
Harwood St. L'boro 6F 7
Haslam St. Midd 4E 39
Haslam St. Roch 5F 13
Hastings Av. W'fld 4A 36
Hastings Clo. W'fld 4A 36
Hastings Rd. P'wich 6A 36
Hastings St. Roch 2H 21
Hathersage St. Oldh 5C 40
Hathershaw. 2F 49
Hathershaw La. Oldh 2F 49
Haugh. 3A 24
Haugh Fold. Miln 3A 24
Haugh Hill Rd. Oldh 6C 32
Haugh La. Miln 3A 24
Haugh Sq. Miln 3A 24
Havelock St. Oldh 6F 41
Haven Clo. Grass 5H 43
Haven Dri. Droy 5C 54
Haven La. Oldh 1C 42
Haverfield Rd. M9 2A 46
Haw Clough La. G'fld 5E 45
Haweswater Cres. Uns 4A 26
Haweswater Dri. Midd 1A 38
Haweswater M. Midd 1A 38
Hawick Gro. Heyw 6C 18
Hawkinge Vw. Heyw 2B 28
Hawkins Way. L'boro 2A 8
Hawkshead Dri. Midd 2A 38
Hawkshead Dri. Rytn 3D 30
Hawkshead Rd. Shaw 1G 31
Hawksley Ct. Oldh 2C 48
Hawksley Ind. Est. Oldh 2C 48
Hawksley St. Oldh 2C 48
Hawksmoor Dri. Shaw 1H 31
Hawkstone Av. Droy 4C 54
Hawk Yd. La. G'fld 6F 45
Hawley Grn. Roch 3F 13
Haworth St. Oldh 2E 41
Hawthorn Cres. Oldh 3F 49
Hawthorn Cres. Shaw 3H 31
Hawthorne Gro. Chad 3B 40
Hawthorn La. Miln 3G 23
Hawthorn Rd. M40 4G 47
Hawthorn Rd. Droy 5G 55
(in two parts)
Hawthorn Rd. Oldh 3B 48
Hawthorn Rd. Roch 1A 20
Hawthorn Rd. S. Droy 5G 55
Hawthorn Wlk. L'boro 6F 7
Hawthorpe Gro. Upperm 3D 44
Haydock Wlk. Chad 4C 40
Hayfield Clo. Midd 6E 29
Hayfield Clo. Oldh 5D 32
Hayle Rd. Oldh 5B 32
Haymaker Ri. Ward 5D 6
Haynes St. Roch 5H 13
Haysbrook Clo. Ash L 6G 49
Hazel Av. Bury 5A 18
Hazel Av. Miln 4G 23
Hazel Clo. Droy 5G 55
Hazeldene Rd. M40 4G 47
Hazel Gro. Chad 3B 40
Hazelhurst Dri. Midd 5B 28
Hazelhurst M. Chad 2H 47
Hazel La. Oldh 3D 48
Hazel Rd. Midd 2D 38
Hazel Rd. W'fld 3A 36
Hazel Ter. M9 6H 37 & 1A 46
Hazelwood. Chad 3G 39
Headlands St. Roch 4G 13
Heady Hill. 5D 18
Heady Hill Ct. Heyw 5E 19
Heady Hill Rd. Heyw 5E 19
Heald Clo. L'boro 2G 15
Heald Clo. Roch 2E 13
Heald Dri. Roch 2E 13
Heald La. L'boro 1G 15
Healds Green. 6H 29
Healds Grn. Chad 6H 29
Healey. 6E 5
Healey Av. Heyw 4A 20
Healey Av. Roch 1F 13
Healey Dell. Roch 1D 12
Healey Dell Nature Reserve. 1D 12
Healey Dell Vis. Cen. 1D 12
Healey Gro. Whitw 6E 5
Healey Hall M. Roch 1E 13
Healey La. Roch 2G 13
Healey Stones. Roch 1F 13
Healey St. Roch 1G 21
Healing St. Roch 2A 22
Heap Bridge. 6A 18
Heap Brow. Bury 6B 18
Heape St. Roch 6E 21
Heapfold. Roch 3D 12
Heap Rd. Roch 3H 11
Heap St. Bury 6B 18
Heap St. Oldh 4A 42
Heathbank Rd. M9 6G 37
Heather Av. Droy 5G 55
Heather Av. Shaw 1B 32
Heather Clo. Heyw 1H 27
Heather Clo. Oldh 2C 42
Heathersett Dri. M9 6A 46
Heatherside Av. Moss 4A 52
Heather Way. Dig 5E 35
Heathfields. 3E 45
Heathfields Rd. Upperm 3E 45
Heathfields Sq. Upperm 3E 45
Heathfield St. M40 2A 54
Heath Rd. Ward 5C 6
Heath St. Roch 1F 21
Heath, The. Ash L 6G 49
Heath, The. Midd 5D 38
Heathway Av. M11 5B 54
Heathwood. Upperm 3E 45
Heatley Rd. Roch 1D 22
Heaton Hall. 6C 36
(Museum)
Heaton Park. 6A 36
Heaton Pk. 6B 36
Heaton Pk. Bowling Pavilion. 5A 36
Heaton Pk. Farm Cen. 6C 36
Heaton Pk. Horticultural Cen. 6B 36
Heaton Pk. Rd. M9 6E 37
Heaton Pk. Rd. W. M9 6E 37
Heaton Pk. Tramway. 6C 36
Heaton Pk. Tramway Mus. 6D 36
Heaton St. Midd 4F 37
Heaton St. Miln 2G 23
Heaton St. P'wich 6A 36
Hebble Butt Clo. Miln 1E 23
Heber Pl. L'boro 6H 7
(off Victoria St.)
Hebron St. Rytn 6G 31
Hector Av. Roch 5B 14
Hedge Rows. Whitw 2E 5
Hedges St. Fail 5A 48
Heights. 3A 34
Heights Av. Roch 3G 13
(in three parts)
Heights Clo. Roch 3G 13
Heights La. Chad 1H 39
Heights La. Del 2H 33
Heights La. Roch 3G 13
Helmshore Av. Oldh 1C 42
Helmshore Ho. Shaw 1H 31
(off Helmshore Way)
Helmshore Way. Shaw 1H 31
Helrose St. M40 2A 54
Helsby Clo. S'head 5E 43
Helston Dri. Rytn 5F 31
Helton Wlk. Midd 2G 37
Helvellyn Dri. Midd 1H 37
Helvellyn Wlk. Oldh 2G 41
Hembury Clo. Midd 1D 38
Hemlock Av. Oldh 2E 49
Hemmington Dri. M9 6A 46
Hemsley St. M9 4A 46
Hemsley St. S. M9 5A 46
Henderson St. L'boro 6G 7
Henderson St. Roch 3B 14
Henderville St. L'boro 5G 7
Hendon Gro. Heyw 2A 28
Hendon Rd. M9 6G 37
Hendriff Pl. Roch 4H 13
Henley St. Chad 2A 48
Henley St. Oldh 3D 40
Henley St. Roch 4G 13
Henley Ter. Roch 2G 21
Henlow Wlk. M40 3F 47
Henry St. Droy 6E 55
Henry St. Fail 6H 47
Henry St. L'boro 2F 15
Henry St. Midd 3B 38
Henry St. P'wich 6A 36
Henry St. Roch 1H 21
Henry St. Ward 4C 6
Henshaw La. Chad 3H 47
Henshaw St. Oldh 4E 41

Henthorn St. *Oldh* 3G **41**	High Down Wlk. *M9* 5A **46**	Hilary Av. *Oldh* 5F **49**
Henthorn St. *Shaw* 3H **31**	*(off Augustine Webster Clo.)*	Hilary St. *Roch* 6F **21**
Heppleton Rd. *M40* 3F **47**	Higher Arthurs. *G'fld* 5D **44**	Hilbre Av. *Rytn* 1D **40**
Hepton St. *Oldh* 3E **41**	Higher Bank Rd. *L'boro* 2G **15**	Hilda St. *Heyw* 4H **19**
Herbert St. *Chad* 4B **40**	Higher Barrowshaw. **1B 42**	Hilda St. *Oldh* 4D **40**
Herbert St. *Droy* 6D **54**	**Higher Blackley. 6F 37**	*(in two parts)*
Herbert St. *Oldh* 2B **42**	**Higher Boarshaw. 1E 39**	Hillbank St. *Midd* 3F **29**
Hereford Clo. *Ash L* 6B **50**	Higher Calderbrook. *L'boro* . . . 2A **8**	Hillbrook Av. *Heyw* 4E **19**
Hereford Clo. *Shaw* 2F **31**	Higher Calderbrook Rd. *L'boro* . . 2A **8**	Hillbrook Av. *M40* 3D **46**
Hereford St. *Oldh* 6B **40**	Higher Carr La. *G'fld* 4D **44**	Hill Clo. *Oldh* 2C **42**
Hereford St. *Roch* 2A **22**	Higher Cleggswood Av.	Hillcrest. *Midd* 6B **28**
Hereford Way. *Midd* 2E **39**	*L'boro* 2G **15**	Hillcrest Av. *Heyw* 4E **19**
Heritage Pk. *Roch* 6A **14**	Higher Crimble. *Roch* 3B **20**	Hillcrest Cres. *Heyw* 4E **19**
Hermon Av. *Oldh* 1E **49**	Higher Crossbank. *Lees* 3D **42**	Hillcrest Rd. *Roch* 5F **21**
Herondale Clo. *M40* 2A **54**	Higher Cross La. *Upperm* 4E **45**	*(in two parts)*
Heron Dri. *Aud* 6G **55**	Higher Fullwood. *Oldh* 5B **32**	Hillcroft. *Oldh* 4G **49**
Heron St. *Oldh* 1C **48**	**Higher Hartshead. 4D 50**	Hilldale Av. *M9* 1A **46**
Herschel St. *M40* 5C **46**	Higher Ho. Clo. *Chad* 1A **48**	Hill End Rd. *Del* 4B **34**
Hersham Wlk. *M9* 4A **46**	Higher Kinders. *G'fld* 5D **44**	Hill Farm Clo. *Oldh* 2G **49**
(off Huncote Dri.)	Higher Lee St. *Oldh* 5D **40**	Hillhouse Ct. *Roch* 4D **20**
Hertford Rd. *M9* 4A **46**	Higher Lime Rd. *Oldh* 5C **48**	Hillier St. *M9* 5A **46**
Hertfordshire Pk. Clo. *Shaw* . . 1H **31**	Higher Lodge. *Roch* 3H **11**	Hillier St. N. *M9* 5A **46**
Hesford Av. *M9* 6B **46**	Higher Lomax La. *Heyw* 5E **19**	Hillington Clo. *Oldh* 5B **48**
Hesketh Av. *Shaw* 4G **31**	Higher Lydgate Pk. *Grass* 5G **43**	Hillington Rd. *M9* 3D **46**
Hesketh Rd. *Roch* 6C **14**	Higher Mouldings. *Bury* 2C **18**	Hillkirk Dri. *Roch* 2E **13**
Hesketh Wlk. *Midd* 1A **38**	Higher Newtons. *Moss* 3H **51**	Hill La. *M9* . . . . 6H **37** & 2A **46**
Hethorn St. *M40* 2A **54**	**Higher Ogden. 2D 24**	Hillside Av. *Dig*. 6D **34**
Heversham Av. *Shaw* 2B **32**	Higher Pk. *Shaw* 5A **24**	Hillside Av. *G'ton* 6E **43**
Hewart Dri. *Bury* 4A **18**	Higher Ri. *Shaw*. 6G **23**	Hillside Av. *Oldh* 4A **42**
Hexham Clo. *Chad* 4C **40**	**Higher Rushcroft. 1F 31**	Hillside Av. *Rytn*. 4E **31**
Hey Bottom La. *Whitw* 6H **5**	Higher Shore Rd. *L'boro* 4E **7**	Hillside Av. *Shaw* 2B **32**
(in three parts)	**Higher Stake Hill. 5H 29**	Hillside Clo. *M40* 4C **46**
Heybrook. *Roch* 4B **14**	Higher Turf La. *Scout* 3F **43**	Hillside Dri. *Midd*. 2D **38**
Heybrook Clo. *W'fld* 3A **36**	Higher Turf Pk. *Rytn*. 6E **31**	Hillside Vw. *Miln* 1G **23**
Heybrook St. *Roch* 5B **14**	Higher Wheat La. *Roch* 5C **14**	Hillside Wlk. *Roch* 1F **13**
Heybrook Wlk. *W'fld* 3A **36**	Higher Wood St. *Midd* 2B **38**	Hillside Way. *Whitw* 2E **5**
Hey Cres. *Lees*. 4D **42**	Highfield. *Miln* 1G **23**	Hills La. *Bury* 1A **36**
Hey Flake La. *Del* 2A **34**	Highfield Av. *Heyw* 5E **19**	Hillspring Rd. *S'head* 5E **43**
Heyford Av. *M40*. 3F **47**	. . . . 2G **21**	Hillstone Av. *Roch* 1E **13**
Hey Head La. *L'boro* 2H **7**	HIGHFIELD BMI HOSPITAL, THE	Hill St. *Heyw* 5G **19**
Heyheads. 6A 52	. . . . 2G **21**	Hill St. *Midd*. 6C **28**
Heyheads New Rd. *Carr* 6A **52**	Highfield Dri. *Midd* 4B **38**	Hill St. *Oldh*. 4H **41**
Hey Hill Clo. *Roch* 4G **31**	Highfield Dri. *Moss* 5G **51**	Hill St. *Roch* 6A **14**
Heyside. 4G 31	Highfield Dri. *Rytn* 1E **41**	Hill St. *Shaw* 3A **32**
Heyside. *Rytn* 6G **31**	Highfield Rd. *Roch* 4A **12**	Hill Top. *Chad* 1H **39**
Heyside Av. *Rytn* 6G **31**	Highfield St. *Midd* 3D **38**	Hilltop. *Whitw* 6E **5**
Heys La. *Heyw* 5E **19**	Highfield St. *Oldh* 4E **41**	Hilltop Av. *M9* 2A **46**
Heys Rd. *P'wich* 6A **36**	*(Kirkham St.)*	Hill Top Dri. *Roch*. 5H **21**
Hey St. *Roch* 5B **14**	Highfield St. *Oldh* 4E **41**	Hilltop Dri. *Rytn* 1E **41**
Hey Top. *G'fld*. 2F **53**	*(Middleton Rd.)*	Hill Top La. *Del* 5G **33**
Heywood. 6G 31	Highfield Ter. *Ash L* 6F **49**	Hill Vw. *Del* 5B **34**
Heywood Av. *Aus* 3E **43**	Highfield Ter. *Oldh* 1B **42**	Hill Vw. *L'boro* 2B **8**
Heywood Ct. *Midd* 4F **37**	High Ga. Dri. *Rytn* 2C **30**	Hill Vw. Clo. *Oldh* 1A **42**
Heywood Distribution Pk.	Highgate La. *Whitw* 5E **5**	Hilson St. *Droy*. 6E **55**
Heyw 1C **26**	Highgrove Ct. *M8*. 6D **36**	Hilton Arc. *Oldh* 4F **41**
Heywood Fold Rd. *S'head* 4D **42**	High Gro. Rd. *Grass & G'fld* . . 6A **44**	Hilton Fold La. *Midd*. 2D **38**
Heywood Hall Rd. *Heyw*. 4H **19**	High Hurst Clo. *Midd* 3G **37**	Hiltons Clo. *Oldh* 6E **41**
Heywood Ho. *Oldh* 6F **41**	Highlands. *L'boro* 2G **15**	Hilton St. *Midd*. 1B **38**
Heywood Ind. Pk. *Heyw* 2D **26**	Highlands. *Rytn* 6C **30**	Hilton St. *Oldh* 3A **42**
Heywood La. *Aus* 4E **43**	*(in two parts)*	Hilton Wlk. *Midd* 3G **37**
Heywood Old Rd.	Highlands Ho. *Moss* 4F **51**	*(in two parts)*
Midd & Heyw 2E **37**	*(off Highlands, The)*	Himley Rd. *M11*. 4A **54**
Heywood Rd. *P'wich* 6A **36**	Highlands Rd. *Roch* 2H **19**	Hinchcliffe St. *Roch* 5F **13**
Heywood Rd. *Roch* 5D **20**	Highlands Rd. *Rytn* 6C **30**	Hinchley Rd. *M9*. 2E **47**
Heywood Sports Complex. 4G **19**	Highlands Rd. *Shaw* 1F **31**	Hindburn Clo. *W'fld* 2A **36**
Heywood St. *Fail*. 6F **47**	Highlands, The. *Moss*. 4F **51**	Hinde St. *M40* 5C **46**
Heywood St. *Oldh* 3C **42**	Highland Vw. *Moss* 3G **51**	Hindhead Wlk. *M40* 3B **54**
Hibbert Cres. *Fail* 6A **48**	Highland Wlk. *M40*. 1B **54**	Hind Hill St. *Heyw* 6H **19**
Hibbert St. *Lees* 4C **42**	High Lee La. *Oldh* 6F **33**	Hindle Dri. *Rytn* 6C **30**
Hibson Av. *Roch* 3A **12**	High Level Rd. *Roch* 1H **21**	Hindle Ter. *Del* 5B **34**
Hibson Clo. *Ward* 5C **6**	High Moor Cres. *Oldh* 2C **42**	*Hinton. Roch* 5G **13**
Higginshaw. 1G 41	Highmoor Vw. *Oldh*. 2C **42**	*(off Redcross St.)*
Higginshaw La.	Highmore Dri. *M9* 2A **46**	Hinton Clo. *Roch* 1A **20**
Oldh & Rytn. 1G **41**	High Peak. *L'boro* 6D **8**	Hinton St. *Oldh* 6F **41**
Higginshaw Rd. *Oldh* 2F **41**	High Peak Rd. *Whitw*. 5E **5**	Hirons La. *S'head*. 6E **43**
Higgs Clo. *Oldh* 4B **42**	High Peak St. *M40*. 6D **46**	Hive St. *Oldh* 3B **48**
Higham Clo. *Rytn* 4G **31**	High Stile La. *Dob* 1F **45**	Hive Vw. *L'boro* 1C **8**
Highbank Cres. *Grass* 6A **44**	High St. *Del*. 5B **34**	Hob Mill Ri. *Moss* 1A **52**
High Bank Rd. *Droy* 6D **54**	High St. *Droy*. 6E **55**	Hobson St. *Fail* 1A **54**
Highbank Rd. *Miln* 3A **24**	High St. *Heyw* 5F **19**	Hobson St. *Oldh* 5F **41**
High Barn Clo. *Roch* 2G **21**	High St. *Lees* 5C **42**	Hodder Av. *L'boro* 5F **7**
Highbarn Ho. *Rytn* 5E **31**	High St. *L'boro* 6F **7**	Hodder Way. *W'fld* 3A **36**
High Barn La. *Whitw* 1E **5**	High St. *Midd* 1C **38**	*(in three parts)*
(Facit)	*(in two parts)*	Hodge Clough Rd. *Oldh* 5A **32**
High Barn La. *Whitw* 2D **4**	High St. *Moss* 3H **51**	Hodge Rd. *Oldh* 6B **32**
(Fold Head)	High St. *Oldh* 4F **41**	Hodge St. *M9*. 4B **46**
Highbarn Rd. *Midd* 4C **38**	*(in two parts)*	Hodson Fold. *Oldh* 4G **49**
High Barn Rd. *Rytn* 5F **31**	High St. *Roch* 5H **13**	Hogarth Ri. *Oldh* 5A **32**
High Barn St. *Rytn* 5E **31**	High St. *Rytn*. 5D **30**	Hogarth Rd. *Roch* 4H **21**
High Birch Ter. *Roch* 3D **20**	High St. *Shaw* 3H **31**	Holbeck Av. *Roch* 1F **13**
Highbury Ct. *P'wich* 6A **36**	High St. *Upperm* 2D **44**	Holborn Av. *Fail* 6B **48**
Highbury Way. *Rytn*. 3D **30**	Highthorne Grn. *Rytn* 1C **30**	Holborn Gdns. *Roch* 2F **21**
Highcroft Way. *Roch* 1H **13**	Highview Wlk. *M9* 2A **46**	Holborn Sq. *Roch* 2F **21**
High Crompton. 2F 31	High Wardle La. *Facit* 2A **6**	Holborn St. *Roch* 2F **21**
	Highwood. *Roch* 4A **12**	Holcombe Clo. *S'head* 4E **43**
	Highworth Dri. *M40* 3F **47**	Holcombe Vw. Clo. *Oldh* 6B **32**

Holden Av. *Bury* 3C **18**	
Holden Clough Dri. *Ash L* 6G **49**	
Holden Fold. 1C 40	
Holden Fold La. *Rytn* 1C **40**	
(in two parts)	
Holden St. *Oldh* 2F **49**	
Holden St. *Roch*. 3A **14**	
Holderness Dri. *Rytn* 1C **40**	
Holford Wlk. *Fir*. 6D **14**	
Holgate St. *Oldh*. 2C **42**	
Holland Clo. *Del* 5A **34**	
Holland Ri. *Roch* 5G **13**	
Holland St. *Heyw* 5H **19**	
(in two parts)	
Holland St. *Hurs* 5G **13**	
Holland St. *Roch* 6G **13**	
Hollies, The. *Oldh* 1D **48**	
Hollin Cres. *G'fld* 1A **52**	
Hollingworth. 2H 15	
Hollingworth Av. *M40*. 3H **47**	
Hollingworth Lake Cvn. Site.	
L'boro 4H **15**	
Hollingworth Lake Country Pk.	
. . . . 3H **15**	
Hollingworth Lake Country Pk.	
Vis. Cen.. . . . . 2H **15**	
Hollingworth Lake Nature Reserve.	
. . . . 3A **16**	
Hollingworth Rd. *L'boro* 2H **15**	
Hollingworth St. *Chad* 2B **48**	
Hollin Hall St. *Oldh*. 4A **42**	
Hollin Ho. *Midd*. 6C **28**	
Hollin La. *Midd* 4A **28**	
Hollin La. *Roch*. 1A **20**	
Hollins. 6C 28	
(Manchester)	
Hollins. 3C 48	
(Oldham)	
Hollins Av. *Lees* 3D **42**	
Hollins Brook Clo. *Uns* 4A **26**	
Hollins Clo. *Bury*. 5A **26**	
Hollins Dri. *Midd* 5A **26**	
Hollins Green. 3E 49	
Hollins Grn. *Midd*. 6C **28**	
Hollins La. *Bury* 5A **26**	
Hollins La. *G'fld* 6F **45**	
Hollins La. *Moss* 4H **51**	
Hollins M. *Uns* 5A **26**	
Hollins Rd. *Oldh*. 3B **48**	
Hollins Rd. *W'head* 3D **42**	
Hollins St. *S'head* 6D **42**	
Hollinwood. 4C 48	
Hollinwood Av. *M40 & Chad* . . 2F **47**	
Hollinwood Bus. Cen. *Fail*. . . . 4B **48**	
Hollowbrook Way. *Roch* 3F **13**	
Hollow Fld. *Roch* 4H **11**	
Hollows Farm Av. *Roch*. 3F **13**	
Hollowspell. *Roch* 2C **14**	
Hollybank. *Droy* 4G **55**	
Holly Bank. *Rytn* 3D **30**	
Hollybrook. *Chad* 6B **30**	
Holly Grove. 6E 35	
Holly Gro. *Chad* 3B **40**	
Holly Gro. *Lees* 3C **42**	
Holly La. *Oldh* 2C **48**	
Hollymount Dri. *Oldh* 6C **32**	
Holly Oak Gdns. *Heyw* 6G **19**	
Holly St. *Droy* 5B **54**	
Holly St. *Oldh* 5B **22**	
Holly St. *Ward* 5C **6**	
Holme Cres. *Rytn* 1C **40**	
Holme Ho. *L'boro* 2B **8**	
Holme Ho. St. *L'boro* 2B **8**	
Holme Pk. Way. *Fail* 6B **48**	
Holmes Rd. *Roch* 6F **13**	
Holmes St. *Roch* 5H **13**	
(College Rd.)	
Holmes St. *Roch* 2C **14**	
(Halifax Rd.)	
Holme Ter. *L'boro* 2B **8**	
Holmfield Av. *M9* 6B **46**	
Holmfield Av. W. *M9*. 6B **46**	
Holmfirth Rd. *G'fld* 6C **44**	
(Greenfield)	
Holmfirth Rd. *G'fld* 6A **44**	
(Saddleworth Moor)	
Holmfoot Wlk. M9 . . . . 6A **46**	
(off Carisbrook St.)	
Holmlea Rd. *Droy* 5C **54**	
Holmleigh Av. *M9*. 4A **46**	
Holroyd St. *Roch* 6A **14**	
Holstein Av. *Roch* 1F **13**	
Holtby St. *M9*. 4A **46**	
Holt La. *Fail* 1E **55**	
Holt Lane End. 6B 48	

Holt La. M.—Juno St.

Holt La. M. *Fail* 6B **48**
Holts 1C **50**
Holts La. *Fail* 6B **48**
Holts La. *Oldh* 1B **50**
Holts Pas. *L'boro* 6G **7**
Holts Ter. *Roch* 3G **13**
Holt St. *L'boro* 1B **8**
Holt St. *Miln* 2G **23**
Holt St. *Oldh* 3A **42**
Holt St. *Whitw* 2E **5**
Holyoake St. *Droy* 5G **55**
Holyoak St. *M40* 1A **54**
Holyrood Clo. *P'wich* 5A **36**
Holyrood Ct. *P'wich* 5A **36**
Holyrood Dri. *P'wich* 5A **36**
Holyrood Gro. *P'wich* 5A **36**
Holyrood Rd. *P'wich* 6A **36**
Holyrood St. *M40* 3C **54**
Holyrood St. *Oldh* 2G **41**
Homebury Dri. *M11* 5A **54**
Home Dri. *Midd* 4B **38**
Homelands Wlk. *M9* 6A **46**
Homerton Rd. *M40* 3A **54**
Homestead Gdns. *Roch* 6D **6**
Honduras St. *Oldh* 4H **41**
Honey Hill. *Lees* 6D **42**
Honeysuckle Way. *Roch* 2F **13**
Honeywell La. *Oldh* 2F **49**
Honister Dri. *Midd* 1A **38**
Honister Rd. *M9* 6B **46**
Honister Way. *Roch* 3D **20**
Honiton Clo. *Chad* 2G **39**
Honiton Clo. *Heyw* 1G **27**
Hood Sq. *G'ton* 6E **43**
Hooley Bridge 3G **19**
Hooley Bri. Ind. Est. *Heyw* 3G **19**
Hooley Brow 4H **19**
Hooley Clough. *Heyw* 3H **19**
Hooper St. *Oldh* 5G **41**
Hopcroft Clo. *M9* 5F **37**
Hope Ct. Roch *5H* ***13***
(off Hope St.)
Hope St. *Heyw* 1B **28**
Hope St. *Oldh* 4H **41**
Hope St. *Roch* (OL11) 6E **21**
Hope St. *Roch* (OL12) 5H **13**
Hope St. *Shaw* 2H **31**
Hopgarth Wlk. *M40* 2B **54**
Hopkin Av. *Oldh* 3H **41**
Hopkins Bldgs. *Moss* 2A **52**
Hopkinson Clo. *Upperm* 3D **44**
Hopkinson Rd. *M9* 6H **37**
Hopkin St. *Oldh* 4F **41**
Hoppet La. *Droy* 5G **55**
Hopwood 6A **20**
Hopwood Av. *Heyw* 1H **27**
Hopwood Ct. *Midd* 5C **28**
Hopwood Ct. *Shaw* 2F **31**
Hopwood Ct. M. *Heyw* 1A **28**
Hopwood Rd. *Midd* 5C **28**
Hopwood St. *M40* 1A **54**
Horden Wlk. Rytn *5E* ***31***
(off Shaw St.)
Horest La. *Dens* 1F **33**
Hornby Av. *M9* 6A **38**
Hornby St. *Heyw* 6H **19**
Hornby St. *Midd* 3C **38**
Hornby St. *Oldh* 6D **40**
Horncastle Rd. *M40* 3D **46**
Hornchurch Cft. *Heyw* 2A **28**
Hornet Clo. *Roch* 4A **22**
Hornsea Clo. *Chad* 2H **39**
Horsedge St. *Oldh* 3F **41**
Horsefield Av. *Whitw* 5E **5**
Horseshoe La. *Midd* 5H **39**
Horsforth La. *G'fld* 1C **52**
Horton Sq. *Shaw* 3H **31**
Hough Clo. *Oldh* 3G **49**
Hough Hall Rd. *M40* 5B **46**
Hough La. *Midd* 5H **29**
Houghton Av. *Oldh* 3D **48**
Houghton Clo. *Roch* 1C **22**
Houghton St. *Rytn* 1E **41**
Houseley Av. *Chad* 2A **48**
Houson St. *Oldh* 6F **41**
Hovingham St. *Roch* 5B **14**
Howardian Clo. *Oldh* 2E **49**
Howard Pl. *Roch* 5H **13**
Howard's La. *Moss* 4A **52**
Howard St. *Oldh* 3C **42**
Howard St. *Roch* 5G **13**
Howard St. *Shaw* 2G **31**
Howard Way. *L'boro* 2A **8**
Howarth Cross 3B **14**
Howarth Cross St. *Roch* 3B **14**
Howarth Farm Way. *Roch* 2C **14**
Howarth Grn. *Roch* 2C **14**
Howarth Knoll. *Roch* 6C **6**
Howarth Pl. *Roch* 3F **21**
Howarth Sq. *Roch* 5A **14**
Howarth St. *L'boro* 5H **7**
Howden Rd. *M9* 6G **37**
Howgill Cres. *Oldh* 2E **49**
Howgill St. *M11* 6B **54**
Hoylake Clo. *M40* 5F **47**
Hoyle Av. *Oldh* 6E **41**
Hoyle's Ter. *Miln* 1E **23**
Hoyle St. *Midd* 5E **39**
Huddersfield Rd. *Carr & Moss* 6A **52**
Huddersfield Rd. *Aus* 3E **43**
Huddersfield Rd. *Del* 5B **34**
Huddersfield Rd. *Dens* 5H **25**
Huddersfield Rd. *Dig* 2F **35**
Huddersfield Rd. *Dob* 6D **34**
Huddersfield Rd. *Miln* 3H **23**
Huddersfield Rd. *Oldh & Aus* 4H **41**
Hudsons Pas. *L'boro* 4A **8**
Hudson St. *Oldh* 3A **48**
Hudson Wlk. *Roch* 6D **12**
Hughes Clo. *Fail* 5G **47**
Hugh Fold. *Lees* 6C **42**
Hughley Clo. *Rytn* 5F **31**
Hugh St. *Roch* 5A **14**
Hughtrede St. *Roch* 4B **22**
Hugo St. *M40* 6C **46**
Hugo St. *Roch* 5F **21**
Hulbert St. *Midd* 2D **38**
Hull Mill La. *Del* 4B **34**
Hulmes Rd. *M40 & Fail* 2C **54**
(in two parts)
Hulme St. *Oldh* 1E **49**
Hulton St. *Fail* 6F **47**
Humber Rd. *Miln* 1G **23**
Hume St. *Roch* 1A **22**
Huncote Dri. *M9* 4A **46**
Hunger Hill. *Roch* 5D **6**
Hunger Hill La. *Roch* 2B **12**
Hunters Hill. *Bury* 5A **26**
Hunters Hill La. *Dig* 3D **34**
Hunters La. *Oldh* 4F **41**
Hunters La. *Roch* 5H **13**
Huntingdon Av. *Chad* 6B **40**
Hunt La. *Chad* 4H **39**
Huntley Way. *Heyw* 6C **18**
Huntsman Rd. *M9* 5B **46**
Hunt St. *M9* 4A **46**
Hurstbourne Av. *M11* 4A **54**
Hurstead 1D **14**
Hurstead Grn. *Roch* 1D **14**
Hurstead M. *Roch* 1D **14**
Hursted Rd. *Miln* 1F **23**
Hurst Mdw. *Roch* 5B **22**
Hurst Nook 6C **50**
Hurst St. *Oldh* 4D **40**
Hurst St. *Roch* 2A **22**
Hurstway Dri. *M9* 2A **46**
Hurstwood Clo. *Oldh* 1A **50**
Husteads La. *Dob* 2A **44**
Hutchins La. *Oldh* 2B **42**
Hutchinson Rd. *Roch* 4H **11**
Hutchinson St. *Roch* 1D **20**
Huxley St. *Oldh* 6A **42**
Hyde Pk. Pl. *Roch* 6C **14**
Hyde Rd. *Midd* 5G **39**
Hyde Sq. *Midd* 2A **38**
Hyde St. *Droy* 3G **55**
Hydon Brook Wlk. *Roch* 3E **21**
Hythe Wlk. *Chad* 5B **40**

I

Ian Frazer Ct. *Roch* 3H **21**
Ibberton Wlk. M9 *4B* ***46***
(off Carnaby St.)
Ibsley. Roch *5G* ***13***
(off Spotland Rd.)
Ilford St. *M11* 5A **54**
Ilfracombe St. *M40* 1B **54**
Ilkeston Wlk. M40 *6C* ***46***
(off Halliford Rd.)
Ilkley Clo. *Chad* 5B **40**
Ilkley St. *M40* 4C **46**
Ilminster. *Roch* 1G **21**
Ilminster Wlk. M9 *6A* ***38***
(off Crossmead Dri.)
Ilthorpe Wlk. *M40* 6C **46**
Inchfield Clo. *Roch* 5A **12**
Inchfield Rd. *M40* 4C **46**
Inchwood M. *Oldh* 5C **32**
Incline Rd. *Oldh* 3B **48**
Industry Rd. *Roch* 4H **13**
Industry St. *Chad* 1A **48**
Industry St. *L'boro* 6H **7**
Industry St. *Roch* 4A **12**
Industry St. *Whitw* 1F **5**
Inghams La. *L'boro* 6H **7**
Ingham St. *M40* 3C **54**
Ingham St. *Oldh* 4G **41**
Ingleby Av. *M9* 1A **46**
Ingleby Clo. *Shaw* 1G **31**
Ingleby Way. *Shaw* 1G **31**
Inglefield. *Roch* 4B **12**
Ingleton Clo. *Rytn* 4D **30**
Ingleton Gdns. *Shaw* 2B **32**
Inglewood Clo. *Bury* 3A **18**
Inglewood Rd. *Chad* 2F **39**
Inglis St. *L'boro* 5G **7**
Ingoe Clo. *Heyw* 4B **20**
Ings Av. *Roch* 3D **12**
Ings La. *Roch* 3D **12**
Inkerman St. *Roch* 4H **13**
Ink St. *Roch* 6H **13**
Innis Av. *M40* 2A **54**
Instow Clo. *Chad* 2H **39**
Intake La. *G'fld* 2C **52**
Invergarry Wlk. *M11* 6A **54**
Inverness Av. *M9* 1C **46**
Inver Wlk. *M40* 3F **47**
Ipswich St. *Roch* 2H **21**
Ireby Clo. *Midd* 1G **37**
Iredine St. *M11* 6A **54**
Iris Av. *Open* 6B **54**
Iris St. *Oldh* 2F **49**
Irk Va. Dri. *Chad* 2G **39**
Irk Way. *W'fld* 1A **36**
Irving St. *Oldh* 3B **48**
Irvin St. *M40* 1A **54**
Irwell Wlk. *Oldh* 2C **48**
Isabella St. *Roch* 3H **13**
Isaiah St. *Oldh* 1F **49**
Isel Wlk. *Midd* 1H **37**
Isherwood Clo. *Heyw* 6H **19**
Isherwood St. *Heyw* 6A **20**
Isherwood St. *Roch* 2A **22**
Ivanhoe St. *Oldh* 2A **42**
Iveagh Ct. *Roch* 1B **22**
Ivor St. *Roch* 4D **20**
Ivy Bank. *Whitw* 1F **5**
Ivy Clo. *Droy* 4D **54**
Ivy Clo. *Shaw* 2H **31**
Ivy Cotts. *Roch* 4F **13**
Ivy Dri. *Midd* 4B **38**
Ivygreen Dri. *S'head* 5D **42**
Ivy St. *M40* 5C **46**
Ivy Ter. *L'boro* 1B **8**
Ivy Villa. *Lees* 6D **42**

J

Jack La. *Droy* 5F **55**
(in two parts)
Jackman Av. *Heyw* 2H **27**
Jack McCann Ct. *Roch* 5A **14**
Jackson Clo. *Oldh* 6E **41**
Jackson M. *Oldh* 2B **42**
Jackson Pit. *Oldh* 5E **41**
Jackson Pl. *Roch* 5B **14**
Jackson St. *Fail* 1B **54**
Jackson St. *Midd* 2D **38**
Jackson St. *Oldh* 4H **41**
Jackson St. *Roch* 1B **22**
Jackson St. *S'head* 5D **42**
Jackson St. *Ward* 5C **6**
Jack Talbot Sports Cen. 4G 19
Jack Taylor Ct. Roch *4B* ***14***
(off Athol St.)
Jacob's Ladder. *Moss* 4G **51**
James Andrew St. *Midd* 2D **38**
James Bentley Wlk. *M40* 2A **54**
James Butterworth Ct. *Roch* 1B **22**
James Butterworth St. *Roch* 1B **22**
Jameson St. *Roch* 5D **20**
James Rd. *Shaw* 1H **31**
James St. *Droy* 5F **55**
James St. *Fail* 5A **48**
James St. *Fir* 6D **14**
James St. *Heyw* 4H **19**
James St. *L'boro* 1E **15**
James St. *Oldh* 2B **42**
James St. *Roch* 5A **14**
(Regent St.)
James St. *Roch* 1C **14**
(Wardle Rd.)
James St. *Shaw* 4G **31**
James St. *Whitw* 1F **5**
James St. S. *Chad* 4A **40**
Jammy La. *Chad* 5C **40**
Jane St. *Chad* 5B **40**
Jane St. *Roch* 5G **13**
Jardine Way. *Chad* 1H **47**
Jarvis St. *Oldh* 5G **41**
Jarvis St. *Roch* 4H **13**
Jasmine Av. *Droy* 5G **55**
Jefferson Way. *Roch* 2H **13**
Jeffrey Wlk. *Heyw* 5E **19**
Jenny St. *Oldh* 3C **48**
Jepheys Pl. *Roch* 4H **13**
Jepheys St. *Roch* 4H **13**
Jericho 3C **18**
Jericho Rd. *Bury* 3C **18**
Jermyn St. *Roch* 5A **14**
Jerrold St. *L'boro* 6H **7**
Jesmond Wlk. M9 *6H* ***37***
(off Claygate Dri.)
Jespersen St. *Oldh* 4F **41**
Jinnah Clo. *Oldh* 6A **42**
Jinnah Clo. *Open* 6A **54**
Joan St. *M40* 6C **46**
John Ashworth St. *Roch* 4B **14**
John Booth St. *S'head* 6D **42**
John Heywood St. *M11* 5A **54**
John Howarth Countryside Cen. 1H 55
John Kemble Ct. *Roch* 3F **21**
John Knott St. *Lees* 5D **42**
John Lee Fold 2D **38**
John Lee Fold. *Midd* 2C **38**
John Roberts Clo. *Roch* 2G **21**
John Robinson Wlk. *M40* 6C **46**
Johnson Av. *Oldh* 4C **32**
Johnson Gro. *Midd* 3A **38**
Johnston. Roch *5G* ***13***
(off Spotland Rd.)
Johnston Av. *L'boro* 2F **15**
John St. *Droy* 6D **54**
John St. *Fail* 4H **47**
John St. *Heyw* 5H **19**
(Adelaide St.)
John St. *Heyw* 4H **19**
(Starkey St.)
John St. *L'boro* 6G **7**
John St. *Oldh* 5E **41**
John St. *P'wich* 3C **36**
John St. *Roch* 2C **14**
(Halifax Rd.)
John St. *Roch* 5H **13**
(St Mary's Ga.)
John St. *Rytn* 5D **30**
John St. *Shaw* 4G **31**
John St. *S'head* 5E **43**
John St. *Whitw* 1F **5**
John William St. *M11* 6A **54**
Jones St. *M9* 5A **46**
Jones St. *Oldh* 3G **41**
Jones St. *Roch* 1A **22**
Jones St. *Rytn* 1E **41**
Jopson St. *Midd* 2D **38**
Jordan Av. *Shaw* 6A **24**
Joseph Dean Ct. *M40* 6C **46**
Joseph St. *Fail* 5H **47**
Joseph St. *L'boro* 5H **7**
Joseph St. *Midd* 2B **38**
Joseph St. *Roch* 3F **13**
Joshua La. *Midd* 4F **39**
Joule St. *M9* 4A **46**
Jowett St. *Oldh* 2A **42**
Jowkin La. *Roch* 6H **11**
Joyce St. *M40* 6D **46**
Joy Pl. *Roch* 3H **13**
Joy St. *Roch* 3H **13**
Jubilee 5A **24**
Jubilee. *Shaw* 5A **24**
Jubilee Rd. *Midd* 2D **38**
Jubilee St. *Shaw* 3A **32**
Jubilee Ter. *Midd* 2D **38**
Judith St. *Roch* 2E **13**
Judy St. *M9* 5B **46**
Julian Ho. *Oldh* 4F **41**
Julia St. *Roch* 5G **13**
Junction All. *Roch* 6H **13**
Junction 19 Ind. Pk.
Heyw 6B **20**
Junction St. *Midd* 5F **39**
Junction St. *Oldh* 1E **49**
Juniper Clo. *Oldh* 5D **32**
Juniper Cres. *Droy* 6D **54**
Juniper Dri. *Fir* 6D **14**
Juno St. *Oldh* 2G **41**

A-Z Oldham & Rochdale 71

Jura Gro.—Langness St.

Jura Gro. Heyw 6F 19
Jutland Av. Roch 5E 13

K

Kathan Clo. Roch 6B 14
Kathleen St. Roch 6F 13
Kay Brow. Heyw 5G 19
Kay St. Heyw 5G 19
Kay St. L'boro 3F 15
Kay St. Roch 2G 21
Keats Av. Droy 5E 55
Keats Av. Roch 4C 12
Keats Rd. Oldh 2H 41
Keb La. Oldh 5G 49
Keble Av. Oldh 2E 49
Keeley Clo. M40 3A 54
Keepers Dri. Roch 3A 12
Keighley Av. Droy 4E 55
Kelham Wlk. M40 4E 47
Kellett St. Roch 5B 14
Kellett Wlk. M11 5A 54
Kelsall Dri. Droy 4D 54
Kelsall St. Oldh 5D 40
Kelsall St. Roch 5A 14
Kelsey Flats. Heyw 5G 19 (off Fearn St.)
Kelsey Wlk. M9 6F 37
Kelso Clo. Oldh 4F 49
Kelverlow St. Oldh 5A 42
Kelvin Av. Midd 5F 37
Kelvington Dri. M9 6A 46
Kelwood Av. Bury 2B 18
Kemnay Wlk. M11 6A 54
Kemp Av. Roch 2F 21
Kempsey Ct. Chad 4B 40
Kempsey St. Chad 4B 40
Kempsey Wlk. M40 4F 47
Kemp St. Midd 3B 38
Kempton Clo. Droy 5G 55
Kempton Way. Chad 4C 40
Kendal Av. Roch 3A 12
Kendal Clo. Heyw 1A 28
Kendal Dri. Shaw 2B 32
Kendal Wlk. Midd 2A 38
Kendrew Wlk. M9 4A 46
Kenilworth. Roch 1G 21
Kenilworth Av. Chad 2G 39
Kenilworth Clo. Oldh 6D 42
Kenilworth Gro. Aud 6G 55
Kenilworth Rd. Roch 1C 30
Kenion Rd. Roch 1D 20
Kenion St. Roch 6H 13
Kenley Dri. Heyw 2B 28
Kenmere Gro. M40 4D 46
Kenmore Clo. W'fld 3A 36
Kenmore Rd. W'fld 3A 36
Kenmore Way. W'fld 3A 36
Kennard Clo. M9 4B 46
Kennedy Dri. Bury 1A 36
Kennedy St. Oldh 6E 41
Kennet Flats. Heyw 5G 19 (off Meadow Clo.)
Kennington Av. M40 3A 54
Kenny Clo. Lees 6B 42
Kensington Av. Chad 3G 39
Kensington Av. Rytn 3C 30
Kensington Clo. Miln 1G 23
Kensington Rd. Fail 5B 48
Kensington Rd. Oldh 1D 48
Kensington St. Roch 3G 21
Kent Av. Chad 5A 40
Kent Av. Droy 6C 54
Kent Clo. Dig 5E 35
Kent Gro. Fail 1C 54
Kentmere Av. Roch 2B 14
Kentmere Ct. M9 1C 46
Kentmere Dri. Midd 6A 28
Kenton Rd. Shaw 2G 31
Kenton St. Oldh 6H 41
Kent St. Oldh 1F 49
Kent St. Roch 1H 21
Kentucky St. Oldh 5A 42
Kent Wlk. Heyw 6E 19
Kenwick Dri. M40 3G 47
Kenwood Rd. Oldh 2C 40
Kenworthy Gdns. Upperm 3D 44
Kenworthy St. Roch 6C 14
Kenworthy Ter. Roch 6C 14
Kenyon Av. Oldh 2F 49
Kenyon Fold 2A 20
Kenyon Fold. Roch 2A 20
Kenyon La. M40 5C 46
Kenyon La. Midd 2D 38
Kenyon La. P'wich 6A 36
Kenyon St. Heyw 5G 19
Kerr St. M9 2A 46
Kershaw Dri. Chad 2F 47
Kershaw Gro. Aud 6F 55
Kershaw La. Aud 6G 55
Kershaw Pas. L'boro 1E 15
Kershaw Rd. Fail 6H 47
Kershaw St. Droy 6D 54
Kershaw St. Heyw 5F 19
Kershaw St. Roch 5H 13
Kershaw St. Rytn 4D 30
Kershaw St. Shaw 2H 31 (in two parts)
Kershaw St. E. Shaw 2H 31
Kersley St. Oldh 5G 41
Kerwood Dri. Rytn 6E 31
Keston Av. M9 2C 46
Keston Av. Droy 6C 54
Keston Rd. Oldh 2A 42
Kestrel Av. Aud 6G 55
Kestrel Av. Oldh 6A 42
Kestrel M. Roch 6B 12
Keswick Av. Chad 4A 40
Keswick Av. Oldh 1G 49
Keswick Clo. Midd 1H 37
Keswick Ct. Midd 1H 37
Keswick St. Roch 5D 20
Keverlow La. Oldh 3A 50
Kevin Av. Rytn 1E 41
Kew Gdns. M40 4C 46
Kew Rd. Fail 5A 48
Kew Rd. Oldh 5H 41 (in two parts)
Kew Rd. Roch 4A 22
Keynsham Rd. M11 4A 54
Khartoum St. M11 5B 54
Kibworth Wlk. M9 6A 38 (off Crossmead Dri.)
Kidacre Wlk. M40 6C 46
Kidderminster Way. Chad 2H 39
Kid St. Midd 2B 38
Kidwall Wlk. M9 4B 46
Kielder Hill. Midd 5B 28
Kilburn Av. M9 5H 37
Kilburn St. Oldh 2A 42
Kildare Cres. Roch 5H 21
Kiln Bank. Whitw 1E 5 (off Tong End)
Kiln Bank La. Whitw 1E 5
Kilnbrook Clo. G'ton 1F 51
Kilner Clo. Bury 5A 26
Kilnerdeyne Ter. Roch 1G 21
Kiln Green 5F 35
Kiln Hill Clo. Chad 1H 39
Kiln Hill La. Chad 1H 39
Kiln La. Miln 1F 23
Kiln Mt. Miln 1F 23
Kilnside Dri. M9 6A 46
Kiln Wlk. Roch 3G 13
Kilworth St. Roch 3F 21
Kimberley St. Oldh 2C 48
Kincraig Clo. M11 6A 54
Kinder Av. Oldh 6A 42
Kinders Cres. G'fld 6D 44
Kinders Fold. L'boro 4F 7
Kinders La. G'fld 6D 44
Kinders M. G'fld 6D 44
Kinder Way. Midd 1B 38
King Albert St. Shaw 2H 31
Kingcombe Wlk. M9 5A 46
Kingfisher Av. Aud 6G 55
Kingfisher Ct. Roch 1C 14
Kingfisher Dri. Bury 3A 18
King La. Oldh 5C 32
Kingsbridge Rd. Oldh 6H 41
Kingsbury Rd. M11 5A 54
Kingscliffe St. M9 5A 46
Kings Clo. P'wich 6A 36
King's Dri. Midd 3A 38
Kings Gro. Roch 1C 14
Kingsheath Av. M11 4A 54
Kingsland. Roch 4E 21
Kingsland Rd. Roch 4D 20
Kings La. Oldh 4C 32
Kingsley Av. M9 6B 46
Kingsley Dri. Lees 4C 42
Kingsley Gro. Aud 6G 55
Kingsley Rd. Midd 1D 38
Kingsley Rd. Oldh 5A 42
Kingsmead M. M9 6G 37
King Sq. Shop. Cen. Oldh 5E 41
Kings Rd. Chad 2G 47
King's Rd. Oldh 6F 41
Kings Rd. Roch 2B 22
King's Rd. Shaw 3G 31
Kingston Av. Chad 1A 48
Kingston Av. Oldh 2H 41
Kingston Clo. Shaw 1H 31
Kingston Dri. Rytn 3C 30
Kingston Gro. M9 1B 46
Kingston M. Fail 6B 48
Kingston Rd. Fail 6B 48
King St. Del 5B 34
King St. Droy 6E 55 (in two parts)
King St. Fail 1B 54
King St. Heyw 6H 19
King St. Midd 2C 38
King St. Moss 4H 51
King St. Oldh 5E 41
King St. Roch 6H 13
King St. E. Roch 2H 21
King St. S. Roch 2G 21 (in two parts)
Kings Wlk. Droy 6E 55
Kingsway. Midd 5B 38
Kingsway. Roch 2B 22
Kingsway Clo. Oldh 6E 41
Kingsway Retail Pk. Roch 6D 14
Kingsway W. Ind. Pk. Roch 2B 22
Kingswood Rd. Midd 6B 28
Kinlett Wlk. M40 3F 47
Kinloch St. Oldh 1G 49
Kinmount Wlk. M9 6A 46 (off Lathbury Rd.)
Kintyre Clo. M11 6B 54
Kinver Rd. M40 3E 47
Kipling Av. Droy 4E 55
Kipling Rd. Oldh 1H 41
Kirby Av. Chad 2F 47
Kirby Wlk. Shaw 1H 31
Kirkbank St. Oldh 4D 40 (in two parts)
Kirkby Av. M40 6D 46
Kirkdale Av. M40 3F 47
Kirkdale Dri. Rytn 4C 30
Kirkfell Wlk. Oldh 2F 41 (in two parts)
Kirkhams 4A 36
Kirkham St. Oldh 4E 41
Kirkhill Wlk. M40 3F 47
Kirkholt 4H 21
Kirkholt Wlk. M9 2A 46
Kirklee Av. Chad 2A 40
Kirklee Rd. Roch 5F 21
Kirklinton Dri. M9 6A 46
Kirkstall. Roch 5G 13 (off Falinge Rd.)
Kirkstall Av. Heyw 4G 19
Kirkstall Av. L'boro 5G 7
Kirkstall Rd. Midd 6B 28
Kirkstone Clo. Oldh 2F 41
Kirkstone Dri. Midd 1A 38
Kirkstone Dri. Rytn 3D 30
Kirkstone Rd. M40 3E 47
Kirktown Wlk. Open 6A 54
Kirkway. M9 1C 46
Kirkway. Midd 4C 38
Kirkway. Roch 5H 21
Kirtlington Clo. Rytn 4G 31
Kirton Wlk. M9 6G 37
Kitchen St. Roch 5A 14
Kitter St. Roch 2B 14
Knacks La. Roch 6C 4
Knarr Barn La. Dob 6H 33
Knarr La. Del 1A 44 (in two parts)
Knight Cres. Midd 5H 27
Knights Clo. P'wich 6A 36
Knoll Hill Vw. Heyw 5E 19
Knoll St. Roch 4D 20
Knoll, The. Moss 4F 51
Knoll, The. Shaw 3A 32
Knott Hill La. Del 6A 34
Knott Hill Local Nature Reserve 6D 50
Knott Lanes 5F 49
Knott Lanes. Oldh 5F 49
Knowl Hill Dri. Roch 3A 12
Knowl La. Roch 1F 11
Knowl Rd. Roch 6D 14
Knowl Rd. Shaw 3A 32
Knowls Lane 6D 42
Knowls La. Lees 6D 42
Knowls, The. Oldh 4B 48
Knowl St. Oldh 3C 48
Knowl Syke St. Ward 4C 6
Knowl Top La. Upperm 4F 45
Knowl Vw. L'boro 3F 15
Knowsley. S'head 4E 43
Knowsley Av. S'head 4E 43
Knowsley Dri. S'head 4E 43
Knowsley Grn. S'head 4E 43
Knowsley St. Roch 5G 13
Knowsley Ter. S'head 4E 43
Krokus Sq. Chad 4A 40

L

Laburnham Rd. Midd 3E 39
Laburnum Av. Aud 6G 55
Laburnum Av. Chad 2B 40
Laburnum Av. Fail 1D 54
Laburnum Av. Shaw 3H 31
Laburnum Ho. Shaw 3H 31
Laburnum La. Miln 4G 23
Laburnum Rd. Oldh 5C 48
Laburnum Ter. Roch 3G 21
Laburnum Vs. Oldh 4G 49
Laburnum Way. L'boro 5F 7
Lacrosse Av. Oldh 1C 48
Ladcastle Rd. G'fld 2B 44
Ladhill La. G'fld 6D 44
Lady House 2E 23
Ladyhouse Clo. Miln 2G 23
Lady Ho. Fold. Miln 3F 23 (off Ashfield La.)
Ladyhouse La. Miln 2F 23 (in two parts)
Ladylands Av. M11 5A 54
Lady Rd. Lees 5C 42
Ladysmith St. Oldh 2C 48
Lake Bank. L'boro 2G 15
Lake Dri. Midd 4B 38
Lakeland Ct. Midd 1H 37
Lakeland Dri. Rytn 1C 30
Lake Side. L'boro 3G 15
Lake St. Roch 1H 21
Lake Vw. M9 3C 46
Lake Vw. L'boro 4F 7
Lakin St. M40 6C 46
Lambeth Av. Fail 5B 48
Lambeth Rd. M40 3A 54
Lambeth Ter. Roch 2F 21
Lambourne Gro. Miln 2F 23
Lambrook Wlk. M40 3B 54
Lamburn Av. M40 3F 47
Lanark Clo. Heyw 6D 18
Lancashire Cotts. Moss 4H 51
Lancashire Ct. Oldh 6C 40
Lancaster Av. Fail 6G 47
Lancaster Av. Midd 4E 39 (in two parts)
Lancaster Ct. M40 3A 54
Lancaster Ho. Rytn 4D 30
Lancaster Rd. Droy 4D 54
Lancaster Sq. Rytn 4D 30
Lancaster St. Chad 1A 48
Lancaster St. Moss 4F 51
Lancaster Ter. Roch 3H 11
Lancing Wlk. Chad 5A 40
Lander Gro. M9 2B 46
Landsberg Rd. Fail 5B 48
Landsberg Ter. Fail 5B 48
Landseer St. Oldh 6G 41
Lands End Rd. Midd 4F 37
Lane Bottom 2C 24
Lane Brow. G'ton 6F 43
Lane Dri. G'ton 6F 43
Lane End 1B 28
Lane End. Heyw 1B 28
Lane End Clo. Fail 1E 55
Lane Head Rd. Oldh & Moss 1D 50
Lane Mdw. Shaw 3G 31
Lane Side 2B 32
Laneside Av. Shaw 2B 32
Laneside Clo. L'boro 5G 7
Laneside Wlk. Miln 6F 15
Langcroft Dri. M40 2A 54
Langdale Av. Oldh 1D 48
Langdale Av. Roch 1C 30
Langdale Dri. Midd 6B 28
Langden Clo. Shaw 1G 31
Langfield Cres. Droy 5G 55
Langham Rd. Oldh 1E 49
Langholme Way. Heyw 6D 18
Langland Clo. M9 1A 46
Langley 1A 38
Langley Av. G'ton 6F 43
Langley Av. Midd 5A 28
Langley Ho. Midd 6C 28
Langley La. Heyw & Midd 5G 27
Langness St. M11 6A 54

Langside Av. *M9* 1A **46**
Langton Clo. *Fail* 5B **48**
Langton St. *Heyw* 4H **19**
Langton St. *Midd* 3C **38**
Langton Ter. *Roch* 3G **21**
Langworthy Rd. *M40* 6C **46**
Lansdowne Av. *Aud* 6G **55**
Lansdowne Ct. *Chad* 5B **40**
Lansdowne Rd. *Chad* 5C **40**
Lansdowne St. *Roch* 6E **13**
Lapwing Clo. *Roch* 6A **12**
Larch Clo. *Fail* 1D **54**
Larches, The. *Moss* 4H **51**
Larch Gro. *Chad* 3B **40**
Larch Gro. *Lees* 3C **42**
Larch St. *Oldh* 6D **40**
Larchview Rd. *Midd* 3E **39**
Larchway. *Fir* 6D **14**
Larchwood. *Chad* 4G **39**
Larchwood Av. *M9* 6B **46**
Larkfield Clo. *Ash L* 6H **49**
Lark Hill. **3C 38**
Lark Hill. *Midd* 3C **38**
Lark Hill Ct. *Midd* 3C **38**
Lark Hill La. *Dob* 5C **34**
Larkhill Pl. *Roch* 4G **13**
Lark Hill Rd. *Dob* 1B **44**
Larks Ri. *Droy* 4H **55**
Lark St. *Oldh* 6B **32**
Larkwood Clo. *Carr* 6A **52**
Lastingham St. *M40* 1A **54**
Lathbury Rd. *M9 & M40* 6A **46**
Lathom Hall Av. *S'head* 4E **43**
Latimer St. *Oldh* 5G **41**
Latin St. *Roch* 1G **21**
Latrigg Cres. *Midd* 1G **37**
Launceston Clo. *Oldh* 1A **50**
Laureate's Pl. *S'head* 4F **43**
Laurel Av. *Chad* 3F **39**
Laurel Bank Gdns. *M9* 2A **46**
Laurel Ct. *Roch* 1B **22**
Laurels Dri. *L'boro* 2F **15**
Laurels, The. *Moss* 4H **51**
Laurel St. *Midd* 3F **39**
Laurel St. *Oldh* 5H **41**
Laurie Pl. *Roch* 4H **13**
Lavender Rd. *Oldh* 1C **50**
Lavenham Av. *M11* 6B **54**
Laverton Clo. *Bury* 6C **18**
Lawers Av. *Chad* 3A **40**
Lawflat. *Ward* 6C **6**
Lawnbank Clo. *Midd* 2A **38**
Lawn Closes. *Oldh* 2A **50**
Lawnswood. *Roch* 4E **21**
Lawrence Clo. *Roch* 4C **12**
Lawson Clo. *Midd* 5C **28**
Laws Ter. *L'boro* 6F **7**
Law St. *Roch* 3E **21**
Lawton Fold. *G'ton* 4F **43**
Lawton Sq. *Del* 5B **34**
Lawton St. *Del* 5B **34**
Lawton St. *Droy* 5F **55**
Lawton St. *Roch* 4A **14**
Laxey St. *M40* 6D **46**
Laycock Cres. *Fail* 6H **47**
Laycock Gro. *Fail* 6H **47**
Laycock St. *Roch* 2C **14**
Laythe Barn Clo. *Miln* 1E **23**
Leabrook Dri. *M40* 5G **47**
Leach Clo. *Roch* 3C **14**
Leach's Pas. *L'boro* 1F **15**
Leach St. *Miln* 2F **23**
Leach St. *Oldh* 3C **42**
Leach St. *Roch* 1B **22**
Leach St. *Shaw* 3A **32**
Leach Wlk. *Oldh* 3C **42**
Lea Ct. *Fail* 6G **47**
Leadale Ri. *S'head* 5E **43**
Lea Dri. *M9* 2B **46**
Lea Fold. *L'boro* 2E **15**
Leaf Ter. *Roch* 1F **13**
League St. *Roch* 2A **22**
Leaholm Rd. *M40* 2B **54**
Leah St. *L'boro* 6H **7**
Leamington St. *Oldh* 3B **42**
Leamington St. *Roch* 5G **13**
Leamore Wlk. *M9* 2A **46**
(off White Moss Rd.)
Lea Mt. Dri. *Bury* 3B **18**
Leander Clo. *M9* 3A **46**
Leander Dri. *Roch* 6F **21**
Leaside Av. *Chad* 1B **40**
Leaside Clo. *Roch* 3F **13**
Lea Vw. *Rytn* 6C **30**

Leaway. *Ward* 5C **6**
Leconfield Dri. *M9* 2A **46**
Ledbury Clo. *Midd* 5C **38**
Ledbury Rd. *Fail*. 3C **54**
Ledsham Av. *M9* 6E **37**
Lee Cross. *Dig* 5F **35**
Leeds Clo. *Bury* 6A **26**
Leefields. *Upperm* 3D **44**
Leefields Clo. *Upperm* 3D **44**
Leegate Dri. *M9* 1B **46**
Leegrange Rd. *M9* 4A **46**
Lee Rd. *M9* 5A **46**
Lees. **5C 42**
Leesbrook. **5B 42**
Leesbrook Pk. *Oldh* 5B **42**
Leesfield. **6C 42**
Lees Gro. *Oldh* 6B **42**
Lees Ho. *Lees* 4C **42**
Lee Side. *Dig* 6F **35**
(in two parts)
Lees New Rd. *Oldh* 2C **50**
Lees Pk. Av. *Droy* 5G **55**
Lees Pk. Way. *Droy* 5G **55**
Lees Rd. *Ash L & Oldh* 6B **50**
Lees Rd. *Moss* 2F **51**
Lees Rd. *Oldh* 4G **41**
Lees St. *Droy* 5F **55**
Lees St. *Midd* 4F **39**
Lees St. *Moss* 3G **51**
Lees St. *Oldh* 5G **49**
Lees St. *Shaw* 2H **31**
(in two parts)
Lees St. E. *Shaw* 2H **31**
(off Lees St.)
Lee St. *L'boro* 5H **7**
Lee St. *Midd* 6B **28**
Lee St. *Oldh* 5D **40**
Lee St. *Upperm* 3D **44**
Leesway. *Lees* 6C **42**
Legh Dri. *Aud* 6F **55**
Leicester Av. *Droy* 4D **54**
Leicester Rd. *Fail* 2E **55**
Leicester St. *Oldh* 5H **41**
Leicester St. *Roch* 2A **22**
Leigh St. *Fir* 6D **14**
Leigh St. *Heyw* 5F **19**
Leighton Av. *L'boro* 3F **15**
Leighton St. *M40* 5C **46**
Leith Pl. *Oldh* 3E **49**
Lemnos St. *Oldh* 4G **41**
Lemonpark Ind. Est. *Heyw* . . 1A **28**
Lenfield La. *Oldh* 2E **41**
Leng Rd. *M40* 2B **54**
Lennox Wlk. *Heyw* 6D **18**
Lenten Gro. *Heyw* 2A **28**
Lentmead Dri. *M40* 4C **46**
Leominster Rd. *Midd* 5D **38**
Leonardin Clo. *Shaw* 1F **31**
Leonard St. *Roch* 6E **21**
Leonard Way. *Rytn* 6F **31**
Leopold Ct. *Roch* 6F **13**
Leopold St. *Roch* 6F **13**
Lepton Wlk. *M9* 1A **46**
Leroy Dri. *M9*. 3A **46**
Leslie Av. *Chad* 2B **48**
Letchworth Av. *Roch* 2A **22**
Letham St. *Oldh* 3F **49**
Levedale Rd. *M9* 1A **46**
Levens St. *M40* 6C **46**
Levens Wlk. *Chad* 6A **40**
Leven Wlk. *W'fld* 3A **36**
Lever St. *Heyw* 4H **19**
Lever St. *Midd* 2C **38**
Lever Wlk. *Midd* 4B **38**
Levington Dri. *Oldh* 5G **49**
Lewes Wlk. *Chad* 5B **40**
Lewis Av. *M9* 4A **46**
Lewis Dri. *Heyw* 6D **18**
Lewisham Av. *M40* 3A **54**
Lewisham Clo. *Rytn* 3C **30**
Lewis Rd. *Droy* 5C **54**
Lewis St. *Heyw* 4A **20**
Lewis St. *Shaw* 4H **31**
Leyburn Av. *Rytn* 5D **30**
Leyburn Rd. *M40* 3E **47**
Ley Dri. *Heyw* 2A **28**
Leyfield Rd. *Miln* 1D **22**
Leyland Av. *M40* 6D **46**
Leyton St. *Roch* 3H **13**
Leywell Dri. *Oldh* 6B **32**
Leywell Rd. *M9* 5B **46**
Library La. *Oldh* 3D **40**
Lichens Cres. *Oldh* 2G **49**
Lichfield Av. *Ash L* 5B **50**
Lichfield Clo. *Dens* 5G **25**

Lichfield Dri. *Chad* 2A **40**
Lichfield Ter. *Roch* 3C **22**
Lightbirches La. *Moss* 3F **51**
Lightbowne Rd. *M40* 6C **46**
Lightburn Av. *L'boro* 1E **15**
Lighthouse. *L'boro* 2A **8**
Lightowlers La. *L'boro* 4B **8**
Lignum Av. *Chad* 3B **40**
Lilac Av. *Miln* 4G **23**
Lilac Gro. *M40* 4C **46**
Lilac Gro. *Chad* 3B **40**
Lilac La. *Oldh* 3D **48**
Lilac Rd. *Roch* 5H **21**
Lilac Vw. Clo. *Shaw* 3A **32**
Lila St. *M9*. 6B **46**
Liley St. *Roch* 6A **14**
Lilmore Av. *M40* 1A **54**
Lilstock Wlk. *M9* 2A **46**
Lily La. *M9*. 6B **46**
Lily Lanes. **5C 50**
Lily Lanes. *Ash L* 5C **50**
Lily St. *Midd* 3E **39**
Lily St. *Miln* 1F **23**
Lily St. *Oldh* 2E **41**
Lily St. *Rytn* 5F **31**
Lima St. *Bury* 4A **18**
Lime Ditch Rd. *Fail*. 4A **48**
Lime Field. **3A 38**
Limefield. *Midd* 3A **38**
Limefield. *Moss* 3F **51**
Limefield. *Roch* 6E **15**
Lime Gdns. *Midd* 3A **38**
Lime Gate. **4C 48**
Lime Ga. *Oldh* 3C **48**
Lime Grn. *Oldh* 4D **48**
Lime Grn. Rd. *Oldh* 5C **48**
Lime Gro. *Heyw* 4G **19**
Lime Gro. *L'boro* 5F **7**
Lime Gro. *Rytn* 3D **30**
Limehurst. **6G 49**
Limehurst. *Oldh* 6G **49**
Limehurst Rd. *Ash L* 6G **49**
Lime La. *Fail* 6C **48**
Lime La. *Oldh* 4C **48**
(in two parts)
Limers Ga. *Whitw* 6H **5**
Lime Side. **4D 48**
Limeside Rd. *Oldh* 3C **48**
Limes, The. *Moss* 4F **51**
(Birches, The)
Limes, The. *Moss* 4A **52**
(Winterford Av.)
Lime St. *Chad* 2C **40**
Lime Tree Gro. *Fail* 6B **48**
Limetrees Rd. *Midd* 3B **38**
Lincoln Av. *Droy* 4E **55**
Lincoln Clo. *Ash L* 5B **50**
Lincoln Clo. *Roch* 1A **22**
Lincoln Clo. Ind. Est. *Roch* . 1A **22**
Lincoln Dri. *M40* 3A **54**
Lincoln Dri. *Roch* 2G **15**
Lincoln Leach Ct. *Roch* . . . 2H **21**
Lincoln Rd. *Fail* 1E **55**
Lincoln Rd. *Midd* 6E **39**
Lincoln St. *Oldh* 6B **40**
Lincoln St. *Roch* 1A **22**
Lincoln St. Bus. Pk. *Roch* . . 2A **22**
Lincoln Wlk. *Heyw* 5E **19**
Lindale Av. *M40* 3F **47**
Lindale Av. *Chad* 5A **40**
Lindale Av. *Rytn* 1C **30**
Lindale Dri. *Midd* 6A **28**
Lindale Ri. *Shaw* 2B **32**
Linden Av. *Oldh* 3B **42**
Linden Way. *Droy* 6C **54**
Lindenwood. *Chad* 3G **39**
Lindisfarne. *Roch* 5G **13**
(off Spotland Rd.)
Lindrick Clo. *M40* 6E **47**
Lindsay Clo. *Oldh* 1B **42**
Lindside Wlk. *M9* 2A **46**
Lindum St. *Heyw* 5A **20**
Lineholme. *Rytn* 1C **40**
Lines Rd. *Droy* 6F **55**
Linfield St. *M11* 6A **54**
Linford Av. *M40* 3E **47**
Lingdale Wlk. *M40* 6C **46**
Lingfield Rd. *M11* 6A **54**
Lingfield Wlk. *Chad* 4C **40**
Lingholme Dri. *Midd* 1G **37**
Lingmell Clo. *Midd* 1H **37**
Lingmoor Clo. *Midd* 1G **37**
Link La. *Oldh* 3E **49**
Link Rd. *S'head* 4D **42**
Links Av. *Fail* 2D **54**

Linkside Av. *Rytn* 4D **30**
Links Pl. *Ash L*. 6C **50**
Links Rd. *Heyw* 1H **27**
Links, The. *M40* 6E **47**
Links Vw. *Roch* 1D **20**
Links Way. *Chad* 3C **40**
Link, The. *Shaw* 1F **31**
Linkway Ind. Est. *Midd* 3D **38**
Linley Dri. *Oldh* 1B **50**
Linnell Dri. *Roch* 5A **12**
Linnet Clo. *Aud* 6G **55**
Linnet Dri. *Bury* 3A **18**
Linnet Hill. *Roch* 1E **21**
Linney La. *Shaw* 2A **32**
Linslade Wlk. *M9* 6A **46**
(off Foleshill Av.)
Linwood St. *Fail* 1A **54**
Lion Brow. *M9* 2A **46**
Lisbon St. *Roch* 5E **13**
Lisburn Rd. *M40* 5C **46**
Lisetta Av. *Oldh* 6H **41**
Liskeard Av. *Rytn* 6F **31**
Liskeard Clo. *Roch* 4C **14**
Lisle St. *Roch* 5A **14**
Lister Rd. *Midd* 5F **37**
Litchfield Ct. *Midd* 4G **37**
Lit. Bank St. *Oldh* 5H **41**
Littleborough. **6H 7**
Littleborough Coach House &
Heritage Cen. 6H **7**
Littleborough Ind. Est. *L'boro* . . 6G **7**
Little Clegg. **3F 15**
Lit. Clegg Rd. *L'boro*. 3E **15**
Littledale St. *Roch* 5G **13**
(in two parts)
Little Flatt. *Roch* 4D **12**
Little Green. **2E 39**
Lit. Hey St. *Rytn* 5G **31**
Littlehills Clo. *Midd* 2A **38**
Lit. Howarth Way. *Roch* . . . 1C **14**
Littlemoor La. *Dig* 5D **34**
Littlemoor La. *Oldh* 3A **42**
Littlemoss. **3G 55**
Littlemoss Rd. *Droy* 4G **55**
Lit. Oak Clo. *Lees* 5C **42**
Little Park. **3C 38**
Little 66. *Bury* 2A **26**
Littletown. *Oldh* 1C **48**
Littlewood. *Rytn* 5H **31**
(off Oldham Rd.)
Littondale Clo. *Rytn* 4E **31**
Liverton Ct. *M9* 6F **37**
Liverton Dri. *M9* 6F **37**
Livesey St. *Oldh* 3A **42**
Livingstone Av. *Moss* 4F **51**
Livingstone St. *Lees* 6C **42**
Livingstone St. *S'head* 5E **43**
Livsey La. *Heyw* 5E **19**
Livsey St. *Roch* 6A **14**
Lizmar Ter. *M9* 5B **46**
Lloyd St. *Droy* 6D **54**
Lloyd St. *Heyw* 6H **19**
Lloyd St. *Roch* 3F **21**
Lloyd St. *Whitw* 2E **5**
Lobden. **4G 5**
Lobden Cres. *Whitw* 4E **5**
Lobley Clo. *Roch* 3B **14**
Lochawe Clo. *Heyw* 6E **19**
Lochinver Gro. *Heyw* 6E **19**
Lock Clo. *Heyw* 1A **28**
Lockhart St. *Roch* 2B **22**
Locking Ga. Ri. *Oldh* 2C **42**
Lockside Vw. *Moss* 2A **52**
Loddon Wlk. *M9* 5A **46**
Lodge Bank Rd. *L'boro* 2F **15**
Lodge Fold. *Droy* 5F **55**
Lodge La. *Del.* 4A **34**
(in two parts)
Lodgeside Clo. *Droy* 5F **55**
Lodge St. *L'boro* 5H **7**
Lodge St. *Midd* 2C **38**
Lodge St. *Ward* 5C **6**
Lodge Vw. *Droy* 5F **55**
Loisine Clo. *Roch* 4D **20**
Lomas St. *Fail* 4A **48**
Lomas St. *Midd* 2D **38**
Lomax St. *L'boro* 4G **7**
Lomax St. *Roch* 4H **13**
Lombard St. *Oldh* 4E **41**
Lombard St. *Roch* 5F **13**
Lomond Ter. *Roch* 3C **22**
London Rd. *Oldh* 2H **41**
Longacres Dri. *Whitw* 1F **5**
Longacres La. *Whitw* 1F **5**
Longdale Clo. *Rytn* 5C **30**

Longdell Wlk.—Market St.

Longdell Wlk. M9 5A 46
(off Moston La.)
Longden Av. Oldh. 6C 32
Longfellow Cres. Oldh 5B 32
Longfield Cres. Oldh. 2A 42
Longfield Pk. Shaw 3G 31
Longfield Rd. Roch. 5E 13
Longfield Rd. Shaw 3G 31
Longford St. Heyw. 5H 19
Long Hill. Roch 3F 21
Longhill Wlk. M40 6C 46
Longhurst Rd. M9 6F 37
Long La. Chad 2H 47
Long La. Dob. 1C 44
(Dobcross)
Long La. Dob 5F 45
(Tunstead)
Longley St. Oldh. 5F 41
Longley St. Shaw. 4H 31
Longmead Way. Midd 2D 38
Longridge Dri. Heyw 5D 18
Long Row. Carr 6B 52
Long Rushes. Shaw 1F 31
Long Sight. 1E 41
Long St. Midd 3B 38
(in two parts)
Longthwaite Clo. Midd 1H 37
Longton Rd. M9. 6G 37
Lonsdale Av. Roch 2B 22
Lonsdale Rd. Oldh 3C 48
Lonsdale St. M40. 1A 54
Lord La. Droy. 3C 54
Lord La. Fail 6H 47
Lordship Clo. M9. 4B 46
Lord Sq. Roch 6H 13
Lord St. Heap B 6A 18
Lord St. L'boro. 6A 8
Lord St. Midd. 2C 38
Lord St. Oldh 3F 41
(in three parts)
Loring St. M40. 2A 54
Lorne Av. Rytn 6B 30
Lorne St. Heyw 6H 19
Lorne St. Moss 4G 51
Lorne St. Oldh 1E 49
Lorne St. Roch. 2B 14
Lorne Way. Heyw. 6D 18
Lorraine Clo. Heyw. 1A 28
Lorton Clo. Midd 1G 37
(in two parts)
Lostock Clo. Heyw 4F 19
Lostock Wlk. W'fld. 2A 36
Loughrigg Av. Rytn 1C 30
Louisa St. M11 6A 54
Louise Clo. Roch 2B 14
Louise Gdns. Roch. 2B 14
Louise St. Roch 2B 14
(in three parts)
Lovers La. Grass 5G 43
Low Bank. Roch. 2C 14
Lowbrook La. Oldh. 2D 42
(in two parts)
Lowcroft Cres. Chad 3H 39
Low Crompton. 3E 31
Low Crompton Rd. Rytn. 3E 31
Lowe Grn. Rytn 4E 31
Lower Arthurs. 5D 44
Lwr. Bamford Clo. Midd 1C 38
Lower Beechwood. Roch 2F 21
Lower Birches. Lees. 1D 50
Lower Calderbrook. L'boro 2A 8
Lwr. Carr La. G'fld 5D 44
Lower Crimble. Roch 3A 20
Lower Crossbank. Lees 3D 42
Lower Dingle. Oldh. 5A 32
Lwr. Edge Av. Oldh 3E 41
Lowerfields. Dob 2C 44
Lowerfields. Oldh. 1H 49
Lowerfields Ri. Shaw. 1H 31
Lower Fold. 2E 13
Lowerfold Av. Rytn. 5G 31
Lowerfold Clo. Roch. 1E 13
Lowerfold Cres. Roch. 1E 13
Lowerfold Dri. Roch 1E 13
Lowerfold Way. Roch 1E 13
Lwr. Frenches Dri. G'fld 6C 44
Lower Fullwood. Oldh. 4B 32
Lower Grn. Midd 6B 38
Lower Grn. Roch 4E 13
Lower Healey. 2G 13
Lwr. Healey La. Roch 3G 13
Lwr. Hey La. Moss 2A 52
Lwr. House La. Ward 4B 6
Lwr. House St. Oldh. 3H 41
Lwr. Jowkin La. Roch. 6H 11
Lwr. Knoll Rd. Dig 4E 35
Lwr. Knowl La. Whitw 1G 11
Lower La. Roch & Miln 4C 22
Lwr. Lime Rd. Oldh 5C 48
Lower Moor. 3G 41
Lower Ogden. 3C 24
Lower Place. 3B 22
Lower Rushcroft. 6G 23
Lwr. Sheriff St. Roch 5G 13
Lower Standrings. Roch. 5C 12
Lower Stones. Del 1A 44
Lower St. Roch 3A 22
Lower Tenterfield. Roch 3H 11
Lwr. Turf La. Scout. 4E 43
Lwr. Tweedale St. Roch 1H 21
Lwr. Victoria St. Chad. 4B 40
Lwr. Wheat End. Roch 5B 14
Lwr. Wrigley Grn. Dig. 6E 35
Lowestead Rd. M11 5A 54
Lowfield Av. Droy. 4D 54
Lowfield Wlk. M9 2A 46
(off Normanton Dri.)
Low Gro. La. G'fld 6A 44
Low Hill. Roch 2C 14
Lowhouse Clo. Miln 6G 15
Lowlands Clo. Midd 6D 38
Low Meadow. Rytn 3D 30
Lowood Clo. Miln 1F 23
Lowrey Wlk. M9. 2A 46
(off Craigend Dri.)
Low Side. 1A 50
Lowside Dri. Oldh 6H 41
Low's Pl. Roch. 3A 14
Lows, The. Oldh. 6H 41
(in two parts)
Lowther Av. Rytn 1C 30
Lowther Cres. Midd 2H 37
Lowther Rd. Roch 3G 21
Lowton Av. M9. 6B 46
Lubeck St. M9 5A 46
Lucas St. Oldh. 4H 41
Lucerne Clo. Chad 5C 40
Lucknow St. Roch 2H 21
Ludgate Rd. M40 3A 54
Ludgate Rd. Roch 5A 22
Ludlow Pk. Oldh. 5B 42
Luke Rd. Droy 6F 55
Lulworth Cres. Fail 5B 48
Lulworth Rd. Midd. 1C 38
Lumb La. Aud 6G 55
(in two parts)
Lumb La. Droy. 4G 55
(in three parts)
Lundale Wlk. M40 6C 46
Lune Gro. Heyw 4F 19
Lune St. Oldh. 1E 49
Lune Wlk. Droy 6F 55
Lurden Wlk. Chad 1B 48
Luzley. 6F 51
Luzley Brook. 4G 31
Luzley Brook Rd. Rytn 4G 31
Luzley Rd. Ash L & Moss 6F 51
Lyceum Pas. Roch. 6H 13
Lyceum Theatre, The. 5F 41
Lychgate Ct. Oldh. 1C 50
Lydden Av. M11 4B 54
Lydford. Roch 1G 21
Lydgate. 5D 8
(Littleborough)
Lydgate. 6G 43
(Oldham)
Lydgate Dri. Oldh. 6A 42
Lydgate Rd. Droy 4C 54
Lyefield Wlk. Roch. 1B 22
Lyme Clough Way. Midd. 5B 28
Lyme Gro. Droy 6D 54
Lymington Clo. Midd 6D 38
Lyndale Dri. L'boro. 5G 7
Lyndene Ct. Heyw 4G 19
Lyndhurst Av. Chad 6H 39
Lyndhurst Av. Roch 1F 29
Lyndhurst Gdns. Midd 3A 38
Lyndhurst Rd. Oldh 2D 48
Lyndon Clo. Scout 3F 43
Lyndon Cft. Oldh 1C 48
Lyneham Wlk. M9 6A 38
Lyn Gro. Heyw 4F 19
Lynham Dri. Heyw 1H 27
Lynmouth Av. Oldh. 2F 49
Lynmouth Av. Rytn. 6C 30
Lynmouth Clo. Chad. 2G 39
Lynn Dri. Droy 5C 54
Lynn St. Oldh. 1C 48
Lynnwood Dri. Roch. 5C 12
Lynroyle Way. Roch 4F 21
Lynthorpe Rd. M40. 2F 47
Lynton Av. Oldh 3C 48
Lynton Av. Roch. 4D 20
Lynton Av. Rytn 6C 30
Lynton Clo. Chad 2H 39
Lynton Dri. P'wich 5A 36
Lynway Gro. Midd 1D 38
Lynwood Clo. Ash L 6G 49
Lynwood Dri. Oldh 3B 42
Lynwood Gro. Aud 6G 55
Lyon St. Shaw 2H 31
Lytham Dri. Heyw 6G 19
Lytham St. Roch 2G 13
Lytton Rd. Droy 5E 55

M

Mabel Rd. Fail 4A 48
Mabel St. M40 2B 54
Mabel St. Roch. 3F 13
Macauley St. Roch 6E 21
Macauley St. Rytn 5E 31
McBride Riverside Pk. Midd 3B 38
Maccles Ct. L'boro 5G 7
McConnell Rd. M40 6C 46
Macdonald St. Oldh 1F 49
McDonough Clo. Oldh 2G 49
Mackenzie Wlk. Oldh 4C 32
McKie Clo. Oldh. 2G 49
Mackintosh Way. Oldh 4F 41
Maclure Rd. Roch 1H 21
McNaught St. Roch 1B 22
McOwen Pl. Roch 6A 14
McOwen St. Roch 6A 14
Maddison Rd. Droy 6D 54
Madeley Dri. Chad 5C 40
Madeley Gdns. Roch. 4F 13
Madens Sq. L'boro. 6H 7
Maden Wlk. Chad. 3B 40
Madison Gdns. Fail 6G 47
Mafeking St. Oldh 2C 48
Magdala St. Heyw 1A 28
Magdala St. Oldh 3E 41
Magpie Clo. Droy. 4G 55
Magpie La. Oldh. 1B 50
Mainhill Wlk. M40 2A 54
Main Rd. Oldh 4C 40
Main St. Fail 5H 47
Mainway. Midd. 5B 38
Mainway E. Midd 5E 39
Maitland Clo. Roch. 2C 14
Maitland Wlk. Chad 3B 40
Major St. Miln 1F 23
Makin Ct. Heyw 6H 19
Malby St. Oldh 3F 41
Malcolm St. Roch. 4F 21
Maldon St. Roch 2H 21
Malham Clo. Rytn 5D 30
Mallaig Wlk. Open 6A 54
Mallard Clo. Oldh. 3D 48
Malley Wlk. M9 2A 46
(off Greendale Dri.)
Mallow Cft. Roch 3C 22
Mally Gdns. Moss 5H 51
Malpas St. Oldh 4F 41
Malta Clo. Midd 3F 39
Malta St. Oldh 5B 42
Maltby Ct. Lees 6D 42
Malton Clo. Chad 2H 39
Malton St. Oldh 6D 40
Malvern Av. Ash L 6A 50
Malvern Av. Droy 5G 55
Malvern Clo. Miln. 6G 15
Malvern Clo. P'wich 6A 36
Malvern Clo. Rytn 6C 30
Malvern Clo. Shaw 1F 31
Malvern Rd. Midd 6B 38
Malvern St. Oldh 6D 40
Malvern St. E. Roch 6E 13
Malvern St. W. Roch. 6E 13
Manchester New Rd. Midd 6A 38
(in two parts)
Manchester Old Rd. Midd 4F 37
Manchester Rd. Aud & Ash L 6H 55
Manchester Rd. Dig & Mars 1H 35
Manchester Rd. Droy 6C 54
Manchester Rd. Moss & G'fld 6G 51
Manchester Rd. Heyw 4G 27
Manchester Rd. Oldh & Chad 3B 48
Manchester Rd. Roch. 4E 21
(in two parts)
Manchester Rd. Shaw 4G 31
Manchester St. Heyw. 5H 19
Manchester St. Oldh 6D 40
(in two parts)
Manchet St. Roch 6D 20
Mandley Av. M40 3F 47
Manesty Clo. Midd. 1G 37
Manley Rd. Oldh. 1E 49
Manley Rd. Roch 3E 21
(Hargreaves St.)
Manley Rd. Roch 4E 21
(Kingsland Rd.)
Mannock St. Oldh 5D 40
Manor Clo. Chad 3C 40
Manor Clo. Grass. 6A 44
Manor Cotts. Moss 3G 51
(off Wilds Sq.)
Manor Dri. Rytn. 6E 31
Mnr. Farm Ri. Oldh. 4B 42
Manor La. Dig 1G 35
Mnr. Mill Clo. Roch 2D 14
Manor Rd. Droy. 6C 54
Manor Rd. Midd. 5B 38
Manor Rd. Oldh 1A 50
Manor Rd. Shaw 2G 31
Manor St. Midd 1C 38
Manor St. Moss. 3G 51
Manor St. Rytn 1G 41
Manor Yd. Upperm 3D 44
(off Wade Row)
Manse, The. Moss 5G 51
Mansfield Av. M9 6H 37 & 1A 46
Mansfield Dri. M9 1A 46
Mansfield Grange. Roch 1E 21
Mansfield Rd. M9 6H 37
Mansfield Rd. Moss. 4A 52
Mansfield Rd. Oldh 6H 41
Mansfield Rd. Roch 6A 12
Mansfield Vw. Moss. 4A 52
Manton Av. M9 3D 46
Manwaring St. Fail. 5G 47
Maple Av. Bury. 4A 18
Maple Av. Dent. 6F 55
Maple Clo. Chad. 2B 40
Maple Clo. Midd. 3F 39
Maple Clo. Shaw. 1F 31
Mapledon Rd. M9 5B 46
Maple Gro. Oldh 3H 47
Maple Gro. Fail. 2C 54
Maple Rd. Chad 2B 40
Maple St. Oldh. 2C 48
Maple St. Roch. 1F 21
Maplewood Clo. Rytn. 1C 40
Marble St. Oldh 3H 41
Marches Clo. Rytn 5H 31
March St. Roch 6A 14
Marcliffe Dri. Roch. 1D 20
Marcroft Pl. Roch. 3A 22
Mardale Av. Rytn 1C 30
Mardale Clo. Oldh 3B 42
Mardale Clo. P'wich 4A 36
Mardale Dri. Midd 2A 38
Mardyke. Roch 5G 13
Marfield Av. Chad. 6A 40
Margaret Ashton Clo. M9 6B 46
Margaret Av. Roch 6C 14
Margaret Rd. Droy 5C 54
Margaret St. Heyw 5F 19
Margaret St. Oldh. 3B 48
Margaret St. Shaw. 3H 31
Margaret Ward Ct. Roch. 2A 22
Margate Av. M40 2A 54
Margrove Clo. Fail 6C 48
Margroy Clo. Roch. 3A 14
Marguerita Rd. M40. 3B 54
(in two parts)
Marigold St. Roch 2H 21
(in two parts)
Marigold Ter. Midd 4F 39
(off Mills Hill Rd.)
Marina Cres. M11 4A 54
Marina Rd. Droy. 5F 55
Marion St. Oldh 2F 49
Markenfield Dri. Shaw 2F 31
Market Av. Oldh 4F 41
Market Brow. M9 3A 46
Market Pl. Droy 6E 55
Market Pl. Heyw. 5H 19
Market Pl. Midd 2C 38
Market Pl. Moss. 4F 51
Market Pl. Oldh 4E 41
Market Pl. Roch. 6H 13
Market Pl. Rytn 5D 30
Market Pl. Shaw. 3H 31
Market Sq. Rytn. 5D 30
Market St. Droy 6E 55
Market St. Heyw 5G 19

Market St.—Milton Rd.

Market St. Midd 2B 38
(in two parts)
Market St. Moss 4G 51
Market St. Rytn 5D 30
Market St. Shaw 3H 31
Market St. Whitw 5E 5
Market Way. Roch 5H 13
Mark Jones Wlk. M40 2A 54
Mark La. Shaw 3A 32
Mark St. Oldh 4D 40
Mark St. Roch 4B 14
Markwood. Del 5B 34
Marland 3D 20
Marland Av. Oldh 4G 49
Marland Av. Roch 3D 20
Marland Clo. Roch 2D 20
Marland Fold. Roch 3D 20
Marland Fold La. Oldh 4F 49
Marland Grn. Roch 3D 20
Marland Hill Rd. Roch 2E 21
Marland Old Rd. Roch 3D 20
Marland St. Chad 2A 48
Marland Tops. Roch 3D 20
Marlborough Clo. Whitw 4E 5
Marlborough Ct. M8 6D 36
Marlborough Dri. Fail 1C 54
Marlborough Gro. Droy 5G 55
Marlborough Rd. Rytn 1E 41
Marlborough St. Heyw 1A 28
Marlborough St. Oldh 5G 41
Marlborough St. Roch 4E 13
Marle Av. Moss 4A 52
Marle Ri. Moss 4A 52
Marleyer St. M40 6E 47
Marlfield Rd. Shaw 1E 31
Marlfield St. M9 4A 46
Marlinford Dri. M40 2A 54
Marlor Ct. Heyw 5F 19
Marlow Rd. M9 4B 46
Marlton Wlk. M9 2A 46
(off Leconfield Dri.)
Marlwood Way. Rytn 1C 40
Marne Cres. Roch 6E 13
Marple Clo. Oldh 3D 48
Marsden Clo. Moss 3F 51
Marsden Clo. Roch 1C 30
Marsden's Sq. L'boro 5H 7
(off Sutcliffe St.)
Marsden St. Midd 4E 39
Marsett Clo. Roch 4C 12
Marshall Ct. Oldh 3E 41
Marshall St. Roch 6C 14
Marsham Clo. G'ton 6F 43
Marsh Head. Dig 4G 35
Marsh Lea. Dig 4F 35
Marslands 1D 44
Marslands. Dig 6D 34
Mars St. Oldh 4C 40
Marston Clo. Fail 1G 55
Marston Clo. W'fld 3A 36
Martha's Ter. Roch 2C 14
Martha St. Oldh 3D 40
Martin Av. Oldh 5A 42
Martindale Clo. Rytn 4E 31
Martindale Cres. Midd 6H 27
Martingale Way. Droy 4H 55
Martin La. Roch 4D 12
Martins Fld. Roch 4B 12
Martin St. Bury 4B 18
Martlett Av. Roch 6A 12
Mary St. Droy 6F 55
Mary St. Heyw 5G 19
Mary St. Roch 1D 14
Masefield Cres. Droy 6E 55
Masefield Rd. Droy 6E 55
Masefield Rd. Oldh 1H 41
Mason St. Heyw 5F 19
Mason St. Roch 6H 13
Massey Av. Fail 5B 48
Massey Clo. Whitw 4E 5
Mather St. Fail 6F 47
Matthew Clo. Oldh 1A 50
Matthew Moss La. Roch 3D 20
Maud St. Roch 3A 14
Maureen St. Roch 3A 14
Mavis Gro. Miln 1G 23
Mavis St. Roch 6E 21
Maxwell St. Bury 4A 18
Mayall St. Moss 4G 51
Mayall St. E. Oldh 4A 42
Maybrook Wlk. M9 5A 46
Mayburn Clo. Midd 6E 39
Mayfair Cres. Fail 5B 48
Mayfair Dri. Rytn 1D 40
Mayfair Gdns. Roch 2F 21
Mayfield 4B 14
Mayfield Av. S'head 4E 43
Mayfield Rd. Oldh 2H 41
Mayfield St. Roch 4B 14
(in two parts)
Mayfield Ter. Roch 4B 14
Maygate. Oldh 3D 40
Mayor St. Chad 4C 40
May Pl. L'boro 1E 15
May Pl. Roch 3A 22
(off Oldham Rd.)
May St. M40 2A 54
(in two parts)
May St. Heyw 1A 28
(in two parts)
May St. Oldh 1C 48
Meadowbank. Ash L 6G 49
Meadowbank Clo. Fail 1E 55
Mdw. Bank Clo. Oldh 1C 50
Meadowbrook Clo. Bury 3A 18
Meadow Clo. Heyw 5G 19
Meadow Clo. Moss 2A 52
Meadow Cotts. Whitw 1F 5
Meadowcroft La. Oldh 2H 41
Meadowcroft La. Roch 1B 20
Meadowfield Clo. Roch 4B 22
Meadow Fold. Upperm 3E 45
Mdw. Head Av. Whitw 5E 5
Mdw. Head La. Roch 3E 11
Meadow La. Oldh 3E 49
Meadow Ri. Shaw 6G 23
Meadow Rd. Midd 5A 38
Meadowside. Miln 4A 24
Meadows, The. G'ton 5E 43
Meadows, The. Midd 5D 38
Meadows, The. Upperm 4D 44
Meadows, The. Whitw 2E 5
Meadow Vw. Roch 4C 12
Meadow Wlk. L'boro 6F 7
Meadow Way. M40 4C 46
Meads, The. Chad 5A 40
Meadway. Chad 3G 47
Meadway. Roch 3E 21
Meanwood Brow. Roch 5F 13
(off Rooley Moor Rd.)
Meanwood Fold. Roch 5F 13
Medley St. Roch 4H 13
Medlock Ct. Oldh 4C 42
Medlock Dri. Oldh 4G 49
Medlock Leisure Cen. 5F 55
Medlock Rd. Fail 3D 54
Medlock St. Droy 5E 55
Medlock St. Oldh 4G 41
Medlock Vale 3E 55
Medlock Way. Lees 5C 42
Medlock Way. W'fld 3A 36
Medway Clo. Oldh 2C 48
Medway Rd. Oldh 2C 48
Medway Rd. Shaw 1G 31
Medway, The. Heyw 4F 19
Meek St. Rytn 1G 41
Megabowl Bowling Alley 3A 26
Megna Clo. Oldh 4D 40
Melbourne Av. Chad 4A 40
Melbourne Clo. Roch 5A 22
Melbourne Rd. Roch 5A 22
Melbourne St. M9 5A 46
Melbourne St. Chad 4B 40
Meldrum St. Oldh 1F 49
Melford Av. M40 4G 47
Melford Gro. Oldh 5B 42
Mellalieu St. Heyw 4G 19
Mellalieu St. Midd 2A 38
Mellalieu St. Rytn 1E 41
Melling Av. Chad 2G 39
Melling Rd. Oldh 5A 42
Mellodew Dri. Oldh 6B 32
Mellor Brow. Heyw 5G 19
Mellor Ho. Rytn 5E 31
(off Westmorland Wlk.)
Mellor St. Droy 6D 54
Mellor St. Fail 1B 54
Mellor St. Lees 5C 42
Mellor St. Roch 5F 13
Mellor St. Rytn 4D 30
Mellor Way. Chad 1B 48
Melrose. Roch 5G 13
(off Spotland Rd.)
Melrose Av. Heyw 4G 19
Melrose Av. L'boro 4G 7
Melrose Ct. Chad 1A 48
Melrose St. M40 2A 54
Melrose St. Oldh 2H 41
Melrose St. Roch 6F 13
Melton Clo. Heyw 6F 19
Melton St. M9 4B 46
Melton St. Heyw 6F 19
Melverley Rd. M9 6E 37
Melville St. Lees 6C 42
Melville St. Roch 6F 21
Mendip Clo. Chad 6A 40
Mendip Clo. Rytn 6C 30
Mendip Dri. Miln 1G 23
Mendip Rd. Oldh 2D 48
Mendips Clo. Shaw 1F 31
Menston Av. M40 4G 47
Mentmore Rd. Roch 6D 14
Mercer La. Roch 5A 12
Mercer's Rd. Heyw 2H 27
Mercer St. Droy 5F 55
Mere Av. Droy 6C 54
Mere Av. Midd 5C 38
Merebank Clo. Roch 5A 12
Mere Clo. Uns 4A 26
Merefield Av. Roch 2G 21
Merefield St. Roch 2G 21
Merefield Ter. Roch 2G 21
Mere La. Roch 2H 21
Mere St. Roch 1H 21
(in three parts)
Mere, The. Ash L 6C 50
Meridian Cen. Oldh 5E 41
Merinall Clo. Roch 6C 14
Merlewood Av. Dent 6F 55
Merlewood Av. Upperm 3D 44
Merlin Clo. L'boro 3G 15
Merlin Clo. Oldh 5G 49
(in two parts)
Merlin Rd. Miln 1F 23
Merrick St. Heyw 6A 20
Merriman Hall. Roch 3B 14
Mersey Clo. W'fld 2A 36
Mersey Dri. W'fld 2A 36
Mersey Rd. Ind. Est. Fail 4B 48
Mersey Rd. N. Fail 4A 48
Mersey Sq. W'fld 2A 36
Merton Av. Oldh 2D 48
Merton Dri. Droy 6C 54
Merton Gro. Chad 2F 47
Merton Rd. P'wich 6A 36
Merton Wlk. M9 6A 46
(off Nethervale Dri.)
Merville Av. M40 4B 46
Metcalfe St. Fir 6D 14
Metcalf M. Upperm 3D 44
Metfield Wlk. M40 3F 47
Metropolitan Ho. Oldh 5F 41
Mevagissey Wlk. Oldh 3A 42
Miall St. Roch 1H 21
Michael St. Midd 3B 38
Micklehurst 5H 51
Micklehurst Rd. Moss 5H 51
Middle Calderbrook. L'boro 2A 8
Middlefield. Oldh 5G 49
Middle Fld. Roch 4A 12
Middlegate. M40 2F 47
Middle Ga. Oldh 3E 49
Middle Healey 1F 13
Middle Hill. Roch 1H 13
Middle Holly Gro. Dig 6E 35
Middlesex Wlk. Oldh 5D 40
Middlestone Dri. M9 6A 46
Middle St. Whitw 2E 5
Middleton 3B 38
Middleton Av. Fail 6H 47
Middleton Cen. Ind. Est.
Midd 3B 38
Middleton Gdns. Midd 3B 38
(in two parts)
Middleton Junction 5F 39
Middleton Leisure Cen. 3C 38
Middleton Old Rd. M9 2A 46
Middleton Rd. M8 & Midd 6D 36
(in two parts)
Middleton Rd. Chad & Oldh 2G 39
(in two parts)
Middleton Rd. Heyw 1A 28
Middleton Rd. Rytn 6B 30
Middleton St Leonard's
Parish Church 2C 38
Middleton Shop. Cen. Midd 3B 38
Middleton Vw. Midd 3D 38
Middleton Way. Midd 3B 38
Middleway. G'ton 6F 43
Middlewood Ct. Chad 3A 40
Middlewood Grn. Chad 3A 40
Middle Wood La. Roch 5E 7
Middlewood Wlk. M9 6A 46
Midge Hall Dri. Roch 1C 20
Midgley Dri. Roch 5C 22
Midgrove. Del 5B 34
Midgrove La. Del 6B 34
Midhurst Av. M40 3A 54
Midhurst St. Roch 2H 21
Midhurst Way. Chad 5B 40
Midmoor Wlk. M9 2A 46
(off Leconfield Dri.)
Midville Rd. M11 4A 54
Milbury Dri. L'boro 3G 15
Mildred Av. G'ton 6F 43
Mildred Av. Rytn 1E 41
Miles St. Oldh 3H 41
Milford Av. Oldh 3C 48
Milford Brow. Lees 4C 42
Milford Cres. L'boro 5H 7
Milford St. Roch 4H 13
Milkstone Pl. Roch 1H 21
Milkstone Rd. Roch 1H 21
(in two parts)
Milk St. Oldh 4A 42
Milk St. Roch 1H 21
Millais St. M40 5C 46
Millard St. Chad 4A 40
Millbank Ct. Heyw 5F 19
Millbank St. Heyw 5F 19
Millbeck Ct. Midd 1H 37
Millbeck Rd. Midd 1H 37
Millbrae Gdns. Shaw 2F 31
Millbrook Bank. Roch 4H 11
Millbrook Clo. Shaw 3B 32
Mill Brow. Ash L 4A 50
Mill Brow. Chad 1A 40
Millbrow Ter. Oldh 1A 40
Millcroft. Shaw 3A 32
Mill Cft. Clo. Roch 3G 11
Millcroft La. Del 3B 34
(in two parts)
Miller Ho. Shaw 4H 31
Miller Mdw. Clo. Shaw 1A 32
Miller Rd. Oldh 2E 49
Millers Brook Clo. Heyw 4H 19
Miller St. Heyw 5H 19
(in two parts)
Millett Ter. Bury 6C 10
Millfield Gro. Roch 1B 22
Millfield Wlk. M40 3E 47
Millfold. Whitw 1F 5
Mill Fold Gdns. L'boro 1F 15
Mill Fold Rd. Midd 3B 38
Millgate. Del 5B 34
Mill Ga. Oldh 2D 48
Millgate. Roch 3B 14
Millgate Cen. Del 5B 34
Mill Ho. Clo. Roch 1D 14
Mill La. Chad 1C 48
Mill La. Dob 2H 43
Mill La. Fail 6E 47
Mill La. Moss 3G 51
Mill La. Rytn 5C 30
Millom Clo. Roch 4C 14
Millrise. Oldh 4E 41
Mills Farm Clo. Oldh 4G 49
Mills Hill 3G 39
Mills Hill Rd. Midd 2F 39
Mills St. Heyw 5F 19
Mills St. Whitw 2F 5
Millstream La. M40 3C 54
Mill St. Fail 6F 47
Mill St. L'boro 2F 15
Mill St. Moss 4G 51
Mill St. Rytn 5D 30
Mill St. Upperm 3D 44
Millview. Dig 5E 35
Millway Wlk. M40 2A 54
Millwright St. M40 2A 54
Milner St. Whitw 3E 5
Milne St. Chad 2C 40
(Burnley La.)
Milne St. Chad 4B 40
(Middleton Rd.)
Milne St. Higg 1G 41
Milne St. Oldh 6C 40
Milne St. Roch 5E 21
Milne St. Shaw 3H 31
Milngate Clo. Roch 4C 22
Milnrow 2F 23
Milnrow Rd. L'boro 3F 15
Milnrow Rd. Roch 6A 14
Milnrow Rd. Shaw 2H 31
Milo Ind. Pk. Droy 4G 55
Milo St. M9 2A 46
Milton Av. Droy 6E 55
Milton Dri. Chad 5A 40
Milton Rd. Aud 6H 55
Milton Rd. P'wich 6A 36

Milton St. *Midd* 2B 38
Milton St. *Moss* 3G 51
Milton St. *Oldh* 6G 41
Milton St. *Roch* 5H 13
Milton St. *Rytn* 4E 31
Milton Vw. *Moss* 3G 51
Minerva Ter. L'boro 6G 7
(off William St.)
Mine St. *Heyw* 3G 19
(in two parts)
Minnie St. *Whitw* 1F 5
Minorca Av. *M11* 5B 54
Minorca Clo. *Roch* 5A 12
Minor St. *Fail* 5A 48
(in two parts)
Minor St. *Roch* 6E 21
Minster Rd. *M9* 5B 46
Minster Way. *Chad* 2A 40
Minton St. *M40* 5E 47
Mirfield Av. *M9* 6H 37
Mirfield Av. *Oldh* 1E 49
Mirfield Dri. *Midd* 2B 38
Mirfield Rd. *M9* 6H 37
Miriam St. *Fail* 1B 54
Mission St. *Heyw* 5G 19
Mitcham Av. *M9* 2C 46
Mitchell Hey. 6G 13
Mitchell Hey. *Roch* 6G 13
Mitchells Quay. *Fail* 6G 47
Mitchell St. *M40* 2A 54
Mitchell St. *Midd* 2B 38
Mitchell St. *Oldh* 3D 40
Mitchell St. *Roch* 2C 14
(John St.)
Mitchell St. *Roch* 5F 13
(Spotland Rd.)
Mitre St. *Fail* 5H 47
Mitton Clo. *Heyw* 5D 18
Mizzy Rd. *Roch* 4G 13
Mode Hill La. *W'fld* 3A 36
Mode Hill Wlk. *W'fld* 3A 36
Mold St. *Oldh* 3E 41
Molesworth St. *Roch* 6A 14
Molyneux St. *Roch* 5F 13
Monarch Clo. *Rytn* 1D 40
Monart Rd. *M9* 4A 46
Monks Clo. *Miln* 1E 23
Monkswood. *Oldh* 4E 41
Monkwood Dri. *M9* 5A 46
Monmouth St. *Midd* 3E 39
Monmouth St. *Oldh* 6C 40
Monmouth St. *Roch* 1H 21
Monsall Rd. *M40* 6A 46
Monsall St. *Oldh* 2E 49
Mons Av. *Roch* 5E 13
Montgomery. *Roch* 1G 21
Montgomery Ho. *Oldh* 4B 48
Montgomery St. *Oldh* 3B 48
Montgomery St. Roch 3E 21
(off Manchester Rd.)
Montreal St. *Oldh* 1F 49
Montrose Gdns. *Rytn* 5F 31
Montrose St. *Roch* 6E 21
Moon St. *Oldh* 4C 40
Moor Bank La. *Miln* 3D 22
Moorby St. *Oldh* 3G 41
Moorclose. 3E 39
Moorclose St. *Midd* 3D 38
(in two parts)
Moorclose Wlk. M9 6A 46
(off Conran St.)
Moor Cres. *Dig* 5E 35
Moorcroft. *Roch* 4H 21
Moorcroft St. *Droy* 6E 55
Moorcroft St. *Oldh* 3C 48
Moordale Av. *Oldh* 2C 42
Moor Edge Rd. *Moss & G'fld* 3B 52
(in two parts)
Mooredge Ter. *Rytn* 1E 41
Moore St. *Roch* 6H 13
Moorfield Av. *L'boro* 4G 7
Moorfield Hamlet. *Shaw* 2F 31
Moorfield Heights. *Carr* 6A 52
Moorfield M. *Shaw* 2H 31
Moorfield Pl. *Roch* 4G 13
Moorfield Rd. *Oldh* 3B 48
Moorfield Ter. *Carr* 6A 52
Moorfield Vw. *L'boro* 5G 7
Moorgate. 6A 52
Moorgate Av. *Roch* 6C 12
Moorgate Cotts. *Carr* 6A 52
Moorgate Dri. *Carr* 6A 52
Moor Ga. La. *L'boro* 4E 7
Moorgate M. *Carr* 6A 52
Moorgate Rd. *Carr* 6A 52
Moorgate St. *Upperm* 3D 44
Moorhey. 5H 41
Moorhey Ind. Est. *Oldh* 5H 41
Moorhey St. *Oldh* 5H 41
Moor Hill. *Roch* 4B 12
Moorhouse Farm. *Miln* 1E 23
Moorhouse Fold. *Miln* 1E 23
Moorings, The. *Moss* 2A 52
Moorland Av. *Del* 6B 34
Moorland Av. *Droy* 6C 54
Moorland Av. *Miln* 1G 23
Moorland Av. *Roch* 5B 12
Moorland Av. *Whitw* 4E 5
Moorland Cres. *Whitw* 4E 5
Moorlands Cres. *Moss* 4H 51
Moorlands Dri. *Moss* 2A 52
Moorland St. *L'boro* 4A 8
Moorland St. *Roch* 4G 13
Moorland St. *Shaw* 2H 31
Moorland Ter. *Roch* 4C 12
Moor La. *Dob* 1E 45
Moor La. *Roch* 2B 12
Moor Pk. Av. *Roch* 5D 20
Moor Rd. *L'boro* 2A 8
Moorsholme Av. *M40* 6C 46
Moorside. 5C 32
Moorside. *L'boro* 5B 8
Moorside. *Roch* 4H 21
Moorside Av. *Droy* 4G 55
Moorside Av. *Oldh* 5D 32
Moorside Cres. *Droy* 5G 55
Moorside Rd. *Moss* 4A 52
Moorside St. *Droy* 5F 55
Moorsley Dri. *M9* 1B 46
Moor St. *Heyw* 5F 19
(in two parts)
Moor St. *Oldh* 4H 41
Moor St. *Shaw* 3G 31
Moortop Clo. *M9* 6G 37
Moor Vw. Clo. *Roch* 3B 12
Moorway Dri. *M9* 1C 46
Moorwood Dri. *Oldh* 1A 50
Mora Av. *Chad* 2B 40
Mora St. *M9* 5B 46
Moray Rd. *Chad* 1A 48
Morden Av. *M11* 5A 54
Morecombe Clo. *M40* 1A 54
Moreton St. *Chad* 3H 39
Morgan St. *L'boro* 6H 7
Morley St. *Oldh* 2C 42
Morley St. *Roch* 4B 14
Morley Way. *G'fld* 6D 44
Morningside Clo. *Roch* 1B 22
Mornington Ct. *Oldh* 3E 41
Mornington Rd. *Roch* 5H 21
Morris St. *Oldh* 6G 41
Mortar St. *Oldh* 3A 42
(in two parts)
Mortimer Av. *M9* 1A 46
Mortimer St. *Oldh* 2G 41
Mortlake Dri. *M40* 2A 54
Morton St. *Fail* 6E 47
Morton St. *Midd* 1C 38
Morton St. *Roch* 6A 14
Mosedale Rd. *Midd* 1H 37
Moss Av. *Roch* 1C 22
Moss Bank. *Shaw* 3H 31
Moss Bank Av. *Droy* 5G 55
Moss Bank Ct. *Droy* 5G 55
Mossbank Gro. *Heyw* 4G 19
Moss Bri. Rd. *Roch* 1B 22
Moss Brook Rd. *M9* 6A 46
Mossclough Ct. *M9* 6A 46
Mossdown Rd. *Rytn* 6G 31
Moss Farm Clo. *Midd* 5D 38
Mossfield Clo. *Bury* 4A 18
Mossfield Dri. *M9* 1C 46
Moss Gate. 6F 23
Moss Ga. Rd. *Shaw* 1F 31
(in two parts)
Moss Grove. 3D 48
Moss Gro. *Shaw* 6E 23
Mossgrove St. *Oldh* 3D 48
Moss Hall Rd. *Bury* 6B 18
Moss Hey. 3A 32
Moss Hey St. *Shaw* 3H 31
Moss Ind. Est. *Roch* 2B 22
Mossland Clo. *Heyw* 1H 27
Moss La. *Ash L* 3H 55
(in three parts)
Moss La. *Midd* 6B 38
(Manchester New Rd.)
Moss La. *Midd* 6C 38
(Mossway)
Moss La. *Roch* 1A 22
Moss La. *Rytn* 6G 31
Moss La. *Whitw* 4D 4
Moss La. Ind. Est. *Rytn* 6G 31
Mossley. 4A 52
Mossley Brow. 4G 51
Mossley Cross. 4F 51
Mossley Rd. *Ash L* 6E 51
Mossley Rd. *Grass* 1H 51
Moss Lynn. *S'head* 4E 43
Moss Mill St. *Roch* 2B 22
Moss Row. *Roch* 4H 11
Moss Side La. *Miln* 2C 22
Moss St. *Dent* 6F 55
Moss St. *Droy* 5F 55
Moss St. *Heyw* 5G 19
Moss St. *Oldh* 3C 42
Moss St. *Roch* 1B 22
Moss Ter. *Roch* 1B 22
Moss, The. *Midd* 5D 38
Moss Vw. *M40* 3E 47
Mossway. *Midd* 6B 38
Moss Way. *Sale* 6H 55
Moston. 5C 46
Moston Bank Av. *M9* 6A 46
Moston Fairway Nature Reserve. 5E 47
Moston La. *M9 & M40* 5A 46
Moston La. *M40* 3E 47
Moston La. E. *M40* 3G 47
Moston Rd. *Midd* 5F 39
Mough La. *Chad* 2F 47
Mountain Ash. *Roch* 2D 12
Mountain Ash Clo. *Roch* 2D 12
Mountain St. *M40* 3B 54
Mountain St. *Moss* 4G 51
Mount Av. *L'boro* 4G 7
Mount Av. *Roch* 1E 15
Mountbatten Clo. *Bury* 1A 36
Mount Fold. *Midd* 4D 38
Mount La. *Dob* 2A 44
Mount Pl. *Roch* 5G 13
Mount Pleasant. *Midd* 3G 37
(in two parts)
Mount Pleasant. *P'wich* 3C 36
Mt. Pleasant Bus. Cen. *Oldh* 4H 41
Mt. Pleasant St. *Oldh* 4H 41
Mount Rd. *Midd* 4B 38
Mount Rd. *P'wich* 4A 36
Mountside Clo. *Roch* 3H 13
Mount St. *Heyw* 6H 19
Mount St. *Roch* (OL11) 6E 21
Mount St. *Roch* (OL12) 5G 13
Mount St. *Rytn* 6E 31
Mount St. *Shaw* 2F 31
Mount Ter. *Droy* 4C 54
Mount Vw. *Upperm* 3D 44
Mt. View Rd. *Shaw* 3A 32
Mowbray St. *Oldh* 5F 41
Mowbray St. *Roch* 4D 20
Mowbray Wlk. *Midd* 1A 38
Mow Halls La. *Dob* 2C 44
Muirfield Clo. *M40* 5E 47
Muirfield Clo. *Heyw* 6H 19
Muirfield Clo. *P'wich* 6A 36
Mulberry Av. *Hey D* 2D 26
Mulberry Clo. *Hey D* 2D 26
Mulberry Clo. *Roch* 2G 21
Mulberry Wlk. *Droy* 6C 54
Mulberry Way. *Hey D* 2D 26
Mulgrove Wlk. M9 2A 46
(off Haverfield Rd.)
Mulmount Clo. *Oldh* 2C 48
Mumps. 4G 41
Mumps. *Oldh* 4G 41
Municipal Clo. Heyw 5H 19
(off Hartland St.)
Munn Rd. *M9* 6F 37
Munslow Wlk. *M9* 2B 46
Muriel St. *Heyw* 5A 20
Muriel St. *Roch* 2B 22
Murrayfield. *Roch* 1A 20
Mutual St. *Heyw* 4A 20
Myerscroft Clo. *M40* 4G 47
Myrtle Clo. *Oldh* 6E 41
Myrtle Gro. *Droy* 5G 55
Myrtle Rd. *Midd* 1E 39
Myrtle St. *Heyw* 6A 20

N

Nadin St. *Oldh* 2E 49
Nallgate. *Roch* 5C 22
Nall St. *Miln* 1E 23
Nantwich Av. *Roch* 2H 13
Napier St. *Shaw* 1H 31
Napier St. E. *Oldh* 6D 40
Napier St. W. *Oldh* 6C 40
Narrow Gate Brow. 2D 30
Naseby Av. *M9* 1B 46
Naseby Ct. *P'wich* 6A 36
Naseby Pl. *P'wich* 6A 36
Naseby Wlk. *W'fld* 3A 36
Naunton Rd. *Midd* 4D 38
Naunton Wlk. *M9* 5A 46
Naylor St. *Oldh* 4E 41
Nazeby Wlk. *Oldh* 6C 40
Naze Ct. *Oldh* 3E 41
Neale Av. *G'fld* 6E 45
Near Barrowshaw. 2C 42
Near Birches Pde. *Oldh* 1C 50
Neath Clo. *W'fld* 4A 36
Neath St. *Oldh* 4D 40
Neild St. *Oldh* 1E 49
Neilson Clo. *Midd* 4E 39
Neilston Av. *M40* 6D 46
Nellie St. *Heyw* 5F 19
Nelson Dri. *Droy* 5B 54
Nelson Rd. *M9* 6H 37
Nelson St. *Heyw* 6H 19
Nelson St. *Lees* 6C 42
Nelson St. *L'boro* 6H 7
Nelson St. *Midd* 4E 39
(in two parts)
Nelson St. *Roch* 6H 13
Nelson Way. *Chad* 1B 48
Nepaul Rd. *M9* 4A 46
Neston Clo. *Shaw* 2B 32
Neston Rd. *Roch* 3C 22
Nether Cft. *Roch* 4A 12
Netherfield Clo. *Oldh* 1C 48
Netherhey La. *Rytn* 1C 40
Nether Hey St. *Oldh* 6H 41
(in two parts)
Nether Ho. Rd. *Shaw* 2G 31
Nether Lees. 6B 42
Netherlees. *Lees* 6B 42
Nethervale Dri. *M9* 6A 46
Netherwood. *Fail* 5B 48
Netley Av. *Roch* 2H 13
Nettleton Gro. *M9* 4B 46
Neville St. *Chad* 4C 40
Nevin Clo. *Oldh* 3B 48
Nevin Rd. *M40* 4F 47
Nevis St. *Roch* 5A 22
Newall St. *L'boro* 5H 7
Newark Pk. Way. *Rytn* 2C 30
Newark Rd. *Roch* 2H 13
Newark Sq. *Roch* 2H 13
Newbank Chase. *Chad* 3A 40
New Barn Clo. *Shaw* 2G 31
New Barn La. *Roch* 2G 21
New Barn Rd. *Oldh* 3G 49
New Barn St. *Roch* 2A 22
Newbarn St. *Shaw* 2G 31
Newbold. 6C 14
Newbold Brow. 5C 14
Newbold Moss. *Roch* 5B 14
Newbold St. *Roch* 5C 14
Newbreak Clo. *Oldh* 3B 42
Newbreak St. *Oldh* 3B 42
Newbridge Vw. *Moss* 5H 51
New Brighton Cotts. Whitw 2F 5
(off Ruth St.)
New Broad La. *Roch* 4B 22
New Bldgs. Pl. *Roch* 5H 13
Newburn Av. *M9* 1B 46
Newbury Gro. *Heyw* 1G 27
Newbury Wlk. M9 6A 46
(off Ravelston Dri.)
Newbury Wlk. Chad 4C 40
(off Kempton Way)
Newby Dri. *Midd* 6B 28
Newchurch. *Oldh* 5G 49
Newchurch St. *Roch* 6E 21
Newcliffe Rd. *M9* 1B 46
New Coin St. *Rytn* 6D 30
Newcroft. *Fail* 1F 55
New Delph. 6B 34
New Earth. 6A 42
New Earth St. *Moss* 3H 51
New Earth St. *Oldh* 6A 42
Newell Ter. *Roch* 4G 13
Newfield Clo. *Roch* 5C 14
Newfield Head La. *Miln* 2H 23
Newfield Vw. *Miln* 1G 23
(in three parts)
Newgate. *Roch* 6G 13
New Hall Rd. *Bury* 3C 18
Newham Av. *M11* 5A 54

Newhey . . . 3H 23
Newhey Rd. *Miln* . . . 2G 23
(in two parts)
Newhouse Clo. *Ward* . . . 5C 6
Newhouse Cres. *Roch* . . . 5A 12
Newhouse Rd. *Heyw* . . . 1H 27
Newhouse St. *Ward* . . . 5C 6
(in two parts)
Newick Wlk. M9 . . . 2A 46
(off Leconfield Dri.)
New Inn Yd. *Roch* . . . 1E 15
Newlands. *Fail* . . . 3C 54
Newlands Av. *Roch* . . . 2H 13
Newlands Clo. *Roch* . . . 2H 13
Newlands Wlk. *Midd* . . . 5A 28
(in two parts)
New La. *Midd* . . . 2C 38
New La. *Rytn* . . . 5D 30
Newman St. *Roch* . . . 2C 14
Newmarket Rd. *Ash L* . . . 2H 55
New Mill. *Roch* . . . 3C 14
New Mill St. *L'boro* . . . 6G 7
New Moston . . . 4G 47
New Oak Clo. *Fail* . . . 5C 48
Newport St. *Midd* . . . 2E 39
Newport St. *Oldh* . . . 6D 40
New Radcliffe St. *Oldh* . . . 4E 41
New Rd. *Oldh* . . . 1E 49
New Rd. *Whitw* . . . 2D 4
New Royd Av. *Lees* . . . 3D 42
Newstead. Roch . . . 5G 13
(off Spotland Rd.)
Newstead Av. *Ash L* . . . 6A 50
New St. *Droy* . . . 6E 55
New St. *Lees* . . . 5C 42
New St. *L'boro* . . . 1F 15
New St. *Miln* . . . 2G 23
New St. *Roch* . . . 3G 13
New St. *Upperm* . . . 3D 44
Newton Cres. *Midd* . . . 1H 37
Newtondale Av. *Rytn* . . . 5C 30
Newtonmore Wlk. *Open* . . . 6A 54
Newton Rd. *Fail* . . . 3C 54
Newton Rd. *Midd* . . . 4F 37
Newton St. *M40* . . . 1A 54
Newton St. *Droy* . . . 4F 55
Newton St. *Fail* . . . 1A 54
Newton St. *Roch* . . . 2A 22
New Town . . . 3H 31
Newtown Ct. *P'wich* . . . 6A 36
Newtown M. *P'wich* . . . 6A 36
Newtown St. *Shaw* . . . 3H 31
New Way. *Whitw* . . . 2E 5
New York St. *Heyw* . . . 5F 19
(in two parts)
Nicholas Rd. *Oldh* . . . 1E 49
Nicholson St. *Lees* . . . 5C 42
Nicholson St. *Roch* . . . 2H 21
Nicker Brow. *Dob* . . . 1C 44
(in two parts)
Nick Rd. La. *Ward* . . . 4H 5
Nield St. *Moss* . . . 3F 51
Nigel Rd. *M9* . . . 6B 46
Nigher Moss Av. *Roch* . . . 6C 14
Nightingale Dri. *Aud* . . . 5G 55
Nile St. *Oldh* . . . 3E 41
Nile St. *Roch* . . . 5A 14
Nimble Nook . . . 6A 40
Nimble Nook. *Chad* . . . 6A 40
Nina Dri. *M40* . . . 2E 47
Ninian Ct. *Midd* . . . 2B 38
Ninth Av. *Oldh* . . . 4D 48
Nixon St. *Fail* . . . 6G 47
Nixon St. *Roch* . . . 4D 20
Noble Mdw. *Roch* . . . 6D 6
Noble St. *Oldh* . . . 1F 49
Nolan St. *M9* . . . 6A 46
Nook . . . 2B 32
Nook Cotts. *S'head* . . . 3E 43
Nook Farm Av. *Roch* . . . 2H 13
Nook Side. *Roch* . . . 2H 13
Nook Ter. *Roch* . . . 2H 13
Nook, The. *Bury* . . . 6B 18
Nook, The. *G'fld* . . . 1E 53
Noon Sun Clo. *G'fld* . . . 1C 52
Noon Sun St. *Roch* . . . 4H 13
(in two parts)
Norbet Wlk. *M9* . . . 6A 46
Norbury Av. *Grass* . . . 5G 43
Norbury Ho. *Oldh* . . . 6H 41
Norbury La. *Oldh* . . . 2B 50
Norbury St. *Roch* . . . 3B 22
Nordale Pk. *Roch* . . . 3A 12
Nordek Clo. *Rytn* . . . 4D 30
Nordek Dri. *Rytn* . . . 4D 30
Norden . . . 4H 11
Norden Clo. *Roch* . . . 3G 11
Norden Rd. *Roch* . . . 2H 19
Nordens Dri. *Chad* . . . 2H 39
Nordens Rd. *Chad* . . . 3H 39
Nordens St. *Chad* . . . 3A 40
Norden Way. *Roch* . . . 3G 11
Noreen Av. *P'wich* . . . 6A 36
Norfolk Av. *Droy* . . . 4D 54
Norfolk Av. *Heyw* . . . 5E 19
Norfolk Clo. *L'boro* . . . 2A 8
Norfolk Clo. *Shaw* . . . 2F 31
Norfolk Cres. *Fail* . . . 1C 54
Norfolk St. *Oldh* . . . 1B 48
(in two parts)
Norfolk St. *Roch* . . . 1G 21
Norfolk Way. *Rytn* . . . 1D 40
Norford Way. *Roch* . . . 5A 12
Norley Clo. *Chad* . . . 1B 40
Norman Clo. *Midd* . . . 2E 39
Norman Rd. *Roch* . . . 1F 21
Norman Rd. W. *M9* . . . 6B 46
Norman St. *Fail* . . . 4A 48
Norman St. *Midd* . . . 2D 38
Norman St. *Oldh* . . . 3D 40
Normanton Dri. *M9* . . . 2A 46
Norman Weall Ct. *Midd* . . . 1C 38
Normington St. *Oldh* . . . 4H 41
Norreys St. *Roch* . . . 5A 14
North Av. *G'fld* . . . 6D 44
North Av. *Uns* . . . 5A 26
North Cres. *M11* . . . 4B 54
North Cft. *Oldh* . . . 2G 49
Northdale Rd. *M9* . . . 6F 37
Northdene Dri. *Roch* . . . 1B 20
N. Downs Rd. *Shaw* . . . 1F 31
North Dri. *Aud* . . . 6G 55
Northerly Cres. *M40* . . . 2F 47
Northfield Av. *M40* . . . 3H 47
Northfield Rd. *M40* . . . 3H 47
North Ga. *Oldh* . . . 3E 49
Northgate. *Whitw* . . . 4E 5
Northgate La. *Oldh* . . . 5C 32
Northland Rd. *M9* . . . 2C 46
North La. *Roch* . . . 5H 13
North Moor . . . 4D 40
Northmoor M. *Oldh* . . . 3E 41
North Nook. *Oldh* . . . 3D 42
Northolt Ct. *M11* . . . 5B 54
Northolt Fold. *Heyw* . . . 2A 28
North Pde. *Miln* . . . 3A 24
Northridge Rd. *M9* . . . 5H 37
North Ri. *G'fld* . . . 6D 44
North Rd. *M11* . . . 5A 54
North Rd. *Aud* . . . 6G 55
North St. *Heyw* . . . 5F 19
North St. L'boro . . . 6A 8
(off East St.)
North St. *Midd* . . . 1C 38
North St. *Roch* . . . 5A 14
North St. *Rytn* . . . 5D 30
(in two parts)
North St. *Whitw* . . . 2E 5
North Vw. *Moss* . . . 4A 52
North Vw. *Whitw* . . . 2F 5
N. View Clo. *Lyd* . . . 6G 43
Northwold Dri. *M9* . . . 2D 46
Norton Rd. *Roch* . . . 2H 13
Norville Av. *M40* . . . 2F 47
Norwich Av. *Chad* . . . 2A 40
Norwich Av. *Roch* . . . 6C 12
Norwich Clo. *Ash L* . . . 6B 50
Norwich St. *Roch* . . . 2A 22
Norwood Clo. *Shaw* . . . 1G 31
Norwood Cres. *Rytn* . . . 1E 41
Norwood Gro. *Rytn* . . . 1E 41
Nottingham Dri. *Ash L* . . . 6H 49
Nottingham Dri. *Fail* . . . 2E 55
Nowell Ct. *Midd* . . . 6C 28
Nowell Ho. *Midd* . . . 6C 28
Nowell Rd. *Midd* . . . 6C 28
Nudger Clo. *Dob* . . . 1B 44
Nudger Grn. *Dob* . . . 1B 44
Nugget St. *Oldh* . . . 5H 41
Nunfield Clo. *M40* . . . 3D 46
Nursery Gdns. *Roch* . . . 5C 14
Nursery Rd. *Fail* . . . 6A 48
Nuthurst Rd. *M40* . . . 4E 47
Nuttall St. *Oldh* . . . 1H 49
Nutt La. *P'wich* . . . 3C 36

O

Oak Av. *Midd* . . . 4C 38
Oak Av. *Rytn* . . . 3D 30
Oak Bank. *Carr* . . . 6B 52
Oak Bank Av. *M9* . . . 4B 46
Oakbank Av. *Chad* . . . 3G 39
Oakcliffe Rd. *Roch* . . . 1C 14
Oakdale Ct. *Del* . . . 6A 34
Oakdene Rd. *Midd* . . . 3E 39
Oakdene St. *M9* . . . 5B 46
Oaken Bank Rd. *Heyw & Midd* . . . 4B 28
Oakenclough. *Oldh* . . . 4E 41
Oaken Clough Dri. *Ash L* . . . 6F 49
Oakenrod Hill. *Roch* . . . 6E 13
Oakenrod Vs. *Roch* . . . 6F 13
Oakenshaw Av. *Whitw* . . . 5E 5
Oakenshaw Vw. *Whitw* . . . 5E 5
Oaken St. *Ash L* . . . 6G 49
Oakfield Av. *Droy* . . . 6D 54
Oakfield Ter. *Roch* . . . 5E 13
Oak Hill. *L'boro* . . . 6F 7
Oaklands Dri. *P'wich* . . . 6A 36
Oaklands Pk. *Grass* . . . 6A 44
Oaklands Rd. *G'fld & Oldh* . . . 6B 44
Oaklands Rd. *Rytn* . . . 1E 41
Oaklands Ter. *Roch* . . . 6E 21
Oak La. *W'fld* . . . 3A 36
Oakleigh Clo. *Heyw* . . . 2A 28
Oakley Clo. *M40* . . . 2A 54
Oakley St. *L'boro* . . . 1E 15
Oakridge Wlk. *M9* . . . 6A 46
Oak Rd. *Fail* . . . 1D 54
Oak Rd. *Oldh* . . . 3C 48
Oakshaw Dri. *Roch* . . . 4C 12
Oak St. *Heyw* . . . 4F 19
Oak St. *L'boro* . . . 6A 8
Oak St. *Midd* . . . 4F 39
Oak St. *Miln* . . . 4G 23
Oak St. *Roch* . . . 6H 13
Oak St. *Shaw* . . . 2A 32
Oak St. *S'bri* . . . 2F 15
Oak Ter. *L'boro* . . . 1B 8
Oak Vw. Rd. *G'fld* . . . 6D 44
Oakville Ter. *M40* . . . 4B 46
Oakway. *Midd* . . . 5B 28
Oakwood. *Chad* . . . 4G 39
Oakwood Av. *M40* . . . 4F 47
Oakworth Cft. *Oldh* . . . 5D 32
Oban Av. *Oldh* . . . 2H 41
Oberlin St. *Oldh* . . . 4B 42
Oberlin St. *Roch* . . . 2F 21
Ockenden Dri. *M9* . . . 6A 46
Octavia Dri. *M40* . . . 3A 54
Oddies Yd. *Roch* . . . 3A 14
Off Duke St. *Moss* . . . 4A 52
Off Green St. *Midd* . . . 2D 38
Off Kershaw St. Shaw . . . 2H 31
(off Kershaw St., in two parts)
Ogden Clo. *Heyw* . . . 5E 19
Ogden La. *Miln* . . . 2B 24
Ogden Rd. *Fail* . . . 1D 54
Ogden St. *Chad* . . . 3C 40
Ogden St. *Midd* . . . 3C 38
Ogden St. *Oldh* . . . 5B 42
Ogden St. *Roch* . . . 5E 21
Ogmore Wlk. *M40* . . . 3E 47
Ogwen Dri. *P'wich* . . . 6A 36
Old Bank Vw. *Oldh* . . . 5A 32
Old Bent La. *Ward* . . . 4A 6
Old Birtle . . . 6C 10
Old Brook Clo. *Shaw* . . . 1B 32
Old Brow. *Moss* (Park St.) . . . 5G 51
Old Brow. *Moss* (Seel St.) . . . 4G 51
Old Brow Ct. *Moss* . . . 5G 51
Old Brow La. *Roch* . . . 2C 14
Oldbury Clo. *Heyw* . . . 2H 27
Old Church St. *M40* . . . 1A 54
Old Church St. *Oldh* . . . 4F 41
Old Clay Dri. *Roch* . . . 1D 14
Oldcroft. *S'head* . . . 5E 43
Old Delph Rd. *Roch* . . . 4A 12
Old Edge La. *Rytn & Oldh* . . . 1E 41
(in two parts)
Oldfield Rd. *P'wich* . . . 4A 36
Oldfield St. *M11* . . . 6A 54
Old Hall La. *P'wich & Midd* . . . 3D 36
(in four parts)
Old Hall Rd. *M40* . . . 6D 46
Oldhall St. *Midd* . . . 3B 38
(in two parts)
Oldham . . . 4F 41
Oldham and Werneth Pk. Study Cen. . . . 6C 40
(Natural History Mus.)
Oldham Art Gallery . . . 5F 41
(off Union St, Library)
Oldham Athletic Football Club. . . . 1D 40
(Boundary Park)
Oldham B'way. Bus. Pk. *Chad* . . . 1G 47
Oldham Central Trad. Pk. *Oldh* . . . 3G 41
Oldham Crematorium. *Oldh* . . . 4C 48
Oldham Edge . . . 3F 41
Oldham Ho. *Shaw* . . . 4H 31
Oldham Mus. . . . 5F 41
Oldham Rd. *Ash L* . . . 6G 49
Oldham Rd. *Del* . . . 3E 33
Oldham Rd. *Fail* . . . 1A 54
Oldham Rd. *Lyd* . . . 5G 43
Oldham Rd. *Midd* . . . 3C 38
Oldham Rd. *Roch* . . . 1A 22
(in two parts)
Oldham Rd. *Rytn* . . . 5E 31
Oldham Rd. *Scout & Dob* . . . 3G 43
Oldham Rd. *Shaw* . . . 5H 31
Oldham Rd. *S'head* . . . 5D 42
Oldham Rugby League Football Club. . . . 1D 40
Oldham Sports Cen. . . . 4F 41
Oldham St. *Droy* . . . 5F 55
Oldham Tourist Info. Cen. . . . 4F 41
Oldham Way. *Dens* . . . 4G 25
Oldham Way. *Oldh* . . . 3D 40
Oldham Way. *Shaw* . . . 5B 24
(Jubilee)
Oldham Way. *Shaw* . . . 5G 23
(Moss Gate)
Oldham Way. *Shaw & Dens* . . . 1D 32
Old Kiln La. *G'ton* . . . 1F 51
Old La. *Aus* . . . 3D 42
Old La. *Chad* . . . 1B 48
Old La. *Dob* . . . 1D 44
Old La. *Grass* . . . 5A 44
Old La. *Upperm* . . . 2F 45
Old Mill Ho. *S'head* . . . 6E 43
Old Mill La. *G'ton* . . . 6E 43
Old Mills Hill. *Midd* . . . 2F 39
Oldmill St. *Roch* . . . 5H 13
Old Packhorse Rd. *Dig* . . . 3D 34
Old Pack Horse Rd. *L'boro & Sower B.* . . . 5D 8
Old Rd. *M9* . . . 3A 46
Old Rd. *Fail* . . . 6G 47
Old School Ho., The. L'boro . . . 5F 7
(off Shore Rd.)
Oldstead Wlk. M9 . . . 6A 46
(off Kelvington Dri.)
Old St. *Oldh* . . . 6B 42
Old Tame . . . 1F 33
Old Thorn La. *G'fld* . . . 5F 45
Oliver Clo. *L'boro* . . . 6F 7
Oliver St. *Oldh* . . . 5F 41
Olive St. *Fail* . . . 5G 47
Olive St. *Heyw* . . . 5A 20
Olive St. *Roch* . . . 6F 21
Ollerton. Roch . . . 5G 13
(off Sheriff St.)
Ollerton Dri. *Fail* . . . 1D 54
Olney. *Roch* . . . 1G 21
Onchan Av. *Oldh* . . . 5H 41
One Ash Clo. *Roch* . . . 3H 13
Onslow Av. *M40* . . . 4G 47
Onslow Clo. *Oldh* . . . 3E 41
Onslow St. *Roch* . . . 3E 21
Oozewood . . . 3C 30
Oozewood Rd. *Rytn* . . . 4A 30
Openshaw . . . 6B 54
Openshaw Wlk. *Open* . . . 6A 54
Orama Mill. *Whitw* . . . 3E 5
Orange Hill Rd. *P'wich* . . . 6A 36
Orchard Brow. *Shaw* . . . 2F 31
Orchard Gro. *Shaw* . . . 2G 31
ORCHARD HOUSE DAY HOSPITAL. . . . 5E 31
Orchard Rd. *Fail* . . . 6H 47
Orchards, The. Heyw . . . 5A 20
(off Rochdale Rd. E.)
Orchards, The. *Shaw* . . . 2F 31
Orchard St. *Heyw* . . . 4A 20
Orchard, The. *Oldh* . . . 2A 50
Orchid Clo. *Oldh* . . . 2D 40
Orchid Way. *Roch* . . . 2F 13
Ordell Wlk. *M9* . . . 2A 46
Oregon Av. *Oldh* . . . 2E 41
Orford Rd. *M40* . . . 2A 54
Oriel Av. *Oldh* . . . 2E 49
Oriel Clo. *Chad* . . . 6A 40
Oriel St. *Roch* . . . 2H 21
Orleans Way. *Oldh* . . . 4E 41

Orley Wlk. *Oldh* 5B **32**
Orme Av. *Midd* 4C **38**
Ormerod Av. *Rytn* 6E **31**
Ormerod St. *M40* 4C **54**
Ormerod St. *Heyw* 6A **20**
Orme St. *Oldh* 6G **41**
Ormrods, The. *Bury* 2D **18**
Ornsay Wlk. *Open* 6A **54**
Orpington Rd. *M9* 6A **46**
Orron St. *L'boro* 6G **7**
Osborne Rd. *M9* 6A **46**
Osborne Rd. *Oldh* 6D **40**
Osborne St. *Heyw* 6H **19**
Osborne St. *Oldh* 3C **40**
Osborne St. *Roch* 2G **21**
Osborne St. *Shaw* 3H **31**
Osborne Trad. Est. *Oldh* 3C **40**
Oscar St. *M40* 6C **46**
(in two parts)
Osmond St. *Oldh* 4A **42**
Osprey Dri. *Droy* 4G **55**
Osterley Rd. *M9* 2B **46**
Ostlers Ga. *Droy* 5H **55**
Oswald St. *Roch* 5A **14**
Oswald St. *Shaw* 1A **32**
Otago St. *Oldh* 2A **42**
Otley Clo. *Chad* 5B **40**
Otmoor Way. *Rytn* 5G **31**
Otterham Wlk. *M40* 2B **54**
Oulder Hill. *Roch* 6D **12**
Oulder Hill Dri. *Roch* 6C **12**
Oulder Hill Recreation Cen. 5D **12**
Ouldfield Clo. *Roch* 1B **22**
Outram M. *Upperm* 2D **44**
Overdale Clo. *Oldh* 2E **41**
Overdell Dri. *Roch* 2E **13**
Overens St. *Oldh* 4H **41**
Overfield Way. *Roch* 3H **13**
Overhill Rd. *Chad* 3H **39**
Over Town La. *Roch* 2E **11**
(in two parts)
Overt St. *Roch* 2H **21**
Owen Fold. *S'head* 4D **42**
Owens Clo. *Chad* 3G **39**
Owen St. *Oldh* 6C **32**
Owler La. *Chad* 2F **47**
Oxendale Dri. *Midd* 2H **37**
Oxford Av. *Droy* 4D **54**
Oxford Av. *Roch* 1C **20**
Oxford Dri. *Midd* 1E **39**
Oxford Ho. *Oldh* 5C **40**
Oxford Pl. *Roch* 2A **22**
Oxford St. *Oldh* 6B **40**
Oxford St. *Shaw* 3H **31**
Oxford Way. *Roch* 3G **13**
Ox Hey La. *Dens* 6H **25**
Oxhill Wlk. *M40* 3F **47**

P

Packer St. *Roch* 6H **13**
Packwood Chase. *Chad* 3H **39**
Paddington Av. *M40* 2A **54**
Paddock Ct. *Fail* 2D **54**
Paddock Head. *L'boro* 1E **15**
Paddock La. *Fail* 2D **54**
Paddock, The. *G'fld* 1B **52**
Pagen St. *Roch* 5H **13**
Pagnall Ct. *Chad* 6B **40**
Pailin Dri. *Droy* 5G **55**
Palace Gdns. *Rytn* 1D **40**
Palace St. *Oldh* 4C **40**
Palatine Av. *Roch* 5C **12**
Palatine Rd. *Roch* 5C **12**
Palatine St. *Roch* 6C **14**
Palatine Ter. *Roch* 5C **12**
Palin Wood Rd. *Del* 4B **34**
Pallotine Wlk. *Roch* 2F **21**
Palm Bus. Cen. *Chad* 4B **40**
Palmer Clo. *Oldh* 1F **49**
Palm Gro. *Chad* 3B **40**
Palm St. *Droy* 5B **54**
Palm St. *Oldh* 3A **42**
Panmure St. *Oldh* 1F **49**
Pares Land Wlk. *Roch* 1B **22**
Parham Wlk. *M9* 2A **46**
Park Av. *Chad* 2B **40**
Park Av. *Fail* 5F **47**
Park Bridge 3A **50**
Pk. Bri. Heritage Cen. 4A **50**
Pk. Bridge Rd. *Ash L* 4H **49**
Pk. Bridge Rd. *Oldh & Ash L* 6G **49**
Park Clo. *Chad* 2B **40**
Park Cotts. *G'fld* 6A **44**
Park Cotts. *Shaw* 1F **31**
Park Ct. *Roch* (Castle Av.) 1G **21**
Park Ct. *Roch* (Suffolk St.) 1H **21**
Park Cres. *Chad* 2H **39**
Parkdale. *Chad* 2B **40**
Parkfield. *Chad* 2A **40**
Parkfield. *Midd* 3B **38**
Parkfield Av. *Oldh* 3B **48**
Parkfield Dri. *Midd* 3A **38**
Parkfield Ind. Est. *Midd* 3A **38**
Park Fld. Rd. *Grass* 5A **44**
Parkfield Rd. N. *M40* 3G **47**
Parkfield St. *Roch* 5B **22**
Parkgate. *Chad* 2B **40**
Parkgate Chase. *Roch* 5C **12**
Parkgate Way. *Shaw* 2B **32**
Park Hill. *Roch* 4H **13**
Parkhurst Av. *M40* 4G **47**
Parklands. *Rytn* 2C **30**
Parklands. *Shaw* 1B **32**
Parklands Cres. *Hey D* 1E **27**
Parklands Ho. *Rytn* 3C **30**
Parklands Way. *Hey D* 1E **27**
Park La. *G'fld* 6E **45**
Park La. *Oldh* 3F **49**
Park La. *Roch* 5H **13**
Park La. *Rytn* 4D **30**
(in three parts)
Parkleigh Dri. *M40* 3G **47**
Pk. Mill Ind. Est. *Moss* 2H **51**
Parkmount Rd. *M9* 4A **46**
Park Pde. *Shaw* 6A **24**
Park Pl. *P'wich* 6A **36**
Park Rd. *Aud* 6H **55**
Park Rd. *L'boro* 5H **7**
Park Rd. *Midd* 3B **38**
Park Rd. *Oldh* 5F **41**
Park Rd. *Roch* 3A **14**
(in two parts)
Parkside. *Midd* 5A **38**
Parkside. *Whitw* 1F **5**
Parkside Av. *Fail* 2C **54**
Parkside Av. *Shaw* 1A **32**
Parkside Ho. *Rytn* 5E **31**
Parkside Ind. Est. *Rytn* 5E **31**
Park 66. *Bury* 3A **26**
Park St. *Droy* 5G **55**
Park St. *Heyw* 1A **28**
Park St. *Moss* 5G **51**
Park St. *Oldh* 6E **41**
(in two parts)
Park St. *Roch* 1H **21**
Park St. *Rytn* 5D **30**
Park St. *Shaw* 2H **31**
Parksway. *M9* 6F **37**
Park Ter. *Heyw* 4H **19**
Park Ter. *Moss* 5G **51**
Park, The. *Grass* 6H **43**
Park, The. *G'fld* 6E **45**
Park Vw. *Aud* 6H **55**
Park Vw. *Chad* 2A **40**
Park Vw. *L'boro* 5H **7**
Park Vw. *Shaw* 1E **31**
Parkville Rd. *P'wich* 4A **36**
Parkway. *Chad* 1A **40**
Parkway. *Roch* 5D **12**
Parrenthorn Rd. *P'wich* 3A **36**
Parr Ho. *Oldh* 6F **41**
Parr La. *Bury* 1A **36**
Parrot St. *M11* 6A **54**
Parsonage Ter. Miln *6F 15*
(off Parsonage Wlk.)
Parsonage Wlk. *Roch* 6F **15**
Parson's Dri. *Midd* 1B **38**
Parsons St. *Oldh* 5C **40**
Parth St. *Bury* 6B **18**
Partington Pk. *Roch* 1E **29**
Partington St. *Fail* 6H **47**
Partington St. *Heyw* 5E **19**
Partington St. *Oldh* 4G **41**
Partington St. *Roch* 5D **20**
Partridge Clo. *Roch* 6B **12**
Partridge Ri. *Droy* 4H **55**
Partridge Rd. *Fail* 1G **55**
Partridge Way. *Chad* 3F **39**
Parvet Av. *Droy* 4D **54**
Passmonds. 4D **12**
Passmonds Cres. *Roch* 5D **12**
Passmonds Way. *Roch* 5D **12**
Pass St. *Oldh* 5D **40**
Pass, The. *Roch* 5A **14**
Pasture Clo. *Heyw* 6F **19**
Pastures La. *Scout* 3F **43**
Patience St. *Roch* 4E **13**
Paton St. *Roch* 2F **13**
Patterdale Clo. *Oldh* 2G **41**
Patterdale Clo. *Roch* 4D **20**
Patterdale Dri. *Midd* 1A **38**
Pattison Clo. *Roch* 2F **13**
Patton Clo. *Bury* 1A **36**
Paulden Av. *Oldh* 2C **42**
Paulden Dri. *Fail* 6A **48**
Paul Row. *L'boro* 2A **8**
Pavilion Clo. *Roch* 3H **13**
Peacehaven Av. *M11* 5A **54**
Peace St. *Fail* 4A **48**
Peach Bank. *Midd* 3C **38**
Peach Rd. *Oldh* 2B **42**
(in two parts)
Peach St. *P'wich* 6A **36**
Peak Clo. *Oldh* 5D **32**
Peakdale Rd. *Droy* 4C **54**
Peak St. *Oldh* 5C **40**
Peanock La. *L'boro* 3F **15**
Pear Av. *Bury* 4A **18**
Pear Clo. *Midd* 5D **38**
Pearl Mill Clo. *Oldh* 1H **49**
Pearl St. *Roch* 5E **13**
Pearly Bank. *Oldh* 4B **32**
Pearson Clo. *Miln* 6F **15**
Pearson Gro. *Lees* 5C **42**
Pearson St. *Roch* 5C **14**
Pear St. *P'wich* 6A **36**
Pebworth Clo. *Midd* 6B **38**
Pedler Brow La. *Roch & L'boro* 5E **7**
Peebles Dri. *M40* 3B **54**
Peel La. *Heyw* 4F **19**
Peels Av. *S'head* 4E **43**
Peel St. *Chad* 5B **40**
Peel St. *Fail* 1B **54**
Peel St. *Heyw* 5F **19**
Peel St. *L'boro* 6H **7**
Peel St. *Roch* 5G **13**
Peel St. *Shaw* 2G **31**
Pegasus Ct. *Roch* 1E **21**
Pelham St. *Oldh* 3F **49**
Pellowe Rd. *Oldh* 2E **49**
Pemberton Ho. Shaw *1H 31*
(off Napier St.)
Pemberton St. *Roch* 5E **21**
Pemberton Way. *Shaw* 1H **31**
Pembridge Fold. *Midd* 3E **39**
Pembridge Rd. *M9* 1B **46**
Pembroke Ct. *Roch* 4H **13**
Pembroke Dri. *Oldh* 5C **32**
Pembroke St. *L'boro* 5H **7**
Pembroke St. *Oldh* 5D **40**
Pendennis. *Roch* 1G **21**
Pendle Clo. *Oldh* 6B **42**
Pendle Gro. *Rytn* 6C **30**
Pendragon Pl. *Fail* 6A **48**
Pendrell Wlk. M9 *2A 46*
(off Sanderstead Dri.)
Penerley Dri. *M9* 6A **46**
Penistone Av. *M9* 2C **46**
Penistone Av. *Roch* 1C **22**
Penmore Clo. *Shaw* 2A **32**
Pennant St. *Oldh* 3H **41**
Pennell St. *M11* 6B **54**
Pennine Av. *Chad* 6A **40**
Pennine Clo. *M9* 1B **46**
Pennine Clo. *Shaw* 2A **32**
Pennine Ct. *Oldh* 5G **41**
Pennine Dri. *Miln* 6G **15**
Pennine Dri. *Ward* 5C **6**
Pennine Precinct. *Miln* 2F **23**
Pennine Va. *Shaw* 1A **32**
Pennine Vw. *L'boro* 1B **8**
Pennine Vw. *Moss* 4H **51**
Pennine Vw. *Rytn* 5E **31**
Pennine Way. *Dig* 1H **35**
Pennington St. *Chad* 2B **48**
Penn St. *M40* 5B **46**
Penn St. *Heyw* 6H **19**
Penn St. *Oldh* 6D **40**
Penn St. *Roch* 5H **13**
Penrhyn Av. *Midd* 4C **38**
Penrhyn Dri. *P'wich* 6A **36**
Penrith Av. *M11* 4A **54**
Penrith Av. *Oldh* 1C **48**
Penrith St. *Roch* 2H **21**
Penrose Gdns. *Midd* 2D **38**
Penrose Wlk. *Midd* 5C **28**
Penryn Av. *Rytn* 5F **31**
Penthorpe Dri. *Rytn* 6F **31**
Pentland Av. *M40* 3E **47**
Pentlands Clo. *Shaw* 1F **31**
Penwell Fold. *Oldh* 2E **41**
Peppermint Clo. *Miln* 3A **24**
Percival Rd. *Droy* 6F **55**
Percival Wlk. *Rytn* 6E **31**
Percy St. *Oldh* 4A **42**
Percy St. *Roch* 2B **22**
Peregrine Cres. *Droy* 4G **55**
Periton Wlk. M9 *2A 46*
(off Leconfield Dri.)
Perivale Dri. *Oldh* 1H **49**
Pernham St. *Oldh* 4A **42**
Perry Clo. *Roch* 2F **21**
Perrymead. *P'wich* 5A **36**
Pershore. Roch *5G 13*
(off Spotland Rd.)
Pershore Rd. *Midd* 6C **28**
Perth Av. *Chad* 1A **48**
Perth Rd. *Roch* 5B **22**
Perth St. *Rytn* 5G **31**
Peterborough Clo. *Ash L* 6H **49**
Peterloo Ter. *Midd* 1C **38**
Peter St. *Midd* 4G **37**
Peter St. *Oldh* 5F **41**
Petrel Clo. *Droy* 4G **55**
Petrel Clo. *Roch* 6B **12**
Petrie St. *Roch* 5H **13**
Petrock Wlk. *M40* 2A **54**
Petts Cres. *L'boro* 5G **7**
Petworth Rd. *Chad* 5B **40**
Pevensey Ct. *M9* 3C **46**
Pevensey Wlk. *Chad* 5B **40**
Peveril Clo. *W'fld* 4A **36**
Peveril Rd. *Oldh* 2A **42**
Pexwood. *Chad* 2G **39**
Philip St. *Oldh* 3A **42**
Philip St. *Roch* 2H **21**
Phillimore St. *Lees* 6C **42**
Phoenix Clo. *Heyw* 6B **20**
Phoenix Ind. Est. *Fail* 5A **48**
Phoenix Pk. Ind. Est. *Heyw* 6B **20**
Phoenix Pl. *S'head* 5D **42**
Phoenix St. *L'boro* 5H **7**
Phoenix St. *Oldh* 5F **41**
Phoenix St. *Roch* 4E **13**
Phoenix St. *S'head* 5D **42**
Phyllis St. *Midd* 4E **39**
Phyllis St. *Roch* 4D **12**
Pickford Wlk. *Rytn* 6E **31**
Pickhill. *Upperm* 3D **44**
Pickhill M. *Upperm* 3D **44**
Pickmere Clo. *Droy* 6F **55**
Pickmere M. *Upperm* 3D **44**
Pickup St. *Roch* 6A **14**
Picton Sq. *Oldh* 5G **41**
Pierce St. *Oldh* 2A **42**
Piercy St. *Fail* 6G **47**
Piethorne Clo. *Miln* 3A **24**
Pike Av. *Fail* 1G **55**
Pike St. *Roch* 2H **21**
Pike Vw. Clo. *Oldh* 6H **41**
Pilkington Dri. *W'fld* 1A **36**
Pilkington Rd. *M9* 3C **46**
Pilkington St. *Midd* 2D **38**
Pilling St. *Roch* 5F **13**
Pilling Wlk. *Chad* 5A **40**
Pilsworth Rd. *Bury* 2A **26**
(in two parts)
Pilsworth Rd. *Heyw* 5F **19**
Pincher Wlk. *Open* 6A **54**
Pine Gro. *Rytn* 3D **30**
Pine St. *Chad* 3A **40**
Pine St. *Heyw* 5H **19**
Pine St. *L'boro* 5H **7**
Pine St. *Midd* 4E **39**
Pine St. *Miln* 4H **23**
Pine St. *Roch* 6B **14**
Pine Tree Rd. *Oldh* 4D **48**
Pineway. *Lees* 5D **42**
Pinewood. *Chad* 4G **39**
Pinfold. *Roch* 1G **21**
Pinfold Av. *M9* 3C **46**
Pingle La. *Del* 4A **34**
Pingot. *Shaw* 6B **24**
Pintail Clo. *Roch* 3D **12**
Pioneer St. *L'boro* 6H **7**
Pioneer St. *Midd* 4F **29**
Pioneer St. *Roch* 1A **22**
Pioneers Villa. *Miln* 3C **24**
Pioneers Yd. *Miln* 2F **23**
Pipers Clo. *Roch* 5H **11**
Pipit Clo. *Aud* 5G **55**
Pirie Wlk. *M40* 1A **54**
Pit La. *Rytn* 1C **30**
(in two parts)
Pitmore Wlk. *M40* 3F **47**
Pitses. 1B **50**
Pits Farm Av. *Roch* 6E **13**
Pitshouse. *Roch* 3A **12**

Pitshouse La.—Regent St.

Pitshouse La. *Roch* 3A **12**
Pit St. *Chad* 1B **48**
Pitt St. *Heyw* 5G **19**
Pitt St. *Oldh* 5G **41**
Pitt St. *Roch* 5H **13**
Pitt St. E. *Oldh* 6H **41**
Plane Rd. *Fail* 2D **54**
Plane St. *Oldh* 4A **42**
Plantagenet Wlk. *M40* 3B **54**
Plantagent St. *Moss* 2H **51**
Plantation Gro. *Uns* 5A **26**
Plant Hill Rd. *M9* 6G **37**
Plate St. *Oldh* 4F **41**
Plato St. *Oldh* 4D **40**
Platt Clo. *Miln* 2G **23**
Platting La. *Roch* 3A **22**
Platting Rd. *Scout & Lyd* 3G **43**
Platt La. *Dob* 1B **44**
Platt St. *S'head* 5D **42**
Playfair Clo. *Heyw* 2A **28**
Pleasant Ct. *Roch* 5E **21**
Pleasant St. *Heyw* 3G **19**
Pleasant St. *Roch* 5E **21**
Pleasant View. **5B 22**
Pleasant Vw. *M9* 6F **37**
Pleasant Vw. *Heyw* 4F **19**
Pleasant Vw. *Lees* 4D **42**
Pleasant Vw. *Shaw* 3B **32**
Pleasington Dri. *M40* 3E **47**
Plover Clo. *Roch* 6B **12**
Plover Dri. *Bury* 3A **18**
Plover Way. *Droy* 4G **55**
Plumpton Clo. *Rytn* 1E **41**
Plumpton Rd. *Roch* 1B **30**
Plum St. *Oldh* 6D **40**
Plymouth Clo. *Ash L* 6H **49**
Plymouth St. *Oldh* 1F **49**
(in two parts)
Pobgreen. **2F 45**
Pobgreen La. *Upperm* 2F **45**
Polden Clo. *Oldh* 3E **49**
Polden Wlk. *M9* 4B **46**
Pole Ct. *Bury* 6A **26**
Polefield App. *P'wich* 5A **36**
Polefield Circ. *P'wich* 5A **36**
Polefield Gro. *P'wich* 5A **36**
Polefield Hall Rd. *P'wich* 5A **36**
(in two parts)
Polefield Rd. *M9* 3A **46**
Polefield Rd. *P'wich* 5A **36**
Pole La. *Bury & P'wich* 6A **26**
Pole La. *Fail* 5H **47**
Pollard Ct. *Oldh* 3E **41**
Pollard Gro. *L'boro* 3A **8**
Polly Grn. *Roch* 2H **13**
Polonia Ct. *Oldh* 2C **48**
Polperro Clo. *Rytn* 5G **31**
Polworth Rd. *M9* 4A **46**
Pomona St. *Roch* 2H **21**
Ponsford Av. *M9* 2C **46**
Pool Bank St. *Midd* 4F **37**
(in two parts)
Pooley Clo. *Midd* 2F **37**
Pool Fold. *Fail* 1E **55**
Pool St. *Oldh* 1F **49**
Poot Hall. *Roch* 2H **13**
Poplar Av. *Bury* 4A **18**
Poplar Av. *Lyd* 1G **51**
Poplar Av. *Oldh* 3D **48**
Poplar Av. *Roch* 4E **13**
Poplars, The. *Moss* 4A **52**
Poplar St. *Fail* 1B **54**
Poplar St. *Midd* 4F **39**
Poplar Wlk. *Chad* 3B **40**
Poppy Clo. *Chad* 4G **39**
Poppyfield Vw. *Roch* 5A **12**
Porritt Clo. *Roch* 1A **20**
Portal Ct. *Midd* 3E **39**
Portal Wlk. M9 *5A* ***46***
(off Alderside Rd.)
Porter St. *Oldh* 6C **40**
Portland Pl. Roch *3A* ***22***
(off Oldham Rd.)
Portman St. *Moss* 4G **51**
Portree Ct. *Heyw* 6E **19**
Port St. *Oldh* 1F **49**
Portwood Wlk. *M9* 6A **46**
Pot Ho. La. *Ward* 6H **5**
Potter Ho. *Oldh* 6F **41**
Potter's La. *M9* 6A **46**
Pottery Wlk. *M40* 3F **47**
Pott St. *M40* 2B **54**
Powell St. *Clay* 5B **54**
Poynter St. *M40* 4E **47**
Poynter Wlk. *Oldh* 5B **32**
Prescott St. *Roch* 3C **14**
Prestbury Dri. *Oldh* 2D **40**
Preston St. *Midd* 3C **38**
Preston St. *Oldh* 5G **41**
Preston St. *Roch* 5E **13**
Prestwick Wlk. *M40* 3E **47**
Pretoria Rd. *Oldh* 2C **48**
Pretoria St. *Roch* 4E **13**
Prettywood. **5C 18**
Prickshaw La. *Whitw* 5C **4**
Priest Hill St. *Oldh* 4E **41**
Priestley Way. *Shaw* 2B **32**
Priestwood Av. *Oldh* 5D **32**
Primley Wlk. M9 *5A* ***46***
(off Edward St.)
Primrose Av. *Upperm* 2E **45**
Primrose Bank. **6E 41**
Primrose Bank. *G'fld* 6D **44**
Primrose Bank. *Oldh* 6E **41**
Primrose Dri. *Bury* 3B **18**
Primrose Dri. *Droy* 4G **55**
Primrose Hill Cotts. *Heyw* 3B **20**
Primrose Ho. *Oldh* 6E **41**
Primrose St. *Roch* 5F **13**
Primrose Wlk. *Oldh* 6E **41**
Prince Charlie St. *Oldh* 3H **41**
Princedom St. *M9* 5A **46**
Prince Edward Av. *Oldh* 4A **42**
Prince George St. *Oldh* 2A **42**
Prince of Wales Bus. Pk. *Oldh* 3A **42**
Princess Av. *Roch* 1C **14**
Princess Clo. *Heyw* 6H **19**
Princess Clo. *Moss* 5A **52**
Princess Dri. *Midd* 3A **38**
Princess Rd. *Chad* 2G **47**
Princess Rd. *P'wich* 6A **36**
Princess Rd. *Roch* 6D **14**
Princess Rd. *Shaw* 3G **31**
Princess St. *Chad* 6A **40**
Princess St. *Fail* 6G **47**
Princess St. *Lees* 5C **42**
Princess St. *Roch* 5H **13**
Prince St. *Heyw* 5H **19**
Prince St. *Oldh* 4G **41**
Prince St. *Roch* 2A **22**
Prince Way. *Rytn* 3C **30**
Printer St. *Oldh* 5F **41**
Prior St. *Oldh* 6H **41**
Priory Clo. *Oldh* 2D **48**
Priory Gro. *Chad* 1A **48**
Privet St. *Oldh* 2B **42**
Progress St. *Roch* 6E **21**
Promenade St. *Heyw* 5A **20**
Propps Hall Dri. *Fail* 1B **54**
Prospect Dri. *Fail* 2D **54**
Prospect Ho. M9 *6A* ***46***
(off Church La.)
Prospect Pl. *Heyw* 4H **19**
Prospect Rd. *Oldh* 4C **40**
Prospect St. *Heyw* 6A **20**
Prospect St. *L'boro* 5H **7**
Prospect St. *Roch* 3G **21**
Prospect Ter. *Roch* 3G **11**
Prospect Vs. *M9* 4B **46**
Provident St. *Shaw* 2H **31**
Puffingate Clo. *Carr* 6A **52**
Pullman St. *Roch* 2H **21**
Pump St. *Oldh* 3B **48**
Purdy Ho. *Oldh* 6F **41**
Purton Wlk. M9 *6A* ***46***
(off Broadwell Dri.)
Putney Clo. *Oldh* 2E **41**
Pym St. *M40* 5B **46**
Pym St. *Heyw* 6H **19**

Q

Quadrant, The. *M9* 2C **46**
Quadrant, The. *Droy* 6D **54**
Quail St. *Oldh* 6A **42**
Quantock Dri. *Oldh* 2F **49**
Quarry Hill. *Roch* 1G **13**
Quarry St. *Roch* 4G **13**
Quarry Vw. *Roch* 2G **13**
Quay St. *Heyw* 6A **20**
Quebec St. *Oldh* 3C **40**
Queen Anne Clo. *Uns* 5A **26**
Queens Av. *Roch* 1C **14**
Queens Dri. *Roch* 4G **21**
Queensferry St. *M40* 1A **54**
Queensgate Dri. *Rytn* 3C **30**
Queen's Pk. Rd. *Heyw* 3H **19**
Queens Rd. *Chad* 4A **40**
Queen's Rd. *L'boro* 6H **7**
Queens Rd. *Oldh* 6G **41**
Queen's Rd. Ter. L'boro *6H* ***7***
(off Queen's Rd.)
Queen St. *Fail* 6G **47**
Queen St. *Heyw* 4H **19**
Queen St. *L'boro* 6H **7**
Queen St. *Midd* 3E **39**
Queen St. *Moss* 4G **51**
Queen St. *Oldh* 4F **41**
Queen St. *Roch* 5H **13**
Queen St. *Rytn* 3H **31**
Queen St. *Shaw* 5D **30**
Queen St. *S'head* 5D **42**
Queens Vw. *L'boro* 2G **15**
Queen's Wlk. *Droy* 6E **55**
Queensway. *G'fld* 5D **44**
Queensway. *Moss* 5H **51**
Queensway. *Roch* 5E **21**
Queensway Neighbourhood Cen. *Roch* 2A **22**
Queen Victoria St. *Roch* 3A **22**
Quick. **1H 51**
Quick Edge. **2G 51**
Quick Edge La. *G'ton* 1F **51**
Quickedge Rd. *Moss & Lyd* 3G **51**
Quick Rd. *Moss* 1H **51**
Quick Vw. *Moss* 2A **52**
Quickwood. **3G 51**
Quickwood. Moss *3H* ***51***
(off Roughtown Rd.)
Quinton. Roch *5G* ***13***
(off Spotland Rd.)

R

Racefield Hamlet. *Chad* 5B **30**
Radcliffe Rd. *Oldh* 1B **42**
Radcliffe St. *Oldh* 3F **41**
(in two parts)
Radcliffe St. *Rytn* 5D **30**
Radcliffe St. *S'head* 5E **43**
Radclyffe St. *Chad* 3B **40**
Radclyffe St. *Midd* 1C **38**
Radclyffe Ter. *Midd* 1C **38**
Radford Dri. *M9* 5A **46**
Radnor St. *Oldh* 6C **40**
Raglan Av. *W'fld* 4A **36**
Raglan St. *Roch* 6E **21**
Railton Ter. *M9* 6B **46**
Railway App. *Roch* 5E **21**
Railway Brow. *Roch* 6E **21**
Railway Rd. *Chad* 3A **48**
Railway Rd. *Oldh* 5D **40**
Railway St. *Heyw* 6A **20**
Railway St. *L'boro* 6H **7**
Railway St. *Miln* 3H **23**
Railway St. *Roch* 6A **14**
Railway Ter. *Heyw* 6H **19**
Railway Vw. *Shaw* 1A **32**
Railway Vw. *S'head* 5D **42**
Raines Crest. *Miln* 1G **23**
Rainham Way. *Chad* 5B **40**
Rainhill Wlk. *M40* 3B **54**
Rainow Av. *Droy* 6C **54**
Rainsdale Flats. Heyw *5G* ***19***
(off Meadow Clo.)
Rainshaw St. *Oldh* 3B **42**
Rainshaw St. *Rytn* 5D **30**
Rain Shore. **1G 11**
Rainton Wlk. *M40* 3F **47**
Rainwood. *Chad* 3G **39**
Rake. *Roch* 6H **11**
Rake Ter. *L'boro* 5A **8**
Rake Top. *Roch* 4D **12**
Rakewood. **4A 16**
Rakewood Dri. *Oldh* 5C **32**
Rakewood Rd. *L'boro* 2H **15**
Raleigh Clo. *Oldh* 3F **41**
Raleigh Gdns. *L'boro* 2A **8**
Ralph Grn. St. *Chad* 2B **48**
Ralph Sherwin Ct. *Roch* 1D **14**
Ralph St. *M11* 6B **54**
Ralph St. *Roch* 4A **14**
Ralstone Av. *Oldh* 1F **49**
Ramsay Pl. *Roch* 5A **14**
Ramsay St. *Roch* 5A **14**
Ramsay Ter. *Roch* 5A **14**
Ramsbury Dri. *M40* 3F **47**
Ramsdale St. *Chad* 4A **40**
Ramsden Clo. *Oldh* 4E **41**
Ramsden Cres. *Oldh* 4E **41**
Ramsden Rd. Ward *5C* ***6***
(off Wardle Rd.)
Ramsden Rd. *Ward* 4C **6**
(Wardle)
Ramsden Rd. *Ward* 2C **6**
(Watergrove Reservoir)
Ramsden St. *Oldh* 4E **41**
Ramsey St. *M40* 6D **46**
Ramsey St. *Chad* 6B **40**
Ramsey St. *Oldh* 3H **41**
Ramsgate Rd. *M40* 3A **54**
Ranby Av. *M9* 1B **46**
Randolph St. *Oldh* 3C **48**
Rand St. *Oldh* 2B **42**
Raneley Gro. *Roch* 5A **22**
Range La. *Dens* 6H **25**
Raper St. *Oldh* 3A **42**
Rapes Highway. *Dens* 2H **25**
Rastell Wlk. M9 *2A* ***46***
(off Ravenswood Dri.)
Ratcliffe Ter. *Moss* 5G **51**
Rathbone St. *Roch* 6C **14**
Rathbourne Av. *M9* 1A **46**
Rath Wlk. *M40* 2A **54**
Ravelston Dri. *M9* 6A **46**
Raven Av. *Chad* 6A **40**
Raven Clo. *Droy* 4G **55**
Ravendale Clo. *Roch* 4C **12**
Ravenoak Dri. *Fail* 5A **48**
Ravensbury St. *M11* 5A **54**
Ravenside Pk. *Chad* 6A **40**
Ravenstonedale Dri. *Rytn* 4E **31**
Ravenstones Dri. *Dig* 6E **35**
Raven St. *Roch* 4A **12**
Ravenswood Dri. *M9* 2A **46**
Ravenwood. *Chad* 4F **39**
Ravine Av. *M9* 6A **46**
Rawstron St. *Whitw* 2E **5**
Raycroft Av. *M9* 3C **46**
Raymond Av. *Chad* 1B **48**
Rayner La. *Ash L* 6H **55**
(in two parts)
Reading Clo. *M11* 6A **54**
Readitt Wlk. *M11* 5A **54**
Recreation Rd. *Fail* 4B **48**
Recreation St. *P'wich* 6A **36**
Rectory Hill. *Bury* 3B **18**
Rectory La. *Bury* 3B **18**
Rectory St. *Midd* 2B **38**
Redbank. *Bury* 1C **18**
Red Brook St. *Roch* 6F **13**
Redcar Clo. *Oldh* 2H **41**
Redcar St. *Roch* 5G **13**
Redcote St. *M40* 5C **46**
Redcross St. *Roch* 5H **13**
Redcross St. N. *Roch* 4G **13**
Reddyshore Brow. *L'boro* 3A **8**
Redesmere Clo. *Droy* 6F **55**
Redfearn Wood. *Roch* 3D **12**
Redfern Cotts. *Roch* 4H **11**
Redfern Way. *Roch* 4H **11**
Redgrave Pl. *Oldh* 3B **42**
Redgrave St. *Oldh* 3A **42**
Red Hall St. *Oldh* 5A **42**
Redland Clo. *L'boro* 5H **7**
Red La. *Dig* 3E **35**
Red La. *Roch* 3B **14**
Red Lumb. **1E 11**
Red Lumb St. *Roch* 1E **11**
Red Pike Wlk. *Oldh* 3G **41**
Redscar Wlk. *Midd* 2H **37**
Redvers St. *Oldh* 3D **40**
Redwood. *Chad* 4F **39**
Redwood Clo. *Roch* 2D **12**
Redwood La. *Lees* 4C **42**
Redwood Pk. Gro. *Fir* 6D **14**
Redwood Rd. *Upperm* 4E **45**
Reed Ct. *Oldh* 3E **41**
Reedham Wlk. *Oldh* 1C **48**
Reed Hill. *Roch* 5H **13**
Reed St. *Oldh* 4F **41**
Reform St. *Roch* 5H **13**
Refuge St. *Shaw* 3H **31**
Regal Wlk. *M40* 1A **54**
Regatta Clo. *Chad* 2A **48**
Regency Clo. *Oldh* 1D **48**
Regency Ct. *Roch* 6B **12**
Regent Clo. *Heyw* 6F **19**
Regent Cres. *Fail* 1C **54**
Regent Cres. *Rytn* 1D **40**
Regent Dri. *Moss* 5H **51**
Regent St. *M40* 2B **54**
Regent St. *Heyw* 6F **19**
Regent St. *L'boro* 6H **7**
Regent St. *Midd* 1B **38**
Regent St. *Oldh* 4G **41**
Regent St. *Shaw* 2H **31**

Reins Lea Av.—Rush Gro.

Reins Lea Av. Oldh 3G 49
Reliance St. M40 6E 47
Reliance St. Enterprise Pk. M40 6D 46
Reliance Trad. Est. M40 1A 54
Rembrandt Wlk. Oldh 5A 32
Rennell St. Roch 6A 14
Renshaw Dri. Bury 4A 18
Repton Av. M40 4G 47
Repton Av. Droy 4B 54
Repton Av. Oldh 2D 48
Reservoir St. Roch 5C 14
Retford Av. Roch 4B 22
Retford St. Oldh 6H 41
Retiro St. Oldh 4F 41
Rex Ct. G'ton 5F 43
Rhodes. 4G 37
Rhodes Av. Lees 6D 42
Rhodes Av. Upperm 2E 45
Rhodes Bank. 5F 41
Rhodes Bank. Oldh 5F 41
Rhodes Cres. Roch 4H 21
Rhodes Green. 3F 37
Rhodes Hill. Lees 6D 42
Rhodes St. Oldh 4G 41
Rhodes St. Roch 2B 14
Rhodes St. Shaw 6G 31
Rhodes St. S'head 4D 42
Rhos Av. Midd 4C 38
Ribble Av. Chad 2G 39
Ribble Av. L'boro 5F 7
Ribble Dri. W'fld 2A 36
Ribble Gro. Heyw 4E 19
Ribble Rd. Oldh 2C 48
Ribblesdale Clo. Heyw 2A 28
Ribble St. Roch 3F 21
Ribble Wlk. Droy 6E 55
Richard St. Fail 6H 47
Richard St. Roch 1H 21
Richard St. Shaw 4G 31
Richmond Av. Chad 1A 48
Richmond Av. Rytn 5D 30
Richmond Clo. Moss 5A 52
Richmond Clo. Roch 4C 22
Richmond Clo. Shaw 4H 31
Richmond Ct. M9 6E 37 (off Deanswood Dri.)
Richmond Cres. Moss 5A 52
Richmond Rd. Fail 5A 48
Richmond St. Droy 5G 55
Richmond Vw. Moss 4A 52 (off Mansfield Rd.)
Richmond Wlk. Oldh 5D 40
Ridd Cotts. Roch 5G 11
Riders Ga. Bury 3D 18
Ridgecroft. Ash L 6H 49
Ridgefield St. Fail 6F 47 (in two parts)
Ridge La. Dig 4F 35
Ridgewood Av. Chad 3G 39
Riding Fold. Droy 4H 55
Ridings Ct. Dob 1C 44
Ridings Way. Chad 5B 40
Ridley St. Oldh 5G 41
Rifle St. Oldh 3F 41
Rigby Ct. Roch 4A 12
Rigi Mt. Rytn 3D 30
Rilldene Wlk. Roch 5H 11
Rimington Fold. Midd 6H 27
Rimmington Clo. M9 3C 46
Ringcroft Gdns. M40 4D 46
Ringley St. M9 5A 46
Ring Lows La. Roch 1H 13
Ringmere Ct. Oldh 3E 41
Rings Clo. Fail 1D 54
Ringwood Av. Aud 6G 55
Ringwood Way. Chad 3C 40
Ripon Clo. Chad 5B 40
Ripon St. Oldh 3D 40
Ripponden Rd. Dens 5G 25
Ripponden Rd. Oldh 3A 42
Ripponden St. Oldh 2A 42
Risbury Wlk. M40 1A 54
Rise, The. S'head 4D 42
Rishworth Dri. M40 5G 47
Rishworth Ri. Shaw 6F 23
Rising La. Oldh 3E 49
Rising La. Clo. Oldh 3E 49
Risley St. Oldh 3F 41
Riverbank. Dob 2B 44
Rivermead. Miln 4H 23
River Pl. Miln 1F 23
Riversdale Dri. Oldh 4G 49
Rivers Edge, The. Whitw 2E 5
Rivershill Dri. Heyw 6F 19
Riverside. Chad 2G 39
Riverside Dri. Roch 3B 14
Riverstone Bri. L'boro 6G 7
River St. Heyw 3H 19
River St. Roch 6H 13
Riversvale Arboretum. 6F 49
River Tame Path. Carr & Stal 6G 51
River Tame Path. Moss 4H 51
Riviera Ct. Roch 3G 11
Rivington Dri. Shaw 2B 32
Rivington Rd. S'head 4E 43
Rivington St. Oldh 2F 41
Rivington St. Roch 4H 13
Rixson St. Oldh 2B 42
Roach Bank Ind. Est. Bury 2A 26
Roach Bank Rd. Bury 2A 26
Roaches. 2A 52
Roaches Ind. Est. Moss 1A 52
Roaches M. Moss 2H 51
Roaches Way. Moss 2A 52
Roach Pl. Roch 5A 14
Roach St. Bury 5A 18
Roach Va. Roch 3C 14
Roachwood Clo. Chad 4G 39
Road End. 6D 44
Road La. Roch 1F 13
Roads Ford Av. Miln 6F 15
Robert Owen St. Droy 5G 55
Robert Saville Ct. Roch 1D 20 (off Half Acre M.)
Robert Sheldon Way. Ash L 6H 55 (in two parts)
Roberts Pas. L'boro 1B 8
Roberts Pl. L'boro 2F 15
Robert St. Fail 4A 48
Robert St. Heyw 1A 28
Robert St. Oldh 2B 48
Robert St. P'wich 6A 36
Robert St. Roch 5A 14
Robins Clo. Droy 4G 55
Robinson Pl. S'head 4F 43
Robinsons Fold. S'head 4F 43
Robin St. Oldh 3E 41
Robson St. Oldh 5F 41
Roch Av. Heyw 5E 19
Rochbury Clo. Roch 1B 20
Roch Clo. W'fld 2A 36
Roch Cres. W'fld 1A 36
Rochdale. 5H 13
Rochdale Art Gallery & Mus. 6G 13
Rochdale Central Leisure Cen. 6A 14
Rochdale Crematorium. Roch 6E 13
Rochdale Exchange Shop. Cen. Roch 6G 13
Rochdale Football Club. 5E 13 (Spotland)
Rochdale Hornets Rugby League Football Club. 5E 13
Rochdale Ind. Cen. Roch 1F 21
ROCHDALE INFIRMARY. 4G 13
Rochdale La. Heyw 5H 19
Rochdale La. Rytn 4D 30
Rochdale Old Rd. Bury 4A 18
Rochdale Pioneers Mus. 5H 13
Rochdale Rd. M9 5A 46
Rochdale Rd. Bury 5A 18
Rochdale Rd. Dens 4F 25
Rochdale Rd. Fir & Miln 6D 14
Rochdale Rd. Heyw 5H 19
Rochdale Rd. L'boro & Sower B. 2H 9
Rochdale Rd. Midd 1C 38
Rochdale Rd. Rytn 2C 30
Rochdale Rd. Rytn & Oldh 2E 41
Rochdale Rd. Shaw 6E 23
Rochdale Rd. E. Heyw 5A 20
Rochdale Tourist Info. Cen. 6H 13
Rochdale Town Hall. 6H 13
Roche Rd. Del 4A 34
Rochester Clo. Ash L 6A 50
Rochester Way. Chad 5B 40
Rochford Pl. Heyw 2B 28
Roch Mills Cres. Roch 2E 21
Roch Mills Gdns. Roch 2E 21
Roch St. Roch 4B 14
Roch Valley Way. Roch 1E 21
Roch Wlk. W'fld 2A 36
Roch Way. W'fld 2A 36
Rock Bank. Moss 4G 51
Rockfield Dri. M9 5A 46
Rockingham Clo. Shaw 1E 31
Rockland Wlk. M40 3E 47
Rocklyn Av. M40 3E 47
Rockmead Dri. M9 2A 46
Rock Nook. L'boro 2B 8
Rock St. Heyw 6A 20
Rock St. Oldh 4F 41 (in two parts)
Rock Ter. Moss 2H 51
Roda St. M9 6B 46
Rodenhurst Dri. M40 6C 46
Rodney St. Roch 5D 20
Roeacre St. Heyw 5A 20
Roebuck La. Oldh 6E 33
Roebuck Low. Oldh 6E 33
Roeburn Wlk. W'fld 3A 36
Roefield. Roch 5F 13
Roefield Ter. Roch 5E 13
Roe La. Oldh 6B 42
Roe St. Roch 4E 13
Roger Byrne Clo. M40 2A 54
Roker Ind. Est. Oldh 3H 41
Roman Rd. Fail & Oldh 5A 48
Roman Rd. Rytn 6D 30
Roman St. Moss 2H 51
Romer Av. M40 4G 47
Romford Clo. Oldh 6E 41
Romney Av. Roch 5H 21
Romney St. M40 5C 46
Romney Wlk. Chad 5B 40
Romsey. Roch 5G 13 (off Spotland Rd.)
Romsey Av. Midd 6B 28
Ronald St. M11 6B 54
Ronald St. Oldh 4A 42
Ronald St. Roch 6E 21
Ronnis Mt. Ash L 6G 49
Roods La. Roch 4G 11
Rook St. Oldh 6A 42
Rookswood Dri. Roch 4D 20
Rookway. Midd 4B 38
Rookwood. Chad 2G 39
Rooley Moor Rd. Roch 2A 4 (Rooley Moor, in two parts)
Rooley Moor Rd. Roch 3D 12 (Stocks Ga.)
Rooley St. Roch 4E 13
Rooley Ter. Roch 5E 13
Ropefield Way. Roch 2G 13
Rope St. Roch 5H 13
Ropley Wlk. M9 4B 46 (off Oak Bank Av.)
Rosary Clo. Oldh 4F 49
Rosary Rd. Oldh 4G 49
Roscoe St. Oldh 5F 41 (in two parts)
Roseacre Ct. Heyw 5H 19
Rose Av. L'boro 2F 15
Rose Av. Roch 3H 11
Rose Bank Rd. M40 3A 54
Roseberry Av. Oldh 2H 41
Roseberry St. Oldh 5D 40
Rosedale Clo. Oldh 2H 41
Rosefield Cres. Roch 6C 14
Rose Hey La. Fail 3C 54
Rose Hill. Del 6B 34
Rose Hill Av. M40 3A 54
Rose Hill Ct. Oldh 3C 42
Rose Hill St. Heyw 5F 19
Roseland Dri. P'wich 5A 36
Rosemary Dri. L'boro 5F 7
Rosemary Rd. Chad 3G 39
Rosemount. Midd 1B 38
Rosen Sq. Chad 4B 40
Rose St. Chad 2A 48
Rose St. Midd 3E 39
Rosethorns Clo. Midd 5B 28
Rosewood. Roch 4A 12
Rosewood Av. Droy 5F 55
Rosewood Cres. Chad 2B 40
Roslin St. M11 5B 54
Rossall Rd. Roch 3A 14
Ross Av. Chad 2H 47
Rossendale Av. M9 4B 46
Rossendale Clo. Shaw 2B 32
Rossendale Way. Shaw 1H 31
Rossington St. M40 2B 54
Rosslyn Rd. Most 4C 46
Rossmere Av. Roch 1E 21
Ross St. Oldh 6D 40
Rosthwaite Clo. Midd 2G 37
Rothay Dri. Midd 6A 28
Rothesay Rd. Oldh 2A 42
Rothesay Ter. Roch 3C 22
Rothman Clo. M40 1A 54
Rothwell St. M40 1A 54
Rothwell St. Fail 6H 47
Rothwell St. Roch 4A 14
Rothwell St. Rytn 6C 30
Rough. L'boro 6D 8
Rough Bank. 2B 24
Rough Bank. Whitw 6E 5
Rough Hey La. Dens 4H 25
Rough Hey Wlk. Roch 1B 22
Rough Hill La. Bury 3B 18
Roughtown. 3H 51
Roughtown Ct. Moss 2H 51
Roughtown Rd. Moss 3H 51
Roundham Wlk. M9 5A 46
Round Hey. Moss 5G 51
Roundhill Way. Oldh 2C 42
Roundthorn. 6A 42
Roundthorn Rd. Midd 4D 38
Roundthorn Rd. Oldh 5H 41
Rouse St. Roch 3E 21
Routledge Wlk. M9 5A 46
Rowan Clo. Fail 1D 54
Rowan Clo. Roch 2C 12
Rowans, The. Moss 4H 51
Rowan Tree Rd. Oldh 4D 48
Rowanwood. Chad 4G 39
Rowbottom Wlk. Oldh 6E 41
Rowden Rd. Oldh 1C 50
Rowland Ct. Roch 1B 22
Rowland Ho. Shaw 5F 31
Rowland St. Roch 1B 22
Rowland Way. Lees 4C 42
Rowrah Cres. Midd 2F 37
Roxbury. 6A 42
Roxbury Av. Oldh 6B 42
Roxby Wlk. M40 3F 47
Royal Av. Droy 5F 55
Royal Av. Heyw 6H 19
Royal George Cotts. G'fld 6A 44 (off Armit Rd.)
ROYAL OLDHAM HOSPITAL, THE. 2D 40
Royal Pennine Trad. Est. Roch 4F 21
Royal St. Roch 2C 14
Royce Clo. Oldh 2F 49
Royden Av. M9 6H 37
Roydes St. Midd 1D 38
Royds Pl. Roch 2A 22
Royds St. L'boro 6A 8
Royds St. Miln 2G 23
Royds St. Roch 2B 22
Royds St. W. Roch 2A 22
Royd St. Bury 3B 18
Royd St. Oldh 1C 48
Royle Barn Rd. Roch 5E 21
Roylelands Bungalows. Roch 4E 21
Royle Rd. Roch 4E 21
Royley. 6C 30
Royley. Rytn 6C 30
Royley Clough. Rytn 5C 30
Royley Cres. Rytn 6C 30
Royley Ho. Rytn 6C 30
Royley Rd. Oldh 1E 49
Royley Way. Rytn 6C 30
Roy St. Rytn 5D 30
Royton. 5D 30
Royton Hall Pk. Rytn 5E 31
Royton Hall Wlk. Rytn 5E 31
Royton Ho. Shaw 4H 31
Royton Sports Cen. 5E 31
Ruby St. Pas. Roch 1G 21
Rudding St. Rytn 1G 41
Rudd St. M40 6C 46
Rudman St. Roch 3G 13
Rudston Av. M40 3D 46
Rudyard Gro. Roch 5H 21
Rudyard Rd. Midd 6E 29
Rufford Av. Roch 3F 21
Rufford Clo. Ash L 6A 50
Rufford Clo. Shaw 2F 31
Rugby Rd. Roch 4A 14
Rugby Rd. Ind. Est. Roch 4A 14
Ruislip Clo. Oldh 1H 49
Rumbles La. Del 5B 34
Running Hill Ga. Upperm 2F 45 (in two parts)
Running Hill Head. 1G 45
Running Hill La. Dob 1F 45
Runnymead Ct. Rytn 5E 31
Rupert St. M40 3C 54
Rupert St. Roch 4E 13
Ruscombe Fold. Midd 6H 27
Rush Bank. Shaw 1F 31
Rushbrooke Av. M11 4A 54
Rushbury Dri. Rytn 5F 31
Rushcroft Ct. M9 3C 46
Rushcroft Rd. Shaw 1F 31
Rushen St. M11 6A 54
Rush Gro. Upperm 4D 44

80 A-Z Oldham & Rochdale

Rush Hill Rd.—Sequoia St.

Rush Hill Rd. *Upperm* 4D 44
Rush Hill Ter. *Upperm* 4D 44
Rushlake Gdns. *Roch* 5A 12
Rush Mt. *Shaw* 1F 31
Rushton Gro. *Oldh* 6C 32
Rushy Hill Vw. *Roch* 4E 13
Ruskin Av. *Chad* 2H 47
Ruskington Dri. *M9* 6A 46
Ruskin Rd. *Droy* 5E 55
Ruskin Rd. *Roch* 5G 21
Ruskin St. *Oldh* 3D 40
Rusland Ct. *M9* 2C 46
Russell St. *Chad* 4B 40
Russell St. *Heyw* 5A 20
Russell St. *Moss* 4G 51
Russet Rd. *M9* 4A 46
Rustons Wlk. *M40* 4G 47
Ruth Av. *M40* 4G 47
Ruthin Av. *M9* 6G 37
Ruthin Av. *Midd* 4C 38
Ruthin Clo. *Oldh* 3B 48
Ruth St. *Oldh* 3F 41
Ruth St. *Whitw* 2E 5
Rutland. *Roch* 1G 21
Rutland Rd. *Droy* 5C 54
Rutland St. *Fail* 5H 47
Rutland St. *Heyw* 4H 19
Rutland St. *Oldh* 6C 40
Rutland Way. *Shaw* 1A 32
Ryburn Flats. Heyw 5G 19
(off Meadow Clo.)
Ryburn Sq. *Roch* 1A 20
Rydal Av. *Chad* 2G 39
Rydal Av. *Droy* 6C 54
Rydal Av. *Midd* 5B 38
Rydal Av. *Rytn* 1C 30
Rydal Gro. *Heyw* 1H 27
Rydal Rd. *Oldh* 4A 42
Rydal Wlk. *Oldh* 4B 42
Ryder St. *Heyw* 5H 19
Rydings La. *Ward* 5A 6
Rydings Rd. *Roch* 1B 14
Ryeburne St. *Oldh* 4A 42
Ryecroft Av. *Heyw* 5A 20
Ryecroft Clo. *Chad* 2H 47
(in two parts)
Ryecroft Vw. *Aud* 6G 55
Ryefields. *Roch* 1D 14
Ryefields Dri. *Upperm* 2D 44
Ryelands Clo. *Roch* 3B 22
Rye St. *Heyw* 4A 20
Rye Top La. *Upperm* 4F 45
Rye Wlk. *Chad* 5A 40
Ryther Gro. *M9* 6F 37

S

Sabden Clo. *Heyw* 5E 19
Sackville Clo. *Shaw* 6G 23
Sackville St. *Roch* 6E 21
Saddle Gro. *Droy* 4H 55
Saddleworth. 3D 44
Saddleworth Bus. Pk. *Del* 5B 34
Saddleworth Fold. *Upperm* 2E 45
Saddleworth Mus. & Art Gallery. 3D 44
Saddleworth Swimming Pool. 4D 44
Saddleworth Tourist Info. Cen. 3D 44
Sadler St. *Midd* 2B 38
Saffron Dri. *Oldh* 1B 42
St Aidan's Clo. *Roch* 2E 21
St Albans Av. *M40* 2A 54
St Albans Av. *Ash L* 6H 49
St Albans Clo. *Oldh* 1F 49
St Albans Ct. *Roch* 1G 21
St Albans Ho. Roch 1G 21
(off St Albans St.)
St Albans St. *Roch* 1G 21
St Alban's Ter. *Roch* 1G 21
St Ambrose Rd. *Oldh* 2A 42
St Andrew's Av. *Droy* 6C 54
St Andrews Clo. *L'boro* 6E 7
St Andrew's Dri. *Heyw* 6H 19
St Anne's Av. *Rytn* 6D 30
St Anne's Cres. *Grass* 6G 43
St Annes Gdns. *Heyw* 5B 20
St Annes Sq. *Del* 5B 34
St Ann's Rd. *Roch* 5C 14
St Anthony's Dri. *Moss* 3H 51
St Asaph's Dri. *Ash L* 6H 49
St Austells Dri. *P'wich* 6A 36
St Barnabas Dri. *L'boro* 5G 7
St Bees Wlk. *Midd* 1A 38
St Chad's Clo. *Roch* 6H 13
St Chads Ct. Roch 6H 13
(off School La.)
St Chads Cres. *Oldh* 4D 48
St Chads Cres. *Upperm* 3E 45
St Christopher's Av. *Ash L* 6C 50
St Christopher's Rd. *Ash L* 6C 50
St Clements Ct. *Oldh* 6E 41
St Clements Ct. *Roch* 5E 13
St Cuthbert's Fold. *Oldh* 4G 49
St David's Clo. *Ash L* 6B 50
St Domingo St. *Oldh* 4E 41
St Dominics Way. *Midd* 4C 38
St Gabriels Clo. *Roch* 6F 21
St Gabriel's Ct. Roch 5E 21
(off Atkinson St.)
St Georges Ct. *Bury* 6A 26
St George's Dri. *M40* 6D 46
St George's Rd. *Bury* 5A 26
St George's Rd. *Droy* 4D 54
St George's Rd. *Roch* 5B 12
St George's Sq. *Chad* 2G 47
St Herberts Ct. *Chad* 4B 40
St Hilda's Dri. *Oldh* 3D 40
St James Clo. *Roch* 1C 30
St James Ct. *Oldh* 3A 42
St James Gro. *Heyw* 5G 19
St James St. *Heyw* 5G 19
St James St. *Miln* 1F 23
St James St. *Oldh* 4H 41
St James St. *Shaw* 2H 31
St James Ter. *Heyw* 5G 19
St Johns Av. *Droy* 5F 55
St Johns Ct. *Lees* 4D 42
St John's Ct. *Roch* 1B 22
St John's Dri. *Roch* 1B 22
St John's Gdns. *Moss* 3H 51
St John's Ind. Est. *Lees* 5C 42
St John's St. *Chad* 6C 40
St John St. *Droy* 6D 54
St John St. *Lees* 5C 42
St John's Wlk. *Oldh* 5C 40
St Joseph's Av. *W'fld* 4A 36
St Joseph's Clo. *Shaw* 1A 32
St Joseph's Dri. *Roch* 3B 22
St Kilda's Av. *Droy* 4D 54
St Leonards Sq. Midd 2C 38
(off High St.)
St Leonards St. *Midd* 2C 38
St Lukes Ct. *Chad* 4A 40
St Lukes Ct. *Roch* 2H 21
St Luke St. *Roch* 2H 21
St Margarets Clo. *P'wich* 5A 36
St Margaret's Gdns. *Oldh* 2C 48
St Margaret's Rd. *M40* 2F 47
St Margaret's Rd. *P'wich* 6A 36
St Marks Av. *Rytn* 5G 31
St Marks Clo. *Rytn* 5G 31
St Mark's Ct. *Chad* 3B 40
St Martin's Clo. *Droy* 4D 54
St Martin's Rd. *Oldh* 3G 49
St Martins St. *Roch* 6F 21
St Mary's Clo. *Roch* 3B 22
St Mary's Ct. *M40* 5D 46
St Marys Ct. *Oldh* 4E 41
St Mary's Crest. *G'fld* 6E 45
St Mary's Dri. *G'fld* 6E 45
St Mary's Ga. *Roch* 6G 13
St Marys Ga. *Shaw* 2H 31
St Mary's Ga. *Upperm* 3D 44
St Mary's Rd. *M40* 6D 46
St Mary's St. *Oldh* 3F 41
St Mary's Way. *Oldh* 4E 41
St Matthews Dri. *Chad* 1A 40
St Pauls Ct. *Oldh* 1F 49
St Peter's St. *Roch* 1B 22
St Phillip's Dri. *Rytn* 2E 41
St Stephens Ct. M9 6A 46
(off Shieldborn Dri.)
St Stephen's Gdns. *Midd* 1C 38
St Stephens St. *Oldh* 3G 41
St Stephens Vw. *Droy* 5E 55
St Thomas Circ. *Oldh* 6D 40
St Thomas St. N. *Oldh* 6D 40
St Thomas St. S. *Oldh* 6D 40
St Wilfred's Dri. *Roch* 2F 13
Salem. 6B 42
Salem Gro. *Oldh* 5B 42
Sales's La. *Bury* 3A 10
Sale St. *L'boro* 5H 7
Salford St. *Oldh* 6A 42
Salik Gdns. *Roch* 2H 21
Salisbury Av. *Heyw* 1G 27
Salisbury Cres. *Ash L* 6B 50
Salisbury Rd. *Oldh* 5H 41
Salisbury St. *Midd* 2D 38
Salisbury St. *Shaw* 1F 31
Salkeld St. *Roch* 2H 21
Salley St. *L'boro* 1A 8
Salmon Fields. *Rytn* 6E 31
Saltburn Wlk. M9 5A 46
(off Naunton Wlk.)
Salterton Wlk. *M40* 6C 46
Salthill Av. *Heyw* 2A 28
Salts Dri. *L'boro* 5G 7
Salts St. *Shaw* 2G 31
Salvin Wlk. *M9* 2A 46
Samlesbury Clo. *Shaw* 2F 31
Sam Rd. *Dig* 4E 35
Samson St. *Roch* 5C 14
Samuel La. *Shaw* 1E 31
Samuel St. *Fail* 5H 47
Samuel St. *Midd* 1C 38
Samuel St. *Roch* 5E 21
Sandbank Gdns. *Whitw* 1E 5
Sandbed. 3F 51
Sandbed La. *Del* 4C 34
Sandbed La. *Moss* 3G 51
Sandbrook Pk. *Roch* 3G 21
Sandbrook Way. *Roch* 3G 21
Sanderstead Dri. *M9* 2A 46
Sandfield Rd. *Roch* 2B 22
Sandgate Av. *M11* 5B 54
Sandgate Rd. *Chad* 5B 40
Sandgate Rd. *W'fld* 4A 36
Sand Hole La. *Roch* 2A 20
(Bury Rd.)
Sand Hole La. *Roch* 6H 21
(Hill Top Dri.)
Sandhutton St. *M9* 4A 46
Sandiway. *Heyw* 5A 20
Sandmere Wlk. *M9* 2A 46
Sandown Clo. *Oldh* 2G 41
Sandpiper Clo. *Roch* 6B 12
Sandpits. *Heyw* 1B 28
Sandringham Ct. M9 6E 37
(off Deanswood Dri.)
Sandringham Dri. *Miln* 1G 23
Sandringham Way. *Rytn* 3C 30
Sands Av. *Chad* 2F 39
Sandstone Rd. *Miln* 6F 15
Sandy Acre. *Moss* 5G 51
Sandy Bank. *Shaw* 1F 31
Sandy Brow. *M9* 3A 46
Sandy La. *Dob* 1C 44
Sandy La. *Droy* 4G 55
Sandy La. *Midd* 3D 38
Sandy La. *Roch* 6E 13
Sandy La. *Rytn* 5D 30
Sandys Av. *Oldh* 2D 48
Sandy Wlk. *Rytn* 5D 30
Sarah Butterworth Ct. *Roch* 6B 14
Sarah Butterworth St. *Roch* 1B 22
Sarah Jane St. *Miln* 1F 23
Sarah Moor. 2F 41
Sarah St. *Midd* 3B 38
Sarah St. *Oldh* 3D 48
Sarah St. *Roch* 1A 22
Sarah St. *Shaw* 4G 31
Sautridge Clo. *Midd* 2F 29
Saville St. *Midd* 4F 39
Savio Way. *Midd* 4C 38
Savoy Dri. *Rytn* 1D 40
Savoy St. *Oldh* 6H 41
Savoy St. *Roch* 5E 13
Sawley Av. *L'boro* 4G 7
Sawley Av. *Oldh* 1B 50
Saw Mill Way. *L'boro* 6F 7
Sawston Wlk. *M40* 2E 47
Sawyer St. *Roch* 4H 13
Saxon Dri. *Chad* 3G 39
Saxon Dri. *Droy* 5F 55
(in two parts)
Saxonholme Rd. *Roch* 2E 29
Saxon Ho. *L'boro* 6A 8
Saxonside. *Midd* 6A 28
Saxon St. *Droy* 5F 55
Saxon St. *Midd* 3D 38
Saxon St. *Moss* 2H 51
Saxon St. *Oldh* 4A 42
Saxon St. *Roch* 6F 13
Saxwood Clo. *Roch* 4B 12
Scafell Clo. *Oldh* 2F 41
(in two parts)
Scarborough St. *M40* 5C 46
Scarfield Dri. *Roch* 4A 12
Scarr Dri. *Roch* 2H 13
Scarr La. *Shaw* 2A 32
Scarr Ter. *Whitw* 1F 5
Scawton Wlk. *M9* 6F 37
Schofield Hall Rd. *L'boro* 4A 16
Schofield Pl. *L'boro* 1B 8
Schofield Rd. *Droy* 6F 55
Schofield St. *M11* 6A 54
Schofield St. *Fail* 5H 47
Schofield St. *Heyw* 5H 19
Schofield St. *L'boro* 5A 8
Schofield St. *Miln* 2G 23
Schofield St. *Oldh* 2E 49
Schofield St. *Roch* 3A 22
Schofield St. *Rytn* 4D 30
Schofield St. *Summ* 1B 8
Scholar's Way. *Midd* 2B 38
Scholes Dri. *M40* 3G 47
Scholes St. *Chad* 1A 48
Scholes St. *Fail* 4A 48
Scholes St. *Oldh* 4G 41
Scholes St. *Roch* 6E 21
School Av. *Ash L* 6B 50
School Ho. Flats. *Oldh* 3B 48
School La. *A'wrth* 5G 11
School La. *Carr* 6A 52
School La. *Roch* 6H 13
School Rd. *Fail* 6H 47
School Rd. *Oldh* 3B 48
Schoolside La. *Midd* 4F 37
School St. *Heyw* 5G 19
School St. *L'boro* 6E 7
School St. *Oldh* 6D 40
School St. *Roch* 5H 13
School St. *S'head* 5E 43
School St. *Upperm* 3D 44
School Ter. Midd 1C 38
(off Rochdale Rd.)
School Ter. Whitw 2E 5
(off Lloyd St.)
Schwabe St. *Midd* 3G 37
Scoltock Way. *Oldh* 4F 41
Scorton Wlk. *M40* 3F 47
Scotland Hall Rd. *M40* 2A 54
Scotland La. *Bury* 5A 10
Scotland St. *M40* 2A 54
Scottfield. *Oldh* 6E 41
Scottfield Rd. *Oldh* 6F 41
Scott Rd. *Droy* 5E 55
Scotts Ind. Pk. *Roch* 1A 22
Scott St. *Miln* 3F 23
Scott St. *Oldh* 6F 41
Scouthead. 3F 43
Scowcroft La. *Shaw* 4G 31
Seabrook Rd. *M40* 3A 54
Seaford Wlk. *Chad* 5B 40
Sealand Ho. *P'wich* 6A 36
Searness Rd. *Midd* 1G 37
Seascale Av. *M11* 4A 54
Seascale Wlk. *Midd* 1A 38
Seatoller Ct. Rytn 5E 31
(off Shaw St.)
Seatoller Dri. *Midd* 2G 37
Second Av. *M11* 5A 54
Second Av. *Bury* 3B 18
Second Av. *Oldh* 3C 48
Sedgefield Pk. *Oldh* 5B 42
Sedgemoor Way. *Oldh* 4E 41
Sedgley Av. *Roch* 3B 22
Sedgley Bldgs. *Droy* 6E 55
Sedgley Clo. *Midd* 4E 39
Sedgley Ct. *Midd* 4E 39
Sedgley St. *Midd* 4E 39
Seel St. *Moss* 4F 51
Sefton Clo. *Midd* 3A 38
Sefton Clo. *Oldh* 5A 32
Sefton Rd. *Midd* 3A 38
Sefton St. *Heyw* 6A 20
Sefton St. *Oldh* 3B 48
Selbourne St. *Oldh* 4G 49
Selby Av. *Chad* 2H 39
Selby Clo. *Miln* 1E 23
Selby Rd. *Midd* 6B 28
Selby St. *Roch* 5B 14
Selden St. *Oldh* 6D 40
Selhurst Av. *M11* 5A 54
Selkirk Av. *Oldh* 1D 48
Selkirk Dri. *M9* 2B 46
Selkirk Pl. *Heyw* 6E 19
Selkirk Rd. *Chad* 1H 47
Sellars Sq. *Droy* 6E 55
Sellers Way. *Chad* 2A 48
Selwood Wlk. M9 6A 46
(off Carisbrook St.)
Selwyn Clo. *Oldh* 6E 41
Selwyn St. *Oldh* 6E 41
Sepia Gro. *Midd* 2B 38
Sequoia St. *M9* 5A 46

A-Z Oldham & Rochdale 81

Settstones La. *Upperm* 2F 45
Sevenacres. *Del* 4B 34
Seven Acres La. *Roch* 3A 12
Seventh Av. *Oldh* 4C 48
Severn Dri. *Miln* 1G 23
Severn Rd. *Chad* 3H 39
Severn Rd. *Heyw* 4E 19
Severn Rd. S. *M11* 5B 54
Severn Rd. *Oldh* 4B 48
(in two parts)
Sevilles Bldgs. *Moss* 3G 51
Seville St. *Rytn* 1E 41
Seville St. *Shaw* 4G 31
Sexton St. *Heyw* 5G 19
Seymour Av. *M11.* 5B 54
Seymour Gro. *Roch* 4B 22
Seymour Rd. S. *M11* 5B 54
Seymour St. *Heyw* 6G 19
(in two parts)
Shackleton Ct. *M40* 3A 54
Shackliffe Rd. *M40.* 3D 46
Shaddock Av. *Roch* 4B 12
Shade Av. *S'head* 6D 42
Shadowbrook Clo. *Oldh* . . . 2E 41
Shadows La. *Moss* 1A 52
Shadows M. *Moss* 1A 52
Shadwell St. E. *Heyw* 4A 20
Shadwell St. W. *Heyw* 4H 19
Shadworth Clo. *Moss* 1A 52
Shadworth La. *G'fld* 2B 52
Shaftesbury Av. *L'boro* . . . 2F 15
Shaftesbury Dri. *Heyw* 1G 27
Shaftesbury Dri. *Ward* 5D 6
Shafton Wlk. *M40.* 3F 47
Shakespeare Clo. *L'boro* . . . 2A 8
Shakespeare Cres. *Droy* . . . 5E 55
Shakespeare Rd. *Droy* 5E 55
Shakespeare Rd. *Oldh* 1H 41
Shakleton Av. *M9.* 2C 46
Shaldon Dri. *M40.* 3C 54
Shanley Ct. *Chad* 3B 40
Shannon Clo. *Heyw* 4E 19
Shapwick Clo. *M9* 5A 46
Sharon. **6A 44**
Sharon Av. *Grass* 6A 44
Sharples Hall St. *Oldh* 2B 42
Sharp St. *Midd.* 3C 38
Sharrow Wlk. M9 . . . . *6A 46*
(off Broadwell Dri.)
Shaw. **3H 31**
Shawbury St. *Midd.* 4E 39
Shawclough. **3G 13**
Shawclough Clo. *Roch* 2F 13
Shawclough Dri. *Roch* 2E 13
Shawclough Ri. Roch *3F 13*
(off Shawclough Rd.)
Shawclough Rd. *Roch* 1E 13
Shawclough Trad. Est. *Roch* . . 2F 13
Shawclough Way. *Roch* . . . 2E 13
Shawcroft Clo. *Shaw* 4G 31
Shaw Edge. **5H 31**
Shawfield. **3B 12**
Shawfield Gro. *Roch* 3B 12
Shawfield La. *Roch* 4A 12
(in two parts)
Shawfold. *Shaw* 2H 31
Shawford Cres. *M40.* 3E 47
Shawford Rd. *M40* 3E 47
Shaw Ga. *Upperm* 4F 45
Shaw Hall. **5B 44**
Shaw Hall Bank. **6B 44**
Shaw Hall Bank Rd. *G'fld* . . 6B 44
Shaw Hall Clo. *G'fld* 6B 44
Shawhead Dri. *Fail* 1D 54
Shaw Ho. *Shaw* 4H 31
Shaw La. *Roch* 4G 15
Shaw Lee. *Dig* 5F 35
Shaw Rd. *Miln* 4H 23
Shaw Rd. *Oldh.* 2G 41
Shaw Rd. *Roch* 6B 22
Shaw Rd. *Rytn* 6E 31
Shaws. *Upperm* 4E 45
Shaws Fold. *S'head* 5F 43
Shaw Side. **4H 31**
Shaws La. *Upperm.* 3E 45
Shaw St. *Bury* 4A 18
Shaw St. *G'fld* 5C 44
Shaw St. *Oldh* 3F 41
Shaw St. *Roch* 3B 14
Shaw St. *Rytn* 5E 31
Shaw St. *S'head* 5E 43
Shayfield Av. *Chad* 4G 39
Shearing Av. *Roch* 4B 12
Shed St. *Whitw* 2F 5
Sheepfoot La. *Oldh* 2D 40
Sheep Gap. *Roch* 4D 12

Shelderslow. **5E 43**
Shelderton Clo. *M40* 6C 46
Shelfield. *Roch* 5B 12
Shelfield Clo. *Roch.* 5B 12
Shelfield La. *Roch* 4A 12
Shelley Av. *Midd* 6D 28
Shelley Gro. *Droy* 5E 55
Shelley Rd. *Chad* 2H 47
Shelley Rd. *Oldh* 2A 42
Shelley St. *M40* 5E 47
Shepherd Ct. *Roch* 1B 22
Shepherds Grn. *G'fld* 6F 45
Shepherd St. *M9* 4A 46
Shepherd St. *Heyw* 5G 19
Shepherd St. *Roch* (OL11) . . 4H 11
Shepherd St. *Roch* (OL12) . . 5H 13
Shepherd St. *Rytn* 5E 31
(in two parts)
Shepherds Way. *Miln* 2F 23
Shepley St. *Fail* 4A 48
Shepley St. *Lees* 5C 42
Sheraton Rd. *Oldh* 1E 49
Sherborne Ho. *Midd.* 6C 28
Sherborne Rd. *Midd.* 6B 28
Sherbourne Clo. *Oldh.* . . . 1A 50
Sherbourne Dri. *Heyw* 4E 19
Sherbrooke Av. *Upperm* . . . 2E 45
Sheridan Way. *Chad* 3G 39
Sheriff St. *Miln* 2G 23
Sheriff St. *Roch* 4G 13
(in two parts)
Sherwin Way. *Roch* 6F 21
Sherwood Av. *Droy* 5G 55
Sherwood Bus. Pk. *Roch* . . 5F 21
Sherwood Clo. *Ash L* 6A 50
Sherwood Ind. Pk. *Roch* . . . 5F 21
Sherwood St. *Oldh.* 2D 40
Sherwood Way. Roch *5F 21*
(off Queensway)
Sherwood Way. *Shaw.* . . . 1E 31
Shieldborn Dri. *M9.* 6A 46
Shield Clo. *Oldh* 5E 41
Shiloh La. *S'head* 1E 43
Shilton Wlk. *M40* 3F 47
Shipla Clo. *Oldh.* 4E 41
Ship La. *Del* 4E 33
Shirburn. *Roch* 1G 21
Shiredale Dri. *M9* 6A 46
Shires, The. *Droy* 4H 55
Shirley Av. *Chad.* 3G 47
Shirley St. *Roch* 5E 21
Sholver. **5B 32**
Sholver Hey La. *Oldh* 5B 32
Sholver Hill Clo. *Oldh.* . . . 5C 32
Sholver La. *Oldh* 5B 32
Shore. **5F 7**
Shore Av. *Shaw* 6A 24
Shore Edge. **1C 32**
Shorefield Clo. *Miln* 6F 15
Shore Fold. *L'boro* 5F 7
Shoreham Wlk. *Chad* 5A 40
Shore Hill. *L'boro* 5A 8
Shore La. *L'boro* 6A 8
Shore Lea. *L'boro* 5F 7
Shore Mt. *L'boro* 5F 7
Shore Rd. *L'boro* 5F 7
Shore St. *Miln* 1F 23
Shore St. *Oldh* 4G 41
Short Av. *Droy.* 6D 54
Short St. *Heyw* 6F 19
Shottwood Fold. *L'boro* . . . 3A 8
Shrewsbury Rd. *Droy.* 5E 55
Shrewsbury St. *Oldh* 3A 42
Shropshire Rd. *Fail.* 1E 55
Shutt La. *Dob.* 1B 44
Sickle St. *Oldh* 6G 41
Siddall St. *Heyw.* 1A 28
Siddall St. *Oldh* 3F 41
Siddall St. *Shaw.* 2H 31
Siddal Moor. **2H 27**
Sidebottom St. *Droy* 6D 54
Sidebottom St. *Oldh.* 3C 42
Side St. *M11* 6A 54
Side St. *Oldh* 3C 48
Sidlaw Clo. *Oldh.* 3F 49
Sidley Av. *M9.* 1B 46
Sidmouth St. *Oldh* 6C 40
Sidney Rd. *M9.* 4A 46
Sidney St. *Oldh* 2G 41
Siebers Bank. *Roch* 3F 13
Sighthill Wlk. *M9* 5A 46
Silburn Way. *Midd* 4G 37
Silchester Wlk. *Oldh* 4F 41
Silk St. *M40* 1A 54
Silk St. *Midd* 3B 38

Silk St. *Roch* 3E 21
Silsden Av. *M9* 6F 37
Silton St. *M9* 6B 46
Silverbirch Way. *Fail.* 6H 47
Silverdale Av. *Chad.* 5A 40
Silverdale Dri. *Lees* 5D 42
Silver Hill. *Miln.* 6F 15
Silverstone Dri. *M40* 3B 54
Silver St. *Oldh* 5E 41
Silverton Gro. *Midd* 6H 27
Silverwell St. *M40* 2B 54
Silverwood. *Chad.* 4G 39
Simeon St. *Miln* 1F 23
Simister. **3C 36**
Simister Grn. *P'wich* 2C 36
Simister La. *P'wich & Midd* . . 3B 36
Simister Rd. *Fail* 6H 47
Simister St. *M9* 5A 46
Simkin Way. *Oldh* 4F 49
Simon La. *Midd* 1E 37
Simpson Clough. **2G 19**
Simpson Hill Clo. *Heyw* . . . 4B 20
Simpsons Pl. *Roch* 4H 13
Simpson Sq. *Chad* 2C 48
Simpson St. *Chad* 2C 48
Sinclair St. *Roch.* 4F 21
Sir Robert Thomas Ct. M9 . . *5A 46*
(off Coningsby Dri.)
Sisson St. *Fail* 6H 47
Sixth Av. *Bury* 3B 18
Sixth Av. *Oldh* 4C 48
Size St. *Whitw* 2F 5
Skilgate Wlk. *M40* 1A 54
Skipton Av. *M40.* 4F 47
Skipton Av. *Chad* 2H 39
Skipton St. *Oldh.* 1H 49
Skye Clo. *Heyw* 6D 18
Slackcote. **2G 33**
Slackcote La. *Del* 2G 33
Slack Ga. *Whitw* 3G 5
Slack Ga. La. *Dens.* 6H 25
Slack Hall. *Aus.* 3D 42
Slack La. *Del* 2G 33
Slack St. *Roch* 6H 13
Sladen Av. *Roch* 4H 13
Sladen Ter. *L'boro* 3B 8
Slades La. *Upperm.* 2G 45
Slades Vw. Clo. *Dig* 4E 35
Slaidburn Clo. *Miln.* 2F 23
Slaithwaite Dri. *M11.* 5A 54
Slate La. *Ash L* 6H 55
(in three parts)
Slater St. *Fail.* 4H 47
Slater St. *Oldh* 5E 41
Slattocks. **3F 29**
Slattocks Link Rd. *Midd* . . . 4F 29
Slaunt Bank. *Roch* 3H 11
Slawson Way. *Heyw.* 4B 20
Sloane Av. *Lees* 3D 42
Smallbridge. **2C 14**
Smallbrook. *Shaw* 1A 32
Small Brook Rd. *Shaw* 5A 24
Smalley St. *Roch* 5E 21
Smallfield Dri. *M9* 5A 46
Smallshaw Rd. *Roch* 1C 12
Smallwood St. *M40* 1A 54
Smethurst Rd. *Bury* 3C 18
Smethurst St. *M9.* 4A 46
Smethurst St. *Heyw* 5F 19
Smethurst St. *Midd* 4F 39
Smith Farm Clo. *Oldh.* . . . 3D 42
Smith Hill. *Miln* 1F 23
Smithies Av. *Midd* 1C 38
Smithies St. *Heyw* 5A 20
Smith St. *Heyw* 5H 19
Smith St. *Lees* 3C 42
Smith St. *L'boro.* 6H 7
Smith St. *Moss* 3F 51
Smith St. *Roch* 6H 13
Smithy Bridge. **2F 15**
Smithy Bri. Rd. *Roch & L'boro* . 1E 15
Smithy Fld. *L'boro* 5G 7
Smithy Fold. *Roch* 4E 13
Smithy Grn. *Miln* 3C 24
Smithy La. *Upperm* 3D 44
Smithy Nook. *L'boro* 2A 8
Smithy Yd. Upperm *3D 44*
(off Smithy La.)
Smyrna St. *Heyw* 6G 19
Smyrna St. *Oldh.* 5A 42
Snipe Av. *Roch* 6B 12
Snipe Retail Pk. *Ash L* 6H 55
(in two parts)
Snipe Rd. *Oldh* 3H 49

Snipe Way. *Aud* 6H 55
Snowden St. *Heyw* 1A 28
Snowden St. *Oldh.* 1F 49
Snowden Wlk. *M40* 3E 47
Snowdon St. *Roch* 5A 22
Society St. *Shaw* 2H 31
Soho St. *Oldh* 6E 41
Solway Clo. *Oldh* 6E 41
Somerset Av. *Shaw.* 2F 31
Somerset Gro. *Roch* 5C 12
Somerset Rd. *Droy* 4D 54
Somerset Rd. *Fail.* 1C 54
Somerset St. *Oldh* 5A 42
Somerset St. *Oldh* 5A 42
Somerton Ct. *M9* 2C 46
Sorrel Dri. *L'boro* 5F 7
Sorrel Way. *Oldh* 1C 42
Soudan St. *Midd* 2E 39
South Av. *G'fld.* 5D 44
South Av. *Heyw* 5F 19
South Cft. *Roch* 5A 14
South Cres. *M11* 5B 54
South Cft. *Oldh.* 5F 41
Southam Clo. *Roch.* 3E 21
Southdown Cres. *M9* 3C 46
S. Downs Clo. *Shaw.* 1F 31
Southerly Cres. *M40.* 2F 47
Southey Clo. *L'boro* 2F 15
Southfields Av. *M11.* 5A 54
Southgate. *Dob* **1C 44**
Southgate. *Whitw* **4D 4**
Southgate Ho. *Oldh* 5F 41
(off Southgate St.)
Southgate Ind. Est. *Heyw* . . 6A 20
Southgate Rd. *Chad.* 2G 47
Southgate St. *Oldh* 5F 41
South Hill. *S'head* 6D 42
S. Hill St. *Oldh* 5G 41
Southlink. *Oldh* 5G 41
Southlink Bus. Pk. *Oldh* . . . 5G 41
Southlink Bus. Pk. Workshops.
    Oldh *5G 41*
(off Southlink)
Southlink Ind. Pk. *Oldh* . . . 4H 41
Southmere Clo. *M40* 2E 47
South Pde. *Roch* 6A 14
South Pl. *Roch.* 5A 14
South St. *Heyw* 5F 19
South St. *Oldh* 3B 48
South Ter. *Roch* 4B 12
S. Terrace Ct. *Roch* 2A 22
South Vw. *Carr.* 6B 52
South Vw. *Roch* 1A 20
Southview Rd. *Roch.* 1E 15
S. View Ter. *Roch.* 1E 15
Southview Wlk. *Oldh* 2C 42
Southway. *M40* 3H 47
South Way. *Oldh* 3E 49
Southwell Gdns. *Ash L* . . . 6H 49
Southwell St. *M9* 6A 46
Southwood Dri. *M9* 6E 37
Sovereign Hall Cvn. Pk. *Moss* . 4F 51
Spa La. *Oldh* 6B 42
Sparrowfield Clo. *Carr* 4E 41
Sparrow Hill. *Roch.* 6G 13
Sparrow St. *Rytn* 1E 41
Sparth Bottoms Rd. *Roch.* . . 1F 21
Sparthfield Av. *Roch* 2G 21
Sparth Rd. *M40.* 2B 54
Spean Wlk. *M11.* 6A 54
Spencer La. *Roch.* 2A 20
Spencer St. *Chad* 1B 48
Spencer St. *L'boro* 5A 8
Spencer St. *Moss* 4F 51
Spencer St. *Oldh* 4G 41
Spen Fold. *L'boro* 1G 15
Spenwood Rd. *L'boro* 6F 7
Spindle Ct. Rytn. *5E 31*
(off High Barn St.)
Spindles, The. *Moss* 5H 51
Spindles, The. *Oldh* 4F 41
Spinks St. *Oldh* 5F 13
Spinners Gdns. *Ward* 1C 14
Spinners Grn. *Roch* 3H 13
Spinners Way. *Oldh* 5C 32
Spinney, The. *Roch* 2F 13
Spinney, The. *Scout* 3E 43
Spinningfield Way. *Heyw* . . 2H 27
Spodden Cotts. *Whitw* 1F 5
Spodden Fold. *Whitw* 3E 5
Spodden St. *Roch* 5F 13
Spodden Wlk. *W'fld* 2A 36
Spod Rd. *Roch.* 4E 13
(in two parts)
Spokeshave Way. *Roch* . . . 3C 14
Sportsmans Dri. *Oldh* 2G 49

Spotland Bridge—Swain St.

Spotland Bridge. 5F 13
Spotland Fold. 4E 13
Spotland Rd. Roch 5F 13
Spotland Tops. Roch 4D 12
Spreadbury St. M40 6C 46
Springbank. Chad. 4A 40
Springbank. Heal 1F 13
Springbank. Upperm 3D 44
Spring Bank. Whitw 2F 5
Spring Bank La. Roch. 5A 12 (in two parts)
Spring Bank St. Oldh 1C 48
Spring Clo. Lees. 6B 42
Springclough Dri. Oldh. 1H 49
Spring Cotts. Moss 3G 51 (off Bk. Mill La.)
Spring Ct. Roch 4H 13
Springfield Av. L'boro 4G 7
Springfield Clo. Fail 5G 47
Springfield Clo. Heyw. 6A 20
Springfield Ind. Est. Fail 5G 47
Springfield La. Roch 2D 14
Springfield La. Rytn 2C 30
Springfield Rd. Droy 5D 54
Springfield Rd. Midd 2B 38
Springfield St. Heyw. 5E 19
Spring Gdns. Midd. 1C 38
Spring Gdns. Roch. 6G 13
Spring Gdns. Rytn 5D 30
Spring Garden St. Rytn 5D 30 (in two parts)
Spring Gro. G'fld 6D 44
Spring Hall Ri. Oldh 5D 32
Springhead. 5E 43
Springhead Av. S'head 6D 42
Spring Hill. 2B 42
Spring Hill. Roch 4B 22
Springhill. Rytn 5D 30
Spring Hill Ct. Oldh 3B 42
SPRINGHILL HOSPICE. 4B 22
Spring La. Lees 6C 42
Spring Lees Ct. S'head 5D 42
Spring Mdw. La. Upperm 3E 45
Spring Mill Wlk. Roch 2C 14
Spring Pl. Whitw 1F 5
Spring Ri. Shaw. 6G 23
Spring Side La. Ward 4A 6
Springs Rd. Midd. 5G 39
Springs, The. Roch 6A 12
Spring St. Moss. 3G 51
Spring St. Oldh 3A 42
Spring St. S'head 5E 43
Spring St. Upperm. 3D 44
Spring Ter. Chad 4A 40
Spring Ter. Miln 4H 23
Spring Ter. Roch 5C 12
Spring Va. Midd. 3C 38
Spring Va. Ct. Midd 2D 38
Spring Va. Ter. L'boro. 6H 7 (off Church St.)
Spring Va. Way. Rytn 4G 31
Springville Av. M9 6B 46
Springwood. Del 4A 34
Springwood Av. Chad. 2G 39
Springwood Hall Rd. Oldh 3G 49
Springwood Way. Ash L. 6G 49
Spruce Av. Bury 5A 18
Spruce St. Roch. 1B 22
Sprucewood. Chad 3F 39
Spurn La. Dig 6D 34
Spur, The. Oldh 2G 49
Square Fold. Droy. 5F 55
Square, The. Dob 1C 44 (Dobcross)
Square, The. Dob. 3D 44 (Uppermill)
Stablefold. Moss 5G 51
Stables, The. Droy 4H 55
Stable St. Chad 3A 48
Stable St. Oldh. 3H 41
Stafford Ct. Roch 1E 15
Stafford Rd. Fail 2E 55
Stafford St. Oldh 1C 48
Stag Pasture Rd. Oldh 4D 48
Staindale. Oldh. 5B 42
Stainmore Av. Ash L. 6A 50
Stainton Dri. Midd 6H 27
Stake Hill. 5F 29
Stakehill Ind. Est. Midd. 5F 29
Stakehill La. Midd. 3F 29
Staley Rd. Moss. 5H 51 (in two parts)
Staley St. Oldh. 5H 41
Staley St. S'head 5D 42
Stamford Dri. Fail 1F 55
Stamford Rd. Lees 3D 42
Stamford Rd. Moss 3G 51
Stamford St. Heyw. 6A 20
Stamford St. Lees 5C 42
Stamford St. Moss 5F 51
Stamford St. Roch 1B 22
Stampstone St. Oldh 3H 41
Stanage Av. M9 1B 46
Stanbury Clo. Bury 6B 18
Standall Wlk. M9 4A 46
Standedge Foot Rd. Dig 2E 35
Standedge Rd. Dig. 6D 34
Standedge Tunnel. 4F 35
Standon Wlk. M40 3F 47
Stanhope St. Moss. 5G 51
Stanhope St. Roch. 2H 21
Stanhope Way. Fail. 5G 47
Stanier St. M9 5A 46
Stanley Pl. Roch 5G 13
Stanley Rd. Chad 1B 48
Stanley St. Chad. 4B 40
Stanley St. Heyw 6H 19
Stanley St. Lees 6C 42
Stanley St. Roch 4G 13
Stanley St. S'head 5E 43
Stanneybrook Clo. Roch 5B 14
Stanney Clo. Miln 2E 23
Stanney Rd. Roch 5B 14
Stannybrook Rd. Fail 6D 48
Stansfield Dri. Roch 4A 12
Stansfield Hall. L'boro 2A 8
Stansfield Rd. Fail 5A 48
Stansfield St. M40 3B 54
Stansfield St. Chad. 6B 40
Stansfield St. Oldh 3E 41
Stanton St. M11 5A 54
Stanton St. Chad 2B 48
Stanway Clo. Midd. 5D 38
Stanway St. M9 5A 46
Stanwell Rd. M40. 4E 47
Stanwick Av. M9. 6E 37
Stanycliffe. 6D 28
Stanycliffe La. Midd 6D 28
Starcross Wlk. M40 1A 54
Starfield Av. L'boro 3F 15
Star Ind. Est. Oldh 6F 41
Starkey St. Heyw 4H 19 (in two parts)
Starling Clo. Droy 4H 55
Starring Gro. L'boro 6F 7 (off Starring Rd.)
Starring La. L'boro 6E 7
Starring Rd. L'boro. 5E 7 (in two parts)
Starring Way. L'boro 6F 7
Station App. Bus. Cen. Roch 1H 21 (off Station Rd.)
Station Cotts. Dig 4F 35 (off Lee Side)
Stationers Entry. Roch 6H 13 (off Butts, The)
Station La. G'fld 6C 44
Station La. G'ton 6E 43
Station Rd. G'ton 6E 43
Station Rd. L'boro 6H 7
Station Rd. Miln 2F 23
Station Rd. Moss 4H 51
Station Rd. Oldh 1G 41
Station Rd. Roch 1H 21
Station Rd. Upperm 4F 35 (Diggle)
Station Rd. Upperm 3D 44 (Uppermill)
Station Rd. Whitw 1F 5 (Hoyle St.)
Station Rd. Whitw 6D 4 (Market St.)
Station Sq. Moss 4G 51
Station St. S'head 5D 42
Staveley Clo. Midd 1A 38
Staveley Clo. Shaw. 3B 32
Stavely Wlk. Rytn 5E 31 (off Shaw St.)
Stavordale. Roch 5G 13 (off Spotland Rd.)
Steadway. G'fld 6E 45
Steeple Vw. Rytn 5D 30
Stella St. M9 6F 37
Stephen Lowry Wlk. M9 6C 46
Stephenson Av. Droy 6E 55
Stephenson St. Fail 4A 48
Stephenson St. Oldh 3B 42
Steps Mdw. Roch. 1C 14
Stevenson Dri. Oldh 5C 32
Stevenson Sq. Roch 2C 14
Stewart St. Miln 4H 23
Stirling Pl. Heyw 6D 18
Stirling Rd. Chad 1H 47
Stirling St. Oldh 4C 40
Stiups La. Roch 3B 22
Stock Brook. 4B 40
Stockburn Dri. Fail 6C 48
Stock Clo. Roch 3G 13
Stockdale Rd. M9. 1A 46
Stockfield Mt. Chad 5B 40
Stockfield Rd. Chad 4B 40
Stock Gro. Miln 6F 15
Stock La. Chad. 4B 40
Stockport Rd. Lyd 6G 43
Stockport Rd. Moss 3G 51
Stock Rd. Roch 3A 14
Stocksfield Dri. M9. 2A 46
Stocks Ga. Roch 3D 12
Stocks St. Roch. 5D 20
Stockton Pk. Oldh 5B 42
Stockton St. L'boro 6G 7
Stockwood Wlk. M9 6A 46
Stokesay Clo. Shaw 5G 31
Stokes St. M11 5B 54
Stoke St. Roch 1B 22
Stone Breaks. 5F 43
Stone Breaks. S'head 4E 43
Stone Breaks Rd. S'head 5E 43
Stonechat Clo. Droy 4G 55
Stonecroft. Oldh 4E 41
Stonefield St. Miln 2F 23
Stoneflat Ct. Roch 5F 13
Stonehead St. M9 6B 46
Stonehill Cres. Roch. 2C 12
Stonehill Dri. Roch. 2C 12
Stone Hill La. Roch 2C 12
Stonehill Rd. Roch 2C 12
Stonelands Way. G'ton 1E 51
Stoneleigh Rd. S'head 4E 43
Stoneleigh St. Oldh 2H 41
Stonesdale Clo. Rytn 4E 31
Stone St. Miln 2F 23
Stoneswood Dri. Moss. 3H 51
Stoneswood Rd. Del. 6A 34
Stoneyfield. 3H 21
Stoney La. Del 2A 34
Stoneyroyd. Whitw. 2F 5
Stoneyvale Ct. Roch. 3H 21
Stonie Heys Av. Roch. 3B 14
Stony Head. L'boro. 1A 8 (off Higher Calderbrook Rd.)
Stopford Av. L'boro. 1E 15
Store Pas. L'boro 6G 7
Stores Cotts. Grass 5A 44
Store St. Roch 4A 12
Store St. Shaw 1A 32
Stottfield. Rytn 6B 30
Stott Ho. Oldh 6E 41
Stott La. Midd 4B 28
Stott Milne St. Chad 6B 40
Stott Rd. Chad 2G 47
Stott's La. M40 1B 54
Stott St. Fail. 1B 54
Stott St. Roch (OL12) 4H 13
Stott St. Roch (OL16) 2D 14
Stourport St. Oldh 2G 41
Stovell Rd. M40 5C 46
Strain Av. M9 1A 46
Strand, The. Roch 5H 21
Strand Way. Rytn 1D 40
Stratford Av. Oldh. 2E 49
Stratford Av. Roch 2G 21
Stratford Rd. Midd 6D 38
Strathaven Pl. Heyw 6D 18
Strathfield Dri. M11 5A 54
Strawberry La. Moss 1G 51
Street Bridge. 6A 30
Street Bri. Rd. Oldh 1A 40
Street End. 5A 48
Streethouse La. Dob. 2B 44
Street Lodge. Roch 6D 20
Street, The. Shaw. 2C 32
Stretford Pl. Roch 2G 13
Striding Edge Wlk. Oldh 2G 41
Strine Dale. 5D 32
Stromness Gro. Heyw 6D 18
Strontian Wlk. Open 6A 54
Stroud Clo. Midd 6C 38
Stuart St. Midd. 3E 39
Stuart St. Oldh 6E 41
Stuart St. Roch 1A 22 (in two parts)
Stuart Wlk. Midd 4B 38
Stubley. 6F 7
Stubley Gdns. L'boro 6G 7
Stubley La. L'boro 6F 7
Stubley Mill Rd. L'boro 1E 15 (in four parts)
Studley Clo. Rytn 5G 31
Styhead Dri. Midd 6H 27
Sudden. 3E 21
Sudden St. Roch 3E 21
Sudley Rd. Roch 2E 21
Sudlow St. Roch 3B 14
Suffield St. Midd 3B 38
Suffolk Av. Droy 4E 55
Suffolk St. Oldh 6B 40
Suffolk St. Roch. 1H 21
Sugar La. Dob 1C 44
Sulby St. M40 5C 46
Sumac St. M11 5B 54
Summer Castle. Roch 6H 13
Summercroft. Chad 2B 48
Summerfield Av. Droy 4C 54
Summerfield Dri. Midd 1E 39
Summerfield Vw. Oldh 2A 50
Summer Hill. Moss 3H 51 (off Greenhill Cotts.)
Summerhill Vw. Dens. 6H 25
Summerseat Clo. S'head. 4E 43
Summersgill Clo. Heyw 6A 20
Summershades La. Grass 5H 43
Summershades Ri. Oldh. 5H 43
Summers St. Chad. 4C 40
Summer St. Roch 6A 14
Summerville Av. M9 6B 46
Summit. 5E 19 **(Heywood)**
Summit. 1B 8 **(Littleborough)**
Summit. 1C 30 **(Oldham)**
Summit Clo. Bury 3D 18
Summit St. Heyw. 5D 18
Sumner St. Shaw. 4H 31
Sunbank Clo. Roch. 3F 13
Sunbury Dri. M40 3B 54
Sundew Pl. Midd 4F 39
Sunfield Av. Oldh 5C 32
Sunfield Cres. Rytn. 6E 31
Sunfield Dri. Rytn. 6F 31
Sunfield Est. Dig. 5E 35
Sunfield La. Dig 5E 35
Sunfield Rd. Oldh. 3E 41
Sunfield Way. Lees. 4C 42
Sun Ga. L'boro 4F 15
Sun Hill. 4C 42
Sunhill Clo. Roch 5B 22
Sunk La. Midd 3C 38 (in two parts)
Sunningdale Av. M11 5A 54
Sunningdale Dri. Heyw. 1H 27
Sunny Bank. Lees 6C 42
Sunnybank Av. Droy. 6D 54
Sunny Bank Rd. Bury 6A 26
Sunnybank Rd. Droy 6D 54
Sunny Brow Rd. Midd 3A 38
Sunnyfield Rd. P'wich 4A 36
Sunnyside. Droy 4D 54
Sunnyside Av. Droy 3D 54
Sunny Side Cotts. Roch 3F 11
Sunnyside Ct. Droy 4D 54
Sunnyside Rd. Droy. 4D 54
Sunrise Vw. L'boro. 2B 8
Sun St. Moss. 4G 51
Surbiton Rd. M40 3A 54
Surma Clo. Oldh 4D 40
Surma Clo. Roch 2B 22
Surrey Av. Droy 4D 54
Surrey Av. Shaw. 2F 31
Surrey Pk. Clo. Shaw 1H 31
Surrey St. Chad 6C 40
Sussex Av. Bury. 6C 18
Sussex Clo. Chad. 5B 40
Sussex Dri. Droy 4E 55
Sussex St. Roch 1H 21
Sutcliffe St. L'boro 5H 7
Sutcliffe St. Midd 3E 39
Sutcliffe St. Oldh 6E 41
Sutcliffe St. Rytn 6G 31
Sutherland Clo. Oldh. 4F 49
Sutherland Flats. Heyw. 5G 19 (off Meadow Clo.)
Sutherland Rd. Heyw 6C 18
Suthers St. Oldh. 5C 40
Sutton Dri. Droy. 4C 54
Swailes St. Oldh. 5H 41
Swaindrod La. L'boro 4C 8
Swainsthorpe Dri. M9. 5A 46
Swain St. Roch 4G 13

Swaledale Clo.—Townfield St.

Swaledale Clo. *Rytn* 4E **31**
Swallow Bank Dri. *Roch* 4D **20**
Swallow Clo. *Carr* 6B **52**
Swallow Dri. *Bury* 3A **18**
Swallow Dri. *Roch* 6B **12**
Swallow La. *Carr* 6B **52**
(in two parts)
Swallow St. *Oldh* 3D **48**
Swan Ct. *Shaw* 3H **31**
Swansea St. *Oldh* 1H **49**
Sweet Briar Clo. *Roch* 3G **13**
Sweetbriar Clo. *Shaw* 2H **31**
Sweet Briar La. *Roch* 3G **13**
Sweetnam Dri. *M11* 5A **54**
Swift Rd. *Oldh* 5C **32**
Swift Rd. *Roch* 6B **12**
Swift Wlk. *M40* 1A **54**
Swinburne Av. *Droy* 4E **55**
Swinburn St. *M9* 4B **46**
Swinford Gro. *Rytn* 4G **31**
Swinford Wlk. *M9* 2A **46**
Swinside Clo. *Midd* 1G **37**
Swinton St. *Oldh* 6A **42**
Sybil St. *L'boro* 5G **7**
Sycamore Av. *Chad* 1H **47**
Sycamore Av. *Heyw* 1A **28**
Sycamore Av. *Miln* 4G **23**
Sycamore Av. *Oldh* 3B **42**
Sycamore Clo. *L'boro* 6F **7**
Sycamore Gro. *Fail* 6B **48**
Sycamores, The. *Lees* 3C **42**
Sycamores, The. *Moss* 4A **52**
Sydenham St. *Oldh* 2G **41**
(in two parts)
Sydenham Ter. *Roch* 2F **13**
Sydney Gdns. *L'boro* 2A **8**
Sydney Jones Ct. *M40* 4E **47**
Sydney St. *Fail* 6G **47**
Sydney St. *Moss* 5H **51**
Syke **1H 13**
Syke La. *Roch* 1H **13**
Syke Rd. *L'boro* 3A **16**
Syke Rd. *Roch* 1H **13**
Sykes Av. *Bury* 5A **26**
Sykes Clo. *G'fld* 6D **44**
Sykes Ct. *Roch* 1B **22**
Sykes St. *Miln* 3G **23**
Sykes St. *Roch* 1B **22**
Sylvan Av. *Fail* 2C **54**
Sylvan Clo. *Midd* 1H **37**
Sylvan St. *Oldh* 4C **40**
Symond Rd. *M9* 6A **38**

T

Tabley Gdns. *Droy* 6F **55**
Tabley St. *Moss* 5H **51**
Tabor St. *Midd* 1B **38**
Tadcaster Wlk. *Oldh* 4F **41**
Talbot Clo. *Oldh* 3A **42**
Talbot St. *Midd* 1C **38**
Talbot St. *Roch* 1H **21**
Talkin Dri. *Midd* 6A **28**
Tall Trees Clo. *Rytn* 5C **30**
Tamar Way. *Heyw* 4E **19**
Tame Bank. *Moss* 2H **51**
Tame Barn Clo. *Miln* 1G **23**
Tame La. *Del* 2G **33**
Tame St. *Moss* 2A **52**
Tame St. *Upperm* 3D **44**
Tame Valley Clo. *Moss* 2A **52**
Tame Vw. *Moss* 3G **51**
Tame Water **2B 44**
Tamewater Vs. Dob *2B* ***44***
(off Brook La.)
Tamworth Av. *W'fld* 4A **36**
Tamworth Ct. *Chad* 6C **40**
Tamworth St. *Oldh* 6C **40**
Tandle Hill Countryside Cen. **3A 30**
Tandle Hill Countryside Pk. **3A 30**
Tandle Hill Rd. *Rytn* 3B **30**
Tandle Hill Ter. *Roch* 1B **30**
Tandlewood M. *M40* 2A **54**
Tandle Wood Pk. *Rytn* 3B **30**
Tangmere Av. *Heyw* 2A **28**
Tangmere Clo. *M40* 2E **47**
Tanhill La. *Oldh* 3G **49**
Tannersfield Lodge. *Fail* 1C **54**
Tanners Fold. *Oldh* 3G **49**
Tan Pit Cotts. *Heyw* 3H **19**
Tara Sports & Leisure Cen. **2A 32**
Tarland Wlk. *Open* 6A **54**
Tarnbrook Clo. *W'fld* 3A **36**
(in two parts)
Tarnside Clo. *Roch* 2C **14**
Tartan St. *M11* 5A **54**
Tarves Wlk. *Open* 6A **54**
Tatchbury Rd. *Fail* 6A **48**
Tate St. *Oldh* 1H **49**
Tatham St. *Roch* 6A **14**
Tattersall St. *Oldh* 5D **40**
Tatton Mere Dri. *Droy* 6F **55**
Taunton Av. *Roch* 6D **12**
Taunton Rd. *Chad* 1A **40**
Taurus St. *Oldh* 3A **42**
Tavern Ct. *Fail* 6B **48**
Tavern Ct. Av. *Fail* 6A **48**
Tavistock Dri. *Chad* 2H **39**
Tavistock Rd. *Roch* 4H **21**
Tay Clo. *Oldh* 6E **41**
Taylor Av. *Roch* 5B **12**
Taylor Grn. Way. *Lees* 4D **42**
Taylor's La. *M40* 2A **54**
Taylor's Pl. *Oldh* 5G **41**
Taylors Pl. *Roch* 4H **13**
Taylor St. *Chad* 4A **40**
Taylor St. *Droy* 6D **54**
Taylor St. *Heyw* 5G **19**
Taylor St. *Lees* 5C **42**
Taylor St. *Midd* 3C **38**
(in two parts)
Taylor St. *Oldh* 3A **42**
Taylor St. *Roch* 4H **13**
Taylor St. *Rytn* 4D **30**
Taylor St. *Whitw* 3F **5**
Taylor Ter. L'boro *6A* ***8***
(off Ealees Rd.)
Teak St. *Bury* 5A **18**
Teal Ct. *Roch* 6B **12**
Teasdale Clo. *Chad* 2G **47**
Tedburn Wlk. *M40* 3F **47**
Tedder Clo. *Bury* 1A **36**
Teddington Rd. *M40* 4E **47**
Teesdale Wlk. *M9* 2A **46**
Tees St. *Roch* 1B **22**
Tees Wlk. *Oldh* 6E **41**
Telford M. *Upperm* 2D **44**
Telford Way. *Roch* 5A **22**
Tell St. *Roch* 6F **13**
Temple Clo. *Lees* 3C **42**
Temple La. *L'boro* 2A **8**
Temple St. *Heyw* 5H **19**
Temple St. *Midd* 2D **38**
Temple St. *Oldh* 4H **41**
Tenbury Dri. *Midd* 6C **38**
Tenby Gro. *Roch* 4E **13**
Tenby Rd. *Oldh* 3B **48**
Tenby St. *Roch* 4E **13**
Tenham Wlk. M9 *2A* ***46***
(off Ravenswood Dri.)
Ten Houses. *Oldh* 3A **50**
Tennyson Rd. *Droy* 5E **55**
Tennyson Rd. *Midd* 1D **38**
Tennyson St. *Oldh* 2A **42**
Tennyson St. *Roch* 2A **22**
Tensing St. *Oldh* 5G **49**
Tentercroft. *Oldh* 4E **41**
Tentercroft. *Roch* 6G **13**
Tenterhill La. *Roch* 3H **11**
Terence St. *M40* 2B **54**
Tern Clo. *Roch* 6B **12**
Terrace St. *Oldh* 4H **41**
Tetley Bye Rd. *Dig* 2G **35**
Tetlow St. *M40* 2A **54**
Tetlow St. *Midd* 3C **38**
Tetlow St. *Oldh* 5D **40**
Tetlows Yd. *L'boro* 1B **8**
Tetsworth Wlk. *M40* 3F **47**
Tewkesbury Av. *Ash L* 6A **50**
Tewkesbury Av. *Chad* 1A **40**
Tewkesbury Av. *Droy* 4E **55**
Tewkesbury Av. *Midd* 6B **28**
Thackeray Gro. *Droy* 5E **55**
Thackeray Rd. *Oldh* 2A **42**
Thames Rd. *Miln* 1H **23**
Thames St. *Oldh* 3G **41**
Thames St. *Roch* 1B **22**
Thankerton Av. *Aud* 6H **55**
Thatcher St. *Oldh* 1G **49**
Thatch Leach **6H 39**
Thatch Leach. *Chad* 6H **39**
Thaxmead Dri. *M40* 3B **54**
Theatre St. *Oldh* 4F **41**
Thekla St. *Oldh* 3D **40**
Thetford. Roch *5G* ***13***
(off Spotland Rd.)
Thimble Clo. *Roch* 1D **14**
Thimbles, The. *Roch* 1D **14**
Third Av. *Bury* 3B **18**
Third Av. *Clay* 4A **54**
Third Av. *Oldh* 3C **48**
Thirlmere Dri. *Midd* 1A **38**
Thirlmere Gro. *Rytn* 3D **30**
Thirlmere Rd. *Roch* 3D **20**
Thirlstone Av. *Oldh* 5D **32**
Thirsfield Dri. *M11* 5A **54**
Thirsk Av. *Chad* 2H **39**
Thistle Grn. *Miln* 6E **15**
Thistle Way. *Oldh* 1B **42**
Thistleyfield. *Miln* 6E **15**
Thomas Henshaw Ct. *Roch* 3E **21**
Thomas Ho. Rytn *5E* ***31***
(off Royton Hall Wlk.)
Thomason Sq. *L'boro* 6G **7**
Thomas St. *Lees* 6C **42**
Thomas St. *L'boro* 1E **15**
Thomas St. *Roch* 5A **14**
Thomas St. *Rytn* 6F **31**
Thomas St. *Shaw* 3A **32**
Thomas St. *Whitw* 1F **5**
Thompson Dri. *Bury* 4A **18**
Thompson La. *Chad* 1A **48**
Thorburn Dri. *Whitw* 4D **4**
Thorgill Wlk. *M40* 6C **46**
Thorley Clo. *Chad* 3H **47**
Thorley St. *Fail* 5H **47**
Thornaby Wlk. M9 *6A* ***46***
(off Lathbury Rd.)
Thorn Av. *Fail* 1C **54**
Thorn Bank. *Carr* 6B **52**
Thornbank Clo. *Heyw* 2A **28**
Thornbury. *Roch* 1G **21**
Thornbush Way. *Roch* 5C **14**
Thorncliff Av. *Oldh* 2E **49**
Thorncliffe Av. *Rytn* 3C **30**
Thorncliffe Pk. *Rytn* 3C **30**
Thorn Clo. *Heyw* 4F **19**
Thorndale Clo. *Rytn* 4E **31**
Thorney Hill Clo. *Oldh* 5G **41**
Thorneylea. *Whitw* 2F **5**
Thornford Wlk. *M40* 3F **47**
Thornham Ct. *Roch* 1C **30**
Thornham Fold **2H 29**
Thornham La. *Midd* 3F **29**
Thornham La. *Rytn* 1C **30**
Thornham New Rd. *Roch* 1F **29**
Thornham Old Rd. *Rytn* 2A **30**
Thornham Rd. *Shaw* 2D **30**
Thornhill Rd. *Droy* 5F **55**
Thornlea. *M9* 3C **46**
Thornlea. *Droy* 6C **54**
Thornlea Av. *Oldh* 4C **48**
Thornlea Dri. *Roch* 3D **12**
Thornlee Ct. *G'ton* 6F **43**
Thornley Clo. *G'ton* 6E **43**
Thornley Cres. *G'ton* 6E **43**
Thornley La. *G'ton* 6E **43**
Thornley Pk. Rd. *G'ton* 6E **43**
Thornley Rd. *P'wich* 4A **36**
Thornley St. *Midd* 2D **38**
Thorn Rd. *Oldh* 2A **50**
Thorns Clough. *Dig* 4E **35**
Thornsett Clo. *M9* 5A **46**
Thornton St. *Oldh* 6F **41**
Thornton St. *Roch* 2H **21**
Thorntree Clo. *M9* 6A **46**
Thorntree Pl. *Roch* 5G **13**
Thorn Vw. *Bury* 4A **18**
Thorp **4C 30**
Thorpebrook Rd. *M40* 6C **46**
Thorpe Clo. *Aus* 3E **43**
Thorpe Hill. *Oldh* 5E **41**
Thorpe La. *Aus & Scout* 3D **42**
Thorpe St. *Midd* 4G **37**
Thorp Rd. *Rytn* 5D **30**
Thorp Vw. *Rytn* 3C **30**
Thorverton Sq. *M40* 5D **46**
Thrapston Av. *Aud* 6H **55**
Three Acre Av. *Rytn* 5G **31**
Three Owls Bird Sanctuary **4H 11**
Three Owls Bird Sanctuary Vis. Cen. **4G 11**
Three Pits. *Midd* 4E **29**
Threlkeld Clo. *Midd* 2G **37**
Threlkeld Ct. *Midd* 2G **37**
Threlkeld Rd. *Midd* 2G **37**
Throstle Ct. *Rytn* 6D **30**
Throstle Hall Ct. *Midd* 2B **38**
Throstles Clo. *Droy* 4G **55**
Thrum Fold. *Roch* 2F **13**
Thrum Hall La. *Roch* 2G **13**
(Daffodil Clo.)
Thrum Hall La. *Roch* 2F **13**
(Gt. Lee)
Thrush Dri. *Bury* 3A **18**
Thrush St. *Roch* 4E **13**
Thurland Rd. *Oldh* 5A **42**
Thurland St. *Chad* 3G **39**
Thurlby Av. *M9* 6A **38**
Thursby Wlk. *Midd* 1G **37**
Thurston Clough Rd. *Scout & Dob* 2G **43**
Tiber Av. *Oldh* 4C **48**
Tideswell Rd. *Droy* 4C **54**
Tiflis St. *Roch* 5G **13**
Tilbury St. *Oldh* 3E **41**
Tilgate Wlk. M9 *2A* ***46***
(off Haverfield Rd.)
Tilton St. *Oldh* 2A **42**
Timbercliffe **2B 8**
Timbercliffe. *L'boro* 2B **8**
Timberhurst. *Bury* 5B **18**
Times Retail Pk. *Heyw* 5G **19**
Times St. *Midd* 3D **38**
Timperley Clo. *Oldh* 3H **49**
Timperley St. *Oldh* 4E **41**
Timson St. *Fail* 6H **47**
Tim's Ter. *Miln* 1F **23**
Tinsdale Wlk. *Midd* 2G **37**
Tintern Av. *Heyw* 3G **19**
Tintern Av. *L'boro* 4G **7**
Tintern Av. *Roch* 2G **13**
Tintern Pl. *Heyw* 3G **19**
Tintern Rd. *Midd* 6B **28**
Tiptree Wlk. *M9* 5A **46**
Titchfield Rd. *Oldh* 1A **50**
Tithe Barn Clo. *Roch* 1D **14**
Titian Ri. *Oldh* 4B **32**
(in two parts)
Toad La. *L'boro & Sower B* 2F **9**
Toad La. *Roch* 5H **13**
(in two parts)
Tobermory Clo. *M11* 6B **54**
Todd St. *Heyw* 5E **19**
Todd St. *Roch* 6A **14**
Todmorden Rd. *L'boro* 1B **8**
Toledo St. *M11* 6B **54**
Tollgate Way. *Roch* 5C **14**
Tolmount Way. *Chad* 3H **39**
Tomlinson Clo. *Oldh* 6E **41**
Tomlinson St. *M40* 2E **47**
Tomlinson St. *Roch* 3E **21**
Tommy Taylor Clo. *M40* 2A **54**
Tonacliffe **5E 5**
Tonacliffe Rd. *Whitw* 6E **5**
Tonacliffe Ter. *Whitw* 4E **5**
Tonacliffe Way. *Whitw* 5E **5**
Tonge Clo. *W'fld* 2A **36**
Tonge Ct. *Midd* 3D **38**
Tonge Hall Clo. *Midd* 3D **38**
Tong End. *Whitw* 1E **5**
Tonge Roughs. *Midd* 3F **39**
Tonge St. *Heyw* 5H **19**
Tonge St. *Midd* 5G **39**
Tonge St. *Roch* 1A **22**
Tong La. *Whitw* 2E **5**
Tongley Wlk. *M40* 3F **47**
Top of Heap **6D 18**
Top of Heap. *Heyw* 5D **18**
Top of Hebers **6A 28**
Top of Moor **3B 42**
Top o' th' Grn. *Chad* 1C **48**
Top o' th' Meadows **2E 43**
Top o' th' Meadows La. *W'head* 2E **43**
Top o' th' Wood **2F 19**
Topping Fold Rd. *Bury* 4A **18**
Top Schwabe St. *Midd* 3G **37**
Topsham Wlk. *M40* 2B **54**
Top St. *Midd* 2B **38**
Top St. *Oldh* 3B **42**
Torcross Rd. *M9* 6F **37**
Torksey Wlk. *M9* 6F **37**
Torness Wlk. *Open* 6A **54**
Torpoint Wlk. *M40* 4E **47**
Torre Clo. *Midd* 6C **28**
Torrington Av. *M9* 3C **46**
Torrington St. *Heyw* 1A **28**
Torver Dri. *Midd* 1H **37**
Torwood Rd. *Chad* 2G **39**
Totnes Av. *Chad* 2H **39**
Tottington Av. *S'head* 4D **42**
Tottington St. *M11* 5A **54**
Totton Rd. *Fail* 6H **47**
Touchet Hall Rd. *Midd* 5F **29**
Towers St. *Oldh* 2B **42**
Tower St. *Heyw* 6F **19**
Towncroft Av. *Midd* 1B **38**
Townfield St. *Oldh* 4H **41**

Town Hall Sq. Roch 6H 13 *(off Packer St.)*
Town Head 5G 13
Town Ho. Rd. L'boro 5H 7 (in four parts)
Townley Pk. Ind. Est. Midd 2C 38
Townley Rd. Miln 1F 23
Townley St. Midd 2C 38
Town Meadows. Roch 6G 13 *(off Esplanade, The)*
Town Mill Brow. Roch 6G 13
Townrow St. Heyw 5H 19
Town Sq. Shop. Cen. Oldh 5F 41
Towns Yd. Rytn 5E 31 *(off Park St.)*
Towton St. M9 5A 46
Trafalgar Sq. Moss 4F 51
Trafalgar Sq. Roch 5A 14
Trafalgar St. Oldh 3E 41
Trafalgar St. Roch 5A 14
Trafford St. Oldh 6E 41
Trafford St. Roch 2G 21
Trajan Ho. Oldh 4F 41
Trans Pennine Trad. Est. Roch 4F 21
Transvaal St. M11 6B 54
Travis Ct. Rytn 5E 31
Travis St. Miln 3H 23
Travis St. Shaw 2H 31
Traylen Way. Roch 4C 12
Tree Av. Droy 4E 55
Tree Ho. Av. Ash L 6F 49
Treetops Clo. Dob 1B 44
Trefoil Way. L'boro 5F 7
Tregaer Fold. Midd 3E 39
Tremain Wlk. M9 6A 46 *(off Stockwood Wlk.)*
Trenchard Ct. M11 5B 54
Trengrove St. Roch 4E 13
Trent Av. Chad 3G 39
Trent Av. Heyw 4E 19
Trent Av. Miln 1G 23
Trentham Gro. M40 4C 46
Trent Rd. Shaw 1G 31
Trent St. Roch 1B 22
Trent Wlk. Droy 6F 55
Trevarrick Ct. Oldh 3A 42
Trevor Dri. M40 3G 47
Trevor St. Roch 4D 20
Trimdon Clo. M11 5A 54
Trinity Bldgs. Moss 3H 51 *(off Roughtown Rd.)*
Trinity Ho. Oldh 3E 41
Trinity St. Midd 3B 38
Trinity St. Oldh 3E 41
Trinity St. Roch 3A 12
Trongate Wlk. M9 6A 46
Troughgate. Oldh 3D 48
Troutbeck Wlk. Rytn 5E 31 *(off Shaw St.)*
Troutbeck Way. Roch 3D 20
Trowbridge Dri. M40 4E 47
Trows La. Roch 6F 21 (in two parts)
Troydale Dri. M40 1A 54
Trub 1F 29
Truro Av. Ash L 6B 50
Truro Rd. Chad 2A 40
Tudor Av. M9 4A 46
Tudor Av. Chad 2F 47
Tudor Clo. Moss 4A 52
Tudor Ct. Heyw 6G 19
Tudor Ct. Roch 4B 14
Tudor Gro. Midd 6H 27
Tudor Hall St. Roch 5E 21
Tudor St. Midd 3D 38
Tudor St. Oldh 6D 40 (in two parts)
Tudor St. Shaw 2H 31
Tulip Clo. Chad 4G 39
Tulip Gro. Roch 2G 13
Tulketh St. Ind. Est. M40 5B 46
Tulpen Sq. Chad 4B 40
Tumbling Bank Ter. Lees 6D 42
Tunshill Gro. Miln 1G 23
Tunshill La. L'boro 6C 16
Tunshill La. Miln 6H 15
Tuns Rd. Oldh 3H 49
Tunstall Rd. Oldh 5A 42
Tunstead 5E 45
Tunstead La. G'fld 5E 45
Turbary Wlk. Miln 1D 22
Turf Clo. Rytn 6E 31
Turf Hill 3B 22
Turf Hill Rd. Roch 2B 22
Turf Ho. Clo. L'boro 4F 7
Turfland Av. Rytn 6E 31
Turf La. Chad 2H 47
Turf La. Rytn 6E 31 (in two parts)
Turf Pk. Rd. Rytn 6E 31
Turf Pit La. Oldh 6C 32
Turf Pits. Oldh 6C 32
Turf Ter. L'boro 5G 7
Turfton Rd. Rytn 6F 31
Turnbull Av. P'wich 4A 36
Turner Av. Fail 1C 54
Turners Pl. Roch 2G 13
Turner St. M11 6A 54
Turner St. Lees 3C 42
Turner St. Roch 4G 13
Turnfield Clo. Roch 2D 14
Turnhill Rd. Roch 4B 22
Turnough Rd. Miln 6F 15
Turnpike Clo. Dig 4E 35
Turton Clo. Heyw 5E 19
Turvin Rd. L'boro & Sower B 2H 9
Tweedale Av. M9 6G 37
Tweedale St. Roch 1G 21
Tweedale Way. Oldh 3H 47
Tweed Clo. Oldh 6E 41
Tweedle Hill Rd. M9 6F 37
Twinegate. Roch 2G 13
Twin St. Heyw 6A 20
Twirl Hill Rd. Ash L 4C 50
Two Acre Dri. Shaw 1F 31
Two Acre La. S'head 1E 43
Two Bridges Rd. Miln 4H 23
Tydden St. Oldh 2F 49
Tydeman Wlk. Miln 2G 23
Tymm St. M40 5E 47
Tyndall Av. M40 4C 46
Tyndall St. Oldh 5A 42
Tyne St. Oldh 4A 42
Tynwald St. Oldh 4A 42
Tyrone Dri. Roch 2A 20
Tywald Mt. Rytn 6E 31

U

Uldale Dri. Midd 2A 38
Ullesthorpe. Roch 5G 13 *(off Sheriff St.)*
Ullock Wlk. Midd 1H 37
Ullswater Av. Roch 4E 13
Ullswater Av. Rytn 3D 30
Ullswater Dri. Midd 6B 28
Ullswater Gro. Heyw 1H 27
Ullswater Wlk. M9 2A 46 *(off Rockmead Dri.)*
Ulster Av. Roch 2G 21
Ulverston Av. Chad 5A 40
Una Rd. Moss 2A 52
Uncouth Rd. Roch 6E 15
Underhill Rd. Oldh 2E 41
Underhill Wlk. M40 3A 54
Under La. Chad 2B 48
Under La. G'ton 1F 51
Under St. Chad 2B 48
Underwood. Roch 6G 13
Underwood Vs. L'boro 1E 15 *(off Oakley St.)*
Underwood Way. Shaw 1B 32
Undsworth Ct. Heyw 5H 19
Union Rd. Roch 1E 15
Union St. Chad 1B 48
Union St. Lees 5C 42
Union St. Midd 2C 38
Union St. Oldh 5E 41
Union St. Roch 5H 13 (in two parts)
Union St. Rytn 5D 30
Union St. Whitw 3E 5
Union St. W. Oldh 5E 41 (in two parts)
Union Yd. Oldh 5H 41
Unity Clo. Heyw 6F 19
Unity Cres. Heyw 6F 19
Unity St. Heyw 6F 19
Unsworth 6A 26
Unsworth Way. Oldh 3E 41
Upland Rd. Oldh 1E 49
Uplands. Midd 4C 38
Uplands, The. Moss 4H 51
Up. Cliff Hill. Shaw 6A 24
Up. Conran St. M9 5A 46
Up. George St. Roch 4H 13
Up. Hayes Clo. Roch 5C 14
Uppermill 2D 44
Up. Passmonds Gro. Roch 5D 12
Up. Stone Dri. Miln 1D 22
Upton. Roch 1G 21
Upton Clo. Midd 6C 38
Upwood Wlk. M9 2A 46
Urmson St. Oldh 2F 49
Usk Clo. W'fld 4A 36
Uttley St. Roch 3E 21
Uxbridge Av. M11 5A 54

V

Vaal St. Oldh 2C 48
Vale Cotts. L'boro 6G 7
Vale Ct. Midd 3D 38
Vale Dri. Oldh 5D 40
Vale La. Fail 3E 55
Valentia Rd. M9 6H 37 & 1A 46
Valentine St. Fail 6G 47
Valentine St. Oldh 5A 42
Vale Rd. Droy 4F 55
Vale Rd. Shaw 3B 32
Vale Side. Moss 5G 51
Vale St. M11 5A 54
Vale St. Heyw 5A 20 (in two parts)
Vale St. Midd 3D 38
Vale, The. Moss 4F 51
Va. Top Av. M9 6B 46
Valiant Wlk. M40 4G 47
Valley Clo. Moss 3F 51
Valley Cotts. Moss 3H 51
Valley New Rd. Rytn 6E 31
Valley Ri. Shaw 6G 23
Valley Rd. Midd 1D 38
Valley Rd. Rytn 6E 31
Vandyke St. Roch 4B 12
Vaughan Av. M40 5C 46
Vaughan Gro. Lees 5D 42
Vaughan St. Rytn 6E 31
Vavasour Ct. Roch 1B 22
Vavasour St. Roch 1B 22 (in two parts)
Vaynor. Roch 5G 13 *(off Spotland Rd.)*
Velmere Av. M9 6E 37
Venetia St. M40 2A 54
Ventnor St. M9 5A 46
Ventnor St. Roch 2H 21
Verdant Way. Roch 4C 22
Verdun Cres. Roch 5E 13
Verdure Clo. Fail 6B 48
Verity Clo. Rytn 1D 40
Verne Dri. Oldh 4C 32
Verney Rd. Rytn 1E 41
Vernon Rd. Droy 5C 54
Vernon St. Harp 6A 46
Vernon St. Moss 3G 51
Verona Dri. M40 3A 54
Vesper St. Fail 5A 48
Vicarage Clo. S'head 4D 42
Vicarage Dri. Roch 2C 14
Vicarage La. Midd 4F 39
Vicarage Rd. N. Roch 6E 21
Vicarage Rd. S. Roch 6E 21
Vicarage St. Oldh 2C 48
Vicarage St. Shaw 2H 31
Vicarage Vw. Roch 6F 21
Vicarage Way. Shaw 3G 31
Vicars Dri. Roch 1H 21
Vicars Ga. Roch 6H 13
Victoria Av. M9 6E 37
Victoria Av. E. M9 & M40 1A 46
Victoria Gdns. Shaw 2H 31
Victoria St. Bar 5F 49
Victoria St. Chad 4B 40
Victoria St. Fail 1B 54
Victoria St. Heyw 6A 20
Victoria St. Lees 5C 42
Victoria St. L'boro 6H 7
Victoria St. Midd 3C 38
Victoria St. Oldh 5G 41
Victoria St. Roch 4H 13
Victoria St. Shaw 3H 31
Victoria St. Whitw 3E 5
Victoria Ter. Heyw 3G 19
Victoria Ter. Miln 2G 23
Victoria Trad. Est. Chad 2B 48
Victoria Wlk. Chad 2C 40
Victoria Way. Rytn 3C 30
Victor St. Heyw 1A 28
Victor St. Oldh 4B 48
Viewfield Wlk. M9 6A 46 *(off Nethervale Dri.)*
Vigo St. Heyw 6A 20
Vigo St. Oldh 6B 42
Viking St. Roch 5E 13
Village Ct. Whitw 2E 5 *(off North St.)*
Village Grn. Upperm 3D 44 *(off New St.)*
Village Wlk. Open 6A 54
Villa Rd. Oldh 1F 49
Villemoble Sq. Droy 6E 55
Villiers Dri. Oldh 6E 41
Vincent Av. Oldh 3A 42
Vincent St. L'boro 5G 7
Vincent St. Midd 1C 38
Vincent St. Roch 2A 22
Vine Clo. Shaw 2H 31
Vine Ct. Roch 6B 14
Vine Fold. M40 4H 47
Vine Pl. Roch 2H 21
Vine St. Chad 2B 48
Vine St. P'wich 6A 36
Vineyard Clo. Ward 4C 6
Vineyard Cotts. Roch 4C 6
Vineyard Ho. Roch 4C 6 *(off Knowl Syke St.)*
Vineyard St. Oldh 5H 41
Viola St. M11 5B 54
Violet Hill Ct. Oldh 3C 42
Violet Way. Midd 4F 39
V.I.P. Centre Ind. Est. Oldh 2A 42
Virginia St. Roch 3G 21
Vivian St. Roch 2G 21
Vorlich Dri. Chad 3H 39
Vulcan St. Oldh 2H 41
Vulcan Ter. L'boro 6F 7 *(off Spenwood Rd.)*

W

Wadcroft Wlk. M9 5A 46
Waddington Fold. Roch 5C 22
Waddington St. Oldh 3C 40
Wade Hill La. Dob 3A 44
Wade Row. Upperm 3D 44
Wade Row Top. Upperm 3D 44 *(off Wade Row)*
Wade St. Midd 5F 39
Wadsworth M. Droy 6D 54
Wagg Fold. L'boro 4F 7
Waggon Rd. Moss 5G 51
Wagstaff Dri. Fail 6H 47
Wagstaffe St. Midd 2C 38
Waingap Cres. Whitw 3F 5
Waingap Ri. Roch 1G 13
Waingap Vw. Whitw 4F 5
Wainwright Clo. S'head 4E 43
Wainwright St. Oldh 6E 41
Waithlands Rd. Roch 1B 22
Wakefield Dri. Chad 2C 40
Wakefield St. Chad 2C 40
Waldeck Wlk. M9 2A 46 *(off Ravenswood Dri.)*
Walden Av. Oldh 1B 42
Walden Flats. Heyw 5G 19 *(off Brunswick St.)*
Walderton Av. M40 6C 46
Wales St. Oldh 2A 42
Walkden St. Roch 4H 13
Walker Av. Fail 1F 55
Walker Rd. M9 1A 46
Walker Rd. Chad 3H 47
Walkers 5D 42
Walkers Clo. Upperm 3D 44
Walkers Ct. S'head 5E 43
Walker's La. S'head 5E 43
Walker's Rd. Oldh 3C 48
Walker St. Heyw 6G 19
Walker St. Midd 4G 37 (Broad St.)
Walker St. Midd 4F 37 (Wilton St., in two parts)
Walker St. Oldh 5D 40
Walker St. Roch 6A 14
Walkers Vw. S'head 4E 43
Walkmill. Dob 2B 44
Walk Mill Clo. Roch 1D 14
Walk, The. Roch 6H 13
Wallace St. Oldh 1F 49
Wallbank 4D 4
Wallbank Dri. Whitw 4D 4
Wall Bank La. Whitw 4D 4
Wallhead Rd. Roch 6D 14
Wall Hill 2A 44
Wall Hill Rd. Dob 2A 44
Wallis St. M40 2A 54

Wallis St.—Whitehall La.

Wallis St. Chad 1A 48
Wallshaw Pl. Oldh 4G 41
Wallshaw St. Oldh 4G 41
(in two parts)
Wall St. Oldh 6F 41
Wallwork Clo. Roch 4A 12
Walmersley Rd. M40 3G 47
Walmsley Av. L'boro 2F 15
Walnut Av. Bury 4A 18
Walnut Av. Oldh 3B 42
Walpole St. Roch 6A 14
Walsden St. M11 5A 54
Walsh St. Chad 5B 40
Walsingham Av. Midd 6C 38
Walter Scott St. Oldh 3H 41
Walters Dri. Oldh 2G 49
Walter St. M9 5A 46
Walter St. Oldh 5F 41
Waltham St. Oldh 1A 50
Walton Clo. Heyw 1H 27
(in two parts)
Walton Clo. Midd 2G 37
Walton Ho. Fail 5H 47
Walton Rd. M9 6H 37
Walton St. Heyw 1H 27
Walton St. Midd 1C 38
Wandsworth Av. M11 5B 54
Wanley Wlk. M9 2A 46
Wanstead Av. M9 2D 46
Warbeck Rd. M40 3F 47
Warcock Rd. Oldh 4A 42
Ward Ct. Dig 5E 35
Warden La. M40 1A 54
Ward La. Dig 5E 35
Wardle 5C 6
Wardle Edge. Roch 2B 14
Wardle Fold 4C 6
Wardle Fold. Ward 4C 6
Wardle Gdns. Roch 2C 14
Wardle Rd. Roch 2C 14
Wardle St. L'boro 5G 7
Ward Rd. Droy 6F 55
Ward St. Chad 4C 40
Ward St. Fail 5G 47
Ward St. Most 5B 46
Ward St. Oldh 3D 40
Wareings Yd. Roch 3A 22
Warfield Wlk. M9 2A 46
Warley St. L'boro 5H 7
Warlow Crest. G'fld 1C 52
Warlow Dri. G'fld 1C 52
(in two parts)
Warmco Ind. Pk. Moss 3H 51
Warne Av. Droy 5G 55
Warner Village Cinema 3A 26
Warnford Clo. M40 3B 54
War Office Rd. Roch 1A 20
Warren La. Oldh 1H 49
Warrington Rd. M9 6G 37
Warrington St. Lees 6C 42
Warth Cotts. Dig 5E 35
Warwick Av. W'fld 4A 36
Warwick Clo. Midd 5C 38
Warwick Clo. Shaw 2F 31
Warwick Ct. Midd 3C 38
Warwick Gro. Aud 6G 55
Warwick Rd. Fail 2D 54
Warwick Rd. Midd 5D 38
Warwick St. Oldh 1C 48
(in two parts)
Warwick St. Roch 3B 14
Wasdale Dri. Midd 1A 38
Wasdale St. Roch 6F 21
Wasdale Wlk. Oldh 3G 41
Wash Brook. Chad 1B 48
Washbrook Ct. Chad 1B 48
Washington St. Oldh 4C 40
Wash La. Bury 5A 18
Wash La. Ter. Bury 5A 18
Wasp Av. Roch 4A 22
Wast Water St. Oldh 2G 41
Watchgate Clo. Midd 6H 27
Watercroft. Roch 4H 11
Waterfield Way. Fail 1E 55
Waterfold. Bury 6A 18
Waterfold La. Bury 6A 18
Waterfold Pk. Bury 5A 18
Water Ga. Upperm 3D 44
Watergate Milne Ct.
Oldh 3B 42
Watergrove Reservoir 2C 6
Waterhead 3C 42
Waterhead. Oldh 3C 42
Waterhouse Clo. Ward 6C 6
Waterhouse St. Roch 5H 13
Water La. Droy 6C 54
(in two parts)
Water La. Miln 2G 23
Waterloo St. Oldh 4F 41
Watermans Clo. M9 5B 46
Waterman Vw. Roch 5C 14
Watermill Clo. Roch 1D 22
Water Mill Clough. Rytn 1C 40
Waters Edge. G'fld 6C 44
Waters Edge Fold. Oldh 5A 32
Watersheddings 2A 42
Watersheddings St. Oldh 2B 42
Watersheddings Way. Oldh 2B 42
Waterside. G'fld 1E 53
Waterside Clo. Oldh 5A 32
Waterside La. Roch 5B 14
Waterson Av. M40 6C 46
Water St. M9 5A 46
Water St. Midd 3B 38
(in two parts)
Water St. Miln 1F 23
Water St. Oldh 4E 41
Water St. Roch 6H 13
Water St. Rytn 5G 31
Water St. Whitw 3E 5
Waterton Av. Moss 3F 51
Waterton La. Moss 3F 51
Waterview Clo. Miln 4H 23
Waterworks Rd. Oldh 2C 42
Watfield Wlk. M9 6A 46
(off Foleshill Av.)
Watkin St. Roch 3A 22
Watlington Clo. Oldh 6B 32
Watson Gdns. Roch 3F 13
Watson St. Oldh 3A 42
Watts St. Chad 4B 40
Watts St. Oldh 3D 48
Watts St. Roch 5A 14
Waugh Av. Fail 1D 54
Waveney Flats. Heyw 5G 19
(off Fox St.)
Waveney Rd. Shaw 1G 31
Waverley. Roch 5G 13
(off Sheriff St.)
Waverley Ct. M9 6E 37
Waverley Cres. Droy 4E 55
Waverley Rd. M9 6B 46
Waverley Rd. Midd 6C 28
Waverley Rd. W. M9 6B 46
Waverley St. Oldh 3H 41
Waverley St. Roch 6E 21
Wavertree Rd. M9 6G 37
Wayne Clo. Droy 3G 55
Weardale Rd. M9 6F 37
Weatherly Clo. Oldh 4F 49
Weavers Ct. Midd 2B 38
Weavers Rd. Midd 2B 38
Webdale Dri. M40 6C 46
Webster St. Moss 3G 51
Webster St. Oldh 6F 41
Webster St. Roch 4G 13
Wedhurst St. Oldh 4A 42
Weeder Sq. Shaw 1C 32
Weedon St. Roch 5B 14
Weir Rd. Miln 6E 15
Weir St. Fail 6G 47
Weir St. Roch 6H 13
Welbeck Av. Chad 2F 47
Welbeck Av. L'boro 5G 7
Welbeck Clo. Miln 1E 23
Welbeck Rd. Roch 3B 22
Welburn St. Roch 2H 21
Welcome Pde. Oldh 2A 50
Weldon Dri. M9 6H 37
Welfold Ho. Oldh 6H 41
Welland Av. Heyw 4E 19
Welland Rd. Shaw 1G 31
Wellbank Clo. Oldh 1G 49
Wellbank Vw. Roch 4B 12
Well Brow. Del 5B 34
Well Brow Ter. Roch 3G 13
Wellbrow Wlk. M9 2A 46
Wellens Way. Midd 4G 37
Wellfield Pl. Roch 2A 22
Wellfield St. Roch 2A 22
Well Grn. L'boro 6H 7
Wellhouse Dri. M40 2E 47
Well-i-Hole Rd. G'fld 1A 52
Welling Rd. M40 5G 47
Wellington Bldgs. Oldh 5F 41
Wellington Ct. Oldh 1D 48
Wellington Lodge. L'boro 5H 7
(off Lodge St.)
Wellington Pl. Roch 5A 14
Wellington Rd. G'fld 5C 44
Wellington Rd. Oldh 1D 48
(Hampton St.)
Wellington Rd. Oldh 1C 48
(Heron St.)
Wellington St. Chad 3B 40
Wellington St. Fail 4A 48
Wellington St. Miln 1G 23
Wellington St. Oldh 5F 41
Wellington St. Roch 4H 13
(in two parts)
Well i' th' La. Roch 2A 22
Well Mdw. La. Upperm 3E 45
Wellpark Wlk. M40 2A 54
Wells Av. Chad 2A 40
Wells Clo. Midd 4G 37
Wells Rd. Oldh 5C 32
Well St. Heyw 6A 20
Well St. Roch 2A 22
Wellwood Dri. M40 6C 46
Wellyhole St. Oldh 5B 42
Wembury St. M9 5A 46
Wembury St. N. M9 5A 46
Wem St. Chad 1A 48
Wendlebury Grn. Rytn 4G 31
Wenfield Dri. M9 2D 46
Wenning Clo. W'fld 2A 36
Wensleydale Clo. Rytn 4C 30
Wensley Way. Roch 1B 22
Wentworth Av. Heyw 1H 27
Wentworth Clo. Midd 3A 38
Wentworth Ct. Fail 1D 54
Werneth 1C 48
Werneth Cres. Oldh 1C 48
Werneth Hall Rd. Oldh 6D 40
Wesley Clo. Roch 2B 14
Wesley Dri. Ash L 6B 50
Wesley St. Fail 4A 48
(in two parts)
Wesley St. Heyw 5G 19
Wesley St. Miln 1E 23
Wesley St. Roch 2B 14
(off Wesley Clo.)
Wesley St. Rytn 6E 31
Wessex Pk. Clo. Shaw 1H 31
West Av. New M 5F 47
West Av. Roch 2C 14
West Bank. G'fld 6B 44
Westbourne Gro. M9 5A 46
Westbourne St. Oldh 4D 40
Westbrook Clo. Roch 1F 29
Westbury Way. Rytn 1D 40
W. Church St. Heyw 5G 19
Westcliffe Ho. Roch 1D 14
West Cotts. G'fld 6B 44
Westcott Gro. Rytn 4G 31
W. Craig Av. M40 2E 47
West Cres. Midd 4B 38
W. Croft Ind. Est. Midd 4H 37
Westdown Gdns. Shaw 1F 31
West Dri. Droy 6D 54
W. End St. Oldh 4D 40
Westerdale. Oldh 5A 42
(in two parts)
Westerdale Dri. Rytn 4C 30
Wester Hill Rd. Oldh 4G 49
Westfield Av. Midd 4C 38
Westfield Clo. Roch 4B 12
Westfield Dri. Grass 6A 44
Westfield Rd. Droy 5C 54
Westfield St. Chad 3C 40
Westgate. Whitw 4D 4
Westgate Clo. Whitw 4D 4
West Grn. Midd 4F 37
West Gro. Moss 4G 51
Westhide Wlk. M9 4B 46
West Hill. Roch 1G 21
Westholme Rd. P'wich 4A 36
West Hulme 2D 40
Westhulme Av. Oldh 3D 40
Westhulme St. Oldh 2D 40
Westhulme Way. Oldh 2C 40
Westland Dri. M9 1A 46
Westleigh St. M9 4A 46
W. Malling Clo. Heyw 2B 28
Westminster Av. Ash L 6B 50
Westminster Av. Rytn 3C 30
Westminster Clo. Shaw 1H 31
Westminster Rd. Fail 5B 48
Westminster St. Oldh 3H 41
Westminster St. Roch 2F 21
Westmorland Dri. Ward 5D 6
Westmorland Wlk.
Rytn 5E 31
Weston Av. M40 4G 47
Weston Av. Roch 3B 22
Weston St. Miln 1E 23
(in two parts)
W. Starkey St. Heyw 4G 19
West St. Droy 5B 54
West St. Fail 6H 47
West St. Heyw 5H 19
West St. Lees 6C 42
West St. L'boro 6A 8
West St. Midd 1C 38
West St. Oldh 5D 40
(Arkwright St.)
West St. Oldh (King St.) 4E 41
West St. Roch (Buckley St.) 5A 14
West St. Roch (Larchway) 6D 14
West Vw. Del 3G 33
West Vw. L'boro 6A 8
Westward Ho. Miln 1F 23
Westway. M9 5F 37
Westway. Lees 6C 42
Westway. Shaw 3H 31
Westwood 4C 40
Westwood Av. M40 4G 47
Westwood Bus. Cen. Oldh 5D 40
Westwood Dri. Oldh 4D 40
Westwood Ind. Est. Oldh 4C 40
Wetherby Dri. Rytn 4C 30
Weybourne Av. M9 3C 46
Weythorne Dri. Bury 2D 18
Whalley Av. L'boro 5G 7
Whalley Clo. Miln 1E 23
Whalley Gdns. Roch 4D 12
Whalley Gro. Ash L 6A 50
Whalley Rd. Heyw 5E 19
Whalley Rd. Midd 6B 28
Whalley Rd. Roch 4D 12
Wham Bar Dri. Heyw 5F 19
Wham Bottom La. Roch 1F 13
Wham La. Dens 6H 25
Wham St. Heyw 5F 19
Wharf Cotts. Moss 4H 51
Wharfedale Av. M40 4C 46
Wharf St. Chad 2B 48
Wharmton Ri. Grass 5H 43
Wharmton Vw. G'fld 6C 44
Wharmton Vw. Moss 2A 52
Wheatfield Cres. Rytn 6C 30
Wheathill St. Roch 3A 22
Wheatsheaf Cen., The. Roch 5H 13
Wheeldale. Oldh 5B 42
Wheelwright Clo. Roch 3D 20
Wheelwright Dri. Roch 2C 14
Whernside Av. M40 4C 46
Whernside Av. Ash L 6A 50
Whetstone Hill Clo. Oldh 1H 41
Whetstone Hill La. Oldh 2A 42
(in two parts)
Whetstone Hill Rd. Oldh 1H 41
Whimberry Lee La. Dig 2F 35
Whinberry Way. Oldh 5C 32
Whinfell Dri. Midd 2G 37
Whingroves Wlk. M40 6C 46
Whinmoor Wlk. M40 6D 46
Whinstone Way. Chad 2G 39
Whipp St. Heyw 4F 19
Whitbrook Way. Midd 4F 29
Whitby Av. Heyw 4G 19
Whitby Rd. Oldh 2A 50
Whitby St. Midd 2E 39
Whitby St. Roch 2A 22
White Ash. Bury 2C 18
White Ash Ter. Bury 2C 18
White Bank Rd. Oldh 3D 48
Whitebeam Clo. Miln 4G 23
Whitebeck Ct. M9 1C 46
White Brook La. Upperm 5F 45
(Greenfield)
White Brook La. Upperm 3E 45
(Uppermill)
Whitecar Av. M40 4G 47
Whitecroft Av. Shaw 2B 32
Whitecroft St. Oldh 2A 42
Whitefield Av. Roch 5B 12
White Gate 2A 48
Whitegate. L'boro 1E 15
Whitegate Av. Chad 1H 47
Whitegate Clo. M40 4G 47
White Gate End 2G 47
Whitegate La. Chad 1H 47
(in two parts)
Whitegate Rd. Chad 2F 47
Whitegates. S'head 1F 43
Whitegates La. S'head 1E 43
Whitegates Rd. Midd 5E 29
Whitehall. Oldh 5D 32
Whitehall La. Oldh 5D 32

Whitehall St.—Wortley Gro.

Whitehall St. Oldh. 3F 41
Whitehall St. Roch. 4H 13
(in two parts)
White Hart Mdw. Midd 1C 38
Whiteheads Pl. S'head 4D 42
Whitehead St. Midd 2E 39
Whitehead St. Miln. 3B 24
(Bethany La.)
Whitehead St. Miln. 1E 23
(Rochdale Rd.)
Whitehead St. Shaw 1F 31
White Hill Clo. Roch 1F 13
Whitehill Dri. M40 6C 46
White Horse Meadows. B'edge. 5C 22
Whitehouse Av. Oldh 5A 42
Whitehouse Clo. Heyw 2H 27
Whitehouse Ter. M9 4B 46
Whitelees M. L'boro 6G 7
Whitelees Rd. L'boro 6G 7
Whiteley Dri. Midd 4E 39
Whiteleys Pl. Roch. 5G 13
Whiteley St. M11 5A 54
Whiteley St. Chad. 1B 48
White Moss. Roch 3D 12
White Moss Gdns. M9 3C 46
White Moss Rd. M9 2A 46
White Moss Rd. E. M9 1B 46
Whiteside Fold. Roch 4C 12
White Swan Ind. Est. Oldh 3A 42
(off Derker St.)
Whiteway St. M9 6A 46
Whitewell Clo. Roch 5C 14
Whitewillow Clo. Fail 1E 55
Whitfield Bottoms. Miln 4H 23
Whitfield Brow. L'boro 4A 8
Whitfield Cres. Miln 4H 23
Whitfield Dri. Miln 2E 23
Whitfield Ri. Shaw 6G 23
Whitland Dri. Oldh 3B 48
Whitman St. M9 5B 46
Whitstable Clo. Chad 5B 40
Whitstable Rd. M40 4E 47
Whittaker. 1B 16
Whittaker Dri. L'boro. 3F 15
Whittaker La. L'boro 1B 16
Whittaker La. Roch 4H 11
Whittaker St. M40 5B 46
Whittaker St. Midd 3B 38
Whittaker St. Roch. 4A 12
Whittaker St. Rytn 5D 30
Whittingham Gro. Oldh 3D 40
Whittle Brook Clo. Uns 4A 26
Whittlebrook Gro. Heyw 2A 28
Whittle Dri. Shaw 1B 32
Whittle La. Heyw 4E 27
Whittles Ter. Miln 3H 23
Whittle St. L'boro 6F 7
Whitworth. 2E 5
Whitworth Mus. 2E 5
Whitworth Rake. Whitw 3F 5
Whitworth Rd. Roch. 1F 13
Whitworth Sq. Whitw 3F 5
Whitworth St. Miln 1F 23
Whitworth St. Roch 3C 14
Whitworth Swimming Pool. 1F 5
Wicken Bank. Heyw 2A 28
Wickentree Holt. Roch 4C 12
Wickentree La. Fail. 4H 47
Wickham Ter. Midd 2C 38
Wickliffe Pl. Roch 1H 21
Wicklow Gro. Oldh 2E 49
Widdop St. Oldh 4D 40
Wiggins Teape Rd. Bury 3A 26
Wigsby Av. M40. 3E 47
Wildbrook Cres. Oldh 2G 49
(in two parts)
Wildbrook Ter. Oldh 3G 49
Wildcroft Av. M40 4C 46
Wild Ho. Oldh. 6F 41
Wildhouse Clo. Miln 5F 15
Wild Ho. La. Miln 5F 15
Wildmoor Av. Oldh 1C 50
Wilds Bldgs. Roch 6D 14
Wild's Pas. L'boro 1B 8
(Chapel St.)
Wild's Pas. L'boro. 1E 15
(New Rd.)
Wilds Sq. Moss 3G 51
Wild St. Heyw 5A 20
Wild St. Lees 5C 42
Wild St. Oldh 4G 41
Wild St. Shaw 3A 32
Wilfred St. M40 5C 46
Wilkes St. Oldh 5B 32
Wilkinson St. Midd. 2B 38
Willan Rd. M9 6G 37
Willbutts La. Roch 5E 13
William Greenwood Clo. Heyw 5G 19
William Henry St. Roch 3A 22
William Lister Clo. M40 3B 54
Williams Cres. Chad 2H 47
Williamson La. Droy 6F 55
Williamson's Yd. Oldh 4H 41
Williams Rd. Most 6D 46
William St. Fail 4A 48
William St. Hurs 1D 14
William St. L'boro 6G 7
William St. Midd 3D 38
William St. Roch 1H 21
William St. Whitw. 2E 5
Willingdon Dri. P'wich 6A 36
Willis Rd. Oldh. 5G 49
Willow Av. Midd 4E 39
Willow Bank. M9 5A 46
(off Church La.)
Willowbank. Lees 3C 42
Willowbrook Av. M40 6C 46
Willowfield Rd. Oldh 1B 42
Willow Fold. Droy 6F 55
Willow Gro. Chad 3B 40
Willowmead Way. Roch 3C 12
Willow Ri. L'boro 2F 15
Willow Rd. Upperm 4E 45
Willows Cotts. Miln 6E 15
Willows Dri. Fail 3D 54
Willows La. Roch 1D 22
Willows, The. Lees 6C 42
Willows, The. Moss 4A 52
Willows, The. Whitw. 6E 5
(off Tonacliffe Rd.)
Willow St. Bury 5A 18
(in two parts)
Willow St. Fail 6F 47
Willow St. Heyw. 5H 19
Willow St. Oldh 4G 41
Willow Wlk. Droy 5G 55
Wilma Av. M9 6G 37
Wilmers. L'boro 1B 8
Wilson Av. Heyw 5E 19
Wilson Rd. M9. 4A 46
Wilson St. G'fld 6C 44
Wilson St. Oldh 1E 49
Wilson St. Roch. 5H 13
Wilson Way. Oldh 3F 41
Wilton Ct. P'wich 3C 36
Wilton Gro. Heyw. 6H 19
Wilton St. Chad 2B 48
Wilton St. Heyw 5F 19
Wilton St. Midd 4F 37
Wilton St. P'wich 6A 36
Wilton Ter. Roch 5G 13
Wiltshire Rd. Chad. 6B 40
Wiltshire Rd. Fail 1E 55
Wimbledon Dri. Roch 2F 21
Wimbledon Rd. Fail 5B 48
Wimbourne Av. Chad 2A 40
Wimpenny Ho. Oldh. 6E 41
Wimpole St. Oldh. 2G 41
Winby St. Roch 3A 22
Wincanton Pk. Oldh 5B 42
Wincebrook. Midd 3C 38
Wince Clo. Midd. 5E 39
Winchester Av. Ash L 5B 50
Winchester Av. Chad 2H 39
Winchester Av. Heyw 1G 27
Winchester Clo. Roch. 6C 12
Windermere M. Midd 6A 28
Windermere Rd. Midd 1G 37
Windermere Rd. Rytn. 2D 30
Windermere St. Roch. 3H 13
Windermere Wlk. Oldh 3A 42
(in two parts)
Windham St. Roch. 2C 14
Windmill Ct. Roch 1B 22
Windmill St. Roch 1B 22
Windrush Dri. M9 6A 46
Windrush, The. Roch 1E 13
Windsor Av. Chad. 1A 48
Windsor Av. Fail. 5B 48
Windsor Av. Heyw 5F 19
Windsor Ct. M8 6D 36
Windsor Ct. Shaw 1H 31
Windsor Dri. Aud 6H 55
Windsor Gro. Ash L 6A 50
Windsor Rd. Droy 5B 54
Windsor Rd. Harp 6A 46
Windsor Rd. Newt H 3C 54
Windsor Rd. Oldh 6D 40
(in two parts)
Windsor St. Fail 5A 48
Windsor St. Newt H 3C 54
Windsor St. Oldh 2G 41
Windsor St. Roch. 2A 22
Windsor Ter. Miln. 1E 23
Windsor Ter. Roch 6C 14
Windybank. M9 6G 37
Winford Rd. Midd. 5E 39
Winford St. M9 5A 46
Wingate St. Roch. 4A 12
Wingfield Vs. L'boro. 4A 8
Wings Gro. Heyw. 2H 27
Winifred Av. Bury. 3D 18
Winifred Rd. M40 6D 46
Winifred St. Roch 4D 12
Winnall Wlk. M40. 1A 54
Winnie St. M40 5C 46
Winsford Dri. Roch 2B 20
Winslade Clo. Oldh. 2B 42
Winster Clo. W'fld 3A 36
Winster Dri. Midd. 1A 38
Winston Av. Roch. 1A 20
Winston Rd. M9. 4B 46
Winston St. M9 5B 46
Winswell Clo. M11 5A 54
Winterbottom St. Oldh 5D 40
Winterdyne St. M9. 6A 46
Winterford La. Moss 3H 51
Winterford Rd. Moss 3H 51
Winton Av. M40 4F 47
Winton St. L'boro. 6H 7
Winwood Dri. Midd 2D 38
Winwood Fold. Midd 5B 28
Wiseman Ter. P'wich 6A 36
Witham Clo. Heyw 4E 19
Withern Flats. Heyw. 5G 19
(off Hill St.)
Withington Grn. Midd. 5C 28
Withington St. Heyw 1A 28
Withins Rd. Oldh 3B 48
Witley Rd. Roch. 6B 14
Woburn Abbey. Upperm 2C 44
Woburn Clo. Miln 1E 23
Wolseley St. Miln. 3H 23
Wolsey St. Heyw 6G 19
Wolstenholme. 4G 11
Wolstenholme Coalpit La. Roch 3F 11
Wolstenholme La. Roch 3G 11
(in two parts)
Wolstenvale Clo. Midd 2D 38
Wolverton Av. Oldh 2D 48
Wolvesey. Roch 1G 21
Woodark Clo. S'head 6D 42
Woodbank Rd. L'boro. 2G 15
Woodbank Ter. Moss 3H 51
Woodbine Pas. L'boro 6G 7
(off William St.)
Woodbine St. Roch 2A 22
(in two parts)
Woodbine St. E. Roch 2B 22
Woodbridge Gdns. Roch. 3E 13
Woodbrook Av. S'head 4E 43
Wood Brook La. S'head 4F 43
Wood Brook Rd. S'head 4E 43
Woodchurch Wlk. Chad 5B 40
Woodcock Clo. Droy 4G 55
Woodcock Clo. Roch 6B 12
Wood Cres. Oldh 2C 50
Woodeaton Clo. Rytn 5G 31
Woodend. 3H 51
(Ashton-under-Lyne)
Wood End. 1H 31
(Oldham)
Woodend. Shaw 1A 32
Woodend Cen. Ind. Pk. Moss 3H 51
Woodend La. Ward 5D 6
Woodend St. Oldh 2E 41
Woodend St. S'head 6D 42
Woodend Vw. Moss 3H 51
Woodfield Av. Roch 3G 13
Woodfield Clo. Oldh 1C 48
Woodfield Rd. Midd 5A 38
Woodfield Ter. Heyw. 4A 20
Woodford Av. Shaw 2B 32
Woodford Ct. Droy 6F 55
(off Williamson La.)
Woodford Rd. Fail 5A 48
Woodgarth Av. M40 2B 54
Woodgate Av. Bury. 3B 18
Woodgate Av. Roch 1C 20
Woodgate Dri. P'wich. 5A 36
Woodgate Hill. 3B 18
Woodgate Hill Rd. Bury 4A 18
(Fern Grove, in two parts)
Woodgate Hill Rd. Bury 3B 18
(Woodgate Hill)
Woodhall St. Fail 5H 47
Woodhead Clo. Lees 4C 42
Wood Hey Gro. Roch 1G 13
Woodheys Rd. L'boro. 3G 15
Wood Hill. Midd 1B 38
Woodhill Clo. Midd. 1B 38
Woodhouse Farm Cotts. Roch 3H 11
Woodhouse Green. 6C 48
Woodhouse Knowl. Del 5A 34
Woodhouse La. Roch. 3H 11
Woodhouse Rd. Shaw 6A 24
Woodhouses. 1G 55
Woodhouse St. Oldh. 6F 41
Woodland Pk. Rytn 3B 30
Woodland Rd. Heyw. 4A 20
Woodland Rd. Roch 3E 13
Woodlands. Fail 3C 54
Woodlands. Roch. 2C 14
Woodlands Av. Roch 1C 20
Woodlands Rd. Ash L. 6B 50
Woodlands Rd. Miln. 2E 23
Woodlands, The. Droy 4C 54
Woodlands, The. Heyw. 1A 28
Woodland St. Heyw 5H 19
Woodland St. Roch 3A 14
Woodlands Vw. Roch. 5C 14
Woodlands Way. Midd 5B 38
Wood La. Midd 4D 38
Woodlea. Chad 4F 39
Woodleigh Dri. Droy. 3G 55
Woodleigh Rd. S'head 4E 43
Woodleigh St. M9 4B 46
Woodlinn Wlk. M9 6A 46
Woodmeadow Ct. Moss 3G 51
Woodmere Dri. M9. 2A 46
Wood Park. 5E 49
Woodpark Clo. Oldh. 2G 49
Woodroyd Dri. Bury 4A 18
Woods Ct. Midd. 4G 37
(off Broad St.)
Woodside. Miln 2A 24
Woodside. Shaw 1B 32
Woodside Clo. Lees 5C 42
Woods La. Dob 2C 44
Woods Pas. L'boro 6F 7
Wood Sq. Droy. 6E 55
Wood Sq. G'fld 5D 44
Woods, The. G'ton 5F 43
Woods, The. Roch 3E 21
Woodstock Clo. Heyw 5A 20
Woodstock Grn. Oldh. 2G 49
Woodstock Rd. Most 4E 47
Woodstock St. Oldh 6F 41
Woodstock St. Roch. 4E 13
Wood St. Heyw 5H 19
Wood St. L'boro. 6G 7
Wood St. Midd. 1H 37
Wood St. Oldh 3H 41
Wood St. Roch. 3A 24
(Huddersfield Rd.)
Wood St. Roch. 1A 22
(Oldham Rd.)
Wood St. Shaw 1E 31
Wood Top Av. Roch 2B 20
Woodvale. Midd. 5C 28
Wood Vw. Heyw. 3G 19
Woodville Ter. M40. 4B 46
Wood Yd. Roch 6D 22
Woollacot St. Oldh 4F 41
Woolmore Av. Oldh 2E 41
Wool Rd. Dob 2D 44
Woolton Clo. M40 3E 47
Worcester Clo. Ash L 5B 50
Worcester Rd. Midd 6B 38
Worcester St. Oldh. 6B 40
Worcester St. Roch 3G 21
Wordsworth Av. Droy 5E 55
Wordsworth Cres. L'boro 3F 15
Wordsworth Rd. Midd 1D 38
Wordsworth Rd. Oldh 2H 41
Wordsworth Way. Roch 1A 20
Workesleigh St. M40 2A 54
Worrall St. Roch. 3F 13
Worsefold St. M40 5C 46
Worsley Av. M40 4B 46
Worsley Pl. Roch 6B 14
Worsley Pl. Shaw. 3G 31
Worsley St. Oldh 6H 41
Worsley St. Roch 6B 14
Worthington Av. Heyw 2A 28
Worthington St. M40 5E 47
Wortley Gro. M40 3D 46

A-Z Oldham & Rochdale 87

Wray Pl. *Roch* 1C **22**
Wraysbury Wlk. M40 . . . . . *6C 46*
(off Hugo St.)
Wrenbury Dri. *Roch* 4C **22**
Wren Clo. *Aud* 6G **55**
Wren Dri. *Bury* 3A **18**
Wren Gdns. *Midd* 2B **38**
Wren Grn. *Roch* 1B **22**
Wrens Nest Av. *Shaw* 1A **32**
Wren St. *Chad* 3B **40**
Wren St. *Oldh* 5A **42**
Wrexham Clo. *Oldh* 3B **48**
Wright St. *Chad* 6B **40**
Wright St. *Fail* 5H **47**
Wright St. *Oldh* 4G **41**
Wrigley Cres. *Fail* 6H **47**
Wrigley Fold. *Midd* 6H **27**
Wrigley Head. *Fail* 5H **47**
Wrigley Head Cres. *Fail* 5H **47**
Wrigley Pl. *L'boro* 2F **15**
Wrigley's Pl. *Oldh* 2E **49**
Wrigley Sq. *Lees* 5D **42**
Wrigley's Sq. *Roch* 5H **13**
Wrigley St. *Lees* 5C **42**
Wrigley St. *Oldh* 4H **41**
Wrigley St. *Scout* 3F **43**
Wroe St. *S'head* 5D **42**
Wuerdle. **1E 15**
Wuerdle Clo. *Roch* 1E **15**
Wuerdle Farm Way. *Roch* 1E **15**
Wuerdle Pl. *Roch* 1E **15**
Wuerdle St. *Roch* 1E **15**
Wycherley Rd. *Roch* 3D **12**
Wychwood Clo. *Midd* 4D **38**
Wye Av. *Fail* 6H **47**
Wye St. *Oldh* 6D **40**
Wykeham Gro. *Roch* 4D **12**
Wyke Pk. *Oldh* 5B **42**
Wyndale Dri. *Fail* 2D **54**
Wyndale Rd. *Oldh* 2F **49**
Wynn St. *M40* 4G **47**
Wyre Clo. *W'fld* 2A **36**
Wyre St. *Moss* 4F **51**
Wythburn Rd. *Midd* 6A **28**
Wyville Dri. *M9* 5F **37**
Wyvis Clo. *Chad* 2A **40**

Y

Yarnton Clo. *Rytn* 4G **31**
Yarrow Clo. *Roch* 2H **21**
Yarrow Wlk. *W'fld* 2A **36**
Yarwell. Roch *5G 13*
(off Falinge Rd.)
Yarwood Clo. *Heyw* 4A **20**
Yasmin Gdns. *Oldh* 3D **40**
Yates St. *Midd* 4G **37**
Yates St. *Oldh* 3G **41**
Yealand Clo. *Roch* 1D **20**
Yeargate Ind. Est. *Bury* 5B **18**
Yeoman's Clo. *Miln* 6F **15**
Yewbarrow Rd. *Oldh* 3G **41**
Yew Ct. *Roch* 3B **14**
Yew Cres. *Oldh* 3B **42**
Yew Dale Dri. *Fail* 5C **48**
Yewdale Dri. *Midd* 2A **38**
Yewdale Gdns. *Roch* 3D **20**
Yewlands Av. *M9* 6H **37**
Yew St. *Bury* 4A **18**
Yew St. *Heyw* 5F **19**
Yew Tree Cotts. *Dig* 3E **35**
Yew Tree Dri. *Chad* 4F **39**
York Av. *Oldh* 1D **48**
York Av. *Roch* 1C **20**
Yorkdale. *Oldh* 4B **42**
York Rd. *Chad* 3H **39**
York Rd. *Droy* 4D **54**
York Rd. E. *Midd* 6E **39**
York Rd. W. *Midd* 6E **39**
Yorkshire St. *Oldh* 4F **41**
Yorkshire St. *Roch* 6H **13**
(in three parts)
York Sq. *Rytn* 5D **30**
York St. *M9* 5A **46**
(in two parts)
York St. *Heyw* 5H **19**
York St. *Oldh* 5E **41**
York St. *Roch* 1B **22**

Z

Zealand St. *Oldh* 3A **42**
Zedburgh. Roch *5G 13*
(off Spotland Rd.)
Zeta St. *M9* 6B **46**
Zetland Pl. *Roch* 5B **14**
Zion Ter. *Roch* 4A **12**